THE POSTCOLONIAL UNCONSCIOUS

The Postcolonial Unconscious is a major attempt to reconstruct the whole field of postcolonial studies. In this magisterial and, at times, polemical study, Neil Lazarus argues that the key critical concepts that form the very foundation of the field need to be reassessed and questioned. Drawing on a vast range of literary sources, Lazarus investigates works and authors from Latin America and the Caribbean, Africa and the Arab world, South, South East, and East Asia, to reconsider them from a postcolonial perspective. Alongside this, he offers bold new readings of some of the most influential figures in the field: Fredric Jameson, Edward Said, and Frantz Fanon. A tour de force of postcolonial studies, this book will set the agenda for the future, probing how the field has come to develop in the directions it has, and why and how it can grow further.

NEIL LAZARUS is Professor of English and Comparative Literary Studies at the University of Warwick. He has published extensively in postcolonial studies and critical social and cultural theory. Previous books include *Resistance in Postcolonial African Fiction* (1990) and *Nationalism and Cultural Practice in the Postcolonial World* (1999). He is the editor of *The Cambridge Companion to Postcolonial Literary Studies* (2004) and co-editor of *Marxism, Modernity and Postcolonial Studies* (2002).

THE POSTCOLONIAL
UNCONSCIOUS

NEIL LAZARUS

CAMBRIDGE
UNIVERSITY PRESS

CAMBRIDGE UNIVERSITY PRESS

Cambridge, New York, Melbourne, Madrid, Cape Town,
Singapore, São Paulo, Delhi, Tokyo, Mexico City

Cambridge University Press
The Edinburgh Building, Cambridge CB2 8RU, UK

Published in the United States of America by Cambridge University Press, New York

www.cambridge.org
Information on this title: www.cambridge.org/9780521186261

First published 2011

Printed in the United Kingdom at the University Press, Cambridge

A catalogue record for this publication is available from the British Library

Library of Congress Cataloging-in-Publication Data

Lazarus, Neil, 1953–
The postcolonial unconscious / Neil Lazarus.
p. cm.
Includes bibliographical references and index.
ISBN 978-1-107-00656-0 – ISBN 978-0-521-18626-1 (pbk.) 1. Postcolonialism in literature.
2. Postcolonialism and the arts. 3. Literature, Modern–20th century–History and criticism–
Theory, etc. 4. Developing countries–Literatures–History and criticism–Theory, etc. 1. Title.
PN56.P555L39 2011
809′.04–dc22

2011001068

ISBN 978-1-107-00656-0 Hardback
ISBN 978-0-521-18626-1 Paperback

For all my family, inherited and acquired

Contents

Acknowledgements

As many of my friends and colleagues already know, I've been beset by illness over the latter half of this decade of the 'noughties'. When I first began writing this book, my expectation was that it would be ready for publication by the end of 2007. It didn't turn out that way. But the truth is that the book in its current form is not simply a delayed version of the one that would have been published if I had not fallen ill. I have benefited from the opportunity provided by periods of enforced inactivity to read more widely and to think some of my ideas through more deeply.

In a strict sense, therefore, I ought to begin by thanking all of the medical personnel – surgeons, specialists, consultants, doctors, nursing staff, administrators – with whom I have come into contact over the course of the past five years, in a rather large number of hospitals in London (and one in Málaga!). Certainly, I will not hear a word said against the British National Health Service. Without a socialised medical care system, I would have been broke, for sure, and quite possibly dead also.

Many of the ideas in this book have been tried out in lectures that I have given over the past several years. I would like to thank all the colleagues who have invited me to speak on these occasions, and who have been so welcoming and so supportive and encouraging in their feedback: David Attwell, Neil Badmington, Deepika Bahri, Anna Bernard, Elleke Boehmer, Bill Boelhower, Timothy Brennan, Louis Brenner, Jim Catano, Kate Chedgzoy, Patrick Corcoran, Tim Cribb, Selwyn Cudjoe, Bo Ekelund, Ziad Elmarsafy, Jed Esty, Erik Falk, Charles Forsdick, Bridget Fowler, Keya Ganguly, Priyamvada Gopal, Helena Grice, Abdulrazak Gurnah, Faye Hammill, Nicholas Harrison, Stefan Helgesson, Tom Hickey, Elaine Hobby, Lyn Innes, David Johnson, Suvir Kaul, Gerri Kimber, Kai Kresse, Andrew Lawrence, Ania Loomba, Michelle Masse, Scott McCracken, V. Y. Mudimbe, David Murphy, Christine O'Dowd-Smyth, Kwadwo Osei-Nyame, Ranka Primorac,

Lyn Pykett, Pallavi Rastogi, Caroline Rooney, Michael Rossington, Anna Rupprecht, Keith Sandiford, Andrew Smith, Rob Spencer, Luke Thurston, Christopher Warnes, Tim Woods, and Asia Zgadzaj.

I am deeply indebted to friends and colleagues with whom I have spent many hours in discussion about postcolonial studies, literature, cultural theory, and politics. I have learned a very great deal from these conversations, which I have treasured also for the fellowship and intellectual solidarity they have offered. For twenty years now, Benita Parry has been so valued and close an interlocutor of mine that she stands as *prima inter pares* in this regard. Tim Brennan, Keya Ganguly, Priya Gopal, John Marx, A. Sivanandan, and Khachig Tölölyan have also been central to the formation and development of my ideas in this book, and I thank them for their comments as well as their friendship. I must also thank in particular my colleagues in the Warwick Research Collective (or WReC, as we like to call ourselves), who continue to bring new ideas and new material to my attention, as we attempt, together, to come up with a plausible theory of 'world literature': Nick Lawrence, Graeme MacDonald, Pablo Mukherjee, Benita Parry, Stephen Shapiro, Sharae Deckard, Rashmi Varma, and Michael Gardiner. My thanks also to friends who have read and commented on parts of this book, or who have contributed, in discussion, to its development, and especially to Bashir Abu-Manneh, Tim Bewes, Fran Bartkowski, Crystal Bartolovich, Michael Bell, Bo Ekelund, Gregory Elliott, John Fletcher, Sean Homer, Peter Mack, and David Savran.

It has been my privilege, over some twenty-five years now, to have worked with some extraordinarily brilliant and intellectually audacious graduate students – at Warwick and, before that, at Brown University in the United States. The fact that so many of these wonderful students should have gone on to make names for themselves in the academy has given me enormous pleasure. I must thank the following, in particular, for the significant contributions that they have made to the development of the ideas in this book, whether through direct feedback or indirectly, through their own, increasingly important, writing: Sadia Abbas, Mai Al-Nakib, Anthony Arnove, Norbert Bugeja, William Clarke, Nicholas Daly, Sharae Deckard, Steven Evans, Rosemary Marangoly George, Elisa Glick, James Graham, Sorcha Gunne, Pranav Jani, Leila Kamali, Touria Khannous, Motochika Kusaka, Lucienne Loh, John Marx, Malachi McIntosh, Kerstin Oloff, Jane Poyner, Nagesh Rao, Robert Spencer, Juliette Taylor-Batty, Jennifer Terry, and Claire Westall.

I would like to thank the British Arts and Humanities Research Council for awarding me a grant under their Research Leave Scheme in 2009, that enabled me to bring this book to completion. I must also thank my copy-editor at Cambridge University Press, Hilary Hammond, with whom it has been a pleasure to work. I am grateful to Malcolm Read, for finding and proposing a suitable cover image for this book.

My greatest debt is to my family, in the UK and in South Africa, who have given me unconditional love and support when I have most needed it in recent years. Their love has immeasurably enriched my life, and I dedicate this book to them.

Thanks are due to the following publications, in which earlier drafts of limited parts of this book have appeared. In all cases, the previously published material has been substantially reworked here.

New Formations, 59 (2006); Neil Lazarus (ed.), *The Cambridge Companion to Postcolonial Studies* (2004); *European Legacy*, 7.6 (2002); Ania Loomba, Suvir Kaul, Matti Bunzl, Antoinette Burton, and Jed Esty (eds), *Postcolonial Studies and Beyond* (Duke University Press, 2005); Douglas Kellner and Sean Homer (eds), *Fredric Jameson: A Critical Reader* (Palgrave, 2004); *Journal of African Cultural Studies*, 17.1 (2005); *Historical Materialism*, 14.4 (2006); *Research in African Literatures*, 36.3 (2005).

Introduction: The political unconscious
of postcolonial studies

Much of my own work since the early 1990s has taken the form of a contestation of particular ideas and assumptions predominant in postcolonial studies. I have sought, in general, to call into question concepts and theories that have seemed to me to lack accountability to the realities of the contemporary world-system that constitutes their putative object; and also to register my disagreement with the partial and tendentious ways in which the work of some key writers in the field has been taken up.[1] In *The Postcolonial Unconscious*, however, I want to move from the 'negative' moment of critique to the more 'positive' moment of reconstruction. While I still believe that it is important to write in the mode of critique, I will be concerned here also to propose alternative readings and conceptualisations, to be set alongside and compared with those currently prevailing. Much of this book will therefore be devoted to an elaboration of concepts, methods, and substantive themes, upon which what I would view as a plausible 'reconstruction' of postcolonial studies might conceivably be based.

The work of reconstruction needs to begin, I think, with a periodisation of postcolonial studies, aimed both at situating its emergence and consolidation as a field of academic enquiry and at contextualising its distinctive emphases and investments. Concerning the latter, we can register immediately the supplementarity of postcolonial studies to post-structuralist theory. This supplementarity has often been noted; and some of the defining theoretical and ideological dispositions in the field have correctly been identified and assessed by critics, accordingly, through reference to post-structuralism.[2] To ring true, however, our periodisation will need to do more than offer an intellectual genealogy of postcolonial studies; it will need in addition to supply a credible sociological account of the relation between the field's problematic and developments in the wider social world.

Emerging at the end of the 1970s and consolidating itself over the course of the following decade and a half, postcolonial studies was very much a creature of its time – or, better, it was a creature *of* and *against* its time. Just behind it lay the post-1945 boom – a 'golden age', as Eric Hobsbawm has called it,[3] of a quarter-century or so of explosive global economic growth accompanied, in the core capitalist countries, by an historically unprecedented democratisation of social resources and, in the 'Third World', by insurgent demands for decolonisation and self-determination. This boom period had come to an end at the beginning of the 1970s, when the world-system stumbled into economic recession and attendant political crisis, from which it has yet to recover. The thirty-plus years since the puncturing of the boom – the 'long downturn', to use Robert Brenner's term[4] – have been marked, economically, by a steady decline of the rate of return on capital investment and, politically, by the global reassertion of US dominance (involving, among other things, the rolling back of the challenge represented by 'Third World' insurgency) and the brutal imposition of 'the logic of unilateral capital'.[5]

The *social* dimensions of the boom era must be emphasised here.[6] In the core capitalist countries, the 'welfare state' was made possible by a strategic compromise between capital and labour. For a combination of reasons – among them the relative strength of organised labour and the relative weakness of 'organised capital' in the immediate postwar years, and an exhausted disenchantment on all sides with the politics of confrontation – postwar reconstruction in these countries took the form of social democracy. Economic growth on the one hand was complemented by the dispersal of social benefits on the other. During this period of thirty years or so, as Colin Leys has written,

> the industrialized countries experienced steady economic growth, distributed the benefits with a degree of equity (however modest) between capital and labour and between town and country, invested in their infrastructure, increasingly recognized and assisted disadvantaged groups and pursued all sorts of other social and cultural objectives, from gender equality to care for the environment, even if such goals were only very imperfectly attained.[7]

Much the same point is made also by Jürgen Habermas, in a rather striking summary that warrants quoting at length:

> Of course, the explosive growth of the global economy, the quadrupling of industrial production, and an exponential increase in the world trade between the early 1950s and the early 1970s also generated disparities between the rich and the poor regions of the world. But the governments of the OECD [Organization of Economic Cooperation and Development] nations, who were responsible for three-quarters of global production and four-fifths of global trade in industrial goods during these two decades, had learned enough from the catastrophic experiences of the period between the two world wars to pursue intelligent

domestic economic policies, focusing on stability with a relatively high rate of economic growth, and on the construction and enhancement of comprehensive social security systems. In welfare-state mass democracies, highly productive capitalist economies were socially domesticated for the first time, and were thus brought more or less in line with the normative self-understanding of democratic constitutional states.[8]

It is worth picking up on Habermas's term 'domesticated' here and stressing that the welfare state was a political *settlement*, reflecting no magnanimous or 'natural' aspiration on capital's part to harmonise its interests with those of labour but, on the contrary, the hard-won ability of organised labour to constrain capital.

If the social gains achieved under the rubrics of the 'welfare state' (in western Europe) and the 'Great Society' (in the United States) were made possible by a temporary truce or stand-off between capital and labour, those in the 'Third World' were powered by the struggle for self-determination. This was a struggle that had to be waged precisely *against* the core capitalist states, of course, whose *domestic* policies might have been 'intelligent', to use Habermas's term – and 'more or less in line with the normative self-understanding of democratic constitutional states' – but whose *foreign* policies continued to rationalise colonial overlordship and to justify imperialist domination. In these terms, the sheer, irreversible advance represented by the achievement of decolonisation in the postwar years needs to be registered decisively. The articulation and elaboration of national consciousness; the mobilisation of popular will or support; the tempering of this will in the fire of the anticolonial campaigns, of campaigns for national liberation, when the least response of the colonial powers was intransigence and the arrogant refusal even to contemplate reform, and the more typical response (from Malaya to Vietnam, Kenya to Algeria) was to call out the police and very often the army to silence dissent and quell resistance – these developments, concerted in their nevertheless uncoordinated appearance across the globe in the immediate postwar period, were (and remain) of huge significance. 'The world became a larger and happier place', as Basil Davidson writes of the decolonising years in Africa[9] – not '*seemed* to become a larger and happier place', note, but actively *became* such. '[T]here were many reasons for optimism', Davidson continues:

The old empires were falling fast and would not be restored. The social freedoms that had provided the real magnet behind nationalism were making themselves increasingly felt; and the grim silence of the colonial years was already shattered by a hubbub of plans and schemes for a more favorable future. People even talked of a 'new Africa', and yet it did not sound absurd. A whole continent seemed to have come alive again, vividly real, bursting with creative energies, claiming its heritage in the human family, and unfolding ever more varied or surprising aspects of itself. (pp. 195–6)

It is important to recollect the energy, dynamism, and optimism of the decolonising and immediate post-independence era, both for the sake of the historical record and also to enable us to register the *successes* of this period, however slender, partial, provisional, or unsustainable they proved to be in the longer term.[10] The Vietnamese army's defeat of the French at Dien Bien Phu in 1954; the staging of the Bandung Conference itself in 1955; Nasser's stand on Suez in 1956; the acquisition of independence in Ghana in 1957 – these were all events that fired the imaginations of millions of people worldwide, in the global 'North' as well as the 'South', placing on to the world stage, perhaps for the first time, the principled and resolute figure of 'Third World' self-determination. Domestically, too, the newly inaugurated postcolonial regimes, initially at least, undertook all manner of ambitious projects intended to improve the livelihood and welfare of their citizenry, from literacy and adult education campaigns to the construction and provision of hospitals, from the building of roads and sewage facilities to irrigation schemes, and from the redistribution of land to the outlawing of feudal rights over the labour of others. Here, women were granted the right to vote and to own property. There, workers won the right to organise and strike. Still elsewhere, compulsory education of children was introduced. Constitutions were framed; new laws were passed; many tyrannical and bitterly resented colonial laws and edicts were struck down, and many equally bitterly resented precolonial customs and practices were officially scrapped or proscribed.[11]

This new sense of uplift and regeneration proved to be of relatively short duration, of course. In *The Black Man's Burden*, Davidson attempts to analyse the processes through which, in the postcolonial era, the gap between 'people' and 'state' widened rather than (as might have been anticipated, and was certainly hoped for) narrowed. Increasingly, he argues, 'social' imperatives – those concerning the distribution of capital, resources, and services – were subordinated to the 'national' requirements of elite entrenchment – that is, where they were not cynically jettisoned altogether. Not only was 'the extraction of wealth from ... already impoverished [societies] ... in no way halted by the [ending of colonial rule]'. The '"national conflict", embodied in the rivalries for executive power between contending groups or individuals among the "elites" ... [took] priority over a "social conflict" concerned with the interests of most of the inhabitants of these new nation-states' (pp. 219, 114). Although his commentary is focused on sub-Saharan Africa, what Davidson says is readily applicable elsewhere in the (post-) colonial world as well. For in territory after territory, leaders and ruling elites came to identify their own maintenance in power as being of greater importance than the broader 'social' goods of democratisation, opportunity, and equality, and they increasingly used the repressive apparatuses and technologies of the state (often inherited from the colonial order) to enforce order and to silence or eliminate opposition.[12]

There are some excellent accounts bringing into clear focus the failures of postcolonial leaderships to extend and democratise the momentous social advance represented by decolonisation. Neil Larsen, for instance, has argued that in what he calls the 'Bandung era' there was an historic failure to steer the anti-imperialist movement worldwide in the direction of proletarian internationalism on the basis of 'a strategic alliance of metropolitan and third world labor against capital as such'.[13] The result of this was that, while the macrosocial schemes of 'development' (or 'modernisation') produced relatively impressive *economic* results throughout the 'Third World' in the quarter of a century following the Second World War, these typically failed to augur *democratisation*, either political or economic. Thus the introduction of 'some aspects of a welfare state in health, social security and housing' in various Latin American states in the post-1945 period, for instance, was never socially dispersed: as Jorge Larrain has written, 'the benefits . . . continued to be highly concentrated and the masses of the people continued to be excluded'.[14]

We should also note here that the Second World War ended with the definitive supersession of European political hegemony by that of the US, and that post-1945 developments unfolded, accordingly, on the frame of a *pax Americana*. It is not only that the 'East–West' conflict, the cold war, continually buffeted postcolonial states about, obliging them to present themselves in certain lights, to implement certain policies and to shut down or abort others, in order to secure favour or forestall disfavour; it is also that decolonisation – the emergence of new autocentric or would-be autocentric regimes in the postcolonial world – was from the outset viewed by the United States, the postwar hegemon, as a potentially dangerous development, to be monitored closely and crushed whenever it seemed too threatening.

There is a remarkable moment in Norman Mailer's great novel of the Second World War, *The Naked and the Dead* (first published in 1949), in which the demented and rabidly right-wing American general, Cummings,

lectures his liberal junior officer, Hearn, about the historical significance
of the war for the United States:

Historically the purpose of this war is to translate America's potential into kinetic
energy ... When you've created power, materials, armies, they don't wither of
their own accord. Our vacuum as a nation is filled with released power, and I can
tell you that we're out of the backwaters of history now ... For the past century
the entire historical process has been working toward greater and greater consolidation of power ... Your men of power in America ... are becoming conscious of
their real aims for the first time in our history. Watch. After the war our foreign
policy is going to be far more naked, far less hypocritical than it has ever been.
We're no longer going to cover our eyes with our left hand while our right is
extending an imperialist paw.[15]

As though performing to Cummings's script, the United States in the
post-1945 period made it its business to export counter-revolution,
working ceaselessly, sometimes directly, sometimes covertly, to undermine, subvert, and overthrow regimes and movements which it deemed
to stand in opposition to its interests and political philosophy.[16]
Brennan refers, in this context, to the 'orchestrated mass killing of leftists
in Indonesia, Chile, Mozambique, Nicaragua, Colombia, Vietnam,
Afghanistan, and elsewhere';[17] and any casual listing of the states and
regimes which the United States actively worked to destabilise in the post-
1945 era must give one pause: such a listing must start, of course, with
Cuba; but it might then move outwards, to such 'middle American' and
Caribbean nations as Guatemala, Nicaragua, Guyana, Grenada, and
Haiti; then on to such properly continental Latin American states as
Venezuela, Bolivia, Peru, and Chile; Africa (Angola, Congo, Libya,
Ghana, for instance); the 'Middle East' (a wide arc from Somalia to
Afghanistan, and including Iran, Iraq, and Syria) and South East Asia
(most notably Vietnam, the Philippines, and Korea, but also Indonesia,
Cambodia, and Laos).

  The setbacks suffered by and the defeats inflicted upon progressive
forces in the 'Third World' in the decades following the end of the Second
World War were considerable. But even they register indirectly the
insurgency, the restless dynamism, of the era. Writing at the end of the
1950s, Frantz Fanon spoke famously of 'the upward thrust of the people'
of Africa, and evoked the 'coordinated effort on the part of two hundred
and fifty million men to triumph over stupidity, hunger, and inhumanity
at one and the same time'.[18] The term 'Third World' itself dates from this
time, and was used, banner-like, to announce a consolidated platform of
resistance to imperialism – one term among many in a distinctive lexicon

of keywords: liberation, revolution, decolonisation, non-alignment, pan-Arabism, pan-Africanism, 'African socialism', nationalism, and so on.

Beginning in the late 1960s, however, a series of related developments combined to bring the postwar boom to a shuddering halt. 'The crisis manifested itself', according to Amin, 'in the return of high and persistent unemployment accompanied by a slowing down of growth in the West, the collapse of Sovietism, and serious regression in some regions of the Third World, accompanied by unsustainable levels of external indebtedness' (*Capitalism*, p. 94). The key point to note here about this crisis is that it provoked capital into the promulgation of a raft of new policies aimed at arresting and turning around the falling rates of profit. As Peter Wilkin has written, these policies formed part of a consolidated attempt on the part of the neo-liberal political elite then rising to hegemony in the core capitalist countries and elsewhere 'to overturn the limited gains made by working people throughout the world-system in the post-war period'.[19] What was labelled 'globalisation' and projected by neo-liberal ideology as a deterritorialised and geopolitically anonymous behemoth – or as a tidal wave (another favoured metaphor) of 'technology and irresistible market forces', 'sweeping over borders . . . [and] transform[ing] the global system in ways beyond the power of anyone to do much to change'[20] – was, on the contrary, a consciously framed political project or strategy. A savage restructuring of class and social relations worldwide was set in train, in the interests of capital.[21]

In the 'West', the practical effects of this restructuring, still ongoing, have been to privatise social provision, thereby crippling or even dismantling the welfare state and stripping vast sectors of metropolitan populations of security across wide aspects of their lives; to drive millions of people out of work, forcing them not only into unemployment but into *structural* unemployment; and to enact legislation that has made it increasingly difficult for people to represent themselves collectively, to campaign and fight for their interests and the rights formally accorded them.[22] In the 'Third World' the effects have been analogous. Economically, '[w]hat was new about this recession and the period that followed it', as Larrain explains,

was that the anti-depression policies followed by most governments produced inflation without adequately stimulating the economy, thus provoking high levels of unemployment. Throughout the developing world the recession had damaging effects: it aggravated the chronic deficits of its balance of payments by bringing down the prices of raw materials and raising the prices of oil and other essential imports, thus producing inflation, unemployment and stagnation. This marked the beginning of the huge expansion of the Third World's international debt, which soon became an impossibly heavy burden for its very weak economies, with the result that several countries defaulted on their obligations. (*Identity and Modernity*, p. 133)

Even during the 'boom' years, the sheer size of the debts owed by 'Third World' states to foreign lending institutions posed a big problem. But once the global downturn commenced, any chance of their 'catching up' and keeping a clean balance sheet disappeared definitively, and probably forever. As John Saul has written, with respect to Africa:

Fatefully [the] ... debt came due, in the 1980s, just as the premises of the dominant players in the development game were changing. The western Keynesian consensus that had sanctioned the agricultural levies, the industrialization dream, the social services sensibility, and the activist state of the immediate post-independence decades – and lent money to support all this – was replaced by 'neo-liberalism'. For Africa this meant the winding down of any remnant of the developmental state, the new driving premise was to be a withdrawal of the state from the economy and the removal of all barriers, including exchange controls, protective tariffs and public ownership (and with such moves to be linked as well to massive social service cutbacks), to the operation of global market forces.[23]

The African case is extreme but not unique. In Latin America, the crippling burden of debt repayment led such major economies as Mexico, Argentina and Brazil to the brink. Growing indebtedness contrived to render states ever more dependent on foreign capital at the very moment when foreign capitalists, themselves concerned with profitability, became unwilling to extend credit and eager to get the highest possible short-term returns on their loans and investments. 'In the aftermath of the debt crisis' of the early 1980s, as Gwynne and Kay have written,

the international financial institutions were by and large able to dictate economic and social policies to the indebted countries, especially the weaker and smaller economies, through structural adjustment programs (SAPs). While Brazil and Mexico were able to negotiate better terms with the World Bank and foreign creditors, Bolivia and other countries were unable to do so. Peru, during the government of Alan García, tried to defy the international financial institutions but was severely punished for it and, after a change of government, the country had to accept the harsh reality of the new power of global capital and implement a SAP. SAPs were used as vehicles for introducing neoliberal policies ... they had particularly negative consequences for the poor of Latin American economies as unemployment soared and wages and social welfare expenditures were drastically reduced.[24]

Throughout the postcolonial world over the course of the final quarter of the twentieth century, Structural Adjustment Programs were imposed as conditions for the distribution of loans, which the recipient nations were not in any position to refuse.[25] Typically mandating huge cuts in government spending and social provision, the slashing of wages, the opening up of local markets to imported goods and the removal of all restrictions on foreign investment, the privatisation of state enterprises and social services, and deregulation in all sectors to ensure that all developments were driven by the logic of the market rather than by social need or government policy, SAPs became a favoured means of disciplining postcolonial states, domesticating them and rendering them subservient to the needs of the global market. They also became a means of ensuring that postcolonial states would retain their peripheral status, neither attempting to delink themselves from the world-system nor ever imagining themselves capable of participating in it from any position of parity, let alone power.

Postcolonial studies emerged as an institutionally specific, conjuncturally determined response to these global developments. The emergent field breathed the air of the reassertion of imperial dominance beginning in the 1970s, one of whose major preconditions was the containment and recuperation of the historic challenge from the 'Third World' that had been expressed in the struggle for decolonisation in the boom years after 1945. After 1975, the prevailing political sentiment in the West turned sharply against anticolonial nationalist insurgency and revolutionary anti-imperialism. The substance and trajectory of the work produced in postcolonial studies was strongly marked by this epochal reversal of the fortunes and influence of insurgent national liberation movements and revolutionary ideologies in the 'Third World'. The decisive defeat of liberationist ideologies within the western (or, increasingly, western-based) intelligentsia, including its radical elements – was fundamental to the emergent field, whose subsequent consolidation, during the 1980s and early 1990s, might then be seen, at least in part, as a function of its articulation of a complex intellectual response to this defeat.

On the one hand, as an initiative in tune with its times, postcolonial studies was party to the general anti-liberationism then rising to hegemony in the wider society. The field not only emerged in close chronological proximity to the enforced end of the 'Bandung era', the era of 'Third World' insurgency. It also characteristically offered, in the scholarship that it fostered and produced, something approximating a monumentalisation of this moment – not, indeed, a celebration, but a rationalisation of, and pragmatic adjustment to, the demise of the ideologies that had flourished during the 'Bandung' years. Especially after the collapse of historical communism in 1989, it was disposed to pronounce Marxism dead and buried also.

On the other hand, however, as a self-consciously *progressive* or *radical* initiative, postcolonial studies was, and has remained, opposed to the dominant forms assumed by anti-liberationist policy and discourse in the dark years since the mid 1970s – years of neo-liberal 'austerity', 'structural adjustment', and political 'rollback'. What Homi K. Bhabha influentially described as 'the postcolonial perspective'[26] might then be conceptualised (in analogy with the liberal cold-war discourse of 'anti-anti-communism') as 'anti-anti-liberationism'. Itself predicated on a disavowal of liberationism, which it understands to have been rendered historically anachronistic by the advent of the new world order represented by 'globalisation', postcolonial studies has nevertheless stood as a firm opponent of 'mainstream' or politically institutionalised anti-liberationism, as expressed both in the frankly imperialist language of leading policy makers and intellectuals in the core capitalist states, and through the punitive policies enacted by such corporate agencies as the World Bank, the International Monetary Fund, and the World Trade Organisation.

A good place to start to unpack this complex placement of postcolonial studies might be to register that, before the late 1970s, there was no field of academic specialisation that went by this name. This is not, of course, to say that there was no work being done before the late 1970s on issues relating to postcolonial cultures and societies. On the contrary, there was a large amount of such work, much of it deeply consequential and of abiding significance. There were political studies of state formation in the newly decolonised countries of Africa, Asia, and the Caribbean; economic and sociological studies of development and underdevelopment; historical accounts of anticolonial nationalism and of the various and diverse nationalist leaderships that had fought or campaigned against colonial rule and that had then themselves come to power when independence had finally been won; literary studies of the new writing that was being produced by writers from these territories; and so on. In every academic discipline, there were presses specialising in the publication of material relating to postcolonial issues. Moreover, in most disciplines, dedicated journals had latterly come into existence to carry the emerging debates and to sponsor wider scholarship.[27]

The word 'postcolonial' occasionally appeared in this scholarship, but it did not mean then what it has come to mean in 'postcolonial studies'. Thus when Hamza Alavi and John S. Saul wrote about the state in 'postcolonial' societies in 1972 and 1974, respectively, they used the term in a strict historically and politically delimited sense, to identify the period immediately following decolonisation, when the various leaderships, parties, and governments that had gained access to the colonial state apparatuses at independence undertook to transform these apparatuses, to make them over so that instead of serving as instruments of colonial dictatorship they would serve these new leaders' own social and political interests, whether socialist or bourgeois, progressive or reactionary, popular or authoritarian.[28] 'Postcolonial', in these usages from the early 1970s, was a periodising term, an historical and not an ideological concept. It bespoke no political desire or aspiration, looked forward to no particular social or political order. Erstwhile colonial territories that had been decolonised were 'postcolonial' states. It was as simple as that. Politically charged and ideologically fraught terms were all around, and were fiercely contested – capitalism and socialism; imperialism and anti-imperialism; 'First World' and 'Third World'; self-determination and neo-colonialism; centre and periphery; modernisation, development, dependency, underdevelopment, mal-development, 'dependent development' – but the notion of 'postcoloniality' did not participate, on any side, in these debates. To describe a literary work or a writer as 'postcolonial' was to name a period, a discrete historical moment, not a project or a politics.[29] It was far more usual to see writers and works characterised in terms of their communities of origin, identity, or identification. Thus Chinua Achebe was described variously as an Igbo writer, a Nigerian writer, an African writer, a Commonwealth writer, a 'Third World' writer, but seldom if ever as a 'postcolonial' one. To have labelled Achebe a 'postcolonial' writer would have been, in a sense, merely to set the scene, historically speaking, for the analysis to come.

To begin to appreciate how much things have changed in this respect, consider the following formulation, drawn from Homi Bhabha's essay, 'The Postcolonial and the Postmodern', first published in 1992:

Postcolonial criticism bears witness to the unequal and uneven forces of cultural representation involved in the contest for political and social authority within the modern world order. Postcolonial perspectives emerge from the colonial testimony of Third World countries and the discourses of 'minorities' within the geopolitical divisions of East and West, North and South. They intervene in those ideological discourses of modernity that attempt to give a hegemonic 'normality' to the uneven development and the differential, often disadvantaged, histories of nations, races, communities, peoples. They formulate their critical revisions around issues of cultural difference, social authority, and political discrimination in order to reveal the antagonistic and ambivalent moments within the 'rationalizations' of modernity. To bend Jürgen Habermas to our purposes, we could also argue that the postcolonial project, at the most general theoretical level, seeks to explore those social pathologies – 'loss of meaning, conditions of anomie' – that no longer simply 'cluster around class antagonism,

[but] break up into widely scattered historical contingencies' . . . The postcolonial perspective . . . departs from the traditions of the sociology of underdevelopment or 'dependency' theory. As a mode of analysis, it attempts to revise those nationalist or 'nativist' pedagogies that set up the relation of Third World and First World in a binary structure of opposition. The postcolonial perspective resists the attempt at holistic forms of social explanation. It forces a recognition of the more complex cultural and political boundaries that exist on the cusp of these often opposed political spheres. (*Location of Culture*, pp. 171, 173)

We can see straight away that in Bhabha's thinking, 'postcolonial' has ceased to be an historical category. The term does not designate what it sounds like it designates, that is, the moment, or more generally the time, *after* colonialism. There *are* temporal words and phrases in Bhabha's formulation – 'no longer', for instance – but these do not appear to relate in any discernible way to *decolonisation* as an historical event, that is, to decolonisation as a 'cut' or break in time, such that one could speak of a colonial 'before' and a postcolonial 'after'. Bhabha writes that 'postcolonial criticism' concerns itself with 'social pathologies' that can 'no longer' be referred to the explanatory factor of class division: 'post-colonial criticism' is thus opposed to (and for Bhabha evidently comes after or supersedes) class analysis. But no explanation is given as to why the term 'colonial' is deemed to be implicated in the putative obsolescence of class analysis. Indeed, on the basis of what Bhabha says, 'postcolonial criticism' could as easily be called 'post-Marxist criticism'.

Or indeed 'post-modern criticism', since Bhabha is at pains to emphasise that the 'post-' in 'postcolonial criticism' is directed against the assumptions of the 'ideological discourses of modernity', which are said to flatten out complexity, to simplify the sheer heterogeneity and unevenness of real conditions, to reduce these to 'a binary structure of opposition'. For Bhabha, 'postcolonial' is a fighting term, a theoretical weapon that 'intervenes' in existing debates and 'resists' certain political and philosophical constructions. 'Postcolonial criticism', as he understands and champions it, is constitutively anti-Marxist – departing not only from more orthodox Marxist scholarship but even from 'the traditions of the sociology of underdevelopment or "dependency" theory'"; it disavows nationalism as such and refuses an antagonistic or struggle-based model of politics in favour of one that empha-sises 'cultural difference', 'ambivalence' and 'the more complex cultural and political boundaries that exist on the cusp' of what 'modern' philosophy had imagined as the determinate categories of social reality.

Between Alavi's and Saul's 'post-colonialism' and Bhabha's, a sea change has occurred. What is at issue is not simply a matter of the changing of the guard, the routine emergence of new theoretical concepts and emphases that supplant or sit alongside the old ones in accordance with shifting generational interests. Rather, there has been a decisive change of paradigms or problematics, such that the retention of particular terms ('postcolonial' itself, for instance) is in fact quite misleading. Aijaz Ahmad's identification of a shift in 'theoretical framework[s] ... from Third World nationalism to postmodernism'[30] is powerfully suggestive here. Even more illuminating, because more precise, is Larsen's observation that what tends, in the new discourse, to be referred to the 'postcolonial', is a 'euphemism' for what used to be referred to the 'Third World' – 'euphemism' because the political meaning of the 'Third World', which used to 'conjure ... up an entire historical conjuncture and accompanying political culture, in which one naturally went on to utter the ... slogans of "national liberation," etc.' has now been eclipsed. '[W]e who once unself-consciously said "third world" now hesitate, if only for a second, to utter it in the same contexts. This hesitation reflects the decline of the national liberation movements of the "Bandung era" ... leaving us with the question of why and with what effect this decline has occurred' ('Imperialism', pp. 24–5).

In 'East isn't East', a brief but important essay from 1995, Edward W. Said differentiated between the thrusts of what he called 'post-modernist' thought and the thought of scholars, writers, and activists from the 'Bandung era', whom he grouped together as 'the first generation of post-colonial artists and scholars': 'The earliest studies of the post-colonial', he wrote,

were by such distinguished thinkers as Anwar Abdel-Malek, Samir Amin, C. L. R. James; almost all were based on studies of domination and control made from the standpoint of either a completed political independence or an incomplete liberationist project. Yet whereas post-modernism, in one of its most famous programmatic statements (by Jean-François Lyotard), stresses the disappearance of the grand narratives of emancipation and enlightenment, the emphasis behind much of the work done by the first generation of post-colonial artists and scholars is exactly the opposite: the grand narratives remain, even though their implementation and realization are at present in abeyance, deferred, or circumvented. This crucial difference between the urgent historical and political imperatives of post-colonialism and post-modernism's relative detachments makes for altogether different approaches and results.[31]

I discuss this passage in detail in Chapter 5 below, drawing out the implications both of what it says and what it fails to say or to make clear. Here, however, I want to focus just on Said's identification of a distinction between the historico-philosophical assumptions of 'Bandung era'

and 'post-modern' discourse. The latter takes its warrant from the conviction that the 'break' between the post-1945 'boom' (within which the
'Bandung era' unfolded) and the subsequent 'long downturn' is not to be
understood as a crisis in analogy with the crises that have been regular
features of capitalist history; nor even in analogy with the great depres-
sions of 1873–93 and 1929–41. Rather, it is to be understood as marking an
epochal transformation from one overarching world order ('modernity')
into another ('postmodernity'). Hence the suggestions that the 'grand
narratives of emancipation and enlightenment' (including, notably, the
'grand narrative' of *capitalist history*) are not merely arguable or susceptible to criticism, but have become definitively *obsolete.*

This 'postmodernist' assumption has been fundamental to postcolonial
studies, structuring the discourse even of some of the field's best-known
dissenting voices. Thus Arif Dirlik, for instance, whose influential 1994
critique of 'the postcolonial aura' nevertheless concedes that what he calls
'postcoloniality' 'represents a response to a genuine need':

the need to overcome a crisis of understanding produced by the inability of
old categories to account for the world. The metanarrative of progress that
underlies two centuries of thinking is in deep crisis. Not only have we lost faith
in progress but also progress has had actual disintegrative effects ... The crisis of
progress has brought in its wake a crisis of modernization ... and called into
question the structure of the globe as conceived by modernizationalists and
radicals alike in the decades after World War II, that is, as three worlds.[32]

Notwithstanding the astringency of his critique of postcolonial theory,
Dirlik shares with its leading proponents key presumptions as to the
eclipse of 'modernity' and the correlative 'metanarrative of progress that
underlies two centuries of thinking'.

Like them he takes it as read that Marxism has been obliterated as an
enabling political horizon[33] and that the eclipse of the idea of the 'Third
World' as an historico-political project is part of a wider – epochal – shift.
This shift is from the 'old' order of 'modernity' (whose constituent
features and aspects – unevenness, revolution, the centrality of the nation,
even imperialism – are seen to have lost their explanatory power) to the
'new world order' of fully globalised capitalism.[34] These presumptions
govern what, drawing on and adapting the resonant title of Fredric
Jameson's 1981 book, we might think of as *the postcolonial unconscious.*[35]

I have argued against the general presumption of epochal change in
postcolonialist theory on several occasions previously, and will not repeat
those arguments here.[36] What I would like to suggest instead (or in

addition), in grounding the central, *reconstructive* thrust of *The Postcolonial Unconscious*, is that developments in the first decade of our new century – above all the US-led and -sponsored invasion and occupation of Iraq and the sorry misadventure in Afghanistan– have exposed the contradictions of this established postcolonialist understanding to stark and unforgiving light. For, conjoining violence and military conquest with expropriation, pillage, and undisguised grabbing for resources, these developments have demonstrably rejoined the twenty-first century to a long and as yet unbroken history, wrongly supposed by postcolonial theory to have come to a close *circa* 1975. This is the history of capitalist imperialism.

It is not, of course, that scholars in postcolonial studies are prone to give any credence to the official rationalisations that present the colossal violence visited on Afghanistan and Iraq – and also the wholesale destruction of civil liberties on the 'home' fronts in 'western' societies – as measured, defensive, and corrective responses to the ghastly Islamist attacks on the World Trade Center towers and the Pentagon on 11 September 2001, or to the subsequent bombings in Bali, Madrid, London, and elsewhere. After all, the lie to this official version of events has been given definitively in any number of subsequent investigative or analytical counter-commentaries, scholarly and journalistic. David Harvey's study of what he calls *The New Imperialism*, for instance, makes clear that '9/11' would better be understood as the 'Pearl Harbor' of which an increasingly organised and powerful American neo-conservativism had long been dreaming, an event that enabled the neo-conservatives at one and the same time to disable liberal opposition, drive towards hegemony, and 'impose [their] ... agenda on government'.[37] Neil Smith, for his part, insists that 'horrific as the loss of life was when those symbols of the military and economic power of the American empire were leveled', the events of 11 September 2001 'did not change the world'; they 'were exceptional ... only for sweeping away the global insularity of the vast majority of the population cocooned within the national borders of the world's one remaining superpower. People in most other parts of the world had faced similar if not far larger traumas'.[38] Writing in 2003, Smith added significantly that 'October 7, 2001 may well come to change the world', this latter marking the date on which 'the US government unleashed what it called its "war on terrorism" by bombing an already devastated Afghanistan ... From the halls of official state power around the world, but from nowhere more than Washington DC, old enemies were converted into terrorists and a hardening of nationally based state power commenced'.[39]

Yet if scholars in postcolonial studies have clearly been critical of the 'war on terror' and reassuringly unimpressed by the sophistries purveyed by the retinue of state ideologists and policy hacks attempting to justify it, they have not typically seen the contemporary developments as requiring them to do any rethinking themselves about the assumptions and common understandings prevailing in their own field. On the contrary, there has been a tendency to insist that what is urgently needed in the context of the debacles in Iraq and Afghanistan is more of precisely the kind of theory that had already been prevalent in the 1980s and 1990s. Thus Sangeeta Ray, who writes in 2005 that '[n]ow more than ever we need to pay attention to the work and role of specular, border intellectuals who have the courage to stand up against the evocation of the horror of alterity by calling attention to intellectually and ethically grounded work on the politics of alterity'.[40] An unintentional irony marks this formulation, and others like it, it seems to me: even though the profuse postcolonialist scholarship on 'the politics of alterity' during the 1980s and 1990s had been predicated fundamentally on assumptions as to the *obsolescence* of imperialism (one of the most important of the received 'modern' categories for 'accounting for the world', after all), Ray now calls for yet more work in this idiom as the best means of addressing the (imperialist) violence unleashed since '9/11'.

Part of the necessary corrective to this way of thinking is provided by the editors of another recent volume, *Postcolonial Studies and Beyond*, who see the need, in the wake of the invasion of Iraq, to call domination by its name:

> The shadow the 2003 US invasion of Iraq casts on the twenty-first century makes it more absurd than ever to speak of ours as a postcolonial world. On the other hand, the signs of galloping US imperialism make the agenda of postcolonial studies more necessary than ever. In a context of rapidly proliferating defenses of empire (not simply de facto but de jure) by policy makers and intellectuals alike, the projects of making visible the long history of empire, of learning from those who have opposed it, and of identifying the contemporary sites of resistance and oppression that have defined postcolonial studies have, arguably, never been more urgent.[41]

The editors' generous suggestion – in their introduction to a large, diverse, and incorporating volume[42] – that postcolonial studies has always been 'defined' as a field by 'the projects of making visible the long history of empire, of learning from those who have opposed it, and of identifying the contemporary sites of resistance and oppression' to it – is eminently contestable. My own view, as will be clear from what I have already written, is that it would be more accurate to maintain that postcolonial studies, in its prevailing and consolidated aspect at least, has been premised on a distinctive and conjuncturally determined set of assumptions, concepts, theories, and methods that have not only *not* been adequate to their putative object – the 'postcolonial world' – but have served fairly systematically to mystify it. But Loomba and colleagues are surely correct to insist that the 'urgent' task facing those in the field today, in the wake of the invasion, occupation and, evidently, the long-term destabilisation of Iraq, is to take central cognisance of the unremitting actuality and indeed the intensification of imperialist social relations in the times and spaces of the postcolonial world.

The full historical significance of the contemporary developments has been well conceptualised in these terms, by Jonathan Schell, as follows:

In the past 200 years, all of the earth's great territorial empires, whether dynastic or colonial, or both, have been destroyed. The list includes the Russian empire of the czars; the Austro-Hungarian Empire of the Habsburgs; the German empire of the Hohenzollerns, the Ottoman Empire, the Napoleonic Empire, the overseas empires of Holland, England, France, Belgium, Italy and Japan, Hitler's 'thousand-year Reich' and the Soviet empire. They were brought down by a force that, to the indignation and astonishment of the imperialists, turned out to be irresistible: the resolve of peoples, no matter how few they were or how poor, to govern themselves.

With its takeover of Iraq, the United States is attempting to reverse this universal historical verdict. It is seeking to reinvent the imperial tradition and reintroduce imperial rule – and on a global scale – for the twenty-first century. Some elements, like the danger of weapons of mass destruction, are new. Yet any student of imperialism will be struck by the similarities between the old style of imperialism and the new: the gigantic disparity between the technical and military might of the conquerors and the conquered; the inextricable combination of rapacious commercial interest and geopolitical ambition and design; the distortion and erosion of domestic constitutions by the immense military establishments, overt and covert, required for foreign domination; the use of one colony as a stepping stone to seize others or pressure them into compliance with the imperial agenda; the appeal to jingoism on the home front.[43]

Analysis of these developments would clearly not be served by an extension of the established postcolonial discussion, in which the term 'capitalism' has tended to be conspicuous largely by its absence (that is, where it has not actively been disparaged as the linchpin in a Eurocentric 'mode of production' narrative), and the term 'imperialism' has tended for the most part to be mobilised in description of a process of cultural and epistemological subjugation, whose material preconditions have been referred to only glancingly, if at all. What is required instead, it seems to me, is a new 'history of the present' – a new reading, above all of the second half of the twentieth century, liberated from the dead weight both of the cold war and of 'Third-Worldism' as its compensatory alternative.

The Postcolonial Unconscious is intended as a contribution to this new reading. In the interests of establishing a research 'archive' different from the one currently prevailing – differently weighted and with different emphases – I adopt a two-pronged approach: on the one hand, critique of ideas and categories that have structured the field in its dominant articulations hitherto; on the other, elaboration and renewal of counter-vailing ideas and categories. Sometimes my aim is to contest the constructions that have been placed upon specific concepts, historical developments, and bodies of writing by influential scholars in the field – constructions that I believe are weak or untenable. At other times, I set out to present new concepts, to defend theories that have been abandoned prematurely, and to discuss writers whose work has either received little attention or else is in urgent need of reinterpretation.

The easiest chapters of the book to introduce, in this respect, are the final two, both of which involve revisionary readings of theorists central to postcolonial studies: Frantz Fanon and Edward W. Said, respectively. In the case of Fanon, I take David Macey's ground-clearing biography, *Frantz Fanon: A Life*, as my point of departure. Macey argues that in the years since his death in 1961, the 'meaning' of Fanon has tended to be framed schematically. He identifies two conflicting and incompatible schemas – the insurgent 'Third Worldist' Fanon and the 'Postcolonial' Fanon. Each is in its own way historically determinate; yet neither plausibly registers the thrust and substance of Fanon's thought or writing. Using '9/11' and 'Iraq' as my pretexts, I re-examine Fanon's writings, attempting to account for their continuing cogency, and discuss and evaluate some of the new approaches to these writings that have emerged over the course of the past decade. In the case of Said, I join a debate already underway between his 'materialist' and 'post-structuralist' champions. Building on the work of Timothy Brennan, particularly, I examine *Orientalism* and Said's work on intellectuals, exploring his theory of knowledge, his nationalitarian politics and his commitment to human-ism, secularity and universalism.

The two longest chapters in the book are concerned with 'postcolonial' *literature*, and reflect my belief that there are vast intellectual resources available to us in this realm that have not remotely been plumbed by scholars working in the field. 'The Politics of Postcolonial Modernism', indeed, proceeds from the dispiriting observation that the range of literary works typically addressed by postcolonial scholars is not only remarkably attenuated, but that, even with reference to this restricted body of works, the same questions tend to be asked, the same methods used, the same concepts mobilised, and the same conclusions drawn. In attempting to understand this state of affairs, I turn to Raymond Williams's critique of literary modernism in his posthumously published *The Politics of Modernism*. There are some questions that have to be raised about Williams's understanding of modernism. But I argue that, even so, his critique retains a striking cogency by analogy in the analysis and critique of postcolonial studies. To challenge the hegemony of modernism, Williams argued that it would be necessary to 'search out and counterpose an alternative tradition taken from the neglected works left in the wide margin of the century'.[44] Pursuing this injunction in the postcolonial context, I propose some interconnected rubrics under which we might begin to reorganise our thinking about 'postcolonial' literature and suggest that thinking in terms of these rubrics would enable us to identify representational schemas that are pervasive, very widely distributed, often cardinal, and even definitive across its vast and hitherto unevenly and indifferently theorised corpus.

In my chapter on representation in 'postcolonial' literature, I demonstrate that in the consolidation of postcolonial studies in the 1980s and 1990s, the signature critique of colonialist (mis-)representation tended to broaden and flatten out. The struggle *over representations* gave way to the struggle *against representation* itself, on the ground that the desire to speak *for*, *of*, or even *about* others was always shadowed by a secretly authoritarian aspiration. The theoretical resort has then often been to a consideration of difference under the rubric of *incommensurability*. While the idea of incommensurability has been given an airing in some very well-known works of the 'postcolonial' corpus, I suggest that the vast majority of 'postcolonial' literary writings point us in a quite different direction, towards the idea not of 'fundamental alienness' but of deep-seated affinity and community, across and athwart the 'international division of labour'. I also attempt to trace and evaluate some of the ways in which 'postcolonial' writers have approached and thought through the difficulties of 'representation' (variously conceived) in their work.

A bridge chapter between the two long chapters on 'postcolonial' literature offers a defence and justification of Fredric Jameson's controversial and widely pilloried argument about 'Third World' literature. Jameson's 'sweeping hypothesis' that 'All third-world texts are necessarily ... allegorical, and in a very specific way: they are to be read as what I will call national allegories'[45] has been the subject of massive repudiation in postcolonial studies, largely following the lines laid down in Aijaz Ahmad's influential rebuttal. In reviewing the debate between these two Marxist theorists, I demonstrate the untenability of Ahmad's reading, draw out the implications of this for subsequent treatments of Jameson by postcolonial critics, and show that it is quite possible to defend Jameson from the charge of 'Third-Worldism', at least as Ahmad lays that charge.

CHAPTER I

The politics of postcolonial modernism

In recent years – since the mid 1990s, say – a more or less concerted materialist critique has arisen of the epistemological and ideological tendencies that have been foremost in postcolonial studies from the time of its initial consolidation as an academic field of enquiry in the elite universities of the anglophone world. While it would clearly be too much to claim that this emergent critique has succeeded in *overturning* the ruling tenets and protocols of the field, it nevertheless exercises a discernibly widening influence there. The specific assumptions and investments predominant in the field from its inception still predominate today, though not nearly as serenely as formerly. Among these assumptions and investments, I would list in particular the following: a constitutive anti-Marxism; an undifferentiating disavowal of all forms of nationalism and a corresponding exaltation of migrancy, liminality, hybridity, and multi-culturality; an hostility towards 'holistic forms of social explanation'[1] (towards totality and systemic analysis);[2] an aversion to dialectics; and a refusal of an antagonistic or struggle-based model of politics. Where, some fifteen years ago, Homi K. Bhabha could characterise these investments quite unilaterally and unselfconsciously as representing '*the* postcolonial perspective' (*Location of Culture*, p. 173), those speaking for the prevailing positions today tend to look over their shoulders while doing so, hedging their bets and introducing all kinds of qualification into what had previously been a relatively untrammelled discourse.

There is no need to rehearse here the arguments that have been adduced by the materialist critics in postcolonial studies. The best known of these will already be familiar to interested readers.[3] What I want to do, instead, is to take up some disciplinary questions concerning 'postcolonial' literature that derive from the materialist critique. Joining a discussion already inaugurated in the scholarly literature,[4] I want to argue, very broadly, that because of the tendentiousness and partiality of the theoretical assumptions that have structured postcolonial studies hitherto, literary scholars working in the field have tended to write with reference to a woefully restricted and attenuated corpus of works. On the one hand, so many works that ought – by the most orthodox criteria, such as representativeness or literary value – to have been taken into consideration, have been ignored entirely; on the other hand, the relatively few works that *have* been taken into consideration have often, and characteristically, been read in the most leadenly reductive of ways. I am tempted to overstate the case, for purposes of illustration, and declare that there is in a strict sense only one author in the postcolonial literary canon. That author is Salman Rushdie, whose novels – especially *Midnight's Children, Shame*, and *The Satanic Verses*[5] – are endlessly, not to say catechistically, cited in the critical literature as testifying to the instability and indeterminacy of social identity, the volatility and perspectivalism of truth, the narratorial constructedness of history, the ineluctable subjectivism of memory and experience, the violence implicit in the universalist discourse of the nation, the corresponding need to centre analysis on the notions of migrancy, hybridity, diaspora, 'in-betweenness', 'translation', and 'blasphemy' (as anti-hegemonic forms of transgression), and so on.[6]

I am sure I am not alone among scholars who read and teach 'postcolonial' *literature* as well as postcolonial *theory* in deploring both the sheer opportunism of so many of the critical readings currently being produced, and also the narrowness of the research base or range of works that is typically canvassed for this production.[7] To read across postcolonial literary studies is to find, to an extraordinary degree, the same questions being asked, the same methods, techniques, and conventions being used, the same concepts mobilised, the same conclusions drawn, about a remarkably small number of literary works (which are actually much more varied, even so, than you would ever discover from the existing critical discussion). For some scholars in the field, evidently, all that is required of the texts evoked is that they permit – which is to say, not actively disallow – a certain, very specific and very restricted kind of reading to be staged through reference to them. Thus, it seems to me, the profuse critical discussions of nationalism as 'imagined community',[8] with their utterly formulaic evocations of *Midnight's Children* or Okri's *The Famished Road* or Ghosh's *The Shadow Lines*;[9] and thus also the industrious commentaries on history as a master-narrative intrinsically complicit with domination, which quite bewilderingly summon Assia Djebar or Patrick Chamoiseau or Arundhati Roy to the bar, as though the writings of these novelists were not themselves insistently historicist in conception. So widespread and routine have such critical readings become that they have even begun to spawn a literary practice in their image. As Timothy Brennan has pointed out in a powerful critique of what he terms 'new cosmopolitan writing', a new literary genre is emerging today, of works that give the impression of having been produced precisely with an eye to their postcolonialist reception. 'Several younger writers', Brennan writes, 'have entered a genre of third world metropolitan fiction whose conventions have given their novels the unfortunate feel of ready-mades' (*At Home*, p. 203).[10]

Let me illustrate the general point I am trying to make here through reference to a 1992 book, *Interviews with Writers of the Postcolonial World*, co-edited by Feroza Jussawalla and Reed Way Dasenbrock. This is a fine book in many ways, certainly one of the more engaging collections of interviews in the postcolonial studies field to have been published to date, noteworthy for its range and theoretical sophistication. Fourteen writers are interviewed: Chinua Achebe, Rudolfo Anaya, Sandra Cisneros, Anita Desai, Buchi Emecheta, Nuruddin Farah, Zulfikar Ghose, Roy Heath, Rolando Hinojosa, Witi Ihimaera, Ngugi wa Thiong'o, Raja Rao, Sam Selvon, and Bapsi Sidhwa. I shall refer only in passing to the obvious problems posed by this collocation of names. What thematic concerns, historical conditions, or existential predicaments can plausibly be said to license the inclusion of such authors as Ngugi, Ghose, and Ihimaera under any shared rubric, let alone that of 'postcoloniality'? Does it make sense to extrapolate the work of US-based Latino writers like Anaya, Cisneros and Hinojosa to the postcolonial?

To do them credit, Jussawalla and Dasenbrock attempt to provide answers to these questions. They propose, thus, that the writers interviewed in the volume all share 'a common heritage of colonialism and post-colonialism, a common heritage of multilingualism and multi-culturalism, a common heritage of displacement and migration'.[11] This, they suggest, not only makes it advisable to situate 'minority' writers from Britain and North America in relation to 'postcolonial' writers from Africa and Asia and the South Pacific; it also explodes the credibility of any nation-based approach to these writers. Jussawalla and Dasenbrock advocate instead a new variant of comparative literature, a 'comparative literature within English' (p. 14) that will be sensitive to the emergence of new traditions of writing while remaining alert to the degree to which these new traditions are being produced 'in some respects against the grain and against the conventions of mainstream Anglo-American writing' (pp. 18–19).[12]

Such a standpoint has something to commend it, at least. Jussawalla's and Dasenbrock's commitment to 'multiculturalism' serves as a credible platform from which to engage urbane and cosmopolitan writers like Ihimaera or Farah or Anaya in conversation. Unsurprisingly, therefore, these are among the most successful interviews in the volume. Certain of the other writers interviewed, however, do not share the editors' cultural or intellectual commitments. With respect to these writers, Jussawalla's and Dasenbrock's determination to place the problematics of hybridity and multiculturalism centre stage is dogmatic, and sometimes strangles conversation rather than facilitating it. Desai, Sidhwa, Heath, and Cisneros are all encouraged to reflect upon their multiculturality, whether or not this seems in keeping with the general tone of the discussion. The interview with Rao quickly goes awry when Jussawalla and Dasenbrock refer in general terms to 'post-colonial' writers' supposed interest in cross-cultural communication. Rao responds both that he is an Indian and not any other kind of writer, and that he is 'not interested in communicating across cultures' (p. 143). But Jussawalla and Dasenbrock seem strangely incapable of grasping the thrust of this authentically conservative position. On the very next page we find them alluding to the 'multiculturalism' of India, which draws from Rao the reproving counter-question: 'Why are you so interested in multiculturality?' (p. 144); and two pages later Rao is obliged to protest that '[h]ere again we are talking too much about internationalism and interculture' (p. 146).

A similar pattern manifests itself in the interview with Zulfikar Ghose. Again, the editors sound their general themes of hybridity and multicul-turalism, translation and accessibility; again, the writer being interviewed demurs from the line of questioning, indicating his commitment to an entirely different aesthetic ideology; and again the editors seem obtusely incapable of recognising the writer's standpoint – or perhaps they are disinclined to do so? Jussawalla asks how Ghose wants his reader to get at the 'larger meanings' in his work. Ghose answers, 'I have no interest in the reader. I never think of the reader. I don't know who the reader is' (p. 186). Jussawalla then asks what Ghose makes of his status as 'a multicultural writer', to which Ghose's response is, 'I'm not multicultural. I'm British. I'm really more Anglo-Saxon than the Anglo-Saxons' (p. 187). It is a firm, if perverse, rejoinder, but the editors wholly disregard it. Within a few pages – as though Ghose had said nothing – they are referring to him once more as a 'multicultural' writer, who embodies in his person 'what's getting to be an increasingly multicultural world'

(p. 195). Ghose is compelled to reiterate that 'this talk about the importance of the multicultural background that supposedly makes some Commonwealth writers so remarkable is utterly inconsequential. The only thing of consequence is the quality of the mind of the writer' (pp. 195–6). It is no wonder that Ghose seems generally testy, snapping back on one occasion that he is 'not an intellectual at all' and that in fact 'I refuse to have ideas. I despise ideas. Ideas have never helped mankind. Only *things* help. Things like penicillin and flushing toilets' (p. 193)!¹³

The sheer appropriativeness of some of the readings regularly put forward in postcolonial studies can still make one gasp: as in the example just cited, where novelists like Ngugi and Heath and Rao are implausibly linked under the sign of 'multiculturalism', so elsewhere we encounter presentations of Wole Soyinka and Kamau Brathwaite as poets closely aligned, in their deepest convictions, with deconstruction; of Bessie Head as a 'difference' feminist, less the Cape Gooseberry than the Southern African Hélène Cixous; of Assia Djebar, Ama Ata Aidoo, and Mahasweta Devi as principled opponents of nationalist discourse *tout court*, rather than of *official* nationalist discourse; and so on. But part of what I want to argue is that even the work of such writers as, say, Rushdie, Vikram Chandra, Maryse Condé, Luisa Valenzuela, Abdelkebir Khatibi, Sony Labou Tansi, or Derek Walcott, all of whom seem undeniably to lend themselves to what we might call pomo-postcolonialist reading ('pomo' as in 'postmodernist'), are not necessarily best or most illuminatingly approached in these terms. There is no need to deny that the concepts, problematics, and methods generated within postcolonial studies have contributed illuminatingly to the interpretation and elucidation of important literary works today called 'postcolonial'. It is also obvious that elective affinities obtain between many such works and the distinctive concepts and methods of postcolonial studies – between J. M. Coetzee's *Waiting for the Barbarians* or *Foe* and the problematics of alterity and incommensurability, for instance; or between Tahar Ben Jelloun's *The Sand Child* and the theory of identity as a performative construct; or between Nuruddin Farah's *Maps* and the critique of essentialist myths of origin.¹⁴ Even so, however, it seems to me that there is so much that we *fail* to attend to when we programmatically refer Coetzee's novels to Lacan, Foucault, or Levinas; or Caribbean literature as a whole to the Deleuzean concepts of extraterritoriality and the rhizome; or the representation of home and belonging in the work of Bharati Mukherjee or Caryl Phillips only to the explicitly post-nationalist debates on diaspora and hybridity.

Moreover, just as important as the fact that works like these are being read so unimaginatively is the fact that so many other extraordinary works, which are not really susceptible to analysis in terms of the received categories and conventions in the field, are being substantially neglected by postcolonialists, if indeed they are known at all. As a number of critics have pointed out, the field of postcolonial studies is structured in such a way that it is much more likely to register the presence of writing in English and, to a lesser extent, French or Spanish,[15] than writing in such other languages as Chinese, Arabic, Yoruba, Zulu, Amharic, Malay, Urdu, Telugu, Bengali, Sinhala, Tagalog, or even in the formerly colonial but 'minor' metropolitan languages of Dutch and Portuguese. Similarly, it is much more likely to register the presence of writers who adopt generic and modal conventions readily assimilable by Euro-American readers than of writers who root their work in other conventions. We should not be particularly surprised, under these circumstances – though we might still find it deplorable – that writers such as Iftikhar Arif, Ismat Chughtai, Mia Couto, Duong Thu Huong, Gamal el-Ghitani, Zulfikar Ghose, Ebrahim Hussein, Hwang Sun-won, Sahar Khalifeh, Clarice Lispector, Abdelrahman Munif, Nirala, Odia Ofeimun, Shu Ting, Pramoedya Ananta Toer, Lesego Rampolokeng, Tarashankar Bandyopadhyay, Trefossa, Fadwa Tuqan, and Nirmal Verma are pretty much completely unknown to a majority of scholars in postcolonial literary studies. More unexpected, however, must be the fact that one could just as easily come up with an equally long list of equally consecrated anglophone, francophone, and hispanophone writers who, despite their formal accessibility and their consecration, again command only slender prestige in the field: Claribel Alegría, Mongo Beti, Ralph de Boissière, Dennis Brutus, Jan Carew, Mohammed Dib, Nissim Ezekiel, Yasmine Gooneratne, Alamgir Hashmi, Abdellatif Laâbi, Amin Maalouf, K. S. Maniam, Gabriela Mistral, Timothy Mo, Nancy Morejón, V. Y. Mudimbe (as a novelist, not as a theorist), Femi Osofisan, Olive Senior, Ninotchka Rosca, Nayantara Sahgal, Albert Wendt, to pluck some names almost at random from my own bookshelves.

Let me pause for a moment here to clarify what I mean. There are, of course, quite substantial critical literatures on at least some of the authors from each of the two lists I have just presented – dedicated books and many articles (perhaps even hundreds), for instance, on each of Brutus, Lispector, Ezekiel, Mistral, and Sahgal. This is precisely why I speak of these as *consecrated* writers. But my point is that their consecration has been bestowed in literary and critical fields *other than that of postcolonial studies*, even if, in abstract terms, abutting and intersecting it – national- or regional- or cultural- or language-literature fields such as 'Nigerian' or 'Chinese' or 'Latin American' or 'Tamil' or 'Arabic', where the principles of selection and hierarchisation are demonstrably different from those operating in the postcolonial studies field. Among the questions that we then need to ask are: How is the relative neglect by literary postcolonialists of writers like these, *especially* when they are so well regarded by scholars working in the adjacent and abutting literary critical fields, to be explained? And what conclusions ought we to draw about the adequacy of what scholars in postcolonial studies have been saying about 'postcolonial' literature or, beyond that, 'postcoloniality', when they so consistently fail to take writers like these into account?

In trying to answer these questions, I have found Raymond Williams's revisionary critique of literary modernism in his posthumously published book, *The Politics of Modernism*, immensely suggestive. Williams's argument is that modernism was the name of a specific and determinate intervention into the field of modern literary production in Europe (and the United States, though Williams has less to say about this) in the first two or three decades of the twentieth century. This intervention succeeded beyond its proponents' wildest expectations. Modernism displaced the received cultural formations of its time and consolidated itself at their expense. Not only did it succeed in establishing itself as the dominant aesthetic formation in its time and place, it construed its own particular dispositions – Williams lists exile and metropolitanism, for instance – as being *uniquely responsive to modernity*. It constructed its own historically, socially, and culturally specific protocols, procedures, and horizons as those of the modern as such. As Williams puts it, modernism recast, rewrote, and rearranged cultural history, producing a selective tradition whose selectivity remained invisible to modernism itself: the authors and 'theoretic contours' usually addressed under the rubric of modernism constituted 'a highly selected version of the modern which then offer[ed] to appropriate the whole of modernity'.[16] The selective tradition that was modernism construed itself in universalistic terms as '*the* literature of modernity'. And because it emerged as the victor in the culture wars of its own time, modernism was able to ground its own definitions as the operative definitions in the fields in which it was active. It was able, to switch theoretical vocabularies for a moment (from that of Williams to that of Bourdieu), to establish for itself the monopoly of legitimacy in the cultural field, 'the monopoly of the *power of consecration* of producers and products'.[17] What this meant was, among other things, that all of the forms of cultural production displaced by modernism – those, that is, that were not modern*ist* – were pronounced *pre*-modern and disparaged as such, as relics, mere anachronisms, forms whose time had definitively come and gone.

To situate modernism in relation to modernity in the context of a discussion of 'postcolonial' literature is to raise some very large and controversial questions. One might argue, for instance, following Theodor W. Adorno, that modernism's essential gesture is to say 'no' to modernity. But then it might immediately be objected that this Adornian formula leaves unresolved the question of the relation of modernism to *colonialism*. The point is that while colonialism is commonly taken as intrinsic to the socio-historical project of *modernity, modernism* is not typically viewed – for all its 'dissidence' – as featuring an *anticolonial* dimension. On the contrary, modernism is typically viewed, for all that it says 'no' to modernity, as a Eurocentric projection, as itself latently if not explicitly colonialist in character. Hence, for instance, the critique of modernism as 'Euro-modernism' in African Marxist and cultural nationalist discourse of the 1950s and 1960s.[18] In a recent article, Simon Gikandi offers a splendid challenge to this received construction of modernism, arguing that, in Africa at least, modernism and anticolonialism have to be understood as mutually enabling and mutually entailing discourses:

In the colonial African context ... the relationship between modernism and modernity was complicated by their contemporaneousness, the fact that the two categories became central to African reflections on their identity and destiny at about the same time. More significantly, while European modernism self-consciously posited itself as a structure opposed to modernity and modernisation, even when it was a consequence of these processes, colonial modernism, like nationalism itself, could not legitimise itself without some kind of self-willed affiliation with modernity. In arguing for the liberation of the African, nationalist intellectuals premised their claim on the fact that modernity could be achieved without the tutelage of colonialism, that indeed, the colonisation of Africa stunted its modernity.[19]

Gikandi argues not only that 'African modernism was produced in relation to mainstream European movements and ideas' and that 'African intellectuals were important players in the European centres of modern art' – two truths very widely accepted nowadays – but that 'while their Western counterparts sought to use the ideology of modernism to undo nationalism, African artists adopted the same aesthetic ideology to imagine and will into being new nations. Nationalism has become a dirty word in some circles, but for the colonised it was a redemptive project that needed an aesthetic dimension in order to fulfil its mandate' (pp. 24–5). The heuristic significance of these words for the argument I am attempting to make in this chapter is significant.

One can – and must, I think – contest the final adequacy of Williams's construction of modernism, which rather tends to write out of the modernist project its critical and even revolutionary dimensions, as evidenced in the intellectual and cultural practice of such figures as El Lissitsky and Eisenstein, Brecht and Benjamin, Lorca and Picasso, among literally dozens of others.[20] The modernism that Williams critiques is in a sense a retrospective modernism, the modernism that would come into existence belatedly or after the fact, as it were – and as a result of what Fredric Jameson has termed the 'canonization and academic institutional-ization' of the modernist movement, 'that can be traced to the late 1950s' (*Postmodernism*, p. 4). Jameson records that the late- and post-Victorian bourgeoisies, at least, were under no illusions about the challenge or affront represented by modernist culture, whose 'forms and ethos' they found 'variously ugly, dissonant, obscure, scandalous, immoral, subversive, and generally "antisocial"'. In undergoing incorporation, canonisation, and institutionalisation after 1945, however, modernist works lost their criticality, according to Jameson; their sting was drawn, their dissonance domesticated, their sheer oppositionality neutralised. Today, he writes, '[n]ot only are Picasso and Joyce no longer ugly; they now strike us, on the whole, as rather "realistic"'. (By 'realistic' here, I take it, Jameson means mundane, routine, everyday, matter-of-fact. Certainly, in the light of the brutal and lurid record of the twentieth century, the occasional extremism, grotesquerie, and excessiveness of modernist representation, which had so offended its contemporary audience, no longer seem particularly shocking or morbid.)

Jameson's periodising commentary is helpful in allowing us to qualify Williams's critique of modernism, which might otherwise seem un-discriminating. Williams is clearly too quick to generalise from that particular tendency *within* modernist literary practice that found conse-cration and academic institutionalisation in the post-1945 period. His conceptualisation of modernism is therefore itself susceptible to criti-cism on historical and definitional grounds. Conversely, however, I think we should also be wary of accepting without reflection Jameson's argument that modernism's erstwhile criticality has been neutralised. We can readily concede that in today's world, what would once have seemed 'ugly' now seems 'realistic'. But to say this is not to say that what is thus represented is no longer disturbing or disquieting or unnerving. Consider for a moment Adorno's evocative claim (in an essay written as late as 1962, interestingly), that '[a]nyone over whom Kafka's wheels have passed has lost both his sense of being at peace with the world and the possibility of being satisfied with the judgment that the course of the world is bad: the moment of confirmation inherent in a resigned acknowledgment of the superior power of evil has been eaten away'.[21] Looking back from our contemporary vantage point, more than forty years on, we might indeed be inclined to nod in agreement with Jameson and declare that whatever truth Adorno's formulation might initially have held (with respect to Kafka's time, or perhaps even to Adorno's own), it is no longer true. (Any teacher of literature who reads Adorno's words and – thinking of how astoundingly blasé today's students often seem – finds himself or herself saying wistfully, 'if only', might be reckoned to be speaking in confirmation of Jameson's point.) For is it not in fact the case that Kafka's wheels today pass over most of his readers without much consequence? With rare exceptions, surely, Kafka's contemporary readers are *not* frozen in their tracks, rocked to their socks, by their encounter with him. Still less does the encounter leave them forever unconsoled, as Adorno would have hoped and even, indeed, expected.[22] The unassimilable Kafka, we might therefore be led to infer, has become the canonised, assimilated Kafka. Modernist writing has lost its erstwhile power, of destabilising or unnerving: on the one hand, the world has changed; on the other hand, in the restricted sphere of literary criticism, the meaning of 'modernism' – skeletalised by New Criticism into a metaphysics and a technique – has changed too, and, along with it, the abilities, sensitivities, and predilections of readers.

Jameson's arguments about the latter-day waning of 'affect' and 'criticality' are certainly challenging and thought-provoking. But I am ultimately unpersuaded by them. My own position differs from both Williams's, on the one side, and Jameson's, on the other. For I want to insist, as neither of these theorists does, upon the *ongoing* critical dimension of modernist literary practice. I am interested in work by *contemporary* writers (including 'postcolonial' ones) that seems (still) to be driven by recognisably modernist protocols and procedures. My suggestion is that, confronted by this work and these writers, we cannot proceed without a theory responsive simultaneously to the notional indispensability and the practical achievement of what, basing myself on Adorno's investigation of the 'Kafka effect' in the formulation cited above, I will call 'disconsolation' in and through literature. Neither

Williams nor Jameson seems to allow – if for different reasons – that there might be a *modernist writing after the canonisation of modernism* – a writing, that is to say, that resists the accommodationism of what has been canonised as modernism and that does what at least *some* modernist work has done from the outset: namely, says 'no'; refuses integration, resolution, consolation, comfort; protests and criticises.[23]

To say that there is only the shortest of distances between 'In the Penal Colony' and Coetzee's *Waiting for the Barbarians*; to identify the affinity between the forms of narration in 'The Metamorphosis' and García Márquez's *One Hundred Years of Solitude*; to propose that the crazy lucidity of *The Trial* or 'A Hunger Artist' finds a compelling echo in Manto's 'Toba Tek Singh': all this is not merely to talk truistically about Kafka's 'influence' on Coetzee and García Márquez and Manto, but to begin to specify the conceptual underpinnings of a particular *kind* of writing, a particular *mode* of literary practice, common to all three authors.[24] *Disconsolation* is the project of this writing, its deepest aesthetic (hence indirectly social) aspiration.[25] *Pace* Jameson, I do not believe that this project has been exhausted over the course of the past sixty years, either as a result of the recuperation of modernism in academic discourse or as a result of more far-reaching changes in the social order. It is still within the compass of art, as Arundhati Roy (writing of the south Indian dance form of Kathakali) puts it in *The God of Small Things*, to 'reveal the nugget of sorrow that happiness contains. The hidden fish of shame in a sea of glory'.[26]

I cannot resist mentioning Kazuo Ishiguro in this context, not least because the title of his fourth novel, *The Unconsoled*, so perfectly captures the essential gesture of modernist literary practice, as I am presenting it here.[27] 'Disconsolation' is also the central aesthetic *effect* of Ishiguro's fiction, as it is of Kafka's. The melancholy that suffuses Ishiguro's work is finally of the order of philosophy. His novels offer us intimate portraits of the wreckage of lives that have been lived wrongly, in the shadow or under the auspices of malign social, cultural, ideological, and familial dispensations. These lives themselves matter, of course – those of Etsuko and Sachiko, of Masuji Ono, of Stevens, for instance, in Ishiguro's first three novels, respectively – and the characters' search in these novels for consolation, justification, reconciliation, is urgent and unceasing.[28] But what seems to me to matter even more in Ishiguro's fiction is that the acts and thoughts that *cannot* be forgiven or apologised for or reconciled be glimpsed in the light of a yearning for fellowship or collectivity – even though it is precisely these acts and thoughts that, in substantive terms, have made fellowship and collectivity impossible. 'Chips of messianic time':[29] a frail light from utopia shines on, or rather, through, the unseeing eyes and unknowing thoughts of Ishiguro's characters. It is this transcendental implication that engenders 'disconsolation' in us as readers, and that enables us to register Ishiguro's work as modernist in its thrust and tendency.[30]

I have been suggesting that Williams's construction of modernism can be faulted both for its relative lack of internal discrimination and for its relative insensitivity to modernism's (ongoing) critical dimension. Even so, it seems to me that his critique of modernism retains a striking cogency by analogy in the analysis and critique of postcolonial studies. The key point here is that in postcolonial studies, as in modernism on Williams's reading of it, a certain limited optic on the world, a '*selective tradition*', has been imagined, and is proposed, as a universal. Like Williams's modernists, postcolonial critics have also been disposed to construe their own particular dispositions – their own particular situations, their own specific locations in the social order, their own specific views on to the world – as cultural universals. (A slippage, or disjuncture, in the analogy must then immediately be noted. The selectivity of the 'tradition' represented by what Gary Pearce helpfully terms 'conscious modernism' was at least partially the product of such modernist writers as Eliot, Pound, and Woolf themselves [aided, of course, and especially after 1945, by New Criticism in the United States and the *Scrutiny* project in Britain and the Commonwealth territories]. In the case of postcolonial studies, by contrast, the attenuated or selective tradition is almost exclusively the product of *critical* discourse. Comparatively few 'postcolonial' *writers* themselves have been involved in the conscious delimitation of postcolonial studies.)[31]

In 'The Postcolonial and the Postmodern', an essay in which he tries, as he puts it, 'to rename the postmodern from the position of the postcolonial', Bhabha writes that

The postcolonial perspective forces us to rethink the profound limitations of a consensual and collusive 'liberal' sense of cultural community. It insists that cultural and political identity are constructed through a process of alterity. Questions of race and cultural difference overlay issues of sexuality and gender and overdetermine the social alliances of class and democratic socialism. The time for 'assimilating' minorities to holistic and organic notions of cultural value has dramatically passed. The very language of cultural community needs to be rethought from a postcolonial perspective. (*Location of Culture*, p. 175)

The political claims lodged in this formulation are serious ones, no doubt. But the presumptive universalism of Bhabha's formulation is without empirical warrant.[32] It quickly collapses when subjected to critical scrutiny. For if the predicates that Bhabha lays out here are what 'the postcolonial perspective' mandates (and he does, after all, say '*forces us to rethink*'), then we are obliged to conclude – on the basis of any representative sampling – that most of the writers who write from locations in the various different postcolonial countries today, as well as most of those who hail from such countries but currently reside – temporarily or permanently – in metropolitan Europe or North America, are not in fact 'postcolonial' writers at all, but must instead be considered somehow 'pre-postcolonial'. For most such writers simply do not write from the perspective that Bhabha spells out for us – and that he himself clearly believes is uniquely responsive to the social and historical condition of 'postcoloniality'. Moreover, in the case of a significant number of these writers, at least, they do not fail to write from this perspective by omission or default, but on the basis of the strictest conviction. Put baldly, their assumptions about identity and community and cultural value and politics are quite different from those revealed in the passage by Bhabha just quoted. Think of Ngugi wa Thiong'o's sustained commentary on the language question in African literature, for instance, in which an emphatically identitarian and unisonant notion of cultural community is presented in order to ground the novelist's opposition to europhone languages as being in a fundamental sense 'alien' to Africa.[33] Think also of Ngugi's later novels, *Petals of Blood, Devil on the Cross, Matigari*, and *Wizard of the Crow* – the latter three composed and originally published not in English but in Gikuyu – with their rigorous insistence on the class basis of social identity in Kenya and Africa.[34] Or think, in a quite different register, of Nayantara Sahgal, whose writing over half a century now, fictional and non-fictional – from *Prison and Chocolate Cake* to *This Time of Morning, A Time to be Happy, Rich Like Us, Mistaken Identity*, and *Lesser Breeds* – has consistently ratified the very 'consensual', 'liberal' (or social democratic) notion of 'cultural community' (her own version of Nehruvianism) that Bhabha describes as being profoundly limited and as needing to be rethought.[35] Or, again changing register radically, think of Timothy Mo's wilful and provocatively essentialist evocation of 'oriental fatalism' – the term he himself uses in *Renegade or Halo²* – as 'something real, not the invention of the West'.[36]

I cite Ngugi and Sahgal and Mo – in one respect they merely stand in for literally hundreds of novelists, poets, and dramatists who could have been mentioned here to make the same point – because there is almost nothing that they have in common as writers and thinkers except, ironically, for the fact that they are not remotely spoken for by Bhabha's 'postcolonial perspective'. (Ngugi is a Marxist, Sahgal a Nehruvian secular socialist, Mo a quirky conservative whose encomium – 'This is one of those rare books ... which will shape the times as well as reflect them' – adorns the back page of the British edition of Samuel Huntington's *The Clash of Civilizations* and keeps company there with Henry Kissinger, Zbigniew Brzezinski, and Francis Fukuyama!)[37] Yet it seems obvious to me that any attempt to theorise 'postcolonial' literature or even 'post-coloniality' will need to come to terms with them, or with writers like them – to contextualise them, assess them, situate them alongside a teeming and heterogeneous (but not for this reason unsystematisable) multiplicity of other writers, *including* pomo-postcolonialist writers. What such a theory *cannot* afford to do, however, without abandoning its claims to validity, is to follow the example of the pomo-postcolonialist critics and misdiagnose a restricted mode of practice as a cultural universal. It ill behoves a theory professing a commitment (however vague and ill-defined) to the world beyond the boundaries of Europe and North America, to mistake a discrete cultural tendency – even if it is held to be a cultural dominant – for the only game in town.

In *The Politics of Modernism*, Williams proposes a double-sided counter-practice to literary modernism. It involves, on the one hand, exploring modernism

with something of its own sense of strangeness and distance, rather than with the comfortable and now internally accommodated forms of its incorporation and naturalization. This means, above all, seeing the imperial and capitalist metropolis as a specific historical form, at different stages: Paris, London, Berlin, New York. It involves looking, from time to time, from outside the metropolis: from the deprived hinterlands, where different forces are moving, and from the poor world which has always been peripheral to the metropolitan systems. This need involve no reduction of the importance of the major artistic and literary works which were shaped within metropolitan perceptions. But one level has certainly to be challenged: the metropolitan interpretation of its own processes as universals. (p. 47)

In the analogous context of postcolonial studies, this kind of work is already well underway. Dozens of scholars have recently undertaken to situate postcolonial studies in sociological and historical terms – both as an intellectual formation and in wider, institutional and ideological, terms; and they have effectively described and challenged the premises and conclusions of its leading proponents. But Williams also calls for another kind of work, which is equally important in challenging the hegemony of modernism. 'If we are to break out of the non-historical fixity of *post*-modernism', he writes,

then we must search out and counterpose an alternative tradition taken from the neglected works left in the wide margin of the century, a tradition which may address itself not to this by now exploitable because quite inhuman rewriting of the past but, for all our sakes, to a modern future in which community may be imagined again. (p. 35)

My sense is that if we take up this injunction in the postcolonial context, we will find no single 'alternative tradition', but rather any number of them. Nevertheless, the injunction is absolutely worth taking up. For while an immanent critique of 'the postcolonial perspective' is both possible and necessary, it is only on the basis of a transcendental critique – that is to say, on the basis of the formulation of an alternative theory – that it can be definitively superseded. It is to this task, I believe – of developing a new approach to 'postcolonial' literature – that we in postcolonial studies are now especially enjoined, and we should not shrink from it.

I want to proceed, accordingly, with a ground-clearing exercise of sorts. When we survey the vast and hitherto unevenly and indifferently theorised corpus of 'postcolonial' literature, our attention is quickly drawn to the fact that, across its full range, certain themes, optics, situations, and kinds of writing are very widely distributed – pervasive, cardinal, and even definitive. I would like to propose that we generate a set of rubrics or headings under which these themes, optics, and so on might be systematised, and that we attempt to reorganise our thinking about 'postcolonial' literature in terms of these. A schema based on this proposal would need to include, at a minimum, the following rubrics, it seems to me:

i.   Mode of production and class relations
ii. Land and environment
iii. State and nation
iv. Structures of feeling

In what follows, I will seek to comment briefly on each of these rubrics, indicating what I take it as incorporating and entailing. I recognise, of course, that the methodological thrust of my list – with its implicit activation of the Marxist metaphor of base and superstructure, and its loose reliance on Williams's formulation of 'cultural materialism' – might strike some readers as partisan.[38] But I see no reason to apologise for this.

The schema that I am proposing is not being presented as in any sense exhaustive or exclusive. Although I am certainly attempting to redress an imbalance in the existing critical discourse, I am not suggesting that we refer *every* literary work that we might classify as 'postcolonial' to one or another of these four rubrics. (This would amount to replacing the reductionism of the current criticism with another form of reductionism, equally unreflexive.) My interest in proposing channels for research that would cut against the narrow grain of mainstream postcolonial criticism springs not merely from my opposition to the ideological and epistemological assumptions that have tended to frame postcolonial studies as a field of enquiry hitherto, but equally from my conviction that postcolonial *criticism* – as an institutionalised mode of academic practice – has tended to turn a blind eye to what 'postcolonial' *literature*, considered in the round, has notably been concerned to put on display.[39] The gap or disjuncture between the purviews of 'literature' and 'criticism' here is no cause for celebration, in my view: I see it as telling decisively against the latter, testifying both to its abstraction and to the tenuousness of its grasp of the central realities of life in the 'postcolonial' world (which of course form the major focus of the literature produced in this world). Part of my ambition in this chapter is therefore to contribute to a bridging of the gap between 'text' and 'critic', on the grounds that the 'world' has to date typically been more adequately registered, and rendered, in 'postcolonial' *literature* than in postcolonial *criticism*.[40]

MODE OF PRODUCTION AND CLASS RELATIONS

Although it is ubiquitously cited in passing (typically as one in a string of such formally equivalent 'identity markers' as race and ethnicity, sex and gender, region and generation), the category of class is seldom afforded sustained or specific attention in mainstream postcolonial criticism. The recoil from Marxism evident across culture studies as a whole in the Anglo-American academy in the post-1975 years – a development discussed in my introduction, above – must of course be adduced in partial explanation here. Within postcolonial studies, it is notable that the core concepts of 'colonialism' and even 'imperialism' are routinely severed from the concept of 'capitalism'. Even on the best postcolonialist accounts, such as Edward Said's in *Culture and Imperialism*, 'imperialism' is typically cast as a *political* dispensation and referred, in civilisational terms, to 'the West', rather than to capitalism. Thus Said holds 'imperialism' to implicate military conquest, alien governance, systematised top-down violence, social asymmetry, cultural and symbolic domination, and Eurocentrism as a set of deeply patterned 'structures of attitude and reference' (p. 61). He makes comparatively little of the fact that it centrally involves the imposition of a particular mode or modes of production and specific regimes of accumulation, expropriation, exploitation in the form of the extraction of surplus value, and so on. Benita Parry's overview of the contradictions deriving from what she calls Said's 'deliberated disengagement' from Marxism in *Culture and Imperialism* is very compelling in this respect. I quote from it at length:

> Said's was the long view of 'imperialism' as 'the practice, the theory and the attitude of a dominating centre ruling a distant territory', and because his interest was in the formation of ideologies underwriting an European hegemony, the study is not concerned with differentiating between mercantile-plantation colonialism, which stimulated the accumulation of capital in Europe, and the subsequent industrial-military interventions of metropolitan nation-states in overseas territories, an era known to historians and political scientists as 'imperialism' and austerely described by Rosa Luxemburg as 'the political expression of the accumulation of capital in its competitive struggle for what remains still open of the non-capitalist environment'. Said wrote with passionate intensity about imperial aggression without referring to the analysis of Lenin or Luxemburg; he distinguished between anticolonial nationalism and liberation movements without alluding to the communist orientation of the latter or the class interests of either; and he placed economic and political machinery and territorial aggrandizement at the center of modern empire without specifying capitalism's world system.[41]

For theoretical reasons alone, therefore, it seems important to fly in the face of the prevailing wind in postcolonial studies and insist that whatever else it might have and, indeed, *did* involve – all the way from the systematic annihilation of whole communities to the cultivation of aesthetic tastes and preferences (needs of the imagination, as Marx called wants of this kind in his chapter on the commodity in *Capital*, as distinct from needs of the stomach)[42] – colonialism as an historical process involved the forced integration of hitherto uncapitalised societies, or societies in which the capitalist mode of production was not hegemonic, into a capitalist world-system. Over the course of a couple of centuries in some territories, mere decades in others, generalised commodity production was imposed: production for exchange rather than use; monetisation; the development of specifically capitalist markets (involving 'free' wage labour and the buying and selling of labour power), or the appropriation, de- and re-centralising of existing markets, and of ancillary systems and institutions designed to enable and facilitate the consolidation, extension, and reproduction of capitalist production and capitalist class relations. Along the way, existing social relations and modes of existence were undermined, destroyed, reconfigured; new social relations and modes of existence were brought into being. Existing circuits of production, distributions of power, constellations of value and meaning, were disturbed, appropriated, reoriented. Peasantries were destroyed, along with subsistence, tributary, and market economies (some of them vast and elaborate), to be replaced by capitalised agriculture in one location, proletarianisation in another, with waves of migratory labour (more or less regulated, sometimes not at all) in between. Ruling elites were made, unmade, and remade, the basis of their power thoroughly transformed.

Yet it is not only for theoretical reasons that it is necessary to insist on the centrality of capitalism to colonialism. It is also because this point is steadily figured (and often given direct emphasis) across the full range of 'postcolonial' literature – in poetry and drama as much as in fiction. Thus what the social scientist Immanuel Wallerstein speaks of as 'the commodification of everything' is registered equally succinctly, also, by the Congolese novelist Sony Labou Tansi in *The Antipeople*: 'The invasion of money into everyday life is something the Belgians left us as a mark of love.'[43] Where the identification of social conditions of existence in the (post-)colonial world is concerned, literature has typically played a vanguardist, not a belated, role.

Indeed, the protracted, brutal, and violently disruptive process through which peasant economies, both material and 'moral' or symbolic, were undermined and disrupted – with capitalist class relations being superimposed over them, historic patterns of land tenure and corresponding modes of community decimated, new forms of community, and of resistance, forged – constitutes the very subject matter of a number of significant literary works. Ngugi wa Thiong'o's panoramic novel, *Petals of Blood*, for instance, centres on Ilmorog, which mutates over its course from a peasant village – 'at its most expansive a haven, but subject still to the ravages of nature'[44] – into the horror of 'New Ilmorog', an industrial wasteland of factories and slums, leaving the bulk of its inhabitants ruined: dispossessed, impoverished, and demoralised. As Tamara Sivanandan observes, '[t]he juxtaposition of the village/city in the story is no mere provider of incidental background, but effectively maps a geography of imperialism, and is a metaphor for the contrast between the potential for autochthonous development – a realisation of the dreams of independence that the common people struggled for – and its supersession by a native capitalism in cahoots with a global imperialism' (p. 15). The same process also forms the backdrop of F. Sionil José's major fiction, most notably the *Rosales Saga*, which, considered as a whole, offers a veritably Balzacian portrait of Filipino culture and society from the mid nineteenth century to the end of the twentieth.[45] One could also cite here such masterworks as Munif's *Cities of Salt*, Fuentes' *The Years with Laura Díaz* and Lovelace's *Salt*, which, as vastly different from one another in form, tone, and ideology as they are in location (an unnamed state in the Persian Gulf, Mexico, and Trinidad, respectively), are nevertheless all directed to the *longue durée* of a specifically capitalist imperialism.[46]

To say that the forced introduction of capitalism in the historical contexts of colonialism spawned the development of new classes and groupings, and of new forms of class domination and struggle, is not, of course, to say that the social relations previously existing were simply overwritten or replaced. On the contrary, capitalism in these contexts was superimposed on the pre-existing relations, strengthening or reinforcing them in some respects or some situations, weakening or ameliorating them in others. As Perry Anderson has argued, an appreciation of the 'complex and differential temporality' of the capitalist mode of production, 'in which episodes or eras were discontinuous from each other, and heterogeneous within themselves' is already observable in Marx's writings from the late 1840s onwards.[47] In these writings there is an awareness of the fact that even within capitalist or capitalising social formations, vast rural populations continued to provide the material ground for the persistence of earlier economic conditions, social relations, cultural practices, and psychic dispositions. This insight was then notably amplified in Trotsky's writings of the 1930s, in which, on the basis of his consideration, first of conditions in Russia in 1905, and subsequently of those in China in 1925–7, he formulated a 'Law of Uneven and Combined Development'. In Russia, China, and other, analogous, contexts, Trotsky suggested, the imposition of generalised commodity production and capitalist class relations tends not to have the effect of supplanting (or is not allowed to supplant) pre-existing modes and structures: rather, capitalism is forcibly conjoined with these pre-existing modes and structures. The outcome, he wrote, is a contradictory 'amalgam of archaic with more contemporary forms' – an urban proletariat working in technologically advanced industries existing side by side with a rural population engaged in subsistence farming; modern plants built alongside 'villages of wood and straw', and peasants 'thrown into the factory cauldron snatched directly from the plow'.[48]

Some of Fredric Jameson's writings – concerned centrally with the relations between capitalist modernity and literary form – begin to sketch in the relevance of this theory of combined and uneven development for the analysis of 'postcolonial' literature. While his essay on 'Third-World Literature in the Era of Multinational Capitalism' has regrettably received attention only because of its claims about 'national allegory' – claims which, as I shall argue in Chapter 2, below, have been tendentiously misunderstood – Jameson's commentary in that essay on the 'crisis of representation' in non-metropolitan cultures that were, and remain, 'locked in a life-and-death struggle with first-world cultural imperialism' (p. 68), strikes me as decisive. It certainly enables him to offer remarkably suggestive readings of Lu Hsun's 'A Madman's Diary' and Ousmane Sembène's *Xala*, the two texts that he chooses to focus on in his essay.[49] His thought-provoking argument that the violence entailed in the imposition of capitalism in such societies made for the 'generic discontinuities' of the literatures subsequently produced (p. 83), receives elaboration also in 'On Magic Realism in Film', another essay addressing 'postcolonial' cultures – published, like the 'Third-World Literature' essay, in 1986 – in which Jameson proposes that magic realism be considered a 'formal mode . . . constituently dependent on a type of historical raw material in which disjunction is structurally present', and in which the content

betrays the overlap or the coexistence of precapitalist with nascent capitalist or technological features. In such a view . . . the organizing category of magic realist film . . . is one of modes of production, and in particular, of a mode of production still locked in conflict with traces of the older mode . . . [T]he articulated superposition of whole layers of the past within the present . . . is the formal precondition for the emergence of this new narrative style.[50]

In a footnote to the 'Third-World Literature' essay, Jameson speculates further that this way of thinking about combined unevenness demands a new type of literary comparativism: namely the 'comparison, not of the individual texts, which are formally and culturally very different from each other, but of the concrete situations from which such texts spring and to which they constitute distinct responses' (pp. 86–7, n. 5).[51]

'Postcolonial' writing is centrally and vitally concerned with the representation of class: in broad terms, as a key determinant (or even *the* key determinant) of social relations, practices, and forms of identity; more narrowly, as a primary source, and site, of social division and violence.

Often, and especially where (inter-)class *relations* rather than the dimensions of (intra-)class *belonging* (*habitus,* forms of consciousness, structures of feeling) are concerned, such representation may be partially abstracted from concrete circumstances, generalised in the interests of articulating and/or mobilising a political critique whose scope exceeds the particular. Consider these lines from 'Don't Ask Me for that Love Again', by the great Urdu poet Faiz Ahmed Faiz, for example:

The rich had cast their spell on history:
dark centuries had been embroidered on brocades and silks.
Bitter threads began to unravel before me
as I went into alleys and in open markets
saw bodies plastered with ash, bathed in blood.
I saw them sold and bought, again and again.
This too deserves attention.[52]

There is much here that would repay investigation: the attitude of the poet to the scenes of destitution that he witnesses and recounts; the aestheticised language of his description (metaphor, tropology, etc.); the relation between poet and audience that is established through the combination of aesthetics and politics in the poem itself; the activation (in the Urdu original, although strangely not in Agha Shahid Ali's translation, undeniably beautiful nonetheless, from which I have just quoted) of the formula, 'What is to be done?', derived of course from Lenin and Chernyshevsky.[53] Here, however, let us note simply that, in Faiz's poem, the rich and powerful are shown to possess the ability, and also the will, to impose themselves (with catastrophic consequences) on the poor and the powerless. The poem transforms the incidents of class violence witnessed by the poet ('[I] saw bodies plastered with ash, bathed in blood') into a metaphysics, thereby 'universalising' them and connecting them to the as yet unbroken spell cast on history by the rich.[54]

Across the range of 'postcolonial' literature, representation of class domination is of course often plaited together with representation of racial domination or what Mahasweta Devi has called 'the pre-historic warfare of casteism',[55] as is called for in the given contexts. In nearly all cases, however – and notwithstanding Foucault's well-known challenge to the 'repressive hypothesis' – power is shown in this work as indeed being held and exercised by a few and as being not held and largely suffered by most. Consider one key moment in Mahasweta's story, 'Paddy Seeds', for instance: when Karan Dusad, a Dalit from the village of Tamadi, appeals to the Harijan Sewa Sangha ('Untouchables' Welfare Association') to help him obtain from the powerful landlord, Lachman Singh, the wages to which he is entitled by law, the landlord simply murders Karan and his brother in full view of all the villagers, and burns their village to the ground. Another impoverished Dalit, Dulan (the story's central protagonist), who lives in a neighbouring village and who had initially persuaded Karan to approach the Harijan Sewa Sangha, draws from this incident the following harsh lesson:

A massive detonation had taken place inside Dulan's mind, setting off landslides in the heaving layers of his consciousness. Things were that simple for the Lachman Singhs of this world? He had always known that human death, like human birth, was bound by time-honored customs and rules. But Lachman Singh had demonstrated how dispensable those rules and customs were, how easily they could be violated. Two dead bodies were thrown on horseback, right in front of all the Dusads of Tamadi, and taken away with the utmost defiance. Lachman knew he did not need to hide the removal of the bodies. Those who witnessed it could not open their mouths. They had read the warrant in his silent glare: whoever talks is dead too. It was not the first time and would not be the last. From time to time, with the flames and the screams of the massacred leaping into the sky, the lowly untouchable must be made to realize that it meant nothing at all that the government had passed laws and appointed officers to enforce them and that the Constitution held declarations. They must not forget that the Rajputs remain Rajputs, the Brahmans remain Brahmans, and all the Dusads, Ganjus, Chamars, and Dhobis remain under their feet.[56]

Mahasweta's approach here is entirely different from Faiz's, and not least because hers is a work of fiction, his of poetry. Using the resources of literary realism, she shuttles between direct, indirect and free indirect speech, and between 'internal' and 'external' narrativisation, thereby opening up a gap between her characters' own understanding of events and actions (including those in which they themselves are implicated) and the meaning of these that is available to her readers but not her characters.[57]

In a passage, towards the end of the story, recounting Dulan's murder of Lachman Singh, Mahasweta writes as follows:

He pounds Lachman Singh's head with a rock. He keeps pounding. Lachman Singh was skilled at murder. He knew the value of bullets, and he was never moved inside by the act of killing. In Dulan's situation, he would have killed with a single bullet. Dulan is not a skilled murderer, and rocks have no value, and this act of killing is for him the culmination of a very long and hard battle inside his mind. So, he goes on pounding Lachman Singh with the rock, long after he is dead. (p. 182)

Here, the reflection on the difference between the brutal Rajput landlord and Dulan is obviously not a registration of Dulan's conscious thoughts. It serves, rather, to focalise his action while at the same time situating it in the long history of Dalit resistance to Rajput overlordship. That is to say, it addresses both how and why Dulan kills Lachman Singh and also the *significance* of this act. Hence the insistence that 'this act of killing' is for Dulan 'the culmination of a very long and hard battle inside his mind': actually, we are made to understand that this 'very long and hard battle' is not Dulan's alone, but that of Dalits, tribals, the peasant masses generally. Dulan's 'pounding' of the ruthless Lachman is psychologically cathartic; but it is also socially redemptive, a 'cleansing force' in pretty much exactly the sense analysed by Fanon in his essay on violence in the pathological theatre of the settler colony (*Wretched of the Earth*, p. 94).

In still another passage, in the midst of Mahasweta's narrative of the bitter dispute between the villagers and the landlord over wages, we encounter this remarkable formulation: 'The pattern of peasant struggle is always stamped by the special characteristics of the region. Lachman's final offer is two rupees plus tiffin' (p. 170). Moving between diegesis and sociological analysis, these two sentences link concrete to abstract, empirical detail to theoretical generality. At the level of diegesis, thus, we learn that three years after Lachman Singh's murder of Karan, and coinciding with the publication of a new 'government circular about farm laborers' wages', a new subdivisional officer is posted to the area – a man 'with a history of being accused of leftist sympathies' (p. 169). Arriving just six weeks before the harvest is due to begin, this SDO duly 'starts his campaign among the farm laborers, assuring them of their right to a daily wage of five rupees and eighty paisa, fourteen times what they have been getting. He also informs the landowners about the wage regulation and his intention to see it implemented' (p. 170). Strengthened in their resolve by the words and deeds of this SDO – who strikes them as 'a genuinely good man' – the villagers again press for their rights, demanding to be paid the legal daily wage. Lachman Singh initially refuses to pay it but, under heavy pressure from 'the government' in the form of the SDO and from the villagers, he eventually offers two rupees plus tiffin. Further protracted negotiation ensues before, as the time of the harvest draws ever closer, and his need for the labour of the villagers becomes correspondingly greater, he finally agrees to pay two rupees and fifty paisa plus tiffin. This concession, still well below the legally stipulated minimum, is accepted by the villagers. The harvest begins. 'The police come to take formal note that the harvest is proceeding peacefully. The laborers get their wages on the seventh day. The SDO, with a sigh of relief, leaves the area, as do the police' (p. 172). Not that this is the end of the affair, of course: 'The storm breaks on the eighth day, when Lachman Singh brings in outside laborers to cut the rest of the paddy.' The villagers protest angrily; again Lachman Singh resorts to violence, and several villagers are shot dead. Upon his return to the area, the shocked SDO orders that Lachman be arrested and charged, but he is quickly acquitted, and in the aftermath the SDO himself 'is demoted for inciting farm laborers and disturbing the traditionally harmonious relations between landlords and laborers in the area' (p. 173).

We must register Mahasweta's emphasis both on the savagery of the violence directed towards the villagers by landlords throughout the region and also on its routine nature.[58] We should take notice also of her identification of intra-class and intra-caste solidarity on the one hand, inter-class and inter-caste antagonism, on the other. As in 'Douloti the Bountiful', where the members of the Nagesia community understand full well that landlords and bond-masters are closely aligned with government officials, merchants, money lenders, labour contractors, and temple leaders – 'What am I telling you?' Bono asks Bhuneswar rhetorically at one point in that story. 'Government – unine – contractor – slum landlord – market-trader – shopkeeper – post office, each is the other's friend' (p. 25) – so too in 'Paddy Seeds' the agents of state and temple and market are transparently in cahoots with Lachman Singh and the other landlords of the area. No sooner has Lachman been acquitted than he and 'the other landlord moneylenders hold *puja* with wild fanfare' at the temple of Hanuman Misra (p. 173). They consolidate their relations with 'the hoodlums working for the Congress party'. The result is that 'Terror reigns under the cover of the Emergency rule'.

The progressivism of the SDO is in this context the exception that proves the rule. He knows from the moment he receives the news of his transfer to the Tohri area that this posting represents the end of his career. The posting is designed precisely to secure his dismissal. The 'impeccable logic' with which his transfer order is written is a trap. The document spells out the antagonism between 'the tribals and untouchables' who are 'the peasants and laborers in the Tohri region', on the one hand, and the 'landlords, the rich farmers, and the moneylenders', who 'are all upper-caste', on the other. It indicates that this antagonism has brought about a situation in which 'there has been no agricultural growth, and the per capita income has not risen. Income, consumption, health, education, and social consciousness – everything has remained backward, subnormal'.

And it disingenuously proposes that '[t]he area needs an enlightened and compassionate officer' – such as himself – to mediate and ameliorate the tension (p. 170). The task is impossible, of course, as the SDO already knows, and as events duly show. In many of her fictions, Mahasweta presents us with sympathetic, politically progressive officials, activists, journalists, and intellectuals who attempt to 'mediate' between subaltern communities and state and civic institutions – law, education, housing, census, agriculture, labour – but whose campaigning and reportage, however personally courageous and sincere, almost always fails to improve the conditions of those communities, and sometimes becomes the unwitting means through which these are worsened.[59]

The violence stemming from class and caste division figures prominently not just in Mahasweta's work, but in Indian writing generally. We read, thus, of the dreadful retribution visited on the 'untouchable', Omprakash Darji, for daring to challenge the authority of Thakur Dharamsi, in Rohinton Mistry's *A Fine Balance*,[60] and similar incidents, recounting casual brutality on the part of elite or upper-caste characters and the devastating effects of these on the lives of subaltern characters, are to be found in such celebrated works (originally written in English, Hindi, Oriya, Bengali, and English again, respectively) as *Untouchable* and *Coolie*, by Mulk Raj Anand; *The Soiled Border*, by Phanisvaranatha Renu; *Paraja*, by Gopinath Mohanty; *So Many Hungers!* and *A Goddess Named Gold*, by Bhabani Bhattacharya; and *The God of Small Things*, by Arundhati Roy.[61] In Vikram Seth's *A Suitable Boy*, the naked exploitativeness and horrifying violence of existing class and caste relations are repeatedly exposed, as when the shoemaker, Jagat Ram, recalls an incident from the year before:

One of the jatavs of his own village, who had spent a couple of years in Brahmpur, had gone back home during the harvest season. After the comparative freedom of the city, he had made the mistake of imagining that he had gained exemption from the generalized loathing of the upper-caste villagers. Perhaps also, being eighteen years old, he had the rashness of youth; at any rate, he cycled round the village singing film songs on a bicycle he had bought from his earnings. One day, feeling thirsty, he had had the brazenness to ask an upper-caste woman who was cooking outside her house for some water to drink. That night he had been set upon by a gang of men, tied to his bicycle, and forced to eat human excreta. His brain and his bicycle had then been smashed to bits. Everyone knew the men who were responsible, yet no one had dared to testify; and the details had been too horrendous for even the newspapers to print.[62]

Elsewhere in his novel, Seth makes a similar point by inversion, when he shows us that the costs of what the rich and powerful do or fail to do are borne not by them, but by those below them in the social order. The sheer weight of the sedimentation (in historical time and social space) of the structures and institutions of class domination and caste rule is sufficient to ensure that there can be no easy commutation of reformist political *intentions* into reformed political *effects*. We are presented with the character of Mahesh Kapoor, the progressive chief minister of the fictional state of Purva Pradesh, who supports the initiative to pass the Zamindari Abolition Bill into law because he has come to deplore the 'immiserating effects' of the land ownership system: 'With his own eyes he had seen the lack of productivity and the consequent hunger, the absence of investment in land improvement, the worst forms of feudal arrogance and subservience, the arbitrary oppression of the weak and the miserable by the agents and muscle-men of the typical landlord' (p. 283). A savage irony then developed in the novel is that the eventual passage of this purportedly progressive act contributes not to the amelioration but in many instances to the greater destitution of those who work the land. The telling case in point is provided by Kachheru, a labourer from Debaria village in Mahesh Kapoor's parliamentary constituency, who finds himself stripped of his land and his livelihood as an unintended consequence of the great politician's reformist activism. As Mahesh Kapoor's son, Maan, subsequently muses, in reflecting on the catastrophe that has befallen Kachheru:

Strange to think that even [Kachheru's] paltry earnings had been undone by – by what? Perhaps by Maan's own father. The two knew nothing of each other as individuals, but Kachheru was the saddest case of the evil practised under the act, and Mahesh Kapoor was almost directly responsible for his utter devastation, his reduction to the forsaken status of a landless labourer. Linked though they were in this sense of the former's guilt and the latter's despair, if they were to pass each other in the street, thought Maan, neither would know the other. (pp. 1288–9)[63]

What we see here also bears comparison with the representation of class relations in fiction by 'postcolonial' writers in other contexts. Peasant experience – centred on the ownership, use, occupation, and disposal of land, on wages and working conditions – is the central subject matter of such works as *One Day of Life* and *Cuzcatlán*, by the Salvadoran Manlio Argueta; *Rope of Ash* and *No Harvest but a Thorn*, by the Malaysian Shahnon Ahmad; *Egyptian Earth*, by the Egyptian Abdel Rahman al-Sharqawi; *Bones*, by the Zimbabwean Chenjerai Hove; *Salt*, by the Trinidadian Earl Lovelace; and *Turbulence*, by the Chinese Jia

Pingwa.[64] An extended passage of external narration in *Cuzcatlán*
surveys the fragility and vulnerability of peasant existence in El Salva-
dor in the late nineteenth and early twentieth centuries, for example, as
the international market for indigo declines, textile mills shut down,
and whole communities, which once upon a time had been self-sus-
taining, are forcibly relocated to the coffee estates in the central
cordillera:

> Unemployment could be added to slavish working conditions as another sign of
> their penurious and miserable state. Thousands of peasants were denied the
> opportunity to find work. Indigo had ceased to be the Old World's vision of
> the ultimate in color. Hence an immense floating population was rounded up
> for vagrancy by the *guardia rural* and forced to work on the new coffee
> estates located at the base of the volcanoes along Cuzcatlán's central cordillera.
> Peasants in the north, like Emiliano, clung to their meager trades and tiny
> parcels in an effort to prevent the Keepers of the Peace from forcibly removing
> them to the volcanoes, where you weren't allowed so much as a roof or a
> garden. Or a *petate* on which to drop dead. They had to prove they had a trade
> or were awaiting harvest, just so they wouldn't have to undergo the transfer to
> the plantations, where people slept under trees or open canopies made of
> avocado leaves or squash vines. Sometimes all the workers on the estate had
> to sleep under collective canopies, lying on the ground with nothing but leaves
> to cover them. Working conditions on the estates were just as harsh as those in
> the textile mills; except that in the latter case you could rent a plot of land or
> work as a tenant farmer. It wasn't easy for the *guardia rural* to uproot the
> peasant masses from the north and move them to the region of the volcanoes.
> (pp. 31–2)

One could make much the same point with respect to the representation
of social relations in urban contexts, where class, whether as an axis of
domination, mode of consciousness or fault line of struggle, is the
defining problematic of work by writers as different – and distant – from
one another as Samaresh Basu, Ralph de Boissière, Carlos Fuentes, Roy
Heath, Festus Iyayi, Lao She, Naguib Mahfouz, and Ousmane
Sembène.[65] Or one could refer, this time in the contexts of migrancy
and trans-nationalism, to such writers as Carlos Bulosan, Jamaica
Kincaid, Timothy Mo, and Sam Selvon.[66]

   In approaching the subject of class relations in 'postcolonial' literature,
we must attend not only to the sheer fact that social conditions of
existence are everywhere represented in this literature, but also to the
forms assumed by this representation – since it is here that writers' own
attitudes to what is being expressed come into focus; and here also,
therefore, that the nature and level of readers' commitment to the text

is negotiated and secured. Consider this 1921 poem, entitled 'Beggar', by the great Hindi poet, Nirala, for example:

> He comes along
> grieving
> down the road,
> his heart in two pieces,
> his belly and his back in one,
> leaning on his stick as he walks,
> with his old tattered bag gaping
> for a handful of grain to kill his hunger.
> Grieving he comes down the road
> with his heart in two pieces.
> Two children with him,
> their hands stretched out always,
> left hand rubbing the stomach as they walk,
> right hand reaching out for a pitying glance.
> When their lips shrivel up from starving
> what recompense
> from the generous Lord of destinies?
> Well, they can drink their tears.
> Sometimes they stand in the road
> licking up the left-overs from a leaf-dish
> and the dogs come hustling and snapping
> to snatch it away from them.
> Only wait – there's nectar in my heart –
> I'll pour it out for you,
> and you can be heroes
> like Abhimanyu
> when I draw your sorrows
> into my own heart.[67]

The opening lines of the poem paint a picture of absolute destitution. To hunger, infirmity, and impoverishment is added anguish: we are told twice that the beggar is 'grieving', and twice also that his heart is broken. The juxtaposition of the image of a heart in two pieces with that of a body so emaciated that belly and back are fused connects physical deterioration to emotional desolation. Rage is silently expressed towards the 'generous Lord of destinies' – for so any prosperous or upper-caste man must seem to the beggar and his two half-starved children – who is unmoved by their plight, indifferent, contemptuous even. The callous dismissal, 'Well they can drink their tears', which the 'generous Lord's' actions say even if the words are not necessarily his directly, is in the style of 'Madame Déficit', Marie Antoinette, when faced by hungry men and women desperate for bread on the eve of the French Revolution. The beggar's children 'reach ... out for a pitying glance' – Nirala's formulation telescopes together the pity that the children's condition arouses in the sympathetic beholder and the gift of money into which the sympathetic beholder customarily 'translates' or commutes this pity, seeking thereby to assuage it.

The poet himself is clearly moved to pity. He calls upon the beggar to 'wait', offering to pour out for him the 'nectar' in his heart. Had the poem ended on this note, this gesture might have struck one as sentimental. But the final sentence of the poem is complex and possesses a much sharper edge than this, which only becomes available to us once we take its *whole* thrust into account. 'I'll pour it out for you, / and you can be heroes / like Abhimanyu / when I draw your sorrows / into my own heart'. The poet pours out the nectar in his heart not merely as an expression of his compassion, but in order to empty a space into which he can then draw the beggar's 'sorrows'. Once he has done this, he says, the beggar and his children 'can be heroes like Abhimanyu'. Concerning 'Abhimanyu', we should note two things. The first is that the Sanskritic word literally translates as 'excessive anger'. The second concerns Abhimanyu's appearance in the *Mahabharata*: the son of Arjuna and Subhadra, he overhears (while still in the womb) his father disclosing to his mother the secret of how to combat and defeat the circular, mazelike battle formation known as the *Chakruvyuha*; but since Subhadra falls asleep in the middle of Arjuna's explanation, the great Pandava warrior stops speaking and does not finish his explanation: Abhimanyu overhears only how to penetrate to the centre of the *Chakruvyuha*, not how to escape from it in the aftermath. At the age of 16, in the context of a war between Pandavas and Kauravas, he breaks into a Kauravan *Chakruvyuha* formation, using his secret knowledge of how to do so. However, his Pandava allies are prevented from following him into the formation, and he is left to fight alone against the entire Kaurava force. Although he fights heroically, he is unable to escape and is ultimately killed. Significantly, the Kaurava do not engage him in one-to-one combat, but fall upon him all at once. The assassination of Abhimanyu is thus interpreted as cowardly: his death is spoken of as marking the end of customary or rule-governed warfare – it is indecent, unworthy.

If we now look again at the final lines of Nirala's poem, we see the poet drawing the 'sorrows' of the beggar into the *Chakruvyuha* of his heart. He drains his heart of pity in order to fill it again with the 'excessive anger' that is Abhimanyu. The beggar and his children are incited to heroism inside his heart: urged, that is, to conduct themselves not so much compassionately or consolingly as militantly, with controlled fury. The image is profoundly discomforting, inasmuch as it admits of no peaceful resolution. Since to overcome anger is to put aside what has made one angry in the first place, to kill 'Abhimanyu' – to still the righteous anger in the heart that he represents – would be to 'forget' that the world is cruelly divided between beggars and 'generous Lords'; and this would be indecent or immoral. We seem once again to be in the territory of 'disconsolation', of the Kafka effect, as discussed above.

In a subsequent poem of 1935, bearing the mordant title 'Giving', Nirala returns to this scene. The poem again describes the encounter between 'one of our glorious Brahmans', ostentatiously devout, 'always deep in the Ramayana / and muttering the holy name Narayana / and faithful in his daily ritual bath', and a beggar, 'black-bodied, skeletal, half-dead – / misery given a human form – / staring unwaveringly in hope of alms / throat shrunk, breath hoarse / merely to live a painful burden'. The Brahman is delighted to scatter rice and cake to some monkeys who come near him on a bridge; but when approached by the beggar, he screams abuse at him. The final words of the poem then record the response of the poet himself, who is not prepared this time merely to bear witness to the incident, but intervenes with bitter irony: 'I said, "Well done, you best of all creation"' (pp. 42–4).

Nirala's move to position himself *between* rulers and ruled – *of* the elite but *for* 'the people' – is of course characteristic of writers, cultural producers, and intellectuals everywhere. As Bourdieu, most notably, has argued, the precarious structural location of cultural production in the total social field – occupying a dominated position within the dominant sphere – disposes writers, artists, and intellectuals to an ideological identification with the socially dominated.[68] In 'postcolonial' contexts, this identification typically takes the form of a *representational* practice, self-consciously and determinedly undertaken – whether of a 'speaking for' or of a 'witnessing'.[69] The writer understands himself or herself as a spokesperson – 'the sensitive point' of his or her community, in Ezekiel Mphahlele's well-known formulation; as at one and the same time 'the record of the mores and experience of his society *and* as the voice of vision in his own time', in Wole Soyinka's, equally well-known.[70]

The politics of identification here are such that we can speak of the pitfall of an 'ideology of the aesthetic'. Striving to represent the aspirations of the disadvantaged majorities of their societies – those whose names are *not* 'preserved on bamboo tablets and silk', as Lu Hsun, rehearsing the ancient Chinese saying, puts it in 'The True Story of Ah Q'[71] – writers are sometimes disposed to the compensatory gesture of romanticisation. The dispossessed and down-trodden emerge in their work as beautiful, heroic, extraordinarily brave or strong or principled. At issue here is what Adorno once described as the 'glorification of splendid underdogs' – a tendency whose attraction to progressive intellectuals he certainly understood but nevertheless thoroughly disavowed: 'In the end, glorification of splendid underdogs is nothing other than glorification of the splendid system that makes them so', he wrote. 'The justified guilt-feelings of those exempt from physical work ought not become an excuse for the "idiocy of rural life".'[72]

In some of Nirala's poetry, we find a very interesting engagement with this problem. A poem of 1935, 'Breaking Stones', depicts the poet watching a young woman who is labouring on a road in Allahabad. Once more the setting is harsh and unforgiving – heat and dust, the hammer heavy, the rock unyielding, the work long and unrelenting. David Rubin has written that 'admiration for [the young woman's] toughness and beauty rather than conventional pathos provides the dominant tone' of the poem; and he argues that this break from convention provides one measure of Nirala's 'originality of approach'.[73] What I find most interesting about the poem, however, is that it stages both the poet's insistent urge to aestheticise the spectacle, to figure the working woman as beautiful and defiant of her circumstances – or beautiful *because* defiant of her circumstances (it is this aspect that Rubin's commentary addresses) – and her evident understanding and refusal of this gesture of his. What the poet seeks to aestheticise, the woman herself seems – or at least this is the poet's intuition – to refuse to look at except with mundane eyes; not because she lacks imagination, but because just as a stone is a stone, so the hard work of breaking stones is nothing but hard work: it pays almost nothing; it is not rewarding, it is not redemptive.

> While I watched she saw me,
> looked at me once,
> then at the house, then at her ragged clothes.
> Seeing no one else was there
> she stared at me with the eyes
> of one who doesn't cry
> even when they beat her.
> As from a tuned sitar
> I heard a strain of music then
> I'd never heard before.
> After a moment she shuddered,
> beautiful,

while the sweat trickled down her forehead,
then once more gave herself to her work
as though to say,
'I'm a woman
breaking stones'.   (pp. 40–1)

We are obviously enjoined, in the general context raised by this discussion, to observe the distinctions drawn across the full range of 'postcolonial' literature between *different kinds of labour* – not only whether peasant, proletarian, or bourgeois, but whether manual or mental, free or unfree, remunerated (and if so, in what forms) or unremunerated, social, familial, or domestic, and so on. In so much of this writing, one encounters extended descriptions of work as an identity-defining activity. Sometimes, work is phrased as being constitutive of self-making, as in this rather Lawrentian passage from near the beginning of Ngugi's *A Grain of Wheat*, describing Mugo's attempts almost literally to root himself through labour:

He turned to the soil. He would labour, sweat, and through success and wealth, force society to recognize him. There was, for him, then, solace in the very act of breaking the soil; to bury seeds and watch the green leaves heave and thrust themselves out of the ground, to tend the plants to ripeness and then harvest, these were all part of the world he had created for himself and which formed the background against which his dreams soared to the sky. (London: Heinemann, 1986 [1967], p. 8)

At other times, though, and, all in all, more typically, labour is viewed in the contexts of exploitation, drudgery, and servitude – as hard, unrewarding, more or less unremitting, sometimes utterly destructive of sociality and even of self-preservation. 'Household Fires', a frequently anthologised poem by the Marathi writer, Indira Sant, for instance explores the effects of the sexual division of labour on women in the urban middle-class Indian family, where their unseen work is not only unceasing, but also monotonous and unfulfilling. The woman at the centre of Sant's poem is depicted as being 'drained by hardship': '[W]hat's left of her? This mother and wife?' the poet asks:

A mass of tatters,
five tongues of flame
licking and licking at her on every side,
fanning the fire in her eyes
till her mind boils over,
gets burnt.[74]

Similarly, in Lao She's *Rickshaw* we read of the central protagonist, 'Camel' Hsiang Tzu (Xiangzi), whose every thought and action registers his own thoroughgoing objectification through labour.[75] Everything that he sees, he reckons as exchange value, in terms of what it costs or how much it might realise; everything that he does, he calculates as investment or expenditure. His 'needs' are merely those that enable his social reproduction as labour power. He eats only what he has to eat to keep himself strong enough to pull his rickshaw; he sleeps just enough to enable him to recover from the day's exertions; he has no friends, and he keeps his dealings with the other rickshaw men with whom he comes into contact to an instrumental minimum; he dislikes drinking, does not gamble, has no interest in women or in conversation – indeed, he regards language with mistrust, as a wasteful indulgence. Lao She makes it clear that Hsiang Tzu's gruff inarticulacy is to be understood as the effect of a systematic repression that is simultaneously social and psychological. When, towards the end of the novel, he is invited by his former employer, the benevolent Mr Cao, to describe the hardships he has undergone, he is surprised to find himself unable to stop speaking:

Hsiang Tzu began with events in the more distant past, starting with how he had left the country and come to the city. He hadn't intended to mention all that useless stuff but his situation would not be completely explained and he wouldn't feel right if he didn't. His memories were composed of layers of bloody sweat and bitter pain and he couldn't speak of them casually or jokingly. He was unwilling to leave anything out once he began. Each drop of sweat, each drop of blood came from the core of his being and every detail had a value that made it worth mentioning ... (pp. 221–2)

In much 'postcolonial' literature, as is to be expected, intellectual work (not only writing, but cultural production of all kinds) is brought into focus *as work*, with its own – specific and irreducible – modalities and materialities. Literature in this idiom is, of course, often realist or naturalist in register, but it is by no means always or exclusively so. Acutely conscious of the gap or discrepancy between manual and mental labour, writers will often deploy the language of craft production metaphorically in description of their work, thereby signalling their recognition of the immateriality – and even, perhaps, insubstantiality – of the social use values that it produces. Thus Laâbi, in a poem from his 1993 volume, *L'Étreinte du monde*:

Writing requires more than one hand.
With things as they are
two would be needed
And the second one would need to learn quickly
the crafts of the ineffable:

to embroider the name of the star
that will rise after the next apocalypse
to recognize among thousands the thread that will not break
to sew into the fabric of passions
swaddling cloths, capes and shrouds
to sculpt dawn in a mound of filth
Writing requires more than two hands
With things as they are
and the snarling miseries
three, four would be needed
so that life might deign to visit
this terrible white desert.[76]

The social value of intellectual and cultural labour is fiercely debated and
disputed, of course, across the range of 'postcolonial' literature. The
attempt is often made to defend such labour – on the one hand against
the instrumentalist charge that since it is 'unproductive' (of exchange
values), it is without warrant; on the other hand against the ultra-leftist
charge that it is decadent or indulgent, something like playing the fiddle
while Rome burns. Hence, for example, the urgent discussions between
Baako and Ocran in Ayi Kwei Armah's *Fragments*, and between Omovo
and Okocha in Ben Okri's *Dangerous Love*, which turn on the question of
how writers and artists can justify themselves in social contexts in which
the most fundamental of material needs – for food, for shelter, for
'freedom' from physical extermination, even – often remain unmet.[77]

   In representing writing as work, 'postcolonial' writers tend to insist, by
and large, on the irreducibility of the social gap (for better or worse)
between it and the majoritarian (and mostly manual) forms of social
labour. In 'To My Poems', written in 1937, for instance, the Bengali
writer Buddhadeva Bose jauntily contrasts 'this work of writing that
I do ... This profession of writing' with the work of chemists, philolo-
gists, astronomers, experts in machines, painters, singers, mechanics,
cobblers, tailors, potters, barbers, and carpenters! All of these latter forms
of work are 'truly respectable'; only writing is not. Perhaps, as the poet
wittily speculates, this is because while all forms of 'real' work require
competence and even skill, anybody can be a writer:

Anybody, but anybody, who has learnt to write his alphabet
and has turned the pages of a few books
can now suddenly, if he wishes,
become a full-scale writer.
Somebody who couldn't have opened his mouth if he had to sing,

would have been in tears if he had to paint,
who hasn't got the qualifications to be either
a mechanic or a cobbler, a tailor or a potter, a barber or a carpenter,
can suddenly, if he so wishes, become
a very great writer.[78]

Like modern writers everywhere, 'postcolonial' writers are perhaps inclined to overvalue the social significance of the work they do (and of cultural labour in general),[79] but they rarely take it as the prototype for, or generic model of, work in general. Indeed, their characteristic representation of writing must be contrasted with that typically obtaining in postmodernist theory (and by extension, therefore, in much postcolonial theory also), in which what might have begun (the case is arguable) as a defensive reconceptualisation of writing as a form of social practice has tended to become the vaulting horse for a thoroughly theoreticist understanding of writing not merely as *a* form of social practice (in other words, not merely as one among all the myriad forms of social practice), but as *the paradigmatic* such form (in other words, as paradigmatic of social practice as such).[80] The upshot, in postmodernist theory, is that all and any forms of social practice come to be seen, ultimately, as scripts, codes, performances, inscriptions, forms of *writing* – and as nothing other than this. To which the correct rejoinder is perhaps still the one that Terry Eagleton once afforded to the 'post-Marxist' arguments of Ernesto Laclau and Chantal Mouffe: 'Laclau and Mouffe deny all validity to the distinction between "discursive" and "non-discursive" practices, on the grounds that a practice is struc-tured along the lines of a discourse. The short reply to this is that a practice may well be organized like a discourse, but as a matter of fact it is a practice rather than a discourse.'[81] To put the matter pointedly – and to draw out its relevance to the discussion of 'postcolonial' literature – let me say that it is important that we recognise the *limits* of the trope mobilised so suggestively and wittily by Rushdie in *Midnight's Children*, of narrativisation as 'chutnification', that is to say, of writing as making chutney and of making chutney as writing. Like making chutney, writing is indeed a form of social practice; but writers and intellectuals, especially, must beware the inclination to construe their distinctive and restricted forms of practice as paradigmatic of social practice in general. I emphasise this truism because of its properly materialist entailment, borne out very widely across 'postcolonial' literature: the denial of the autonomy or primacy of ideas in social life. In 'postcolonial' literature we very often find an insistent and studied emphasis on the *inability* of ideas or words or memories or narratives to assume consequence – or, still less, to change things. (Which is not to say, of course, that ideas or words or memories are not held to be uniquely illuminating, enabling or socially indispensable in other respects.) Consider this little passage from Mistry's *A Fine Balance*, for instance: it can be read, I think, as a self-conscious rejoinder to pomo-postcolonialist constructions of writing and thinking as emblems of social practice in general:

Dina Dalal seldom indulged in looking back at her life with regret or bitterness, or questioning why things had turned out the way they had, cheating her of the bright future everyone had predicted for her when she was in school, when her name was still Dina Shroff. And if she did sink into one of these rare moods, she quickly swam out of it. What was the point of repeating the story over and over and over, she asked herself – it always ended the same way; whichever corridor she took, she wound up in the same room. (p. 15)

LAND AND ENVIRONMENT

'Land and environment' is preferred to the potential alternative represented by the Williamsian rubric of 'country and city'. The formula draws attention immediately to the contemporary concern with 'environment' in the sense of 'ecology', which is at the heart of much 'postcolonial' writing, literary as well as critical, and to which, indeed, Williams's own work makes an important early contribution.[82] It also allows for a consideration of 'land' as a site of multiple forms of contestation, both material and representational, that exceed the limits of Williams's more restricted notion of 'country'. The commentary in *The Country and the City* is focused, as Williams himself makes clear, on the English historical experience, 'based on a highly developed agrarian capitalism, with a very early disappearance of the traditional peasantry'.[83] Williams himself tends to argue for the modal quality of these English developments – 'the English experience remains exceptionally important: not only symptomatic but in some ways diagnostic' (p. 2) – a controversial view even in 1973, and still more so today.[84] But it is clear at least that the specific forms of the pastoral and more generally of aesthetic ruralism, central to the unfolding of English literature (as the literature of *England*), are not equally central to literature in the 'postcolonial' context. (I discuss the examples of Jibanananda and Walcott, some of whose work might be considered in the light of a qualified exception to this statement, below.) What one more typically finds in this context is rather what James Graham, in his study of southern African writing, has presented as a dialectics of 'Land' and 'land' – a fraught discourse in which 'land' is struggled over and negotiated in all of its meanings: as abstract expanse, as ground of subsistence, as domesticated territory ('home' or 'country'), as reservoir of history and culture, and as potentially privatisable 'property'.[85] The question that animates Graham's study – 'when does land become Land?' – is certainly fundamental to 'postcolonial' literature at large.

What Williams's relational focus on 'country' and 'city' *does* allow, however – and in fact demands – is attention to what we might call the psycho-dynamics of urbanism and land-based experience. Concerning the latter, it has always seemed to me that the opening to Thomas Mofolo's *Chaka* is exemplary, inasmuch as it does not simply set the scene and place the plot into motion, but serves rather to introduce us to a whole symbolic economy – or 'structure of feeling', to use the term that Williams himself favoured in his early writings. Mofolo's narrative opens on to a world, as all narratives do; but it gives us in addition the means to understand how this world is experienced, and how meaning and value are produced in it. The text begins with a topographical description of South Africa. An enumeration of the different peoples who inhabit this landmass then leads to the observation that the story will be set among one of these peoples, the Bokone. Mofolo then proceeds as follows:

The greater portion of the land of Bokone, which lies between the Maloti and the sea is covered by forest. Besides, the crops there are never bitten by frost, for there are only light frosts because of the nearness of the sea. It is a land of lush greenness, and of extremely rich pasturage. Its soil is dark, and that means that it produces much food; its indigenous grass is the luxuriant *seboku*; its water lies in marshes, and that means that its cattle grow very fat. There are numerous rivers, and that means that rain is plentiful. It is a land of dense mists which often clear only after the sun has risen high, and that means that there are no droughts since the moisture takes long to dry up.[86]

It is of course the studied repetition of instances of inferential logic that is so striking here: the darkness of the soil *means* that 'it produces much food'; the presence of marshland *means* that 'cattle grow very fat'; the fact that the land is often shrouded in mist *means* that 'there are no droughts'. No doubt any – or, indeed, all – of these inferences might have been drawn by a sympathetic reader. But what needs to be registered as distinctive is that the events in *Chaka* unfold in a socio-natural order in which the conceptual movement from 'dark soil' to 'much food' is so fundamental, and at the same time (and no doubt for this reason) so completely axiomatic, as to correspond to strict common sense. If you have to *think* your way from marshland to fat cattle, or from mists to the absence of droughts, then your symbolic economy is different from that obtaining in the novel. The burden assumed by the author, in these terms, is to 'ground' his readers in the novel's *mise-en-scène*, thereby making it possible for these readers (ourselves) to appreciate the full human implications of his story.

This sort of 'grounding' receives explicit general theorisation in the *Éloge de la créolité* of Jean Bernabé, Patrick Chamoiseau, and Raphael Confiant, with its repeated reference to the irreducibility of Creole culture – the uniqueness of its 'world', 'values', and 'interior architecture'.[87] It receives further exemplification in Chamoiseau's novel, *Texaco*. The *present-day* narrative strand of this novel investigates the contestation between the social logics implicated by Fort-de-France, on the one hand – a (phantasmatic) 'occidental' logic of order, regulation, normalcy – and by the slum of Texaco itself, on the other – 'Fort-de-France's mess',[88] the Creole city with its 'open profusion' (p. 220) and its sprawling, insurrectionary dis-order. Much of the novel's *historical* narrative strand, however, is set on the land and describes the struggle against slavery and the attempt, in the aftermath of its abolition, to people the land – not merely to subsist on it, but 'to understand, and to inhabit it' (p. 82).

In a remarkable section of Book One of *Texaco*, devoted to 'The Age of Straw (1823[?]–1920)', and entitled 'The Noutéka of the Hills',[89] Chamoiseau describes the cultivation, by a small group of former slaves, in the aftermath of slavery, of land up in the hills, beyond the boundary limits not only of the erstwhile plantations, but even of the scattered communities of maroons. The narrative presents us with the *process* of settlement, as the members of the group battle to discover, through trial and error, how to live in this particular environment, which is like no other they have ever encountered – to learn what the land will tolerate and what it will not allow:

We learned not to settle too high up . . .
   Too high, the land was badly chabinous, that is ill-tempered, nervous, unfaithful, betraying the hutches and the crops. Carrying on its old affair with the rain, it would suddenly elope, ruining lives, tools, and gardens in its wake.
   How many hutches we buried before we understood. (p. 127)

One senses, in this description, the reciprocal interpenetrations of social being and consciousness. The carrying capacity of the land sets untranscendable limits on the forms of cultivation that can be practised, and on their productivity. At the same time, the encoding of the land within an intricate, gendered, symbolic imaginary ('chabinous', 'ill-tempered', 'unfaithful', 'it would suddenly elope') works to bring it, for all its gross materiality and relative intractability, within the sway of a unique and historically specific culture: 'We learned that here the ground was richer than below, newer, still flitty, not yet milked by etcetera harvests. And we learned to find the right slope' (p. 128). In time, the members of the group learn how 'to read the landscape', which means that they have learned to render this land as 'their Land', to inhabit it as a powerful source of cultural meaning in addition to living off it:

The difficult thing was to survive without having to go back down. We grew what békés call secondary crops and we call food crops. Near the food crops you have to plant medicine plants, which bring luck and disarm zombies. Growing them all tangled up with each other never tires the soil. That's Creole gardening . . .
   First, plant the providence of the breadfruit tree. Reduce oil shortage by planting avocado. Mind the shade and the watering. Watch for the moon: the moon which rises makes all things rise with her, the moon which goes down flattens everything. Plant on an empty stomach and the tree will bear no fruit. Plant on a full stomach, the tree will be generous. Put up barriers against salt winds. Where the soil shivers plant thickets with roots like claws: sweet pea, local pear, rose-apple, orange trees. From far away this seems all due to chance; in reality . . . it is fate's beckoning. You've got to read the landscape. (pp. 128–9)

In turning from 'country' to 'city', let us begin by referencing the important work of such theorists as David Harvey and Marshall Berman, that sought to theorise the relationship between modernisation, modernity, and modernism – that is, between capitalist urbanisation, consciousness, and cultural representation.[90] This scholarship contains much that is of direct relevance to the 'postcolonial' context – and Berman, indeed, was presumably already thinking along broadly 'postcolonialist' lines when he turned his attention to St Petersburg, under the rubric of 'the modernism of underdevelopment', in one section of his book. The radical transformation of the built space of the city, subject to the 'creative destruction' of capitalist development, in the latter half of the nineteenth century and the first decades of the twentieth, is not peculiar to London, Paris, Berlin, or New York. Strictly contemporary with developments in these cities – and linked precisely to them – are analogous developments in St Petersburg, Calcutta, Buenos Aires, Shanghai, Istanbul, and Cairo.
   In these latter contexts, also, we can note the existence of a crisis of representation – an attempt to register 'the shock of the new', as the forms of space consciousness and time consciousness demanded by life in urban

contexts in which the commodity has become the dominant social form are counterposed with inherited ways of seeing and knowing, now under acute pressure if not already obsolete. The divide between 'old' and 'new', between urban and land-based forms of consciousness, is acutely registered in Lao She's *Rickshaw,* for instance: the author tells us that when Hsiang Tzu first arrives in Shanghai, 'he was a country boy and not like the city folks who hear the wind and expect the rain' (p. 12). Very quickly, however, Hsiang Tzu's sensibilities are remoulded in accordance with the rigours of life in the city. What Lao She deplores as 'individualism' is nothing other than the social logic corresponding to capitalist urbanism:

Rumors, truths – Hsiang Tzu seemed to have forgotten the farmer's life he once led. He didn't much care if the fighting ruined the crops and didn't pay much attention to the presence or absence of spring rain. All he was concerned about was his rickshaw; his rickshaw could produce wheat cakes and everything else he ate. It was an all-powerful field which followed obediently after him, a piece of animated, precious earth.

The price of food went up due to drought and news of warfare; this much Hsiang Tzu knew. But like the city folk, he could only grumble about the high cost of food. There was nothing he could do about it at all. So food was expensive; did anyone know how to make it cheaper? This kind of attitude made him concerned only about himself; he put all other disasters and calamities out of his head. (pp. 12–13)

In 'The Welsh Industrial Novel', an article first delivered as the inaugural Gwyn Jones lecture at Cardiff University in 1978, Raymond Williams drew attention to the struggle of English writers in the mid nineteenth century to develop a literary register adequate to the task of representing the newly industrialised landscape that confronted them in cities and towns like Manchester and Preston. There was at first, he wrote, a tendency to render an 'authentic sense of shock at the unaccustomed sight' of such a landscape through 'received conventional images: the panorama of Hell as painted by Bosch, or the irruption of the classical Vulcan'.[91] Writing of this kind tended to the panoramic: produced by middle-class writers, 'for the most part not themselves living in the industrial areas', it was mediated by an 'external, incorporating perspective'; dark, blasted, infernal, the canvas depicted was typically empty of people, except as correlatives of the general horrific spectacle.

Thus Dickens initially describes Coketown in *Hard Times* as 'a town of red brick, or of brick that would have been red if the smoke and ashes had allowed it; but as matters stood it was a town of unnatural red and black, like the painted face of a savage' (qtd Williams, 'Welsh Industrial Novel',

p. 215). The representation is precisely class-based: the narrative voice issues from outside the frame of what it describes, whose almost inhuman – and certainly dehumanising – otherness it is concerned to emphasise. Coketown, on Dickens's initial description, defies the logic of *Gemeinschaft*. It has been built according to a different social logic. There can be no *people* living in it, only automatons coursing through its lattice of effectively indistinguishable streets – and themselves effectively indistinguishable, inasmuch as each of them is merely the bearer of a certain quantum of labour power. Williams argues that this initial style of representation in *Hard Times* was atypical of Dickens; and notes that it was falsified the moment the author 'touched other springs and made his always variable people – Dickensian people very unlike one another – move and relate'. This subsequent move, to animate and humanise the figures initially described as mere indices of an industrial landscape, conceived in terms of ruthless functionality and hideous denaturalisation, strikes Williams as being very important. '[T]hat second look is the significant transition', he writes:

> Not only are you not a devil if you live in this new sketch of Hell; you are not an automaton if you are a secular Vulcan; you are not a savage if you live in this savage-looking landscape. But you are still, perhaps, a labouring man and only a labouring man. Certainly that external, representative and as a matter of fact highly class-conscious perspective is the method of other novels in this group; of Disraeli, in *Sybil*; of Kingsley, in *Alton Locke*; even of Dickens among the workers in *Hard Times*. But the true second look came from the one novelist who lived in her landscape; Elizabeth Gaskell, especially in *Mary Barton*, and even more, if we could get back to it, in the abandoned first version of that novel, *John Barton*, when the crisis was not to be observed but experienced, internalized; the world of industrial conflict seen from the point of view of a militant who is at the same time 'my hero, *the* person with whom all my sympathies went'. Under pressure she drew back from that transforming identification, but still what she wrote was the best of these early English industrial novels: a story of these changes happening to people who were, are and remain individual human beings through all the fierce and dynamic trajectories of social and economic transformation and conflict. (pp. 215–16)

This is enormously suggestive for the analysis of 'postcolonial' literature, I think. Consider the following passage in Rohinton Mistry's *A Fine Balance*, for instance. The passage is focalised through the consciousness of Dina Dalal, a downwardly mobile Parsi widow, of young middle age and lower middle-class origins, resident in Bombay and struggling to maintain what the novel itself describes as her 'fragile independence' – domestic and financial – in increasingly difficult circumstances. As her limited savings diminish, Dina attempts to establish herself as a seamstress, and searches for tailors with the requisite skills to work with and for her. Her searching takes her further and further from the parts of Bombay that she knows. In describing her as 'taking the train to the northern suburbs, to parts of the city she had never seen in all her forty-two years' (p. 66), Mistry is specifically telling us that Dina is venturing across class lines. Then we read:

> One evening, while the slow local waited for a signal change, she gazed beyond the railway fence where a stream of black sewer sludge spilled from an underground drain. Men were hauling on a rope that disappeared into the ground. Their arms were dark to the elbows, the black slime dripping from hands and rope. In the slum behind them, cooking fires smouldered, with smoke smudging the air. The workers were trying to unblock the overflowing drain.
>
> Then a boy emerged out of the earth, clinging to the end of the rope. He was covered in the slippery sewer sludge, and when he stood up, he shone and shimmered in the sun with a terrible beauty. His hair, stiffened by the muck, flared from his head like a crown of black flames. Behind him, the slum smoke curled towards the sky, and the hellishness of the place was complete.
>
> Dina stared, shuddering, transfixed by his appearance, covering her nose against the stench till the train had cleared the area. But the underworld vision haunted her for the rest of the day, and for days to come. (p. 67)

In its attempts to register the perceived 'hellishness of the place', the passage draws upon what Williams called 'received conventional images' – which now include not only 'the panorama of Hell as painted by Bosch, or the irruption of the classical Vulcan', but also, quite patently, Blake's chimney-sweeper and dark satanic mills, and Dickens's Coketown itself. Elsewhere in the novel, we become accustomed to reading in the context of a gap or distance between the narratorial consciousness and the consciousness of the protagonists. Here, however, Dina's consciousness and that of the narrator seem to coincide. In his descriptions of the activities, thoughts, and feelings of the novel's other principal characters, Mistry tends to look through the welter of things as they present themselves or are given, by way of reflecting or commenting upon them, and hence perhaps of extracting their social *meaning*. A characteristic passage, thus, describes the arrival of Omprakash and Ishvar in Bombay and their attempts to find their way to the place where they have been promised shelter:

> Someone they asked for directions pointed them down the right road. The shop-cum-residence was a ten-minute walk from the station. The pavements were

covered with sleeping people. A thin yellow light from the streetlamps fell like tainted rain on the rag-wrapped bodies, and Omprakash shivered. 'They look like corpses,' he whispered. He gazed hard at them, searching for a sign of life – a rising chest, a quivering finger, a fluttering eyelid. But the lamplight was not sufficient for detecting minute movements. (p. 153)

Here, too, there is a 'hellish' scene, and a principal character who shivers or shudders in recoiling from it. But here the poetic formula that has 'thin yellow light' falling 'like tainted rain on the rag-wrapped bodies' cannot be located within Omprakash's consciousness. These cannot be his interior words; they neither stage his situation nor correspond to his particular way of seeing. They register, instead, a *commentary* on what he sees. They show us, readers, not only what Omprakash sees and how he sees it, but also how it might be conceptualised or understood, beyond the compass of his own awareness.

Dina Dalal possesses, in these terms, a certain ontological priority in *A Fine Balance*. To be sure, we are shown what she sees, just as we are shown what Omprakash or Ishvar or Maneck sees. But whereas these other characters are not figured as recognising what the narrative guides us to recognise, Dina's character *is* figured thus. The shock that she experiences at the sight of the slime-covered boy who rises before her, evidently from the bowels of the earth, is shared by the narrator. *What* is shared here, to be precise, is not merely the experience of shock itself, but the perceptual and conceptual disposition that determines this experience, both giving rise to it and shaping its content and form of expression. Dina's experience is class-based; the narrative representation of it issues from the same class location. The relation between subject and object within this representation is external: a passenger in a train, Dina is located only temporarily within the landscape she contemplates, from which, moreover, she attempts to distance herself as far as possible by holding her nose against its intrusive smell. The narrative voice, similarly, discloses its distance from what it describes through rhetorical means, through its aestheticised and ethicised encoding of the slime-covered boy as a 'terrible beauty'.

In his essay, Williams argues that the next step in the evolution of 'the industrial novel' is, in the terms we have been using, 'towards describing what it is like to live in hell, and slowly, as the disorder becomes an habitual order, what it is like to get used to it, to grow up in it, to see it as home' (p. 214). This can happen only when the 'crisis' represented by existing conditions is 'not to be observed but experienced, internalized' (p. 215). This formulation points Williams beyond Dickens and Gaskell and George Eliot's *Felix Holt*, towards a writer like Joseph Keating. In the 'postcolonial' context, similarly, we would need to move beyond Mistry – whose particular achievement, like Dickens's or Gaskell's, might be said to consist in his ability to conjure his characters into existence with such sympathy and moving generosity as to burn them indelibly into our conscience[92] – to such other writers as Ousmane Sembène, Carlos Bulosan, or Samaresh Basu, whose writing stems from a different class experience and a different class ethic.

STATE AND NATION

The identification of the *colonial* state as a dictatorship, and the corollary celebration (or at least documentation) of the struggle against its repressive violence, lies at the heart of anticolonial writing. Even on a casual approach to poets like Martin Carter or David Mandessi Diop, for instance, one will encounter such modular lines as

> In that time
> With civilization's mouthings
> With splashes of holy water on domesticated brows
> The vultures built in the shadow of their claws
> The bloody monument of the tutelary era.[93]

and

> I come from the nigger yard of yesterday
> leaping from the oppressors' hate
> and the scorn of myself;
> from the agony of the dark hut in the shadow
> and the hurt of things;
> from the long days of cruelty and the long nights of pain
> down to the wide streets of to-morrow, of the next day
> leaping I come, who cannot see will hear.[94]

The idiom of this writing – not merely its idiom, indeed, but its very *raison d'être* – is nationalist. But 'nationalism' here is not at all the cramping, reductive, and authoritarian discourse typically identified, and uniformly deplored, by postcolonialist critics. On the contrary: in the historical context of anticolonialism, this nationalism is the engine of collective daring, ingenuity, and capacious social imagination – a 'magnificent song that [makes] the people rise against their oppressors', in Fanon's resounding words (of which most of his postcolonialist readers, notwithstanding their adulation of him, have taken absolutely no notice) (*Wretched of the*

Earth, p. 203). In its appearance in works of literature, anticolonial nationalism is seldom narrow, sectarian, or chauvinistic; it seeks instead to open the community up to the globe. The fostering of nationalism is also the fostering of internationalism and transcultural solidaristic affiliation. Nor does anticolonial nationalist literary discourse merely reflect or transmit a pregiven 'national consciousness'. One can see, in the grappling with landscape and seascape, flora and fauna, in the identification, indexing, and weighting of these, and also of objects and relationships, history and memory, a forging of the imaginative currency, the symbolic capital, of national(ist) identification and self-understanding. The *cri nègre* that grounds Aimé Césaire's refusal of colonialist politics, ethics, and aesthetics, for instance – most famously in the *Cahier d'un retour au pays natal* (*Notebook of a Return to the Native Land*) – also serves to instantiate a Caribbean people, whose right to a self-determining existence it both demands and (literally) authorises.[95] The very title of Césaire's 1960 volume, *Ferrements*, presents us with the image of the poet working to refunction the 'chains' or 'fetters' that continue to constrain Caribbean selfhood even after the abolition of racial slavery – a case, not so much of 'beating swords into ploughshares and spears into pruning hooks', as of turning manacles (including those that have been 'mind forg'd') into ironwork, expressive of an autonomous Caribbean imaginary.[96]

Through their contestatory troping, counteridentification, valorisation and revalorisation of community, environment, and social order, writers in the historical context of decolonisation bring the 'worlds' of the 'new' nations to conceptuality and cognition. They 'world' these nations, so to speak, defining them through grammars, lexicons, registers, habitus that have had to be fought for and fought over, seized from the grasp of colonial definition, colonial understanding, colonial discursivity, and conceptuality.

> Here in prison
> rage contained in my breast
> I patiently wait
> for the clouds to gather
> blown by the wind of History
> No one
> can stop the rain.[97]

Written from an Angolan prison in 1960, Agostinho Neto's apparently simple lines activate the elementary opposition between social and natural orders – injustice and incarceration on the one hand, on the other rain, wind, and clouds – but do not confirm it, resignedly. Instead, taking his cue from the metaphor famously deployed by Harold Macmillan in his 'Wind of Change' speech, delivered to the South African parliament a few months earlier (in February 1960), Neto proposes both that rain, clouds, and wind are not impersonal forces, above the fray, but partisan, socially interested; and that, like these natural elements, the pulse of freedom cannot be stilled. The very elementalism of rain provides a guarantee of the victory of the nationalist cause.

A similar logic obtains in Badr Shakir al-Sayyab's marvellous 'Rain Song' (written, incidentally, in the same year as Neto's poem), in which rain again loses its purely natural aspect to become instead a socionatural force. It becomes *time*, in fact – the present time of hunger and destitution, the bitter 'now' that nevertheless arcs into the future, towards the redemptive arrival of 'a new dawn'. The reiterated formula, 'drip, drop', assumes meaning in al-Sayyab's poem also as 'tick, tock', as the *passing* of the time of hardship and struggle, as the *passage* towards 'the young world of tomorrow':

> Since we had been children, the sky
> Would be clouded in wintertime,
> And down would pour the rain,
> And every year when earth turned green the hunger struck us.
> Not a year has passed without hunger in Iraq.
> Rain . . .
> Drip, drop, the rain . . .
> Drip, drop . . .
> In every drop of rain
> A red or yellow color buds from the seeds of flowers.
> Every tear wept by the hungry and naked people,
> Every spilt drop of slaves' blood,
> Is a smile aimed at a new dawn,
> A nipple turning rosy in an infant's lips,
> In the young world of tomorrow, bringer of life.
> Drip, drop, the rain . . .
> Drip . . .
> Drop . . . the rain . . .
> Iraq will blossom one day.[98]

In this context, lines from 'Poem of the Land' by the great Palestinian poet Mahmoud Darwish (who was much influenced by al-Sayyab) might be taken to testify generally, not only to the centrality of the category of resistance in anticolonial nationalist literature,[99] but also to the power and cogency of the literary imagination in the construction of national consciousness. Like Neto and al-Sayyab, Darwish works with ready-to-hand symbolic materials (soil, pebbles, birds, figs, almonds); but they emerge transfigured in his poem, as constellated images in a singular, charged landscape:

> I name the soil I call it
>   an extension of my soul
> I name my hands I call them
>   the pavement of wounds
> I name the pebbles
>   wings
> I name the birds
>   almonds and figs
> I name my ribs
>   trees
> Gently I pull a branch
>   from the fig tree of my breast
> I throw it like a stone
>   to blow up the conqueror's tank.[100]

Postcolonial scholarship has tended to slight writings of this kind, sometimes programmatically. An example is provided by Ania Loomba's generally praiseworthy text, *Colonialism/Postcolonialism*.[101] In the section of her primer addressed to 'Challenging Colonialism', Loomba indeed devotes an initial chapter to the topic of 'Nationalisms and Pan-nationalisms', in which she dutifully discusses organised struggle-based forms of resistance to colonialism. But she then follows this with *three* chapters urging a critique or deconstruction of the received paradigms of anticolonialism, including nationalism and revolution. The suggestion progressively and sometimes explicitly elaborated across these latter three chapters – 'Feminism, Nationalism and Postcolonialism'; 'Can the Subaltern Speak?'; and 'Post-modernism and Postcolonial Studies', respectively – is that 'challenging colonialism' ought also, and centrally, to involve 'challenging *anti*-colonialism'. Hence, presumably, Loomba's relative lack of interest in the nationalist registration of violence and repression, protest and resistance, revolution and liberation struggle.

Earlier, I quoted Fanon's celebratory identification of nationalism as a 'magnificent song'. What Fanon actually says, of course, is that 'nationalism, that magnificent song that made the people rise against their oppressors, stops short, falters, and dies away on the day that independence is proclaimed' (*Wretched of the Earth*, p. 203). 'The Pitfalls of National Consciousness', from which these words are taken, in fact argues that while nationalism plays a critical and progressive role in mobilising and orchestrating popular resistance to colonialism, in the aftermath of decolonisation it typically becomes a barrier to progress, inasmuch as it is used by the newly ascendant political elite to divert attention from their failure to transform the 'independent' nation, which therefore assumes the aspect of a 'neo-colony'.[102] Nationalism, as Fanon puts it, 'is not a political doctrine, nor a program. If you really wish your country to avoid regression, or at best halts and uncertainties, a rapid step must be taken from national consciousness to political and social consciousness' (p. 203).

In an interview with Jennifer Wicke and Michael Sprinker conducted in 1989, Edward Said returned to this Fanonian formula, speaking of the widespread failure of the political elites in the newly independent states, in the years following decolonisation, to transform 'national consciousness into political and social consciousness'.[103] In South, South East and East Asia, the Maghreb and the Mashriq, Latin America and the Caribbean, as in Africa, leaders and ruling elites have come to identify their own maintenance in power as being of greater importance than the broader 'social' goods of democratisation, opportunity, and equality, and they have increasingly used the repressive apparatuses and technologies of the state (often inherited from the colonial order) to enforce order and to silence or eliminate opposition: Pinochet and the Duvaliers, Mobutu, Babangida and Mugabe, Zia ul-Haq and Ferdinand Marcos – the list is dispiritingly long. As Arundhati Roy puts it, in a summary consideration of developments in postcolonial India: 'Over the past fifty years ordinary citizens' modest hopes for lives of dignity, security and relief from abject poverty have been systematically snuffed out. Every "democratic" institution in this country has shown itself to be unaccountable, inaccessible to the ordinary citizen, and either unwilling or incapable of acting in the interests of genuine social justice.'[104] The grim irony borne in Roy's formulation is that the Indian state is in fact to be distinguished from the vast majority of postcolonial states in having preserved at least its formal commitment to democratic governance. As Sunil Khilnani has written, '[t]he historic persistence of India's democratic routines, interrupted only by Mrs Indira Gandhi's Emergency – a twenty-two month eclipse during the mid-1970s – is the single most remarkable fact about post-1947 India, distinguishing it from almost all the new nation-states that emerged out of the disintegration of European empires'.[105] How much worse than in India, then, have been developments in such states as Burma and Indonesia, Somalia and Egypt, Guatemala and Paraguay!

Perhaps it is understandable that the overwhelming bulk of the literature on the subject of nationalism in postcolonial studies should have taken the form of categorical disavowal. Scholars in the field have evidently not known how – other than through this wholesale repudiation – to account for the setbacks and defeats of the post-independence years, and more particularly for the stupefying violence and criminality of postcolonial governance. Their outlook puts one in mind of Teacher, the character in Ayi Kwei Armah's *The Beautyful Ones are not yet Born*, who responds to the rapid and squalid unravelling of the great expectations that had attended political independence in Ghana by turning his back on all ideologies, including most notably the progressive nationalism to which he had earlier been drawn. Teacher draws the melancholy conclusion that the impoverished, depleted state of the nation a decade after independence is the secret truth of the buoyantly hope-filled promise represented by Nkrumah's nationalist campaign in the decolonising years. The current malaise seems, to him, to falsify that earlier promise. He retreats into political agnosticism and abandons his erstwhile activism, resolved never again to heed the inspirational voice of hope: 'I will not be entranced by the voice, even if it should swell as it did in the days of hope. I will not be entranced, since I have seen the destruction of the promises it made. But I shall not resist it either. I will be like a cork.'[106] Postcolonialist scholars rather resemble Teacher in this respect, it seems to me. For them, too, the fact that the postcolonial era has borne witness to defeat and despotism, barbarism and brutality, is taken to prove that even in its most progressive avatars – as represented by Castro, Nkrumah, Mandela, Nehru, Sukarno, for instance – anticolonial nationalism was never really a 'magnificent song', but only the sound of the siren; that it was never really a means of speaking truth to power, of 'awakening' the powerless (that is to say, of arousing, conscientising, and mobilising them), but only a seductive lie.

To be sure, the fact that even – and perhaps especially – the most repressively violent postcolonial regimes have been concerned, very self-consciously, to disseminate a particular, singular, and self-serving narrative of the nation, designed to cast them as the heirs of the 'heroes' and 'veterans' who struggled for 'liberation' – and hence to legitimate their power – might seem to ratify postcolonialist scholars' theoretical inclination to repudiate nationalism as such. Tirop Simatei, for instance, has written of the Kenyan 'political establishment's desire', in the immediate postcolonial era, 'to fashion a monolithic history of the new nation that [would] firmly legitimize … its power'.[107] He suggests that the construction of this monolithic nationalist narrative entailed not only the falsification of the actual history of decolonisation, but the repression of those who dared to remember it. The apparently unifying national(ist) slogan – 'forgive and forget' – in fact enabled the postcolonial Kenyan state to instantiate and entrench an official amnesia. 'To remember the past, according to Jomo Kenyatta, [was] an expression of disloyalty to the nation, [was] "to stoke fires of revenge or animosity".' The 'state-enforced amnesia' served to 'criminalise … remembrance' (p. 91). Nationalism in this context had the deliberated function, as Fanon had presciently warned, of 'pacifying' the people, of '[putting] them to sleep' (*Wretched of the Earth*, pp. 168, 169).[108]

In Armah's novel, of course, Teacher's alienated stance is ultimately disconfirmed. It is rather the stubborn, pedestrian commitment, against all the odds, to precisely the sort of vision that had been projected in Nkrumah's campaigning speeches – a commitment represented in the novel by Armah's central protagonist, identified only as 'the man' – that is valorised. Yet in postcolonial studies, it is Teacher's general outlook that has typically prevailed. Nearly all of the discussion has centred on the 'Janus face' of nationalism in general (which is therefore not to be trusted in any particular); very little of it has addressed the specific agency of the postcolonial *state*, captured by the political class at independence, and actively deployed by it – for better and, mostly, worse – thereafter. There has been relatively little attempt to suggest that not all forms of nationalist discourse are reducible to the statist master-discourse – indeed, that some of the most adamantine and far-reaching resistance to the violence and repressiveness of the postcolonial state has been undertaken precisely in the name of alternative nationalisms, of different national imaginings.

The general discrepancy between postcolonial *criticism* and 'postcolonial' *literature* is at its most marked here. For the programmatic disavowal of nationalism in the criticism is brought strongly into question by the sheer ubiquity of representations (including, crucially, *positive* representations) of nation-ness – whether nationalist in the strict sense or not, that is, whether written in solidarity with political movements claiming nationally representative status, or in the name of countries 'yet to be born' (Laâbi, *World's Embrace*, p. 135) – across the full range of 'postcolonial' literature. The critique of official or statist nationalist discourse in this work ought not to be mistaken for a critique of nationalism itself. We should take note of the sheer prodigiousness of the texts that put themselves forward explicitly and self-consciously as vehicles of national consciousness, speaking the language of what Wole Soyinka, in his powerful poem 'Elegy for a Nation', terms 'voluntary patriotese' – the word 'voluntary' distinguishing the poet's imagination of the nation from that projected in official statist discourse.[109] A preliminary representative sampling here might include such novelists as Etel Adnan, Manlio Argueta, Patrick Chamoiseau, Zee Edgell, F. Sionil José, Elias Khoury, Earl Lovelace,[110] Pepetela, Pramoedya Ananta Toer, Sergio Ramirez, Manuel Rui, A. Sivanandan, Etienne van Heerden, and Yvonne Vera – not to mention the Salman Rushdie of *Midnight's Children* and *The Moor's Last Sigh*, both of which purport to figure and indeed speak for India, their opposition to the statist discourse of the nation notwithstanding.[111] An analogous list could easily be produced of dramatists and poets.[112]

I should also mention the vast array of other texts which, while they do not necessarily assume this burden of national(ist) representation, nevertheless stage or situate themselves very explicitly and self-consciously in terms of the nation's experience. I am thinking here, for instance, of such poetical works as A. K. Ramanujan's *Relations* and Agha Shahid Ali's *Rooms are Never Finished*, and such novels as Anita Desai's *Clear Light of Day* and Mo Yan's *Red Sorghum*, all of which evoke and examine the links between private and public realities, the familial and the national: aspirations, experiences, memories, the ties that bind and those that separate.[113] The temporal framing of Desai's novel, for instance, is so scrupulously marked as to bring the question of the nation and its fate inevitably and unavoidably into view. Set in the late 1960s (the novel's 'present') and recounting events from 1947–8 (tumultuous both for the nation and the family represented in the novel), *Clear Light of Day* is written in the late 1970s, from which extradiegetical viewpoint the depicted events of 1947–8 and the 1960s – and the relation between them – are implicitly revalued. A similarly implicit revaluation is also in evidence in the framing of Seth's *A Suitable Boy*, which mobilises the temporal gap between the early 1990s – the time of the novel's composition – and 1951 – the time of its setting – to pose questions about the trajectory and progressiveness of developments in India since decolonisation.[114] And, again, much the same device is mobilised by Agha Shahid Ali in his 2003 poem, 'Summers of Translation', when he casts his mind back to 1989, just before the outbreak of full-scale war in Kashmir, when he and his mother read the work of Faiz Ahmed Faiz together:

> so many summers, so many monsoons, dimmed on Time's shelf,
> return, framed by the voice you gave to each story,
> as when – in the last summer of peace – the heart itself
> was the focus. You read all of Faiz aloud to me:

> We chose poems that would translate best. So strange:
> Why did we not linger just a bit on 'Memory'?
> It was '89, the stones were not far, signs of change
> everywhere (Kashmir would soon be in literal
> flames). Well, our dawns were so perfectly set to arrange
> our evenings in color that liberty with each ghazal
> was my only way of being loyal to any original
>   (*Rooms are Never Finished*, p. 30)

In an exceptionally illuminating and suggestive commentary, Edward Said has drawn attention to the socially (and nationally) representative aspect of the fractured and unstable narrative forms utilised by such writers as Ghassan Kanafani, Emile Habiby, and Elias Khoury. Said contrasts these writers – the first two of them Palestinian, the third Lebanese – with the grand old man of Egyptian fiction, Naguib Mahfouz: 'The thing about Mahfouz', he writes,

> is that he can and has always been able to depend on the vital integrity and even, cultural compactness of Egypt. For all its tremendous age, the variety of its components and the influences on it – the merest listing of these is inhibitingly impressive: Pharonic, Arab, Muslim, Hellenistic, European, Christian, Judaic, etc. – the country has a stability and identity that in this [twentieth] century have not disappeared. Put differently, this is to say that the Arabic novel has flourished especially well in twentieth-century Egypt because throughout all the turbulence of the country's wars, revolutions, and social upheavals, civil society was never eclipsed, its existence was never in doubt, was never completely absorbed into the State. Novelists like Mahfouz had it always *there* for them, and accordingly developed an abiding institutional connection with the society through their fiction.[115]

Narrative form in Mahfouz, as Said construes it, reflects and registers the integrity, depth, and relative stability of Egyptian (and still more Cairene) civil society, in which Mahfouz is, and knows himself to be, an active participant. Said speaks, thus, of 'the discursive patterns of a narrative structure that [is] not merely a passive reflection of an evolving society, but an organic part of it' (p. xiii). One senses this as much in Mahfouz's social realist work – *The Cairo Trilogy*, for example – as in such formally more dispersed, avowedly modernist novels of his as *Adrift on the Nile*.[116]

With Kanafani, Habiby, and Khoury, however, the situation is entirely different. 'For one [thing]' as Said puts it,

> in some Arab countries you cannot leave your house and suppose that when and if you return it will be as you left it. For another, you can no longer take for granted that such places as hospitals, schools, and government buildings will function as they do elsewhere, or if they do for a while, that they will continue to

do so next week. For a third, you cannot be certain that such recorded, certified, and registered stabilities in all societies – birth, marriage, death – will in fact be noted or in any way commemorated. Rather, most aspects of life are negotiable, not just with money and normal social intercourse, but also with guns and rocket-propelled-grenades. (Foreword, p. xiv)

It is impossible in such circumstances to write like a Mahfouz. Instead, in the fiction of Palestinian writers and that of their Lebanese counterparts after the outbreak of civil war in 1975, 'form is an adventure, narrative both uncertain and meandering, character less a stable collection of traits than a linguistic device, as self-conscious as it is provisional and ironic' (p. xv). Said considers the 'peculiarly disintegrating prose' of Kanafani's *Men in the Sun*,[117] 'in which within a group of two or three sentences time and place are in so relentlessly constant a state of flux that the reader is never absolutely certain where and when the story is taking place' (p. xv). In Kanafani's later novel, *All That's Left to You*,[118] the 'technique is even more pronounced, so that even in one short paragraph multiple narrators speak without, so far as the reader is concerned, adequate markers, distinctions, delimitations' (p. xv). Habiby's *The Secret Life of Saeed, the Ill-Fated Pessoptimist*[119] is quite as unstable – disoriented and disorienting – in its own way as Kanafani's work. Absurd, excessive, carnivalesque, vertiginous, and careering in its formal and narrative aspects, it differentiates itself sharply from the received proprieties and conventions of the novel in Arabic. As Said puts it, '[i]t is as if the Palestinian situation ... produces a wildly erratic and free-wheeling version of the picaresque novel, which in its flaunting of its carelessness and spite is in Arabic prose fiction about as far as one can get from Mahfouz's stateliness' (p. xvi). Khoury's *Little Mountain*, for its part, is introduced in terms of 'rejection, drift, errance, uncertainty' (p. xxi) – which might be taken for postmodern thematics except that Said insists that their manifestation in Khoury's work be grasped as objective correlatives of the social disintegration specifically contingent upon the Lebanese civil war. In this Lebanon, 'the novel exists largely as a form recording its own impossibility, shading off or breaking into autobiography (as in the remarkable proliferation of Lebanese women's writing), reportage, pastiche, or apparently authorless discourse' (p. xvi).

Analogous arguments could, I think, be advanced with respect to the work of many other writers in 'postcolonial' contexts, whose specific inflections (formal and substantive) of received traditions and idioms of poetry, drama, or prose writing are too often abstracted from their particular contexts by postcolonialist critics and read as expressions or variants of a (putatively) globally dispersed aesthetic mode, such as 'magical realism' or 'the gothic' or 'postmodernism'. In such readings there is often a fatal disposition to situate the aesthetic mode of the 'postcolonial' work as derivative of that of a categorically prior 'Western' instance.[120] Moreover, the 'internal' thrust of the work under review – that is, its engagement with and reciprocal effect on the 'local' traditions upon which it is substantially predicated – is typically neglected.

Consider, for instance, the label, 'magical realism', as it has been applied to the work of such African writers as Kojo Laing, Sony Labou Tansi, Mia Couto, and Ivan Vladislavic. The conclusion typically drawn by critics[121] is that the formal experimentalism of works like *Search Sweet Country* and *Woman of the Aeroplanes* (Laing), *The Antipeople* and *The Seven Solitudes of Lorsa Lopez* (Labou Tansi), *Voices Made Night, Every Man is a Race*, and *The Last Flight of the Flamingo* (Couto), and *Propaganda by Monuments, The Restless Supermarket*, and *The Exploded View* (Vladislavic) registers the exhaustion of the received 'modern' political projects (including nationalism) that – or so the implication goes – had been entailed by 'realism'.[122] However, there is no need to suppose that the combination of fantasy and naturalism in Vladislavic's writing, say, functions to this end. Certainly, his work produces a disorienting image of an alternative world that, while mirroring the 'real' world with sufficient regularity to guarantee recognition of it, displaces or subverts or challenges it in other respects. But to refer this effect abstractly to 'postmodernism' is to fail to see just how committed it is to representing the psychosocial dynamics of *South African* life during the last years of the apartheid era and in the contemporary period of 'normalisation'. The distinguishing features of Vladislavic's fiction – the informal, not quite casual prose, the relentless accumulation of detail, the general fastidiousness, the concern, identified by Patrick Lenta, with 'everyday abnormality',[123] the obsessive, willed tranquillity of the surface that hints at, and intermittently breaks apart to reveal, an inner core of hysteria and repressed violence – are all predicated precisely on the questions of what 'South Africa' is and what it has been, and to what extent what it has been continues to determine what it is and what it might be capable of becoming.[124] The story that begins, 'Wednesday afternoon, mid-winter, finds me at the counter in the United Building Society (Hillbrow), minding my own business, making a cash withdrawal, when my hands burst into flames',[125] for instance, simply cannot be understood outside of the specific ideological/experiential context of South Africa in the final years of apartheid, the 'interregnum' as Nadine Gordimer called it[126] – the

South Africa in which 'total strategies' were being devised paranoically by the state to defeat phantasmatic 'total onslaughts', with the result that the mere presence, the mere physical existence, of most of the nation's people was projected as incipient criminality, latent terrorism. Vladislavic's protagonist initially responds to his 'condition' with 'horror and fear': his hands unquenchably and inexplicably alight, he 'wander[s] aimlessly for half an hour' (p. 102). At some point, however, he begins to inhabit the identity capriciously imposed upon him – to find himself in it: 'Finally I enter a shoe-shop with the express intention of setting something alight ... I am starting to enjoy myself. I am highly inflammable. Better, I am incendiary' (pp. 102–3). By the story's end, he has started to 'live the dream', even though it was not his dream to begin with, but the state's nightmare: 'Later I think I will torch the park across the street. Meanwhile, I am content to play with fire' (p. 103).

It is the actuality of 'South Africa' as implied (and also explicit) context within this story that enables it to gain representational purchase. To read the story is to be reminded of other South African works addressed to the same fundamental issue, albeit coming at it in different ways and from different directions. One thinks, for instance, of Achmat Dangor's work, above all *Kafka's Curse*,[127] of Zakes Mda's *Ways of Dying*,[128] or of the work of Etienne van Heerden, especially the story, 'My Cuban', with its absolutely simple – if humanistically unthinkable[129] – opening sentence, 'I have a Cuban on a leash',[130] and whose narrator's initial projection of the blank, psychotic calm of the world-defying, and increasingly reality-denying, Afrikaner nationalist discourse of the late 1970s and early 1980s, has, by the end of the narrative, collapsed into the hysteria it was devised to conceal:

Swearing, I tried to disentangle myself from my harness, the winged anchor that bound me. At last I was free, the short carbine in my hands, warm with the sun that had already penetrated the metal still half in the bush I fell and the carbine started to chatter beneath me and the dust rose in small vertical spurts around the Cuban's boots but yet he still came on smiling and I cursed him and his line and his whore of a mother and his island and still smiling he kept coming but he never got to me where I lay and shot my carbine empty, sobbing, still half in my harness, with the parachute languidly rising and falling in the breath of Africa. (p. 83)[131]

The point I am trying to make here is not simply that Vladislavic's work, or van Heerden's – or that of any writer – is best approached contextually, in terms of its precise sociological and also literary-institutional coordinates. I am also suggesting that, inasmuch as the *nation* – nationalism, the nation-state form, the very idea of nation-ness – is, for the most transparent of historical reasons, a foundational political horizon for writers from the 'postcolonial' world, it tends to figure centrally as a generative matrix or object of representation in their work. Thus Vladislavic's and van Heerden's writings are not only 'South African' in their formation, but are cardinally *about* South Africa. The same could also be said of Laing in relation to Ghana, Okri in relation to Nigeria, Couto in relation to Mozambique, and so on.[132] In speaking *in* its time and place, the work of these writers also speaks *of* (or even *for*) its time and place.

In their intense focus on violence and social repression, 'postcolonial' writers have taken up the idea of the state as a particular (and privileged) instrument of political domination – hence as simultaneously *at stake in* and *the site of* struggles for power and justice, hegemony and freedom. The actions and specific instrumentality of the postcolonial state have been scrupulously and even obsessively documented and troped, not least by way of ensuring that a counter-memory of what has happened survives – that, in limit cases, the truth is not buried along with the bodies of those murdered by predatory states, east, west, north, and south.[133]

> They shake their heads and say
> 'we want evidence'.
> How can I explain
> that there cannot be any evidence.
> For when the state rapes
> the streets are empty.[134]

These lines are taken from Keki N. Daruwalla's 1980 volume, *Winter Poems*, which, as Bruce King has recently observed, provides both a record and an indictment of a decade of state-sponsored 'scarcity, discontent, and barrenness' in India during the 1970s.[135] But much the same point could be made through citation of such other remarkable poems as 'Exit Left, Monster, Victim in Pursuit (Death of a Tyrant)' and 'Vain Ransom' by Wole Soyinka[136] – the latter written 'for the dead and maimed of Kenya and Tanzania' – or 'Marginal Notes on the Book of Defeat' by Nizar Qabbani, with its pointed observation, in the aftermath of Israel's victory in the 1967 war, that autocracy in the Arab world has caused the Arab people to lose the war not once, but twice – or, rather, to have lost not one war, but two. Not only has the army been defeated, by the Israeli forces; but the nation, represented by the people, has been defeated by the state:

> O Sultan, O my lord,
> Because I came close to your deaf walls,
> Trying to reveal my sadness and my misfortune,

I was beaten with shoes.
Your soldiers forced me to eat out of my shoes.
O Sultan, O my lord,
You have lost the war twice
Because half of us has no tongue
What value are people with no voice?[137]

The violence and repressiveness of the postcolonial state are at the centre of the canvases painted in such works of poetry as Frank M. Chipasula's *Nightwatcher, Nightsong*, Ariel Dorfman's *In Case of Fire in a Foreign Land*, Claribel Alegría's *Woman of the River*, and Kim Chiha's *Heart's Agony*;[138] and such works of fiction as Nuruddin Farah's trilogy, *Sweet and Sour Milk*, *Sardines*, and *Close Sesame* – to which he has given the general title, *Variations on the Theme of an African Dictatorship* – and Mongo Beti's sequence, *Perpetua and the Habit of Unhappiness*, *Remember Ruben*, and *Lament for an African Pol* – not to mention the entire subgenre represented by the Latin American 'Dictator' novel, among the best-known examples of which are Alejo Carpentier's *Reasons of State*, García Márquez's *The Autumn of the Patriarch*, and Augusto Roa Bastos's *I the Supreme*.[139] We should also take into account here such novels as Nayantara Sahgal's *Rich Like Us* and Rohinton Mistry's *A Fine Balance*, both of which reckon the human and political costs to the cause of democracy of Mrs Gandhi's Emergency; Luisa Valenzuela's *The Lizard's Tale*, with its harrowing, surrealist exploration of intersubjectivity (especially as between the sexes) deformed by terroristic state violence;[140] the 'scar literature' that emerged in China after the Cultural Revolution, and that weighed the psychic and physical costs of that disastrous era – for example Dai Houying's *Stones of the Wall* and Bei Dao's short-story collection, *Waves*.[141] To these lists can be added still another, of writers – like the Arabic poet, Adonis, for instance, in such powerful and disturbing poems as 'A Mirror for the Executioner' (1984), or Assia Djebar, in her remarkable *Algerian White* (2000 [1995]) – who chronicle the violence meted out by the postcolonial state specifically to intellectuals, and especially those intellectuals determined, in Edward Said's celebrated phrase, to speak truth to power.[142] If the names of Victor Jara, Abdellatif Zéroual, and Ken Saro-Wiwa might be said to stand for all the artists, writers, and intellectuals permanently silenced by state terror, there are, thankfully, other courageous artists, writers, and intellectuals who have emerged to testify in their stead. As Bei Dao puts it in his poem, 'An End of a Beginning', written in the context of the Cultural Revolution:

Here I stand
Replacing another, who has been murdered
I have no other choice
And where I fall
Another will stand.[143]

The sadly still flourishing genre represented by such texts as Abdellatif Laâbi's *Rue du retour*, Ngugi's *Detained*, Alicia Partnoy's *The Little School*, Pramoedya's *The Mute's Soliloquy*, and Graciliano Ramos's *Prison Memoirs* demands not only due critical regard but adequate *theorisation*.[144]

There are signs that the sheer scale of some of the horrific develop-ments over the past twenty years or so – especially but not exclusively in sub-Saharan Africa (where it is enough merely to name Liberia and Sierra Leone, Somalia and Sudan, Rwanda, the Congo and Zimbabwe, for example) – has been such as to cause scholars in postcolonial studies to turn their attention from the idea of the nation to that of the state.[145] In the emergent discussion of genocide, terror, and statist violence, the one-dimensional postcolonialist focus on the constructedness of nationalist discourse – and the disavowal of nationalism as such that tended to follow from this abstracting theoretical focus – seems finally to be giving way to more nuanced and, indeed, more ideologically and historically discriminating lines of enquiry.[146] A 2004 essay by Elleke Boehmer, for instance, juxtaposing the work of Arundhati Roy and Yvonne Vera, concludes that in 'keeping the possibility of a liberatory or *women's nation* alive', these novelists 'reject the rhetoric of negativity through which the nation is almost always conventionally addressed in a postcolonial discourse which privileges diasporic border crossings, dialogic migrancy, and so on'.[147] Even though Boehmer does not take up questions concerning the various forms of state that might corres-pond to the alternative nationalist imaginaries figured in *The God of Small Things* or *The Stone Virgins*[148] – questions in which these novels themselves have an investment, incidentally – her identification of the 'experiment[ation] with alternative, heterogeneous constructions of community' in the two works as 'characteristically nationalist in certain key respects' marks a significant advance on the received treatment of nation and nationalism in postcolonial studies (p. 175). In this light, one might mention the recently burgeoning scholarly production on Zimbabwean literature since independence, much of which has been exemplary in undertaking a politicised critique of statist nationalism – especially as it has been used in justification of the brutal, violent, and socially devastating 'third *Chimurenga*' of the post-2000 years – that does not make the mistake of supposing that what is therefore entailed is a repudiation of nationalism as such. As Ranka Primorac has argued,

representing nationalism as inherently detrimental is especially counter-productive in the Zimbabwean context, because in Zimbabwe, anti-colonial nationalism has from the outset embodied ideals of freedom, democracy and equality as well as the restoration of land to the people. References to early nationalist goals continue to be among the principal means through which the Zimbabwean state can be held to account, and twenty-first century struggles over the meanings of freedom and democracy are still conceptualised by their participants as struggles over the nature of the nation.[149]

STRUCTURES OF FEELING

In what I have written above, I have been attempting to register the materialist heartbeat of much 'postcolonial' writing. But I would like to draw attention also to a *phenomenological* dimension in this literature, an attempt on the part of many writers to capture or represent the 'structure of feeling'[150] of lives lived in particular ways in particular places and times, framed by particular conditions of existence, predicated on particular meanings, values, and assumptions and oriented towards particular goals. In an article on Aimé Césaire's poetics, Carrie Noland has argued that our 'responsibility' as readers to literary texts 'is to respond to [their] call, not by determining unilaterally what [they] mean ... but by patiently taking a fuller inventory of all the ways in which [they] might achieve meaning and agency in a complex world'.[151] What is at issue here is not the anthropo-logical or philosophical specification of the sheer *actuality* of daily or customary life (what V. Y. Mudimbe terms *la chose du texte*, that is, the existentially intransitive zone of social practice that precedes and exists outside of any discursive commentary on it)[152] – important though that specification undoubtedly is in its own right. Rather, I have in mind the attempt to portray the texture of life as it is experienced, not merely in its objective but also in its subjective aspects – to afford the reader a lens on to lives that might be socially restricted and miniature in scope, but which are nonetheless construable in representative terms, as 'typical' or, if not quite so much, as 'emblematic'.

What is being celebrated here is the writer's ability to show us what it *feels* like to live on a given ground – to show us how a certain socionatural order (a physical world, a mode of production, a specific set of social relationships, forms of belonging, customs and obligations) is encoun-tered, experienced, lived. The success of writers in 'opening up' for us structures of feeling or fields of vision, in enabling us as readers imaginatively to 'inhabit' these structures or fields, depends on their ability to find the words, concepts, figures, tropes, and narrative forms to mediate between and thread together – in ways that are not merely plausible but, more importantly, *intelligible* and *transmissable* – what are in fact discrepant and discontinuous aspects of reality: for example, landscape, forces and relations of production, community, awareness of self, gender, language. When Tayeb Salih's narrator in *Season of Migration to the North* returns to his home village in the Sudan for the first time after a period of years spent studying in England, for instance, he records his impressions as follows:

I awoke, on the second day of my arrival, in my familiar bed in the room whose walls had witnessed the trivial incidents of my life in childhood and the onset of adolescence. I listened intently to the wind: that indeed was a sound well known to me, a sound which in our village possessed a merry whispering – the sound of the wind passing through palm trees is different from when it passes through fields of corn. I heard the cooing of the turtle-dove, and I looked through the window at the palm-tree standing in the courtyard of our house and I knew that all was still well with life. I looked at its strong straight trunk, at its roots that strike down into the ground, at the green branches hanging down loosely over its top, and I experienced a feeling of assurance. I felt not like a storm-swept feather but like that palm tree, a being with a background, with roots, with a purpose.[153]

The passage provides us not only with a description of the setting of a house in a Sudanese village, but also with a phenomenological image of a way of thinking attuned to this house and village from the inside, as it were. It is true that the language in the passage is complexly overdetermined – marked by the narrator's deep desire to 'ground' himself in half-forgotten sights and sounds, forms of understanding, by way of 'unthinking' what he has learned in the North. The ineradicable shadow of 'the North' in 'the South' – which disturbs the narrator's homecoming search for origins (and gives Salih's novel its overarching theme) – implies that what is experienced or recovered as autochthonous is not necessarily so. Despite this, we do receive sufficient information in the passage to enable us to register the presence of a discrete universe of meaning and value, precisely adjusted (in phenomenological terms) to its location in time and space: an elective affinity appears to hold at this point in the novel between the landscape, the space of the village and the household, the forms of labour undertaken by the villagers, the prevailing orders of sociality and discourse, the operative moral codes and symbolic economies. To say 'I heard the cooing of the turtle-dove, and I looked through the window at the palm-tree standing in the courtyard of our house and I knew that all was still well with life' is to implicate a social order of meaning, which it becomes our task as readers to situate, as completely as we can.

As further illustrations of what I am driving at here, consider the 'mutuality' of land, labour, and consciousness in Asturias's extraordinary novel, *Men of Maize*, or in such novels as Gopinath Mohanty's *Paraja*, Shahnon Ahmad's *Rope of Ash* and *No Harvest but a Thorn*, al-Sharqawi's *Egyptian Earth*, or N. V. M. Gonzalez's *A Season of Grace*.[154] Or consider Lewis Nkosi's striking and perceptive assessment of Bessie Head's novel, *When Rain Clouds Gather*:

> the evocation of the sun-parched waste of Botswana, with an occasional desert 'bloom' such as the village of Golema Mmidi, the slow almost imperceptible changes of the seasons and the unhurried accumulation of the physical details of everyday life, these are just some of the achievements of this South African novelist. This materiality of everyday existence happens to be the most difficult thing to achieve in a novel; and yet recreating in fiction the microcosm of the larger social world, and breathing a new life into the harshly familiar and the unrelentingly dull, is what writing novels used to be about; Bessie Head manages her task with immense skill and sympathy.[155]

Nkosi celebrates Head's success in rendering the 'materiality of everyday existence' in Golema Mmidi. He has in mind not simply her intuitive and extraordinarily sensitive descriptions of men and women at work, but – more broadly – her descriptions of how these men and women live together: how they think and act and interact, given the people that they are, in the precise circumstances in which they find themselves. He values the way Head writes in *When Rain Clouds Gather*, thus, because she is able to move so dexterously and compellingly from the detailed description of daily practice to the forms of consciousness of cattlemen in their isolated posts in the bush. Mistry achieves a similar effect in *A Fine Balance*, when he has Ishvar tell Dina, in response to a query from her, that his way of talking about his life, which involves searching for wider meanings in the smallest incidents and events, and in connecting these one to another, is linked to his craft: 'Must be my tailor training' he speculates. 'Tailors are practised in examining patterns, reading the outlines' (p. 395).

It might be objected that to prize the recreation in literature of 'the microcosm of the larger social world' is to betray a bias towards fiction and, more narrowly, towards realist or naturalist representation. Although all of the writers I have mentioned thus far in this section (Salih, Asturias, al-Sharqawi, Shahnon, Mohanty, Head, Mistry) are indeed novelists (if not by any means all literary *realists*), I do not think that this objection holds water. For what I have been calling the 'phenomenological' dimension of 'postcolonial' literature – the attempt to render and register structures of feeling – is just as insistently foregrounded in *poetry*.

Just before turning to poetry, however, let me note in passing my conviction that we ought, today, to begin to redress a long-standing imbalance in postcolonial literary studies by focusing anew on realist writing. The point is that, inasmuch as the dominant aesthetic dispositions in postcolonial literary studies have from the outset reflected those in post-structuralist theory generally, the categorical disparagement of realism in the latter field has tended to receive a dutiful – if wholly unjustified and unjustifiable – echo in the former. The situation in postcolonial literary studies has been accurately described in the following way by Laura Moss:

> there has been a critical elevation of writing perceived to be experimental or writing that plays with non-realistic form. Within postcolonial criticism, these simultaneous developments have converged in the production of a profusion of studies linking, and sometimes suggesting the interdependence of, political or social resistance and non-realist fiction. If a text does not fit the profile of postcolonial resistance, as realist texts seldom do, it is generally considered incapable of subversion … In spite of many examples of recent politically charged realist texts, the critical expectations about the form often hold that it is a reinforcement of conservative, specifically imperialist, ideology … [This assumption] has led to the virtual dismissal of the realist novel by those critics looking for an apparently radical form to hold disruptive content.[156]

Moss goes on to 'challenge the idea, as it has been developed or assumed by many postcolonial critics, that realism is almost necessarily conservative, and non-realist forms are inherently somehow *more* postcolonial – and therefore subversive' (p. 158).[157] This challenge is pertinent: scholars of eighteenth- and nineteenth-century fiction, for instance, have long since rebutted the view, widely prevalent in avant-gardist theoretical circles in the 1970s and early 1980s, that realism is an authoritarian aesthetic form; there is no good reason for scholars in postcolonial studies to hang on to this dogma today.

If fiction is able to recreate the materiality of everyday life through its density, accumulation of detail, and ability to mediate between and thread together divergent aspects of reality, poetry is capable of achieving a similar end through its own peculiar means of representation.[158] In much 'postcolonial' poetry we witness the attempt to find words, tones, registers, grammars, syntaxes, sensitive to and capable of registering landscapes as well as patterns of social relationship shaped by particular histories of dispossession and resistance, conquest and reclamation, subjection and struggle. In work composed in the languages of the former colonial powers, especially – as, most notably, in the Carib-bean – the socially and historically sedimented resources and symbolic freightage of these languages are first deconstructed and then reformu-lated so as to enable them to shoulder the burden of *post*colonial representation. 'The final mission was to lead the word astray into teeming deafness scorched Tropics. Like an addition of fruits drunk with memories in the banana-trees' mute desire', Édouard Glissant writes in his prose poem, 'November'.[159] This idea of 'leading the word astray' is worth emphasising: the suggestion, I take it, is that the given word, the received lexicon, the inherited vocabulary, has to be stripped down, possibly even disassembled, and then revarnished if not rebuilt, before it can be made to fit the Caribbean landscape or equipped to represent the problematics of social being in the 'New World' – *after* the middle passage and slavery, *after* indenture, *after* colonialism. The poem that follows 'November' in Glissant's volume is entitled '*Lecture sauvage*' ('Wild Reading'), a phrase that captures brilliantly the sense that in the Caribbean context the 'reading' of social being – the repre-sentation of the local *chose du texte* – ought not to be a matter of taming or domestication, of subordinating world text to pre-given concept, but rather of submitting conceptuality to the irreducible topography and social forms of the 'New World'. New words need to be minted, old words and forms of understanding stretched and revised. In all of his work, as Betsy Wing writes, Glissant

celebrates not only the countries rising from the ravages of colonialism but also all geography – all writing-of-the-earth. While frequently personal in tone, the poems insistently cross conventional borders between personal, emotional contact and contact with the world-totality the poet is struggling to know and put into words ... Setting himself apart from the followers of the Symbolists, [Glissant] never attempts to write the unsayable, the inexpressible. The premise of his writing is that all can be said. His would be a poetry of duration (*durée*) and accumulation, as opposed to the poetry of the revelatory instant, the momentary fulguration epitomized for Glissant in the work of Rimbaud. Glissant does not seek privileged moments of individual revelation that may come from some external source or even from 'deep within'. He strives, rather, to locate himself precisely by the concrete contacts produced by all his intelligence, sensory as well as intellectual, in touch with the world. The words of these poems are part of the physical continuum of his existence – frail and receptive, powerful and resistant, dense and alive: 'I say that poetry is flesh'.[160]

In Derek Walcott's poetry, we often bear witness to an analogous attempt to model (or, better, remodel) the 'new' world in and through language. Poetic discourse is here conceived as a glove made to fit a particular hand. Setting his sail against the abstract, classificatory dimension of language, Walcott offers us instead, in many of his poems, words, metaphors, figures that aim to mirror the local world – not in the sense of mimetic representation, but in gestaltist or impressionist terms: what is conveyed, ultimately, is the effect on the subject of the objectivity of the world. In 'Islands', from the 1962 volume, *In a Green Night*, for example, the poet observes that '[m]erely to name' islands 'is the prose of diarists'.[161] Such taxonomic naming is not only objectifying, it is scientist in the precise sense understood by Maurice Merleau-Ponty when he wrote, in his celebrated essay 'Eye and Mind' (written at almost exactly the same time as Walcott's poem, incidentally) that 'Science manipulates things and gives up living in them. It makes its own limited models of things; operating upon these indices or variables to effect whatever transformations are permitted by their definition, it comes face to face with the real world only at rare intervals.'[162] The counter-premise to such scientism is then stated by Walcott: 'But islands can only exist / If we have loved in them'. It is the interiorisation of islands, not their mere mapping – their 'occupation' in the sense of inhabitation and not of externally projected power – that transforms them into objects of social consciousness. This, then, provides the poet with his task, which is less to write *about* islands than to show us how, for those who live in them, social being in the widest sense (subjectivity, sensuality, sexuality and gender, forms of embodiment, community, family, friendship, class relations) is in part an effect of their materiality and presence. Hence:

> I seek,
> As climate seeks its style, to write
> Verse crisp as sand, clear as sunlight,
> Cold as the curled wave, ordinary
> As a tumbler of island water.   ('Islands', p. 52)

In 'Names', a poem from the 1976 collection, *Sea Grapes*, and which is dedicated, significantly, to Edward Kamau Brathwaite (whose own verse is also concerned to explore the political ontology of language, the relation between word and world in the context of Caribbean history), Walcott takes as his topic the birth of Caribbean subjectivity. A key moment in the poem occurs when the poet observes that while the settler colonists sought to domesticate the Caribbean world-text through its reduction to 'new' Europe, the Afro-Caribbean population responded to this world-text as 'wild readers':

> And when they [the settler colonists] named these bays
> bays,
> was it nostalgia or irony? ...
> Their memory turned acid
> but the names held;
> Valencia glows
> with the lanterns of oranges ...
> Being men, they could not live
> except they first presumed
> the right of every thing to be a noun.
> The African acquiesced, repeated, and changed them   (pp. 306–7)

In the poem, the course of the struggle over language – over naming, in fact – is figured as emblematic of the emergence of Caribbean subjectivity. It is, again, a matter of allowing language to resonate with the actuality (and difference) of what it represents:

> Listen, my children, say:
> *moubain*: the hogplum,
> *cerise*: the wild cherry,
> *baie-la*: the bay,
> with the fresh green voices
> they were once themselves
> in the way the wind bends
> our natural inflections   (p. 307)

The evocation of 'fresh green voices' here ought to be distinguished, in passing, from what Raymond Williams, in his discussion of William Wordsworth and John Clare in *The Country and the City*, has termed 'the green language' of pastoralism. Pastoral poetry, as Williams describes it, involves the 'projection of personal feeling into a subjectively particularised and objectively generalised Nature' (*Country and City*, p. 134). 'Closer description of nature – of birds, trees, effects of weather and of light – is a very marked element' in this mode of writing. 'It is often a prolonged, rapt, exceptional description: an intricate working of particularity, as opposed to the more characteristic attribution of single identifying qualities in most earlier writing' (p. 133). In the contexts of 'postcolonial' literature, we might think of a writer like Jibanananda Das, and especially of the sonnets that make up *Bengal the Beautiful*, posthumously discovered and published only in 1957. These sonnets seem to accord closely with Williams's understanding of pastoralism. Consider the following, for example:

> Evening. All around is silent peace.
> A *shalik* softly flies off carrying straw.
> A bullock-cart travels along at its ease.
> Straw's gold is piled high on the courtyard floor.
>
> All the doves in the world are singing in the wood.
> All the beauty of the world is on the grass.
> All the love in the world is in our mood.
> Sky-high sky-wide sky-long peace comes to pass.[163]

Schooled by Williams, we immediately notice, of course, that *work* in this poem has been relegated to the margins, if not eliminated altogether. The *shalik* is building a nest, to be sure; but the fact that it flies off 'softly' indicates not only that it does so silently but also that its labours are less than arduous. More to the point, the bullock-cart travels along not only 'at its ease' but also, for all we can know from the poem, unaccompanied; certainly, human labour is not seen to be involved. Above all, the work that has had to be done to pile the straw high on the courtyard floor is swallowed up by the poet's use of the present tense: to say that the straw 'is piled high on the courtyard floor' is to situate the work of piling it there beyond the visual and temporal purview of the poem.

However, the fact that the social world of production has been eliminated from Jibanananda's poem as an explicit referent is not to suggest that the materialities of 'society' and 'history' are not registered by it. Of Jibanananda's work at large, his English translator Joe Winter has written:

The natural landscape informs the writing as if by right. The presence of the trees and plants and rivers, the ground reality he grew up with, is breathtaking. His poetry is earthed in these sights and smells, in the overt and hidden force of Bengal's living land. It has been said Nature is a character in his work. An uncanny sense of individuality is there, an idiosyncratic disposition, everything except a voice for which the poet's becomes a proxy.[164]

This description not only helps us to identify the affective intensity of Jibanananda's writing; it also prompts us, more generally, I think, to grapple with the twin registers of pastoralism, as both celebration and elegy or lament. The objectivity and ineluctability of the socio-material world seem to enter Jibanananda's poem in the forms of longing and desire – longing and desire for what has been lost, for what has been broken, for what has been displaced or forcibly set aside. It is not only that inasmuch as the 'peace' that the poet invokes in the final line of his poem is spoken of as having 'come to pass', it cannot be thought of as a given or natural occurrence, or indeed as anything other than exceptional. It is also that in its very registration of fulfilment (of the poet in and by his world), the poem suggests that that fulfilment is no longer capable of being achieved, if in fact it ever was.

It is in this respect, I think, that Walcott's poetry takes its distance from pastoralism. My own interest lies in emphasising the *materialist* gesture of Walcott's writing: what is sought is a language alert to the pulse of the Caribbean *chose du texte*. The world as represented in Walcott's poetry is the world lived in; the poetry is not cast as a means of remembering – nor, indeed, of re-membering – a unity (of the poet and the landscape or community that his poetry recalls or reveals) that 'life' or 'history' or 'society' has broken or dissolved. With Jibanananda it is otherwise. Reading John Clare's work more than a century and a half after it had been written, Williams comments:

I can recognise what Clare is describing: particular trees, and a particular brook, by which I played as a child, have gone in just this way, in the last few years, in an improved use of marginal land. And then what one has to consider is the extension of this observation – one kind of loss against one kind of gain – into a loss of 'Nature'. It is not only the loss of what can be called – sometimes justly, sometimes affectedly – a piece of 'unspoiled' country. It is also, for any particular man, the loss of a specifically human and historical landscape, in which the source of feeling is not really that it is 'natural' but that it is native ... And then what is most urgently being mourned ... is a loss of childhood through a loss of its immediate landscape. (*Country and City*, p. 138)

So, too, in the case of Jibanananda. In the great poem, '1946–47', for instance, he counterposes a yesterday – 'only the other day' – when 'the harvest festival was in the air' to today, when '[i]n many thousand Bengali villages, silent, dark, listless, the lamp of hope's out' (*Naked Lonely Hand*, p.). The image conjured up of the earlier time admits the diversity of customary practice, village to village: 'in this place eldest and next eldest, / in that place low-caste wives blew the conch ... / crow-hordes came flying in the sun for the nectar'. But whatever the forms of social life assumed – in history, in tradition, in legend – today 'all's erased', 'the sun is extinct', 'there's no glimmer of light': 'of all those crows not a whisper is heard'. Even the mature acknowledgement that the image of village life evoked in legend and tradition (and perhaps even in his own poetry) has been nostalgic and sentimental,

glossing over hardship and destitution, merely serves to sharpen the
focus of the poet's fundamental insight:

> There in the night of the moon peasants would dance in the meadow
> after a good drink of the paddy's strange juice – shortly before
> the marriage of Majhi Bagdi's daughter Ishwari
> and shortly after – and before the birth of her child.
> All these children today are crushed nearly to death
> in the exhausted, crowded community
> of this age's stupid misrule: and of all these village children
> the great-grandfathers laughed and played and loved – and went to sleep
>   in the dark
> after flinging out the *zamindars'* Permanent Settlement to the top
>   of the *charak*-tree.
> Not that they had such a fine time of it; but still,
> compared with the blind and ragged village creatures of today
> in their famine and riot and unhappiness and illiteracy,
> they were of a distinct and quite separate world ...

CHAPTER 2

Fredric Jameson on 'Third-World Literature': a defence

In 1986, Fredric Jameson published an essay entitled 'Third-World Literature in the Era of Multinational Capitalism' in *Social Text*, a left-identified, New York-based journal of cultural politics. In retrospect, I'm sure he wishes that he hadn't. For the essay has brought him nothing but brickbats.

Jameson's work has always been marked, somewhat paradoxically, by both its magisterial erudition and its eminent contestability. I don't mean by the term 'contestability' that what he has written has proved controversial, necessarily. I mean, rather, that his work has demonstrated a rather remarkable tendency to provoke its readers to take issue with its premises and arguments, its terms and conclusions. Jameson has always attracted a lot of readers, most of whom, from the beginning, have liked to disagree with him, in whole or in part. My sense is that this is because, while he has characteristically worked with material – ideas, concepts, theories, bodies of work, modes and styles of cultural practice – that possesses, or is beginning to possess, wide currency, his own approach to this material has invariably been off-centre: not only consistently dialectical and deeply committed to systematicity (in an age in which dialectics and systematicity have been almost universally reviled), but also heterodox and distinctly underivative, though never lapsing into mere idiosyncrasy. Not only has Jameson tended to get to this material *first*, as it were, to think about it significantly in advance of most other scholars, he has also tended to think about it in a significantly *different* way from most other scholars.[1] The precedence – so consistent a feature of his work as to amount almost to a prescience – is what has brought the wide readership (or is at least *part* of what has brought the wide readership); the off-centredness – a function and effect of Jameson's sustainedly *Marxist* commitments – is what has ensured that his own interpretation of a particular phenomenon or text or tendency, while being duly and dutifully referenced in the subsequent scholarly literature, has never quite emerged as the representative one, the institutional standard.

Thus the 1971 *Marxism and Form*, for instance:[2] while Jameson's audacious and illuminating engagement with twentieth-century Marxist aesthetics in this study predated by a good half-dozen years the burgeoning of interest in this body of work in wider literary critical circles in the anglophone world, his decisive emphasis on its political and dialectical aspects – although it was regularly cited – found symptomatically little purchase when, later in the 1970s, such theorists as Adorno, Bloch, Lefebvre, Bakhtin, and especially Benjamin began to receive widespread attention from American and British academics. In the scholarship that emerged in the later 1970s the work of these Marxist theorists tended to be configured in radically decontextualised and depoliticised form. By 1981, revealingly, Terry Eagleton would feel the need, in introducing his own book on Benjamin, to protest that his subject was 'in imminent danger of being appropriated by a critical establishment that regards his Marxism as a contingent peccadillo or tolerable eccentricity'.[3] For all its remarkable insight, Jameson's reading of Benjamin in *Marxism and Form* had evidently cut no lasting ice with critics in the 'establishment'.

A similar story could be told about *The Prison-House of Language*, which, as early as 1972, had offered a brilliant – indeed, to this date unsurpassed – critique of the genealogy and epistemology of post-structuralist thought at the very moment of its entry (as 'Theory', with a capital 'T') into Anglo-American academic circuits.[4] As so often, Jameson had done the reading – in English, French, German, Spanish, Italian, and Russian, to judge by his footnotes! – before most of his colleagues. Typically, however, when these colleagues came to do the reading themselves in the years that followed, they did so, not without reference, but without *deference*, to Jameson's study.[5]

The pattern does not change even in the case of the celebrated work on postmodernism. Perry Anderson is, I think, wrong to argue for the hegemonic effect of Jameson's theory of postmodernism, which he sees as coming to 'command the field' and as 'setting the terms of theoretical opposition in the most striking imaginable way'. As Anderson presents it, the effect of Jameson's writing on postmodernism has been to take 'a concept whose visionary origins [had been] ... all but completely effaced in usages complicit with the established order' and to wrest ... [it] away by a prodigious display of theoretical intelligence and energy for the cause of a revolutionary Left. This has been a discursive victory gained against all the political odds, in a period of neo-liberal hegemony when every familiar landmark of the Left appeared to sink beneath the waves of a tidal reaction. It was won, undoubtedly, because the cognitive mapping of the con-temporary world it offered caught so unforgettably – at once lyrically and caustically – the imaginative structures and lived experience of the time, and their boundary conditions.[6]

The problem with this formulation rests in its idealism. I recognise that this is not a complaint that one can typically level against Anderson. Yet in his discussion of Jameson, Anderson confuses intellectual reach or cogency or rhetorical power with institutional effect – incidentally just the slippage to which, if we were thinking structurally, we might suppose an intellectual historian to be objectively disposed by virtue of his disciplinary formation.[7] That Jameson's theory of postmodernism is rich and resourceful – perhaps even without equal in these respects – need not be disputed. But this has not, *contra* Anderson, been sufficient to win for the American theorist 'command [of] the field'. For the fact is that, institutionally speaking – that is, among other things, at the level of routine practice in the interlocking academic fields of culture studies – almost everybody who reads the famous essay on 'Postmodernism, or, The Cultural Logic of Late Capitalism',[8] for instance, tends to register *both* that they find it suggestive *and* that it seems to them profoundly deficient or misguided in key respects or instances. The vast bulk of the scholarly work produced on postmodernism tips its hat to Jameson, to be sure, even makes use of such concepts of his as 'cognitive mapping'; but it is no more *Jamesonian* in general tendency than it is *Marxist* – indeed, it is arguably seldom the former precisely *because* it is not the latter. Anderson supposes that, as a result of Jameson's daring, insight, and ingenuity, the concept of 'postmodernism' has come to wear his colours in the academy. My own view is that it would be truer to say just the opposite – that in the circuits of actually existing culture studies, Jameson is typically (mis-)read as himself a postmodernist, in the over-arching context of a politically indifferent (and, specifically, *post-Marxist*) conception of 'postmodernity'.

I have been commenting on what I have called the contestability of Jameson's work, the fact that engagement with his arguments has typically taken the form of a disputation of them. In the case of his 'Third-World Literature' essay, however, a quite different explanatory schema is required. For in this case, and in the specific context of the then still

emergent field of postcolonial studies, there was no contestation or
disputation of Jameson's arguments, only a blanket and largely *a priori*
dismissal of them. Both the pervasiveness and the ferocity of this response
were remarkable. It was as though, for postcolonialists, Jameson had
suddenly fallen foul of the standards not only of intellectual credibility
but also of *decency*. Anyone teaching postcolonial studies in the Anglo-
American academy during the late 1980s or early 1990s would, I think, be
able to attest to this development. There was a distinctly moralistic tinge
to the discussions of Jameson's essay. I myself was teaching at Brown
University in the United States at the time, and I recall that, almost
overnight, 'Jameson' seemed to have become a dirty word to my students,
both undergraduate and postgraduate. And I discovered the same reaction
among colleagues in the academy whom I encountered at conferences
devoted to postcolonial studies.

Everybody objected to, took offence at, the same passage in Jameson's
essay. Even today, when the polemics have long since echoed themselves
to silence, I am sure that postcolonialists who were active at that time will
know which passage I am referring to, even before I cite it. It is, of course,
that in which, having made a couple of 'initial distinctions' (I will return
to these in due course), Jameson moves to advance a 'sweeping hypothesis': '[L]et me now', he writes,

> try to say what all third-world cultural productions seem to have in common and
> what distinguishes them radically from analogous cultural forms in the first
> world. All third-world texts are necessarily, I want to argue, allegorical, and in
> a very specific way: they are to be read as what I will call *national allegories*, even
> when, or perhaps I should say, particularly when their forms develop out of
> predominantly western machineries of representation, such as the novel.[9]

Acknowledging the dangers of simplification, Jameson nevertheless adds,
in an attempt at clarification, that while in 'capitalist culture' there is 'a
radical split between what we have come to think of as the domain of
sexuality and the unconscious and that of the public world of classes, of
the economic, and of secular political power', in 'third-world culture' the
relations between the 'subjective' and the 'public or political' are 'wholly
different':

> Third-world texts, even those which are seemingly private and invested with a
> properly libidinal dynamic, necessarily project a political dimension in the
> form of a national allegory: the story of the private individual destiny is
> always an allegory of the embattled situation of the public third-world culture
> and society. (p. 69)

II

To understand why this passage, and Jameson's essay as a whole, should have come to be viewed as so profoundly objectionable, it is necessary to introduce Aijaz Ahmad into the discussion. For without Ahmad's forceful and damaging rejoinder to Jameson, which initially appeared in a subsequent issue of *Social Text* and was reprinted in *In Theory: Classes, Nations, Literatures*, the postcolonialist disparagement of Jameson would never have proceeded as it did.[10] Whether or not Ahmad's rebuttal represented the first discussion in print of Jameson's essay – and I have not been able to find an earlier discussion – it quickly emerged as paradigmatic. Ahmad it was who identified Jameson's postulation of the 'national allegory' hypothesis as *colonialist* in character and tendency. This is what he wrote:

There is doubtless a personal, somewhat existential side to my encounter with this text, which is best clarified at the outset. I have been reading Jameson's work now for roughly fifteen years, and at least some of what I know about the literatures and cultures of Western Europe and the USA comes from him; and because I am a Marxist, I had always thought of us, Jameson and myself, as birds of the same feather, even though we never quite flocked together. But then, when I was on the fifth page of this text (specifically, on the sentence starting with 'All third-world texts are necessarily . . .' etc.) I realized that what was being theorized was, among many other things, myself. Now, I was born in India and I write poetry in Urdu, a language not commonly understood among US intellectuals. So I said to myself: '*All? . . . necessarily?*' It felt odd. Matters became much more curious, however. For the further I read, the more I realized, with no little chagrin, that the man whom I had for so long, so affectionately, albeit from a physical distance, taken as a comrade was, in his own opinion, my civilizational Other. It was not a good feeling. (*In Theory*, p. 96)

I want to consider the rhetorical dimensions of this passage; for it seems to me that what is *actually said* is powerfully supplemented by what is assumed and suggested but *not actually said* – by what is said in *not being said*, by the forms of identification and of dis-identification that Ahmad mobilises and instantiates. The passage opens, thus, with his protestation of long-standing respect for Jameson. He has been reading him for a long time, he says, and has learned a lot from him – or, at least, a lot about 'the literatures and cultures of Western Europe and the USA'. The inference is going to be that Jameson has not repaid this compliment in kind; he has not been similarly respectful – at least, not where literatures and cultures from *outside* Western Europe and the USA are concerned. The respect Ahmad attests that he used to feel for Jameson is of a specific kind: not that of a student for a teacher, nor of a reader for a writer, but of one Marxist intellectual for another, of a *comrade* for another comrade. But even before the publication of the 'Third-World Literature' essay, it seems, this was a virtual rather than an actual comradeship. A silent but not unexpressed reprimand – of Jameson's aloofness, perhaps even of the fact that the circles in which he travels as a superstar in the American academic firmament are not those in which 'Marxists' and 'comrades' ought to travel – is contained in Ahmad's witticism that 'I had always thought of us, Jameson and myself, as birds of the same feather, even though we never quite flocked together.' Be this as it may, Ahmad reiterates that the 'affection' in which he had held Jameson 'for so long' had had to be conducted 'from a physical distance'. And he now realises – the realisation has been forced upon him – that what separates him from Jameson is more than mere physical distance: it is *ideological* distance, too – specifically, the 'distance' or, better, the yawning divide, between incompatible optics deriving ultimately from the colonial encounter. Marxist intellectual though Jameson might be (or might profess himself to be), he continues – this is how Ahmad sees it – to replicate the essential gesture of colonialist thought in conceiving of the 'non-West' in terms of its otherness from the normative 'West'. Hence Ahmad's resort to the trope of 'civilisation': Jameson, he says, supposes himself to be 'my civilizational Other'.

Substantively, Ahmad's words home in on the categorical universalism of Jameson's hypothesis: 'All third-world texts are necessarily'. Ahmad questions Jameson's elementary competence to formulate such an hypothesis: 'I was born in India and I write poetry in Urdu, a language not commonly understood among US intellectuals', he writes, drawing attention to the fact that, for all Jameson's polyglottism, nearly all of the languages implicated by the term 'third world' remain unavailable to him. On what authority, therefore – by what mandate – could his hypothesis possibly justify its universalism? Propositionally, its generalism seems to Ahmad unwarranted – indeed, absurd: he insists that 'one knows of so many texts from one's own part of the world which do not fit the description of "national allegory"' (*In Theory*, p. 107). And what then adds ideological insult to propositional injury, drawing his particular ire and indignation, is the fact that Jameson – who has, after all, taken the time and the trouble to learn a lot about the cultures and societies of the 'non-West' (Ahmad acknowledges that Jameson's interpretation of the Chinese writer Lu Xun and the Senegalese writer Ousmane Sembène in his essay is 'marvellously erudite' [p. 95]); and who, precisely for this reason, might presumably have been relied upon to know how much he had *still* to discover – does not hesitate to put forward a categorical global hypothesis, in the language of 'all' and 'necessarily'. The gesture strikes Ahmad as frankly colonialist.[11] As he puts it:

> The mere fact ... that languages of the metropolitan countries have not been adopted by the vast majority of the producers of literature in Asia and Africa means that the vast majority of literary texts from those continents are unavailable in the metropolises, so that a literary theorist who sets out to formulate 'a theory of the cognitive aesthetics of third-world literature' will be constructing ideal-types, in the Weberian manner, duplicating all the basic procedures which Orientalist scholars have historically deployed in presenting their own readings of a certain tradition of 'high' textuality as *the* knowledge of a supposedly unitary object which they call 'the Islamic civilization'. (p. 97)

Now I want to register in passing my view that Ahmad overstates his case here. He seems to have 'forgotten', in the passage just cited, that the literatures of South America and the Caribbean, which are unquestionably constitutive of the Jamesonian category of the 'third-world', *are* overwhelmingly produced in 'languages of the metropolitan countries', to which Jameson *does* have direct access, and over which he has long demonstrated an impressively broad academic command. The 'Third-World Literature' essay is full of references to the literatures and cultures of the hispanophone 'New World' – particularly Cuba, in which (not least for political reasons, of course) Jameson has held a long-standing interest. (Witness, for instance – among many other publications that could be cited in this respect – the foreword that he wrote to a translation into English of Roberto Fernández Retamar's classic text, *Caliban*.)[12] Moreover, as elsewhere in his writings, Ahmad's statement also betrays the fact that he knows comparatively little about Africa, or sub-Saharan Africa, at least: for in *that* subcontinent, unlike the Indian subcontinent, and for historical reasons that would repay close examination, the languages of the metropolitan countries *have* in fact been adopted by the majority of the producers of literature. As it happens, well over half of the literary works produced in sub-Saharan Africa are composed in the metropolitan languages, chiefly of French, English, and Portuguese.

Still, the main thrust of Ahmad's argument against Jameson is not that the universalism of his hypothesis concerning 'third-world' literature is unwarranted or even that his method is latently Orientalist. Rather, it is that his foundational category of the 'third-world' – hence also the binary opposition which structures his essay, between 'first-world' and 'third-world' cultures – is untenable. Ahmad is quite unambiguous on this point. The notion of the 'third-world', he tells us, is, 'even in its most telling deployments, a polemical one, with no theoretical status whatso-ever' (p. 96). Because of this, it is impossible to elaborate a theory – any theory – of 'Third World Literature':

> there is no such thing as a 'Third World Literature' which can be constructed as an internally coherent object of theoretical knowledge. There are fundamental issues – of periodization, social and linguistic formations, political and ideo-logical struggles within the field of literary production, and so on – which simply cannot be resolved at this level of generality without an altogether positivist reductionism. (pp. 96–7)

Jameson's mobilisation of the category of the 'third-world' is specious, according to Ahmad, on two separate accounts. First, while he defines the 'first-world' and the 'second-world' in terms of their modes of production (capitalism and socialism, respectively), he defines the 'third-world' in terms of its 'experience of colonialism and imperialism'.[13] This means, as Ahmad puts it, that '[t]hat which is constitutive of human history itself is present in the first two cases, absent in the third case. Ideologically, this classification divides the world between those who make history and those who are mere objects of it' (*In Theory*, p. 100). Second, Jameson's binary opposition between 'first-world' and 'third-world' formations – and which, to repeat, Ahmad sees as being 'empirically ungrounded in any facts' (p. 101) – has the effect of flattening out the divisions *within* each of these (non-)formations in the interest of accentuating the opposition *between* them. Where a Marxist analysis ought to have emphasised class struggle, Jameson's 'third-worldist' analysis emphasises instead the struggle for national liberation, the struggle of colonial societies to emerge into nationhood in a world of nation-states. Inasmuch as Jameson pro-ceeds from the ground of 'third-worldism', Ahmad argues, he is more or less *bound* to valorise nationalism as the overarching political value, such that the 'national allegory' hypothesis emerges as something in the nature of a truism or tautology, constructed internally and immanently in accordance with the terms of his theory rather than being addressed to, and shedding light on, a tendency or reality outside itself:

> If [the] 'Third World' is *constituted* by the singular 'experience of colonialism and imperialism', and if the only possible response is a nationalist one, then what else is there that is more urgent to narrate than this 'experience'? In fact, there is *nothing else* to narrate. For if societies here are defined not by relations of production but by relations of intra-national domination; if they are forever

suspended outside the sphere of conflict between capitalism (First World) and socialism (Second World); if the motivating force for history here is neither class formation and class struggle nor the multiplicities of intersecting conflicts based upon class, gender, nation, race, region, and so on, but the unitary 'experience' of national oppression (if one is merely the *object* of history, the Hegelian slave) then what else *can* one narrate but that national oppression? Politically, we are Calibans all. (*In Theory*, p. 102)

III

Ahmad's critique of Jameson was first published in 1987 and, as I have already intimated, quickly became paradigmatic. It still serves as the point of departure for any sustained discussion of the merits of the 'national allegory' hypothesis – as even my own procedure in this chapter must be taken to confirm. Especially remarkable, in my view, is the fact that the critique is typically construed as unanswerable, so that it serves in effect as the accepted means of focalising Jameson's text, which therefore comes before us, readers in the field of postcolonial studies, as to a significant degree predigested, already read. There are, to be sure, some splendid exceptions to this rule, commentaries which address the debate between the two theorists but contrive to read Jameson's article with fresh eyes.[14] More generally, however, the authority of Ahmad's reading tends quite simply to be taken for granted. Thus Frederick Buell repeats point for point the terms of Ahmad's critique, in fact identifying his own views so seamlessly with Ahmad's that he moves in closing to claim Ahmad for his own globalisation theory standpoint. Ahmad, he tells us, 'invok[es] a profound recent change in modes of world organization'.[15] (In fact, Ahmad invokes no such thing, but Buell himself certainly does.) Sara Suleri, similarly, praises the 'eloquence' of Ahmad's critique of Jameson's 'third-worldist' discourse – a discourse that, for her, 'bespeaks a theoretical fear that has still to reconcile the uneasy distance between alterity and the problematic of national specificities'.[16] It is true that Suleri qualifies her appreciation of Ahmad somewhat – he is 'perhaps too heavily invested in a reading of the "real" to provide an adequate theoretical alternative to the potentially alteritist allegory of Jameson's argument'. But this is very much in the nature of a quibble: for her commentary is centrally predicated on Ahmad's diagnosis of a 'rhetoric of otherness' in Jameson's essay, and on his construction of this rhetoric as neo-Orientalist if not neo-colonialist in character. As Suleri puts it in introducing the Jameson–Ahmad debate:

contemporary rereadings of colonial alterity too frequently wrest the rhetoric of otherness into a postmodern substitute for the very Orientalism that they seek to dismantle, thereby replicating on an interpretive level the cultural and critical fallacies that such revisionism is designed to critique … In contravention of the astounding specificity of each colonial encounter, alteritism enters the interpretive scene to insist on the conceptual centrality of an untouchable intransigence. Much like the category of the exotic in the colonial narratives of the prior century, contemporary critical theory names the other in order that it need not be further known; more crucially, alteritism represses the detail of cultural facticity by citing otherness as a universal trope, thereby suggesting that the discursive site of alterity is nothing other than the familiar and unresolved confrontation between the historical and the allegorical.[17] (*Rhetoric of English India*, pp. 12–13)

What Ahmad calls Jameson's 'rhetoric of otherness', Suleri terms his 'alteritism'. In Rosemary Marangoly George's discussion of the debate, Jameson's 'reading practice' is construed, analogously, in the light of Johannes Fabian's critique of the colonialist logic of anthropological discourse.[18] The binary opposition between 'first-world' and 'third-world' cultures in the 'Third-World Literature' essay is read as registering not the engineered geopolitical unevenness of imperialism, but a *temporal* unevenness, which Fabian has termed 'allochrony'. Allochrony denies 'coevality': the scandal of anthropology, Fabian has argued, is that through its methodology and disciplinary practice it presents other people, who are in fact contemporaries of the anthropologists who write about them, as though they are living in another time, specifically in the past. The anthropologist who writes about Africans or Pacific Islanders or Amerindians positions them as 'primitive': they live in the present but are actually of the past; the anthropologist's encounter with them is therefore an encounter not merely of different social and cultural orders but of different, and of course differently *valued*, temporalities. (Christopher Miller has used this conception in a very interesting reading of Conrad's *Heart of Darkness*, arguing that, in Conrad's text, Marlow's voyage to the centre of the African continent is phrased as a voyage backwards in time, beyond the beginning of civilisation.)[19] For George, Jameson's binarisation of 'first-world' and 'third-world' cultures functions to similar effect: it situates 'third-world' cultures as backward and, more specifically, as embroiled still in tasks and projects which have already been undertaken, and completed, in the 'first-world': 'Jameson, it seems … would like to convince us that nationalism is the *only* authentic cultural attribute of the non-western parts of the world. And even this "fundamental" attribute has already been experienced in the past of western literature' (*Politics of Home*, p. 109). Exactly the same point is made by Gayatri Chakravorty Spivak (writing *after* both Ahmad and George but citing neither of them, incidentally) in

A Critique of Postcolonial Reason, when she essays to identify 'what is most problematic in Jameson's "Third-World Literature." Psychoanalysis (such as it is) for us. Anthropology (as, in Jameson, nationalism), for them. As Johannes Fabian has pointed out, for the anthropologist, "[d]ispersal in space [can] reflect ... directly ... sequence in Time"'.[20]

In the passage from Ahmad to George and Spivak, and certainly to Buell and Suleri, a curious inversion occurs. The critique mutates from a Marxist critique of 'Third-Worldism' into a 'Third-Worldist' critique of Marxism. Ahmad himself was the first to recognise this mutation, although he failed, I think (for understandable reasons), to grasp fully the role that he had played in bringing it about. Already by 1992, when he republished 'Jameson's Rhetoric of Otherness' as a chapter in his book, *In Theory*, it had become clear to him that an ideologically consequential gap had opened up between his strategic intentions in criticising Jameson and the conclusions that postcolonialist readers were increasingly drawing from that critique. As he wrote in the introductory chapter of *In Theory*, 'Literature Among the Signs of Our Time':

> It has been a matter of considerable personal irritation for me that my essay appeared at a time when Jameson was very much under attack precisely for being an unrepentant Marxist. There remain at least some circles where almost anything that was so fundamentally critical of him was welcome, so that my article has been pressed into that sort of service, even though my own disagreement had been registered on the opposite grounds – namely, that I had found that particular essay of his not rigorous enough in its Marxism. Meanwhile, my disagreement with Jameson on Third-Worldist nationalism has also been assimilated far too often into the sort of thing which we hear nowadays from the fashionable poststructuralists in their unbridled diatribes against nationalism as such. (pp. 10–11)

Ahmad is right to argue that his readers have ridden on his coat-tails in order, not to challenge Jameson's Marxism for its lack of 'rigour', but to repudiate Jameson precisely *for his Marxism*. In postcolonial studies, the Jameson–Ahmad debate has been mobilised very centrally as a way of routing Marxism, of pointing to its alleged complicities with Orientalism, cultural supremacism, colonialism, and the like.[21] The internal links in this chain of argument proceed something like this:

i. Jameson's binarisation of 'First World' and 'Third World' formations bespeaks a cultural essentialism.
ii. This cultural essentialism is readable as a latter-day Orientalism.
iii. Jameson's methodology is Marxist.
iv. Therefore, Marxism is culturally essentialist and Orientalist.

Ahmad deplores this postcolonialist appropriation of his critique of Jameson, finding it at one and the same time 'irritating' and culturally symptomatic. He deplores it, but he argues that it has nothing to do with him. It is an effect, rather, of the ideological tendencies prevailing in postcolonial studies in the late 1980s and early 1990s. This latter proposition is certainly true, or at least it is true to a degree. Ahmad clearly cannot be identified and isolated as the *fons et origo*, or even as the exclusive agent, of the curious process through which his intended Marxist critique of Jameson's 'Third-Worldism' came to be taken up as a 'Third-Worldist' critique of Jameson's Marxism and of Marxism as such, and in terms of which, in its crudest and most programmatic form, the fact that he, Ahmad, is a South Asian and Jameson a white American, contributed significantly to his readership's preference for his views (even misunderstood) over those of his American Marxist interlocutor.

I think this is an important point. We need a materialist and institutionally grounded reading of this process – a reading that would situate both Ahmad's initial critique of Jameson and the subsequent taking up of this critique as *overdetermined*. As position-takings in a field already structured by previously taken positions (including Jameson's), both Ahmad's critique and the appropriation of it were in a sense objectively mandated. Such a reading would enable us to make sense to those many readers of Jameson's essay who would otherwise complain, and perfectly truthfully, that they had come to the 'Third-World Literature' essay without having read Ahmad's critique first – indeed, without previously ever having *heard* of Aijaz Ahmad. A significant number of these readers – particularly, I think, those who were reading Jameson's essay in the late 1980s and early 1990s – responded to it in much the same way as Ahmad had, with disquiet or even outrage.[22] (If and when these readers then went on to encounter Ahmad's critique, they often identified with him, felt that he had articulated at least some of their criticisms of Jameson's essay.) What needs to be emphasized, then, is that although Ahmad's formulation was obviously his and his alone, the content of what he wrote was, so to speak, 'there to be written'; it was 'in the air', which is why these other readers are able to report having responded to Jameson's essay in the same way as Ahmad had.

But I wonder, even so, whether we should allow Ahmad to wash his hands quite so easily of any involvement, any implication, in the way his readers came to take up his critique of Jameson? He was writing, within the United States, in an academic (and wider cultural) climate of fervid identity politics (even though he was himself an opponent of such politics). This was a climate in which the strategic production of the race card was becoming a formidable weapon in the competition for symbolic capital, within the academy as well as in the wider circuits of culture and society; in which a mobile, radically contingent and hierarchically organised lexicon of 'oppressions' was beginning to displace more foundationalist schemas of domination and exploitation (whether liberal or radical). Within the university sectors of the arts, humanities and social sciences, the curious and unstable combination of post-Marxist and anti-nationalist philosophical discourse, identity politics, postmodernism, and multiculturalism (the whole ensemble sometimes leavened by post-structuralist epistemology) resulted in the distinctive emphases that Ahmad sought to analyse in *In Theory* under the rubric of 'Third-Worldism', and that were also notably addressed at much the same time, in their different ways, by Kwame Anthony Appiah and Arif Dirlik.[23] The dispositions of the field were so tilted that even as principled an opponent of identity politics as Gayatri Spivak was led, on occasion, to resort to them as a rhetorical means – as when, for instance, she sought to bat away Benita Parry's fierce, class-based argument that in much postcolonialist writing in its post-structuralist aspect, there was a paradoxical tendency to silence 'native' speech, by responding that

When Benita Parry takes us to task for not being able to listen to the natives, or to let the natives speak, she forgets that the three of us [Parry had criticised Homi Bhabha and Abdul JanMohamed in addition to Spivak], postcolonials, are 'natives' too. We talk like Defoe's Friday, only much better. Three hundred years have passed, and territorial imperialism has changed to neo-colonialism. The resistant post-colonial has become a scandal.[24]

In such an intellectual climate, Ahmad could not have been unaware, I think – or, at least, he *ought not* to have been unaware – of the rhetorical effect that his *language* in his Jameson article would be likely to engender. I say 'language' rather than 'argument'. In fact, I do not believe that Ahmad *was* unaware of this. The invocation in his essay of a 'rhetoric of otherness' in Jameson; the suggestion that Jameson's 'first-world'–'third-world' opposition had had the effect of 'otherising' him (Ahmad) along an axis of 'civilisation'; the classification of Jameson's reading practice as Orientalist – this is not the vocabulary of a *Marxist* critique. If Ahmad was not *consciously* smuggling 'Third-Worldist' rhetoric into his own Marxist critique of Jameson's 'third-worldism', the incorporation of such rhetoric into the critique is nevertheless indisputable. One need not doubt that Ahmad intended to criticise Jameson from the standpoint of a more 'rigorous' Marxism. But when, in strict accordance with the prevailing temper of the field, his postcolonialist readers duly appropriated him for their 'Third-Worldist' critique of Jameson's Marxism, this appropriation did not need to be cut from whole cloth.[25]

IV

The irony of this is considerable, but it is doubled by the fact that it is also quite possible to defend Jameson *on Marxist grounds* from the charge of 'Third-Worldism', at least as Ahmad lays that charge. Let us return briefly to the opening pages of the 'Third-World Literature' essay and undertake a close reading of them, by way of exploring the problematic out of which Jameson writes.[26]

The essay opens with a statement about the radical discrepancy obtaining between contemporary discussions of the nation and nationness among 'American' and 'third-world' intellectuals. In the discourse of the 'third-world' intellectuals, 'the name of the country ... returns again and again like a gong'; there is 'a collective attention to "us" and what we have to do and how we do it', a collective attention to 'us' as a 'people' or imagined community (p. 65). (Jameson refers explicitly to Benedict Anderson's influential *Imagined Communities*, which had then only recently appeared.) There is no similar discussion on the 'American' side: indeed, Jameson speculates that from the standpoint of the 'American' intellectual, 'one might feel' that the topic being discussed by 'third-world' intellectuals 'is nothing but that old thing called "nationalism," long liquidated here and rightly so'. We can immediately note that although Jameson is himself an American, he is not spoken for in the discourse of 'American' intellectuals as he represents it. The 'American' ideology is evidently not the ideology of all Americans, but a particular (and of course severely restricted) view of the world, issuing from a particular standpoint.

Having introduced the idea that 'America' functions in his essay as an ideological construct – the field of vision of the discourse of 'American' intellectuals – Jameson then moves directly to offer a typological repre-sentation of 'American' or, indeed, 'first-worldist' thought. The 'first-worldist' perspective would have it that nationalism has been put to bed on *this* side of the imperial divide ('we' have outlived 'our' nationalist pasts), and had better not be mentioned in the context of the *other* side, since it only ever emerges there as a blood-drenched, politically regressive atavism. Jameson explicitly disavows this 'first-world wisdom': 'The predictable reminders of Kampuchea and of Iraq and Iran do not really seem to me to settle anything or suggest by what these nationalisms might be replaced except perhaps some global American postmodernist culture' ('Third-World Literature', p. 65). Ahmad contrives to misread Jameson quite spectacularly here, claiming that *Jameson* stipulates that 'the only choice for the "Third World" is ... between its "nationalisms" and a "global American postmodernist culture"' (*In Theory*, p. 101). What Jameson actually proposes, I am trying to argue, is that this is the way that things *seem* from the standpoint of the 'First-Worldist' ('American') intellectual – who is precisely *unable* to imagine the possibility either of socialism or even of progressive forms of nationalism, and who therefore envisages the only 'choice' confronting 'Third World' societies as being between Americanism and barbarism.

It is worth reminding ourselves here of the occasion for which the 'Third-World Literature' essay was originally written: a memorial lecture at the University of California, San Diego, honouring Jameson's colleague and friend, Robert C. Elliott, who had published widely on satire and utopia ('Third-World Literature', p. 86 n. 3). Jameson is writing in the first instance to and for US students and scholars of literature, people, in the main, whose exposure to 'postcolonial' writings will have been very limited. With respect to these students and scholars, he believes, there is a particular problem where postcolonial writings are concerned. This prob- lem takes the form of a schooled inability to grapple with cultural difference. Again using the foil of the typological 'American' intellectual, Jameson argues that while such an intellectual has been trained to imagine herself or himself receptive to literary value wherever it might arise, s/he has also been trained to recognise it only in the restricted 'western canon'. On the one hand, thus, s/he celebrates what s/he finds in canonical texts as the epitome of literary value; on the other hand, s/he holds literary value to be locatable only in canonical texts. To which Jameson responds that '[i]f the purpose of the canon is to restrict our aesthetic sympathies, to develop a range of rich and subtle perceptions which can be exercised only on the occasion of a small but choice body of texts, to discourage us from reading anything else or from reading those things in different ways, then it is humanly impoverishing' (p. 66).

Jameson suspects that 'third-world' texts tend to be apprehended by 'first-world' readers in one of two equally unsatisfactory ways (and some- times in both of these ways at the same time): either as aesthetically inferior or as derivative: 'The third-world novel will not offer the satisfac- tions of Proust or Joyce; what is more damaging than that, perhaps, is its tendency to remind us of outmoded stages of our own first-world cultural development and to cause us to conclude that "they are still writing novels like Dreiser or Sherwood Anderson"' (p. 65). Jameson is again ventriloquising his putative 'first-world' reader here. Those postcolonialists who have taken offence at his formulation, believing that Jameson is patronisingly consigning 'third-world literature' to third-class status, have misread him. It is not in the least that 'third-world literature' is not, in his eyes, 'as good as' ('western') canonical literature. It is rather that the ('western') canon serves in 'first-world' thought as a false universal, preventing any concrete engagement with 'third-world' (or culturally different) texts. The 'first-world' reader of 'third-world' texts who hopes to find the 'Tolstoy of Africa' or the 'Flaubert of India' is inevitably disappointed, of course. But instead of recognising the parochialism of this hope – premised as it is on the assumption that only those who write like Tolstoy or Flaubert (as though the two of them wrote in anything like the same manner!) deserve to be considered great writers – our ideal-typical reader construes the 'gap' between Tolstoy or Flaubert and, say, Pramoedya Ananta Toer or Tayeb Salih or George Lamming, as signalling the deficiency of the latter writers, not the reader's own failure of cultural competence. Because what is encountered is only referred back, unreflexively, to the ('western') canon, it cannot be brought to life, deciphered in its actuality, its adequacy – and, indeed, brilliance – in its own particular field(s). De-realised, it is found wanting. Ultimately, the failure to engage with cultural difference prevents the 'First World' reader from having to contemplate the contingency of what is presented to him/her, ideologically, as uncontingent, universally true:

> We sense, between ourselves and this alien text, the presence of another reader, of the Other reader, for whom a narrative, which strikes us as conventional or naïve, has a freshness of information and a social interest that we cannot share. The fear and the resistance I'm evoking has to do, then, with the sense of our own non-coincidence with the Other reader, that Other 'ideal reader' – that is to say, to read this text adequately – we could have to give up a great deal that is individually precious to us and acknowledge an existence and a situation unfamiliar and therefore frightening – one that we do not know and prefer *not* to know.[27] ('Third-World Literature', p. 66)

It is at precisely this juncture that Jameson moves to comment on his use of the term 'third-world':

> I take the point of criticisms of this expression, particularly those which stress the way in which it obliterates profound differences between a whole range of non-western countries and situations ... I don't, however, see any comparable

expression that articulates, as this one does, the fundamental breaks between the capitalist first world, the socialist bloc of the second world, and a range of other countries which have suffered the experience of colonialism and imperialism ... I am using the term 'third world' in an essentially descriptive sense, and objections to it do not strike me as especially relevant to the argument I am making. (p. 67)

It is obvious that Jameson concedes the danger of reductionism in using a term like 'third-world', which tends to emphasise the conflict between 'worlds' rather than classes within given social formations. In his essay, he scrupulously skirts this pitfall, managing to say some penetrating things about class consciousness and class conflict in 'third-world' literature. (Ahmad seems not to have noticed any of these.) But Jameson retains the term – 'third-world' – in the absence of any other capable of registering the structurality of the contemporary world order. Ahmad suggests that in analytically decoupling the 'third world' from the 'capitalist first world' and the 'socialist bloc of the second world', Jameson effectively defines it as outside of human history: because it is distinguished from both the 'first world' and the 'second world', the 'third world' must, on his reading, be neither 'capitalist' nor 'socialist'. Indeed, he sees Jameson as arguing that the 'third world' comes into being only on the basis of its '"experience" of externally inserted phenomena' (*In Theory*, pp. 99–100).

It seems to me, however, that to speak of social formations as having 'suffered the experience of colonialism and imperialism' is scarcely to define them as being divorced from human history, or even the history of capitalism. What does Ahmad suppose *imperialism* is, for goodness sake? According to him, Jameson's classification 'leaves the so-called Third World in limbo; if only the First World is capitalist and the Second World socialist, how does one understand the Third World?' (*In Theory*, p. 100). But nowhere does Jameson state or even imply that only the 'first-world' is capitalist and only the 'second-world' socialist. Ahmad's critique fails signally to reckon with Jameson's clear awareness that some 'third-world' societies are socialist and others are not – as when he speaks of a trip to Cuba, on which he 'had occasion to visit a remarkable college-preparatory school on the outskirts of Havana. It is a matter of some shame for an American to witness the cultural curriculum in a socialist setting which also very much identifies itself with the third world' ('Third-World Literature', pp. 74–5). To speak of 'Third World' societies as having suffered the experience of colonialism and imperialism is, as I understand it, to speak of their having been forced into the capitalist world-system, of their having been yoked, on the basis of conquest and political domination, into a global order predicated on inequality and exploitation. Hence Jameson's observation that

none of these cultures can be conceived as anthropologically independent or autonomous, rather, they are all in various distinct ways locked in a life-and-death struggle with first-world cultural imperialism – a cultural struggle that is itself a reflexion of the economic situation of such areas in their penetration by various stages of capital, or as it is sometimes euphemistically called, modernization. (p. 68)

The banner of the 'third-world' was raised at a specific moment in the history of anti-imperialist struggle in the twentieth century. I take it that in Jameson's essay it functions more as the name of a political desire (as in: Cuba 'very much identifies itself with the third-world') than as the descriptor of any actual place or historical location or, of course, mode of production. Thus, while there is indisputably an 'India' or an 'Indonesia' or an 'Iraq' or an 'Ivory Coast' (although the truth of this formulation is not quite as self-evident as it appears), there is no 'third-world' in the same political-ontological sense. 'Third-worldness', as a regulative ideal, is born of anticolonialist and anti-imperialist struggle. It gestures towards a world in which autonomy and popular self-determination will be politically meaningful concepts, in which 'independence' will not correspond merely to 'flag independence'. In a world of colonies and nation-states, such an aspiration can only be imagined as coming into being through nationalism – not that nationalism is necessarily a terminus (indeed, Marxists must hope it is not), but that it is unforgoable as a site of liberation struggle. As Jameson writes at the very beginning of his essay, therefore, 'a certain nationalism is fundamental in the third world' (p. 65). Ironically, Ahmad has written most eloquently about this himself, arguing that '[f]or human collectivities in the backward zones of capital … all relationships with imperialism pass through their own nation-states, and there is simply no way of breaking out of that imperial dominance without struggling for different kinds of national projects and for a revolutionary restructuring of one's own nation-state' (*In Theory*, p. 11).

In these terms, it seems plausible to propose that literature which rises to the challenge of 'third-worldness' will of necessity allegorise the nation.[28] 'If it can be allowed', as Neil Larsen has written, 'that the third world nation itself exists, on one plane at least, only as an abstract possibility … then it follows that attempts to represent this nation, to portray it in a narrative or symbolic medium, will reflect this abstraction within the formal elements of the medium itself.'[29] My suspicion is that, if Jameson had not postulated his 'national allegory' hypothesis, we would have had to invent it. This is not primarily for theoretical reasons (though these are not trivial), but in order to keep pace with, to be accountable to, modern and contemporary writings from the 'postcolonial' world, the 'Third World', the 'backward zones of capital' – whatever term one chooses to apply here. For considered in the round, these writings seem to *require* such an hypothesis. Jameson's conceptualisation of the relationship between such writings and nationalism is neither definitive nor the end of the discussion. But it seems to me to raise massively consequential questions and to go at least some way towards answering them. Scholars in postcolonial studies should therefore seize the opportunity today to reread it, as though for the first time.

v

It remains for us only to explore one further way in which Jameson tends to use the notion of the 'third-world' – with reference, this time, not to the 'Third-World Literature' essay but to his other writings, especially those published since the early 1980s. The following passage, drawn from the concluding chapter of his book, *Postmodernism, or, The Cultural Logic of Late Capitalism,* can serve as a way into this discussion. Following a brief discussion of reification in the Marxian-Lukácsian sense of commodity fetishism, Jameson turns to another 'definition of reification that has been important in recent years': namely, the idea of reification as social forgetting, involving 'the "effacement of the traces of production" from the object itself, from the commodity thereby produced'. Concerning this latter definition, he writes:

This sees the matter from the standpoint of the consumer: it suggests the kind of guilt people are freed from if they are able not to remember the work that went into their toys and furnishings. Indeed, the point of having your own object world, and walls and muffled distance or relative silence all around you, is to forget all those innumerable others for a while; you don't want to have to think about Third World women every time you pull yourself up to your word processor, or all the other lower-class people with their lower-class lives when you decide to use or consume your other luxury products: it would be like having voices inside your head; indeed, it 'violates' the intimate space of your privacy and your extended body. For a society that wants to forget about class, therefore, reification in this consumer-packaging sense is very functional indeed: consumerism as a culture involves much more than this, but this kind of 'effacement' is surely the indispensable precondition on which all the rest can be constructed. (*Postmodernism*, pp. 314–15)

The passage ascribes a consciousness to an archetypal 'First World' figure, 'the consumer', who construes his or her private use and consumption of commodities, especially luxuries, as identity-bestowing, but who – and precisely for this reason – requires the activity of using/consuming to be 'guilt free'. 'Guilt free' in this context means that the social prehistory of the commodities being used or consumed – above all, the social conditions under which they were produced – must have been effaced from the material form in which the commodities themselves are presented, or must at least be effortlessly disposable or neglectable at the point of their use/consumption.

Generalising from this example, we could say that if 'First World' culture is by and large intent on 'forgetting' not only depredations past[30] but – even more important, perhaps – depredations *present* (the *continuing* violence upon which the current order rests – not merely the existence of classes per se, but the unremitting and globally dispersed actuality of domination, exploitation, inequality, and dispossession staged through them), then one of Jameson's preferred and characteristic counter-strategies is to allow, or even to demand, the *return of the repressed*. He insists that the repressed elements that a culture structured in dominance 'forgets', denies, or disregards are nevertheless unforgoably and inescapably constitutive of it. Thus, private consumption of luxury goods anywhere in the 'First World' turns out to rely upon the exploitation of 'Third World' labour. Elsewhere, 'the inner forms and structures' of modernist literature turn out to rely upon 'the structure of imperialism'.[31] The 'Third World' emerges, as in the passage cited above, as a favoured weapon in Jameson's critical arsenal in this respect. To insist upon its intrinsicality to the system as a whole (and at the same time to draw attention to the degraded status it occupies there, of course) is to disturb the pacific image projected by those who speak for the dominant order. So when the intellectuals of the transnational capitalist class 'pop up and feverishly reassure us as to the richness and excitement of the new free market all over the world',[32] for example, Jameson's production of the term 'third-world' negates or unsettles their celebratory discourse: the concept of the 'third-world', as he deploys it, is incapable of being accommodated, recuperated, or *totalised* by the dominant (globalist) concept of the world-system.

The counter-concept to the 'third-world' is of course that of the 'West', which Jameson also uses, often by way of demonstrating the partiality or tendentiousness of situated notions or forms of practice that have nevertheless contrived to install themselves snugly as cultural universals or self-evident truths. Consider the following passage, for instance, drawn from

the *Postmodernism* book and concerned to reflect upon the relation
between 'postmodernism' and the 'modernism' that it affects to have
superseded. Jameson has just been arguing that

> Modernism must … be seen as uniquely corresponding to an uneven moment of
> social development, or to what Ernst Bloch called the 'simultaneity of the
> nonsimultaneous', the 'synchronicity of the nonsynchronous' (*Gleichzeitigkeit
> des Ungleichzeitigen*): the coexistence of realities from radically different moments
> of history – handicrafts alongside the great cartels, peasant fields with the Krupp
> factories or the Ford plant in the distance. (*Postmodernism*, p. 307)

Within the space/time of capitalist modernity, in other words, emergent
features, including those rising to dominance, exist alongside other
features – whether themselves dominant or residual, 'major' or 'minor'
– of earlier historical provenance. Jameson then invites us to distinguish
this 'modernism' from a hypothetical 'postmodernist' order in which,
almost by definition, unevenness has been superseded, harmonised, van-
quished, or ironed out:

> What follows paradoxically as a consequence is that in that case the postmodern
> must be characterized as a situation in which the survival, the residue, the
> holdover, the archaic, has finally been swept away without a trace. In the
> postmodern, then, the past itself has disappeared (along with the well-known
> 'sense of the past' or historicity and collective memory). Where its buildings still
> remain, renovation and restoration allow them to be transferred to the present
> in their entirety as those other, very different and postmodern things called *simu-
> lacra*. Everything is now organized and planned; nature has been triumphantly
> blotted out, along with peasants, petit-bourgeois commerce, handicraft, feudal
> aristocracies and imperial bureaucracies. Ours is a more homogeneously modern-
> ized condition; we no longer are encumbered with the embarrassment of non-
> simultaneities and non-synchronicities. Everything has reached the same hour on
> the great clock of development or rationalization (at least from the perspective of the
> 'West'). This is the sense in which we can affirm, either that modernism is
> characterized by a situation of incomplete modernization, or that postmodernism
> is more modern than modernism itself. (*Postmodernism*, pp. 309–10)

At the risk of overstating the obvious, it is important to note that this is
not how Jameson himself understands the 'globalised' world. The effect
of the parenthetical qualification in the sentence that reads, 'Everything
has reached the same hour on the great clock of development or
rationalization (at least from the perspective of the "West")' is, I take
it, to make clear that everything has *not* in fact reached the same hour on
the great clock of development or rationalisation, but that this is how it
seems from the 'western' standpoint. The term 'West' here evidently

names not a geographical location, but an episteme or line of vision. By the same token, the fact that the characterisation of 'the postmodern' in the passage as a whole is conceptually rather than empirically derived ('What follows paradoxically as a consequence is that in that case the postmodern must be characterized') indicates that its propositional content must be understood as speculation, theory-driven projection, rather than as a description of reality. Certainly Jameson raises the spectre of a 'post-historical' order in which modernity as a sociocultural project, underpinned by the logic of progressive modernisation, has (will have?) eclipsed itself through self-realisation. 'Postmodernism is what you have when the modernization process is complete and nature is gone for good', he writes (*Postmodernism*, p. ix), calling up the image of a fully modernised 'postmodern' world in which all unevennesses have (will have?) been overcome, all lags, gaps, residues, survivals, and hold-overs closed or harmonised or smoothed away. There is (will be?) only a more or less seamless, history-less, eternal present. (Jameson himself acknowledges how much this characterisation owes to the work of Jean Baudrillard.) But the image thus invoked is less 'sociological' than it is 'philosophical': it centres on the key categories of a *theory* of the present that sees itself as needing to supersede all previous such theories because their enabling sociocultural ground ('modernity') has itself supposedly been superseded. The idea that history (in the sense of [class] struggle) has come to an end; the idea that unevenness (in the sense of inequality, exploitation, immiseration) has been transcended; the idea that nature (in the sense of sheer and potentially recalcitrant externality) has been superseded – it is these *ideas*, and also the implication that they are unforgoable, given the *problematic* of 'the postmodern', that interest Jameson here, rather than the question of whether or not they are true, or even tenable.

To introduce the Althusserian concept of the 'problematic' is, of course, to emphasise that all theories are situated or perspectival. We can hypothesise that inasmuch as Jameson understands 'postmodernism' as 'the cultural logic of late capitalism', one of his main aims is to demonstrate that people 'in the postmodern' map or conceptualise the world as they do – in terms of 'postmodern' categories – because this is how the world *is given* to them or, even more starkly, because this is how the world *is*, for them. Social being determines consciousness. When, therefore, he writes that '[w]hat follows paradoxically as a consequence [of the definition of the modern in terms of unevenness] is that in that case the postmodern must be characterized as a situation in which the survival, the residue, the holdover, the archaic, has finally been swept away without a trace', he is writing about a lens on to the world rather than about the world itself; to put it in Althusserian terms, he is not describing 'real conditions of existence' but rather a 'representation' of an 'imaginary relationship' to such conditions.[33] In conjuring up the thought-figure of a 'postmodern' social universe in which modernisation had fully realised itself and so had come to an end, and with it all forms of unevenness, Jameson is then not characterising the way things *are* (or even the way they *might be*), but the way they *seem* from a specifically delimited and historically determinate vantage point.

In his compelling critique of dominant assumptions in globalisation theory, Paul Smith has drawn attention to the tendency of globalisation theorists to *annunciate* – that is, to treat as *having been* actualised or instantiated – a 'version of capitalism which has not yet arrived' (and which, moreover, cannot plausibly be imagined as *ever* arriving).[34] In what he calls 'millennial dreaming', Smith suggests that '[m]agical notions such as that of fully global space replete with an ecstatic buzz of cyber communication, or of an instantaneous mobility of people, goods and services, or of a global market place hooked up by immaterial money that flashes around the globe many times a minute ... are regularly projected' (*Millennial Dreams*, p. 13). 'Such images' he adds, 'have effectively become shibboleths, appearing to construe a kind of isochronic world wherein the constrictions of time and space have been overcome, where the necessary navigational and communicational means are so fully developed and supremely achieved that they can eclipse even reality itself.'

Now there is, in my opinion, a certain problem here, having to do with Jameson's own tendency to overestimate the significance of changes in the structuration of capitalist social relations at the level of the world-system since the early 1970s, to present these changes in the light of an epochal and world-historical transformation. The important 1984 essay 'Postmodernism, or, The Cultural Logic of Late Capitalism', for instance, undertook, as its title suggests, to situate 'postmodernism' within the historical and ideological contexts of a newly emergent, post-monopoly, stage of capitalism.[35] By the term 'late capitalism', Jameson would subsequently write, he meant to designate not merely 'the emergence of new forms of business organization (multinationals, trans-nationals) beyond the monopoly stage but, above all, the vision of a world capitalist system fundamentally distinct from the older imperialism, which was little more than a rivalry between the various colonial powers' (*Postmodernism*, pp. xviii–xix).

This conception of an emergent system or new capitalist world order 'fundamentally distinct from the older imperialism' is, of course, precisely what scores of other commentators, starting in the late 1980s, have written about under the rubric of 'globalisation'; and some dissenting commentators have therefore moved to criticise Jameson as being himself guilty of a degree of 'millennial dreaming'. To be sure, the diffusion of the term 'globalisation' through the social sciences and humanities proved to be so thoroughgoing and rapid that Jameson himself came to find its usage unavoidable by the mid 1990s – hence, most notably, his publication of the volume *The Cultures of Globalization*, co-edited with Masao Miyoshi, in 1998. In his writings on postmodernism from the mid to late 1980s, however – just prior to the avalanche of scholarly work on 'globalisation' – he tended to favour the term 'late capitalism', which at least allowed an emphasis on *continuity* with earlier stages of capitalism that such other then topical terms as 'post-industrial society', more inclined to emphasise 'break, rupture, and mutation', discouraged (*Postmodernism*, p. xix).

The internal constituents of Jameson's characterisation of 'late capitalism' are indeed readily recognisable to readers familiar with the literature on globalisation. The formation includes, he tells us, not only 'new forms of business organization' but

the new international division of labor, a vertiginous new dynamic in international banking and the stock exchanges (including the enormous Second and Third World debt), new forms of media interrelationship (very much including transportation systems such as containerization), computers and automation, the flight of production to advanced Third World areas, along with all the more familiar social consequences, including the crisis of traditional labor, the emergence of yuppies, and gentrification on a now-global scale. (*Postmodernism*, p. xix)

This limited inventory is both unexceptional and, on its own terms, unexceptionable. Jameson's analysis becomes susceptible to criticism only when he moves further, as he intermittently does, to suggest that the trends he has identified have consolidated themselves so deeply that they now effectively *define* the contemporary social order.[36]

For the most part, however, it seems to me that he keeps himself relatively aloof from the more outlandish claims of 'globalisation theory'. Arguing against Anthony Giddens, for instance, he insists – following Jürgen Habermas – that it remains necessary to characterise 'modernity' as an 'unfinished project' above all because 'it never could be completed by the middle class and its economic system' (*Singular Modernity*, p. 11). 'Postmodernism', that is to say, represents the world as it is given to some (a small minority: 'the middle class') but could never be in sum:

it is possible to conceive the universalisation of capitalism, but not the totalisation of modernity, if by 'modernity' is meant 'bourgeoisification'. As we have seen, Jameson considers the suggestion that

[w]here modernity was a set of questions and answers that characterized a situation of incomplete or partial modernization, postmodernity is what obtains under a tendentially far more complete modernization, which can be summed up in two achievements: the industrialization of agriculture, and the colonization and commercialization of the Unconscious or, in other words, mass culture and the culture industry. (*Singular Modernity*, p. 12)

To reach any adequate understanding of this formulation, we need to set alongside it the significant qualification entailed in the explicit mobilisation of the idea of *periodisation* in the 'Cultural Logic of Late Capitalism' essay: 'periodisation' is precisely designed, Jameson tells us, to 'allow . . . for the presence and coexistence of a range of very different, yet subordinate features' (*Postmodernism*, p. 4). This means that we cannot think of modernisation in terms of a drive towards a kind of steady state to which a society might gain access once and for all – such that once it had been 'modernised', it would exist in a relation of equality and equivalence with all other 'modernised' societies. (Hence, I take it, the cogency of Jameson's observation in his 1998 essay entitled 'Notes on Globalization as a Philosophical Issue', 'that the United States is not just one country, or one culture, among others, any more than English is just one language among others. There is a fundamental dissymmetry in the relationship between the United States and every other country in the world, not only third-world countries, but even Japan and those of Western Europe' [p. 58]). Jameson is a close reader of dependency and world-systems theory: he does not need to be told that 'modernisation' *intensifies* rather than *diminishes* inequality, unevenness, and difference. The fact that what we have seen him call 'the perspective of the "West"' is culturally dominant, means that the future that it holds out for the rest of the world is incorporation rather than inclusion, heteronomy rather than autonomy. 'Combined and uneven', as the old Marxist slogan had it.

CHAPTER 3

'A figure glimpsed in a rear-view mirror': the question of representation in 'postcolonial' fiction

'Representation' is perhaps the single most fraught and contentious term within postcolonial studies. 'Who is speaking?' 'Of and for whom?' 'How, where, and to what ends?' 'On what authority?' 'In which languages?' 'Through means of which concepts and categories?' 'On the basis of which problematics and epistemological assumptions?' Like all revisionist modes of knowledge production, postcolonial studies has been centrally concerned with questions like this from the outset. It would not be too much to suggest, in fact, that one defining gesture of scholarship in the field has consisted precisely in its critique of *a specific set of representations* – those famously addressed by Edward Said under the rubric of 'Oriental- ism'. Building upon Said's canonical formulation, scholars working in postcolonial studies have produced a considerable amount of valuable work over the past thirty-odd years on 'western' conceptions of the 'non- West', in which they have been concerned to demonstrate not only the falsity or inaccuracy of these conceptions but also their systematicity and their capacity to ground, engender, or constitute social practices, policies, and institutions.[1]

There is, of course, no single theory of representation in postcolonial studies. However, I want to suggest that while the issue has been broached and thought about in a variety of different ways by different theorists, it has been somewhat fetishised in the scholarship. There has been a great deal of formidable philosophising, which has led to the elaboration of some rather grand and categorical propositions. In substantive terms, however, the results seem, to me, to have been mixed at best. My own view is that much of what has been said is pretty deeply misconceived, while much else is clearly in the nature of sheer academic adventurism. A small number of the ideas that have been put forward *do* strike me as illuminating and valuable; but I do not find even these to be as decisive or as original as most of my colleagues in the field clearly imagine them to be.

In this chapter I will explore the degree to which the debate over representation in postcolonial studies has related (or, more particularly, has failed to relate) to the strategic negotiation of representation in the corpus of 'postcolonial' literature – or, better, in the vast, scattered, heterogeneous, but still, in principle, *systematisable* archive of literary works that, considered in the round, might be taken to constitute the corpus of 'postcolonial' literature. There is a clear discrepancy or disjuncture in this respect between what a very large amount of this literature has tended to show and what most postcolonialist critics have tended to register as significant. My proposal is that where the two forms of discourse (that is, '"postcolonial" literature' and 'postcolonial criticism') diverge, we would do well to think hard about the understandings at play in the former before moving to ratify those prevailing in the latter. I will restrict my comments in this chapter to fiction, although I believe that the inclusion of other literary genres would not change the nature of the argument that I am concerned to make.

THE CRITIQUE OF 'EUROCENTRIC' REPRESENTATION

Colonial rule, as V. Y. Mudimbe notes in *The Invention of Africa*, was established and consolidated on the basis of 'the domination of physical space, the reformation of natives' minds, and the integration of local economic histories into the Western perspective. These complementary projects constitute what might be called the colonizing structure, which completely embraces the physical, human, and spiritual aspects of the colonizing experience' (p. 2). To the extent that the ideological legitimation of colonialism took the forms of a belittling of 'native' cultures and a silencing of 'native' voices, the responses of the colonised to colonialism always included, centrally, an ideological dimension, in which colonial representations were contested and the validity and integrity of 'native' cultures reclaimed. Among the best-known instances of such resistance is that offered by Aimé Césaire, in his searing *Discourse on Colonialism*. In a key passage in this polemic, Césaire self-consciously assumes the agency and sovereignty of the speaking subject in order to throw the various apologies for colonialism back in the faces of the colonisers. 'They talk to me about progress, about "achievements," diseases cured, improved standards of living', he says. But

I am talking about societies drained of their essence, cultures trampled underfoot, institutions undermined, lands confiscated, religions smashed, magnificent artistic creations destroyed, extraordinary *possibilities* wiped out.

They throw facts at my head, statistics, mileages of roads, canals, and railroad tracks.

I am talking about thousands of men sacrificed to the Congo-Océan. I am talking about those who, as I write this, are digging the harbor of Abidjan by hand. I am talking about millions of men torn from their gods, their land, their habits, their life – from life, from the dance, from wisdom . . .[2]

In postcolonial studies, this kind of rhetorical-political gesture has come to be known under the deceptively playful-sounding rubric of 'the empire writing [or striking] back'.[3] It is a ubiquitous if still arresting feature of much 'postcolonial' literature – so widely recurrent and well known, perhaps, as to require little sustained elaboration here. In the cultural domain, decolonisation calls for both a critique of the colonial record and a counter-demonstration of how things really are or were. Both the negative and the positive moments are indispensable if the task, as Basil Davidson has put it, is 'to save or restore the sense and fact of community against all the pressures of the colonial system'.[4] The insistence that 'it was not like that' – that the colonial record is false, indeed, systematically distorted – must be complemented by a corrective exposition, a 'setting straight of the record'.

Thus the Sesotho writer, Thomas Mofolo, for instance, who in his great novel, *Chaka* (submitted to a missionary press in South Africa in 1910, first published in 1925), offers a reinterpretation of the life and death of the legendary Zulu king, in which his ambition is to retrieve Southern African history and culture from the depredations of colonial historiography. Mofolo's novel seeks to subvert the supremacism and to challenge the tendentiousness of colonial discourse by demonstrating the sophistication of African social existence, contemporaneously and in the past. Sections of the work are clearly 'pedagogical' in this sense – indeed, Daniel Kunene has noted the existence, in Mofolo's original manuscript but revealingly not in the published version, of 'at least two chapters which describe in some detail the history and customs of the Zulus, as well as their military system'.[5] Mofolo takes an historical figure uniformly vilified in the annals of imperial history and reinterprets him. He transforms a tyrant, a 'blood-thirsty monster of motiveless malignity',[6] into an intelligible if still exceptional individual. His concern is not to apologise for Chaka – no Basotho of Mofolo's era with any sensitivity to history could have failed to hold misgivings about the expanionist militarism of the Zulu leader – but to render his actions meaningful against a background of lived culture.

This gesture of specifying the 'thematics of existence' of a particular culture[7] by way of challenging (explicitly or implicitly) the authority of colonial discourse, is an important feature of the representational practice of 'postcolonial' fiction, readily identifiable in work by such diverse authors as Premchand and Ngugi wa Thiong'o, Patrick Chamoiseau and N. V. M. Gonzalez.[8] We might also refer in this context to Chinua Achebe, who has famously written that 'I would be quite satisfied if my novels (especially the ones I set in the past) did no more than teach my readers that their past – with all its imperfections – was not one long night of savagery from which the first Europeans acting on God's behalf delivered them'.[9] If there is clearly an 'ethnographic' element to much revisionist fiction of this kind – Achebe's own *Things Fall Apart* and *Arrow of God*, for instance[10] – we need to distinguish its thrust from that of colonialist (and neo-colonialist) ethnography, whose disciplinary gaze is allochronic, even – or perhaps especially – when, as quite often, it is tinged with nostalgia. As Eleni Coundouriatis has demonstrated compellingly with respect to *Things Fall Apart*, the novel 'reflects ... the ethnographic impulse to reconstruct a whole culture' precisely because it is a work of its time:

unlike the 'salvage ethnography' of European ethnographers who sought ... to preserve what was already lost, Achebe's autoethnography aims at affirming the contemporaneity of native cultures with those of the West. Ibo culture is decidedly not a finished thing looked at nostalgically at the moment of the novel's composition but the very perspective from which an Ibo writer of the late 1950s is looking at his own continuous history.[11]

We are right to celebrate the brilliance of the recovery of culture and community – as resources in and for the present – in the work of writers such as Mofolo and Achebe.[12] Yet as Coundouriatis's phrase 'continuous history', to describe the work of remembrance in Achebe's fiction, might already be taken dialectically to acknowledge, recovery in the 'postcolonial' context sometimes comes up against obstacles that Mofolo or Achebe did not have to surmount. Let us consider two such obstacles here: the first is historiographic; the second, epistemological.

The historiographic problem is relatively easy to describe. It is sometimes the case that a writer's access to a situation and its existential and experiential correlates – what Mudimbe calls its *chose du texte* – is blocked. Sometimes the information that the writer needs has been lost – whether intentionally, in the sense that it has been destroyed as a matter of official policy (often the case where colonial policing was concerned, for instance, and specifically where this involved the systematic use of torture), or more casually, as the effect (not least through time) of the uneven social distribution of power: records have not been kept, memory has died, dominant or hegemonic narratives have rendered subordinate or subaltern narratives irretrievable, and so on. At other times, information exists, but is so compromised by its tendentiousness that even where it stands alone it can only be approached through means of a symptomatic reading.

Assia Djebar's work grapples with this historiographic problem directly and to illuminating effect. In *Fantasia*, for instance, the first volume of her *Algerian Quartet*, Djebar's narration of the French conquest of Algeria becomes at the same time a deconstructive commentary on her reading of the available sources. 'Five in the morning', she writes, of the joining of hostilities on 30 June 1830:

A Sunday; and what is more, it is the Feast of Corpus Christi in the Christian calendar. The first lookout, wearing the uniform of a frigate captain, stands on the poop of one of the craft of the reserve fleet which will sail past ahead of the battle squadron, preceding a hundred or so men-o'-war. The name of the lookout man is Amable Matterer. He keeps watch and that same day will write, 'I was the first to catch sight of the city of Algiers, a tiny triangle on a mountain slope'.[13]

'I, in my turn, write, using his language, but more than one hundred and fifty years later', Djebar notes (p. 7). As her narrative proceeds, additional chroniclers enter its frame: Baron Barchou, J. T. Merle, Hajj Ahmed Effendi (the Hanefite Mufti of Algiers), and some three dozen others. She positions these diverse chroniclers as her interlocutors, poring intently over what they have written. But it becomes clear that if what she is looking for is an Algerian *chose du texte*, it cannot be found in these documents. This is not only because, of the thirty-seven reports of the events of July 1830 that are extant and capable of being read, 'only three are from the viewpoint of the besieged' (p. 44), but rather because neither the thirty-seven considered together nor even the three considered by themselves afford access to the consciousness of those under siege. What is felt by those being invaded; what being besieged, and being defeated, did to their world, their sense of place and time – in short, their culture – finds no registration in the available reports. It is only approached, never rendered, by the words written by the various chroniclers. It lies, one could say, on the other side of the silence that these words themselves memorialise and to which they even contribute.[14] It can only be inferred from these words.

Let us consider two specific episodes in Djebar's text:[15] a first, dealing with the massacre of Ouled Riah tribespeople in 1845; a second, a small incident deriving from the brutal war of liberation of 1954–62, more than a hundred years later. In Charles-Robert Ageron's historical study, *Modern Algeria: A History from 1830 to the Present*, first published in

France in 1964, we read that in 1845 an uprising of the tribe of the Ouled Riah in the mountains of the Dahra region was summarily crushed. 'In the Dahra ... the future Marshal of France and governor-general of Algeria, Pélissier, did not hesitate to smoke to death eight hundred of the tribe of the Ouled Riah in the caves in which they had taken refuge', Ageron writes.[16] Actually, that is *all that he writes* about this atrocity. Djebar, however, scours the available testimonies, attempting, as she puts it, to 'piece together a picture of that night' (*Fantasia*, p. 70). She quotes from a document subsequently assembled by a French doctor and also from two eyewitness reports – one written by a Spanish officer serving in the French army, which appeared in a Spanish newspaper; the other written as a letter to his family by an unnamed French soldier and subsequently published by the French doctor. These describe the blocking up of all but one of the exits to the caves in which the Ouled Riah had taken refuge, the piling of brushwood into the remaining aperture, setting it on fire, stoking the furnace through an entire night, the sounds, smells, and spectacle of the event: 'What pen could do justice to this scene?' the French soldier asks in his letter home. 'To see, in the middle of the night, by moonlight, a body of French soldiers, busy keeping the hellfire alight! To hear the muffled groans of men, women, children, beasts, and the cracking of burnt rocks as they crumbled, and the continual gunfire!' (p. 71). Following the mass asphyxiation, French soldiers enter the caves the next morning. (Djebar corrects the official record, replicated in Ageron's study of 1964: it was not 800 men, women, and children who perished, but almost double that number, 1,500.) The Spanish officer is one of this advance guard. He describes '[a]n appalling sight ... All the corpses are naked, in attitudes which indicated the convulsions they must have experienced before they expired. Blood was flowing from their mouths; but the most horrifying sight was that of infants at the breast, lying amid the remains of dead sheep, sacks of beans etc.' (p. 72). By the afternoon, the smoke has begun to clear; Pélissier orders that the bodies be dragged out of the caves into the sunlight and counted.

Djebar is fascinated especially by Pélissier's own report of the incident, which will be deemed 'too realistic' when it comes to be read at a parliamentary session in France and 'unleash[es] an uproar of controversy: insults from the opposition, embarrassment on the part of the government, fury of the warmongers, shame throughout Paris in which the seeds of the 1848 Revolution are germinating' (p. 75). She uses the report to delve beneath what it says, to reach beyond what it shows. 'After the spectacular, brutal killing carried out in all naïveté', she writes, Pélissier is overcome with remorse and describes the slaughter he has organized. I venture to thank him for having faced the corpses, for having indulged a whim to immortalize them in a description of their rigid carcasses, their paralysed embraces, their final paroxysms. For having looked on the enemy otherwise than as a horde of zealots or a host of ubiquitous shadows. (p. 78)

Unlike Conrad's Kurtz, Pélissier survives, even prospers. But below the surface of his frank, exculpatory and self-justifying words, in which he freely assumes responsibility for what has been wrought under his command, Djebar locates a certain awareness of the horror of it in precisely the Conradian sense. We are left to consider the idea that this is the sort of event that even the victors do not survive intact. Two months after the massacre of the Ouled Riah, Colonel Saint-Arnaud uses identical tactics to smoke out the Sbeah tribe. This time, however, he refuses to allow the bodies of the tribespeople to be exhumed. 'Enter not the caves! Let no man keep the tally! No auditing. No conclusions', as Djebar writes (p. 76). And she then quotes from a letter that Saint-Arnaud writes to his brother after his asphyxiation of the Sbeah: 'Brother, no-one is more prone to goodness by nature and disposition than I! ... From 8 to 12 August I have been ill, but my conscience does not trouble me. I have done my duty as a leader and tomorrow I shall do the same again, but I have developed a distaste for Africa!' (p. 76). It is in these terms that Djebar 'accepts' Pélissier's report as 'a palimpsest on which I now inscribe the charred passion of my ancestors' (p. 79). Before leaving the scene of the atrocity, she begins this reconstructive labour of inscription, telling us that even at the point of 'victory', with the 'entire Ouled Riah tribe' annihilated, the struggle has only just been joined, and nothing is finished:

Victory had apparently been won on this hillside. But the next day, 23 June, Nature has her revenge: the stench of death is so strong (ravens and vultures fly ceaselessly over the ravine, and the soldiers even see them carrying off the remains of human corpses!) that Pélissier gives the order, that same day, to move the camp half a league further away ...
   As if the sun, the summer bearing down its incalescent burden, and all nature join forces to expel the French army. (p. 75)

The second episode from *Fantasia* that I want to consider is to be found towards the end of the work. It is set in 1956, a couple of years into the war of liberation in Algeria, in a small mountain village named El-Aroub. French paratroopers occupy the village, driving off the maquisards who had previously been using it as a base. They subsequently capture two men in maquisards' uniform and subject them to brutal interrogation under the gaze of the villagers, torturing them until one of them breaks, disclosing the whereabouts of an arms cache. The two captives – who by this point have been so badly beaten that they are 'unrecognizable' (p. 209) – are then shot to death. A couple of days later the paratroopers leave the village, under orders to repair to Constantine.

Djebar derives her information about 'these days in El-Aroub' from the chronicle of a French legionnaire, one Pierre Leulliette, who would go on to publish his record under the title of *Saint Michel et le Dragon* in 1961. 'I come at length upon what [Leulliette] ... wrote', she observes in *Fantasia*: '[I] turn the pages at random, read as if I were shrouded in the ancestral veil; with my one free eye perusing the page, where is written more than the eye-witness sees, more than can be heard' (p. 209).

During the retreat to Constantine, Leulliette is befriended by a para-trooper named Bernard, who tells him that while stationed in El-Aroub, he had broken camp one night and made his way to a run-down farm in the village where, as he puts it, 'a pretty Fatma [had] smiled at me during the day!' (p. 210). Djebar renarrates the story that Bernard had told to Leulliette as follows:

He slips in without knocking. It must be half past one in the morning. He hesitates in the darkness, then strikes a match: facing him, a group of women squat in a circle, staring at him; they are nearly all old, or look it. They huddle close to one another; their eyes gleam with terror or surprise ...

The Frenchman takes food out of his pockets and hurriedly distributes it. He walks around, he strikes another match; finally his eyes light on the 'pretty Fatma' who had smiled at him. He seizes her hand, pulls her to her feet.

The match has gone out. The couple find their way to the back of the vast room, where it is pitch-black. The old women squatting in a circle have not moved; companions and sisters of silence, they crouch, staring with dim pupils which preserve the present moment: could the lake of happiness exist?

The Frenchman has undressed. 'I could have been in my own home,' he will admit. He presses the girl close to him; she shudders, she holds him tight, she begins to caress him.

'What if one of the old women were to get up and come and stick a knife in my back?' he thinks.

Suddenly two frail arms are round his neck, a gasping voice begins to whisper: strange, fond, warm words come tumbling out. The unknown hot-blooded girl pours these words in Arabic or Berber into his ear.

'She kissed me full on the mouth, like a young girl. Just imagine! I'd never seen anything like it! ... She was kissing me! Do you realize? ... Kissing me! It was that little meaningless action that I shall never be able to forget!' (pp. 210–11)

This is a powerful and disturbing passage. We realise, to begin with, that Bernard cannot even keep out of his *own* account the glimmering aware-ness that what he is concerned to represent to Leulliette as an escapade governed by passion – *shared*, importantly, between him and 'the pretty Fatma' – is falsified by the violence of the situation that alone makes his actions possible. It is not only that he cannot fail to see not only the 'surprise' but also the 'terror' registered in the eyes of the village women huddled together in the farmhouse at his arrival; and that, cognisant of this terror, he himself fears that these women will stab him if he turns his back on them (and recognises, moreover, that this would mark an *appropriate* response to what he is doing). It is also that, even as he reaches – in the form of 'the pretty Fatma' who, he says, had 'smiled at [him] ... during the day' – for the rationale of mutual desire to justify his conduct, he discloses his own *rejection* of this schema. What disturbs him, after all, is precisely the thought that 'the pretty Fatma' might have responded to him in the guise of a lover. He is disquieted by the thought that in kissing him on the mouth, she had behaved 'like a young girl' – that is to say, like a young *white, French* girl, with whom, in ordinary circumstances, a man like himself might have fallen in love or at least have had a fling. The 'pretty Fatma's' kiss seems to insist on agency – in other words, on subjectivity and, more to the point, inter-subjectivity – an expectation that, Bernard dimly recognises, is inconceivable in this con-text. It is not to be wondered at that, having returned to camp, he should start awake immediately after falling asleep, certain that 'he must leave the village for ever' (p. 211).

While the deconstruction of Bernard's story offered in Djebar's renarration of it is indispensable to the task of cultural decolonisation, it does not allow an authoritative counter-representation of the con-sciousness of the village women implicated in the story, and still less of 'the pretty Fatma' at its (absent or empty) centre.[17] The women's stillness cannot be made to move; their silence cannot be made to speak. They are unreadable in Bernard's story, and Djebar makes no attempt to attribute consciousness to them in her renarration of it. In the case of 'the pretty Fatma', however, there is neither immobility nor silence. But while her words and actions are manifestly meaning-bearing (and Bernard himself is therefore forced to describe them as 'meaningless' precisely in order to neutralise this truth, which is potentially damaging to his own equanimity and integrity), we can never be sure that the interpretation that we give them, no matter how compelling and evidentially rich we make it, will be conclusive or definitive. What do 'the unknown hot-blooded girl's' shudders, caresses, whispers, kisses signify? What is she thinking? There will always be a gap here between 'interpretation' or 'adequation', on the one hand, and 'how things really were', on the other. The latter, Leopold von Ranke's historiographic ideal, is constitutively irrecoverable by us.

I have been discussing Djebar's *Fantasia* by way of exploring a methodological problem confronted by many 'postcolonial' writers eager to challenge, subvert, or, indeed, 'unwrite' the colonial archive as part of their contribution to the wider social project of decolonisation. Another problem that sometimes arises in this same context concerns the question of the truth of history, or, better, of truth in history. In one of his most celebrated essays, Ranajit Guha, founder of the enormously influential 'subaltern studies' historiographical project, bids us to consider the idea that inasmuch as the anticolonialist (or indeed, the postcolonialist) 'setting straight of the record' takes the form of counter-representation, it, too – like the colonial representation that it seeks to demolish – must be understood as *appropriation*, that is to say, as in the first instance politically contingent *invention*, rather than as *recovery* or *retrieval*. 'There was one Indian battle that Britain never won', Guha writes, in opening his essay 'Colonialism in South Asia: A Dominance without Hegemony and its Historiography': 'It was a battle for appropriation of the Indian past.'[18] But his main point is that in the context of India, this battle was never about the past *as it really was*:

[T]he appropriation of a past by conquest carries with it the risk of rebounding upon the conquerors. It can end up by sacralizing the past for the subject people and encouraging them to use it in their effort to define and affirm their own identity ... [T]he appropriated past [comes] to serve as the sign of the Other not only for the colonizers but, ironically for the colonized as well. The colonized, in their turn, reconstruct ... their past for purposes opposed to those of their rulers and [make] it the ground for marking out their differences in cultural and political terms. History [becomes] thus a game for two to play as the alien colonialist project of appropriation [is] matched by an indigenous nationalist project of counter-appropriation. (p. 3)

Some of what Guha suggests here must be conceded even if we would wish, as I myself do, to dissent from the sweeping conclusions that many in postcolonial studies have drawn from it.[19] Much counter-colonial representation, above all that proffered in the midst of consolidated nationalist struggle, is, in its interventionist aspects, at least, demonstrably of the order described by Guha. Thus, when Le Duan, for instance, opens his pamphlet, *The Vietnamese Revolution*, with an historical synopsis, we can see clearly that his reconstruction of the past is profoundly overdetermined by contemporary – that is to say, by liberationist – political insights and imperatives:

During the long process of struggle to build and defend their country, our heroic people developed a national consciousness at an early date and evinced extremely ardent patriotism. Under French colonialist rule, which lasted nearly a century, they refused to resign themselves to servitude and repeatedly rose up in arms against the aggressors and the traitors.[20]

The same observation can also be made about a text such as Govan Mbeki's *South Africa: The Peasants' Revolt*, which, while more distanced in its register than Le's, is no less activist in intent. In the first chapter of his study, Mbeki surveys and attempts to demolish the colonialist rationality underlying apartheid in South Africa:

Historical arguments that justify the White claim to exclusive rights in 88 per cent of the country are absurd. The true record is that brown and black people were spread throughout the subcontinent long before the first Whites arrived. Van Riebeeck found the Nama at the Cape when he landed in Table Bay. Boers found and fought the Khoikhoi and Batwa when they trekked into Namaqualand – an area which still bears the name of its original inhabitants. Xhosa lived on the banks of the Buffalo River in 1686 and settled at what is now Somerset East in 1702. Whites fought Xhosas in the 1770s on the fringes of the tsitsikama forest, and drove them back from the Gamtoos to the Fish River in 1778. Zulu tribes once occupied the whole of Natal, down to the borders of Pondoland. Whites drove deep into tribal territories in the Orange Free State and the Transvaal before their expansion was halted at last late in the nineteenth century. The White man's claims to rights of first occupancy are false.[21]

It is evident that the reconstruction of the past is no mere academic exercise but directly serves contemporary ideological interests. What consequences might be said to follow from this? Does the fact that the counter-colonial discourse is ideologically interested undermine or otherwise compromise the truth-claims that it lodges, or that might be lodged for it? (Mbeki, after all, is quite insistent that he is counterposing 'the true record' to the 'false' claims of South African whites.) Statements like Guha's – '[h]istory became thus a game for two to play as the alien colonialist project of appropriation was matched by an indigenous nationalist project of counter-appropriation' – have been taken by many in postcolonial studies to imply that, inasmuch as all histories are to be understood as politically interested narratives, critics ought to devote themselves to the study of their *rhetorics* and bracket as undecidable the question of their *epistemological* adequacy.[22]

My own view is that we lose something indispensable when we go down this road. It is certainly the case that the concepts mobilised by Le and Mbeki, and the arguments produced by them, are *contingent* – that is to say, are strictly of the present, deriving from the intellectual and ideological universe of the times of writing rather than of the times being written about. And it is certainly the case that, among other things, this positions them as *readings* and, more specifically in their particular contexts, as *counter-readings*. But this ought not to cause us to suspend enquiry into their truth-value. We should not rush too quickly past the fact that in the writing of Le and Mbeki, the claims to representational adequacy in the spheres of politics and knowledge are submitted in concert. Le and Mbeki speak at one and the same time *of* – that is, about – and *on behalf of* their people, inviting us to contemplate the idea that, in these instances, at least, 'speaking the truth about' and 'acquiring the authority to speak for' implicate one another. We do not have to choose between attention to truth – as propositional correspondence with reality – and attention to rhetoric – as the discursive shaping and mobilisation of ideas, including about what is true.

This way of putting things ought not to come as a surprise to students of literature: for in the study of literature it is more or less taken for granted that questions concerning the social truth of texts cannot be answered through reference to their content alone. Truth in literary works is never reducible to what is said directly in them. What they say is never *just* what they say, if I might put it that way. Rather, as Bourdieu has suggested, the writer 'is the one who is capable of *making a sensation*, which does not mean being sensational, like television acrobats, but rather, in the strong sense of the term, putting across on the level of sensation – that is, touching the sensibility, moving people – analyses which would leave the reader or spectator indifferent if expressed in the cold rigor of concept and demonstration'.[23] Consider the moment in *Max Havelaar* when the author, Multatuli, speaking in his own voice, attempts, desperately and almost despairingly, to justify and defend the truth of what he is writing about the Dutch Indies, against public and institutional cynicism and disbelief. He could, he says, produce documentary evidence to support his allegations of colonial maladministration, corruption, and injustice: he has this evidence to hand. But it is precisely because, as the real historical figure Eduard Douwes Dekker (Multatuli is his pen-name), he *has already produced* this evidence, both in the state circuits of the colonial office and in the public sphere in Holland, only for it to fall on deaf ears, that he resorts now to fiction, hoping through this means to 'make a sensation' in the Bourdieusian sense. His novel is peopled by characters like Adinda and Saïjah, representatives of the colonised Netherlands Indies population. 'I know, *and I can prove*', writes Multatuli,

> that there were many Adindas and many Saïjahs, and that *what is fiction in particular is truth in general* ... Hence, instead of bare names of persons and places, with dates – instead of a copy of *the list of thefts and extortions which lies before me* – instead of these, I have tried to give a sketch of what *may* go on in the hearts of poor people robbed of their means of subsistence, or, more precisely: I have only *suggested* what may go on in their hearts, fearing that I might be too wide of the mark if I firmly delineated emotions which I never felt myself.
>   But ... as regards the *underlying truth*?[24]

This is astounding, I think, in a work published in 1860. The tactics of representation in *Max Havelaar* are marked by a strikingly 'postcolonial' ethical sensibility, whose governing impulse is not empathy (although empathy is plainly and appropriately in evidence) but an acute awareness of the violence entailed in any insufficiently mediated attribution of consciousness across the colonial divide. It is this awareness, above all, that sets *Max Havelaar* apart from colonial fiction generally – even from that by such liberal authors as, say, Forster, Plomer, or Cary.[25]

THE CRITIQUE OF 'REPRESENTATION ITSELF' (AS EUROCENTRIC)

The attempt to 'unthink Eurocentrism'[26] is lodged as a foundational aspiration of postcolonialist scholarship. There is wide disagreement, however, as to what is entailed in and by such 'unthinking'. A predominant tendency in the field has been to situate Eurocentrism less as an *ideological* formation (selective, interested, partial, and partisan) than as an *episteme* (a trans-ideologically dispersed field of vision, or conceptual atmosphere). If we understand Eurocentrism as an *ideology* (as I myself do), then it could become subject to critique. One's general methodological assumption would be that it is always possible in principle (and indeed in practice) to stand outside a given problematic in order to subject its claims to scrutiny. This, of course, is the classical notion of critique as encountered in Kant and exemplified most significantly for radical scholarship in Marx's various critiques of bourgeois political economy and idealist philosophy. It is ideology critique on this model that had been activated in anti-colonialist writing and scholarship prior to the advent of postcolonial studies: in Césaire's *Discourse on Colonialism*, for instance, but also in the publications of such activist intellectuals as C. L. R. James, Frantz Fanon, and Walter Rodney (to draw examples only from the Caribbean), and in the many critiques of anthropology or modernisation theory or development studies (not least by practising anthropologists, sociologists, and political scientists themselves) published during the 1960s and 1970s.

Scholars in postcolonial studies, however, have tended to address Eurocentrism less in terms of ideology and more as an episteme – as, so to speak, the very air that must be breathed by anybody engaging in questions relating to 'Europe and its Others'. Eurocentrism emerges on this conceptualisation as an untranscendable horizon governing thought – its forms, contents, modalities, and presuppositions so deeply and insidiously layered and patterned that they cannot be circumvented, only deconstructed. And in these terms it is not susceptible to critique, since it is entailed in the very fabric of disciplinarity and institutionalised knowledge production. In retrospect, I think it can be seen that even as the signature critique of Eurocentric thought was first being produced in postcolonial studies, during the early 1980s, its thrust was already tending to broaden and flatten out. What might have begun as a critique of ideology changed *qualitatively* as scholars in the field, in step with their colleagues elsewhere in the circuits of post-structuralist theory, moved to junk the concepts of truth and thence, by negative association, of ideology too, as so much metaphysical or essentialist baggage. In this process, *the critique of Eurocentric representation was increasingly subsumed by a critique of representation itself, as Eurocentric.*

Consider V. Y. Mudimbe, for instance, both as a theorist and as a writer of fiction. In his preface to *The Idea of Africa*, Mudimbe makes a point of stating the obvious, perhaps because he wishes to tweak the noses of his anti-foundationalist readers for their excessive theoreticism: 'there are natural features, cultural characteristics, and, probably, values that contribute to the reality of Africa as a continent and its civilizations as constituting a totality different from those of, say, Asia and Europe'.[27] Sadly, however, such *plumpes Denken* is not typical of Mudimbe. On the contrary, the bulk of his work has tended to focus on the difficulty or even the impossibility of producing commonsensical descriptions or elaborations like this where Africa is concerned. The central point is made on many separate occasions in his work. 'How does one think about and comment upon alterity without essentializing its features? . . . In African contexts, can one speak and write about a tradition or its contemporary practice without taking into account the authority of the colonial library that has invented African identities?' he asks in one place.[28] In another, he speaks of the relative unforgoability, or inescapability, of 'the colonial library' and its framing of the epistemological object of Africa:

> I do not doubt that there is in the primary discourses of African cultures a reading that could possibly relate to *la chose du texte*, to its fundamental local authorities. Yet, the fact is there: African discourses have been silenced radically or, in most cases, converted by conquering Western discourses … Western interpreters, as well as African analysts, have been using categories and conceptual systems that depend on a Western epistemological order. Even in the most explicitly 'Afro-centric' descriptions, models of analysis explicitly or implicitly, knowingly or unknowingly, refer to the same order. (*Idea of Africa*, pp. xiv–xv)

Such ideas receive a fascinating, complementary gloss in Mudimbe's fiction, in which we find a sustained meditation on, and enactment of, the problems posed by the relation, or, more accurately, the breach, between the African *chose du texte* and all available forms of representation of it. In his 1979 novel, *L'Écart* (translated into English as *The Rift*), these problems are thematised explicitly not only in the work's title but in the research project undertaken in the novel itself by the central protagonist, Ahmed Nara, and in his remembered and re-presented conversations with his former lover, the Frenchwoman, Isabelle. Engaged in ethnographic research, Nara records in his journal that the 'tropical ethnic groups' he is studying have been the object of much previous research:

> I have gone through the work of the ethnologists on several occasions, gone back to all of their sources with great care … I would like to start from scratch, reconstruct the universe of these peoples from start to finish: decolonize the knowledge already gathered about them, bring to light new, more believable genealogies, and be able to advance an interpretation that pays more careful attention to their environment and their true history.[29]

The novel frames this aspiration as unrealisable, however. Dispute between interpreters is, of course, a structuring principle of scholarly practice. Nara's differences from 'the ethnographers' can readily be accommodated by ethnography itself. It is 'starting from scratch' that proves elusive. All the counter-arguments that Nara can adduce (that is to say, all of his attempts to write against the material lodged in the colonial library) remain of necessity at the same level as those he is attempting to subvert or demolish: they share with these arguments a form, a protocol, a set of assumptions as to what would constitute significance, proof, disproof, rigour, evidence. It begins to seem to Nara that the ethnocentrism of ethnography resides not merely in the propositions that have been advanced in the field, subject to its protocols – many of which, demonstrably false, have duly been demonstrated to be false, and have hence been discarded, *without any change to the ethnocentric character of ethnography* – but in what we might call the essential gesture of the discipline, and perhaps even of disciplinarity as such. 'Anthropology and philology and all social sciences', Mudimbe writes in *The Invention of Africa*, in words that clearly presage Dipesh Chakrabarty's later argument in *Provincializing Europe*[30] as well as underlying Nara's conclusions in *The Rift*, 'can be really understood only in the context of their epistemological region of possibility. The histories of these sciences as well as their trends, their truths as well as their experiences, being derived from a given space, speak from it and, primarily, about it' (*Invention of Africa*, p. 18). And in these terms,

Ethnocentrism is both ... anthropology's virtue and its weakness. It is not, as some scholars thought, an unfortunate mishap, nor a stupid accident, but one of the major signs of the possibility of anthropology ... From this ethical point of view, some scholars have wondered whether it was possible to think of an anthropological science without ethnocentrism ... It is surely possible, as functionalism and structuralism proved, to have works that seem to respect indigenous traditions. And one could hope for even more profound changes in anthropology ... But so far it seems impossible to imagine any anthropology without a Western epistemological link. For on the one hand, it cannot be completely cut off from the field of its epistemological genesis and from its roots; and, on the other hand, as a science, it depends upon a precise frame without which there is no science at all, nor any anthropology. (p. 19)

Nara's record of his conversations with Isabelle register the same philosophical conundrum, but come at it – appropriately enough, for what is being narrated is a love story, or the failure of one – from the perspective of damaged intersubjectivity. 'Isabelle,' Nara says to her in one of their exchanges, 'it's always the same with us ... permanent misunderstanding. Europe and Africa ... between you and me.' 'So, if I understand you correctly,' she asks in response, '[l]ove between us isn't possible ...?' 'No,' he protests, 'that's not it. What I am wondering is rather under what conditions it would be possible ... under what conditions would it be not thinkable but possible' (*The Rift*, p. 90). It is not that between Nara and Isabelle love is unthinkable. It is that the social and subjective conditions of possibility for love – reciprocity, mutuality, a space within which, as Theodor W. Adorno once put it in a wonderful aphorism, one might show oneself weak without provoking strength[31] – do not exist, cannot be made to take root while the relationship between Europe and Africa, and hence between Europeans and Africans in the real world, continues to be poisoned by the 'atmosphere' of an overdetermining ethnocentrism. Nara accuses Isabelle of 'us[ing] Africa as a refuge'. But Mudimbe's novel has him 'recognise' that this is not merely a contingent, characterological flaw but a saturating, determinate, social disposition:

To use Africa as a refuge is amusing. Obviously, she could bring me hundreds of scholarly works to substantiate doing so ... Entire libraries ... Africa dancing ... The Africa of emotions, of desire ... The unleashing of the senses in the image of intertwining lianas and the branches of a tropical forest. Green. Debauchery, like the ecstasy from hashish, is green. A tanager has conversations with a nightingale in the dense foliage of trees ... Green lizards play hide-and-seek with puff adders in the underbrush. Along the swamps, overripe fruits are sweating gold and vermilion: pineapples, mangoes, papayas ... In the dusk, closing in around the forest, the rhythm of drums covers the buzzing of the insects and proclaims the glory of all carnality: on open squares encircled by mud huts and naked men, firm-breasted women, mothers with pendulous breasts, all beating time with their feet and their hands, hips swaying in rhythm, their bodies dripping sweat ... the fascination and the thrill of unmentionable yearnings ... 'If that's what Africa is, Isabelle ...' (*The Rift*, pp. 84–5)

One is reminded of the relationship between Mustafa Sa'eed and Ann Hammond (or Sheila Greenwood or Jean Morris or Isabella Seymour!) in Tayeb Salih's *Season of Migration to the North*. (Surely the echo of Salih's Isabella in Mudimbe's Isabelle is not merely coincidental?) In Salih's novel, the attraction that Mustafa Sa'eed holds for his European lovers (later victims) is indistinguishable from his association in their eyes with primitivism. Of Isabella Seymour, he writes at one point that '[s]he gazed hard and long at me as though seeing me as a symbol rather than reality' (p. 43). Like Mudimbe's Isabelle, Isabella also 'uses Africa as a refuge': 'Sometimes she would hear me out in silence, a Christian sympathy in her eyes. There came a moment when I felt I had been transformed in her eyes into a naked, primitive creature, a spear in one hand and arrows in the other, hunting elephants and lions in the jungles' (p. 38).[32]

Neither Mustafa Sa'eed nor Ahmed Nara is able to devise an effective strategy to resist or even withstand the constituting violence – what Mudimbe in his scholarly capacity calls the 'rational violence' – of Eurocentric discourse. In *Why Are We So Blest?* – another novel allegorising colonial relations as intersubjective ones – Ayi Kwei Armah has his central protagonist, Solo, describe the romantic encounter between Africans and Westerners in the language of warfare: of the African,

Modin, who has fallen in love with the white American, Aimée, Solo writes: 'Why could he not see his companion? This was an object, destructive, powerfully hurled against him from the barrel of a powerful, destructive culture. Why could he not see that?'[33] Both Salih and Mudimbe avoid the conspiratorialism of Armah's presentation, by way of emphasising that although racism and Eurocentrism might, of course, be consciously assumed, they are not in the first instance matters of consciousness or intentionality.

This goes some way towards explaining their intractability. I have already cited Mudimbe's observation that even 'the most explicitly "Afrocentric" [of] descriptions' – and whether by 'Western interpreters' or 'African analysts' – are invariably premised on 'categories and conceptual systems which depend on a Western epistemological order'. In *The Rift*, this situation is registered technically through a form of inversion. Nara is able to protest that Isabelle's idea of Africa 'comes straight out of a Tarzan movie' (p. 85). But when she asks him to put her right, to correct her, his words and concepts prove woefully inadequate to the task. He has been hoping that the 'contact with a tradition and the practice of its rigors' that he has been striving towards in his research will 'subject me to its norms so that my words could represent them faithfully' (p. 14). Nothing of the sort happens. All he can say to Isabelle – and it is no wonder that she is not persuaded – is that she 'can't know how demanding Africa is' (p. 88). In substantive terms, he can produce only the woolly abstraction that while 'Europe is, before anything else, an idea, a legal institution ... Africa ... is perhaps primarily a body, a multiple existence' (p. 88).

What is at issue here, I think, is a knowing inversion of the strategy through which colonialist discourse had tended to represent Africa. The notorious excess of signification in *Heart of Darkness*, emblematic of what Conrad himself clearly knew to be the unfulfillable desire to fill in a blankness or absence, becomes in Mudimbe's novel a self-conscious inarticulacy, emblematic of an equally unfulfillable desire *not* to fill in a presence. The 'presence' in question here would be the African *chose du texte*, which *is* – that is to say, has an actuality – but which is constantly constructed as something else, the object of an objectifying gaze, whenever it suffers representation. The refusal to represent, in other words, is for Mudimbe the necessary response to a situation in which representation is either a specification of absence or deficiency (the Eurocentric episteme) or a reactive ('Afrocentric') specification of presence or plenitude as the determinate opposite of the prior Eurocentric representation.

These questions receive a somewhat different airing in *Le Bel immonde* (the French title is unpromisingly rendered in Marjolijn de Jager's English translation as *Before the Birth of the Moon*), first published in 1976. Kenneth Harrow has argued that in this novel, Mudimbe

[moves] further and further away from conventional Western formulations ... situat[ing] Africa's present marginality in the chaotic urban landscapes where past loyalties, forged in forsaken villages, are in the process of dissolving, and where new ties, based on class, nation, school, church, work, or other institutional entities, have not yet supplanted old ones. The basis for identity lies somewhere between the inherited adherence to 'tradition', to the sacred ground on which Lords and Masters erected society, established its certainties and truths, and the new play of parodic masks that bring an end to previous notions of authority. The present becomes an age of role playing and power, with knowledge a viaduct of untruth leading to rule, grounded in force, and legitimized by material gain.[34]

Sensitive to the instability of contemporary African sociality – a recurrent feature of his work since the 1990s[35] – Harrow's suggestion is not that Mudimbe seeks to establish a convergence between 'moving away from conventional Western formulations', on the one hand, and 'situating' the actuality of Africa, on the other, as though the two operations were, in a sense, mutually entailing. For the assumptions governing *Before the Birth of the Moon* are less identitarian than this. The African *chose du texte* – 'tradition', in Harrow's formulation – proves irrecuperable even to 'Afrocentric' enquiry. Near the end of *The Invention of Africa*, Mudimbe proposes that for all 'the cleverness of discourses and the competency of authors', they 'do not necessarily reveal *la chose du texte*, that which is out there in the African traditions, insistent and discrete ... African discourses today, by the very epistemological distance which makes them possible, explicit, and credible as scientific or philosophical utterances, might just be commenting upon rather than unveiling *la chose du texte*' (p. 185). He adds:

[O]ne wonders whether the discourses of African gnosis do not obscure a fundamental reality, their own *chose du texte*, the primordial African discourse in its variety and multiplicity. Is not this reality distorted in the expression of African modalities in non-African languages? Is it not inverted, modified by anthropological and philosophical categories used by specialists of dominant discourses? Does the question of how to relate in a more faithful way to *la chose du texte* necessarily imply another epistemological shift? Is it possible to consider this shift outside of the very epistemological field which makes my question both possible and thinkable? (p. 186)

Consider two moments in *Before the Birth of the Moon*. The first is that in which representatives from Ya's village come to Kinshasa to inform her lesbian lover and herself of the murder of her father and to recruit her into the struggle of 'her people' against the state. Her father has died, Ya is told, 'for the cause of his people'.[36] He has been killed

because he knew that things were not as they should be: there are the rich and the poor. The rich stand guard so that this difference will continue, so that there will always be the poor to be their slaves ... In earlier days, in our villages, things were not like that ... That is why we fought the Whites. They left ... and now it is our people, people of our own race, who ... (p. 69)

The problem for Ya is that she finds no points of personal identification in this schema. She remembers her father with love, as a 'wise and just' man, but as an anachronism, 'lord of another era', the 'incarnation of a past which, from your childhood on, seemed insignificant to you compared to the efficiency of the Whites' (p. 68). Similarly, her recollection of Mulembe, the village of her childhood, is less in the nature of a remembrance of the place in which she had once lived than a fabricated image, a backward projection from the present, a picture postcard, shot through with nostalgia and an impossible longing for lost origins: 'Your eyes opened roughly, windows exposed to a forgotten world: the green forests, the underbrush of wild ferns, the quiet waters full of fish, a savannah with gazelles, the plentiful fields surrounding a small, prosperous village' (p. 68). What is *real* to Ya is neither the world she now pretends to remember nor the world proposed in the political discourse of the men who have come to visit her, but the parallel universe of Kinshasa: 'You were quite well aware that you had slid into another universe in order to survive. From your school years on, you had judged it right to cast aside the old aristocratic concepts of your class. A whole new world was out there waiting for you' (p. 70). Especially because she is a woman, for Ya all forms of identification with the discourses of the 'tribe' now seem irremediably restrictive – or had she perhaps always felt this way?

For the men there were construction sites; for the best among them there were medical schools or schools of agronomics. For a woman, for you, there was only marriage, the only possibility in what was a completely nonexistent future. The city had seduced you with its liberties: a strange upward mobility that had carried you to the sidewalks of Kinshasa ... (p. 71)

Learning of her father's murder, Ya comes to accept that 'it was necessary to take part in the drama of [her] own people, without any uproar, to allow [herself] to be included' (p. 72). But it is not quite clear what she has accepted in accepting this. For she does not so much embrace the cause of 'her people' as allow it to wash over and absorb her. She acts not out of subjective solidarity but out of an almost impersonal sense of accountability:

> With small nods of their heads, the two young women [Ya and her lover] indicated their agreement and understood that they were becoming knots in a large fishnet thrown out to sea. They would walk the open road in front of them, without questions, without problems either, ignorant of both the sources and the direction of the winds, and, if need be, they would do so for the rest of their lives: the tribe required no less. (p. 73)

It is difficult to locate an African *chose du texte* – a culture, a form of sociality, a way of life lived or experienced – in this discourse of obligation. Outside, there is only the sun (indeed a perduringly objective presence, materially effective) and 'a large Dutch batik'; inside, Ya and her lover sit with the three representatives from 'her people'. We read:

> The three men and the two women seemed at the same time sad and savage, reduced to nothingness in a suffering and a nameless hatred. They knew that they were to hurl themselves at the horns of mad animals, they each nurtured the same desire to survive the struggle, to be able to find their roots again afterwards: a communion in the same hope. (p. 74)

The second moment from *Before the Birth of the Moon* that I would like to consider occurs precisely at the mid-point of the novel, where we encounter what Mudimbe himself, in an 'Author's note', terms a 'cannibalist farce'. In this ritualised ceremony, the government minister who serves as the novel's central male protagonist participates in the murder of Ya's lover. It is noteworthy that Mudimbe scrupulously resists attributing consciousness to the young woman herself at the scene of her execution. She is, in fact, barely humanised at first: we read that '[the minister] saw the Master sit down, and it was at that moment that he noticed a form whose hands and feet were bound together, lying flat on the ground in front of the Master' (p. 104). Only later does she emerge as 'the victim' and 'the young girl'. Even as the moment when she will be murdered approaches, she is not represented as thinking, as being a subject. The meaning of her death for her – that is to say, the meaning of her own death – remains, if not quite unreadable, at least undecidable, at the level of the text's enunciation:

> He found himself on his knees, next to the young woman. He could feel a light, tepid breath on his calves. He directed his attention to the Master who was reciting the formula of the Sacrifice. He heard an assistant light the fire behind

his back and, at the same time, saw the white knife flat in the hands of the priest. It shone in the moonlight. Another assistant, a little old man, all bones and silver hair, came to sit down at the victim's left side; as he chanted, he put his hands over her eyes and her mouth and stretched her throat forward. The young woman let them do as they pleased, either possessed by the atmosphere of the mystery which she beheld, or completely submissive because she had been drugged. (pp. 106–7)

At the very moment when the text might be supposed to be, as it were, 'most African' – when, immediately prior to the ritual murder, it breaks from French and transcribes a Nkundo prayer – it might, in fact, be at its most Eurocentric. For this is the moment in which, on the text's own evidence, a scene of cannibalism unfolds. (The killing itself is not represented; there is an elision in the text, and then we read: 'Sitting in the hut, across from the Master, he was holding her liver in his hands. The fire had shriveled it' [p. 109].) And yet the 'Author's note' informs us that 'the cannibalist farce is imaginary, from beginning to end. The ritual litany, however, is from a Nkundo prayer. In its proper cultural context it has nothing to do with human sacrifice' (p. 203). In *Parables and Fables*, Mudimbe recalls that in *Before the Birth of the Moon* he had 'patiently conjugated the "French Nouveau Roman" techniques with a critical yet impatient reading of 1960s Central African politics' (*Parables*, p. x). This account is revealing, but it leaves out one of the more remarkable features of the novel: the fact that its political critique is premised not upon the association of political dictatorship and cannibalism (already long since a cliché), but of political dictatorship *with the discourse of cannibalism*,[37] such that what Harrow calls 'Africa's present marginality' cannot be thought of independently of its construction in and through the dynamics of modernity or the 'colonial library'. When he first arrives at the scene of the sacrifice, the minister is rendered 'ill at ease' by the prospect of murder, and by what this collective act will demand of him: 'To divert his attention, he called to mind the catechism and the religious lessons: the truth of another spiritual universe that precludes neither massacres nor murders on a grand scale, sometimes for the world balance of power, often for the possession and accumulation of great wealth. He heard that he was being called' (*Before the Birth*, p. 105). The minister's recognition of the ethnocentrism of Catholicism becomes the justification for his cynical, ethically relativist, embrace of an Africanist discourse of authenticity. The novel, however, demonstrates that no African *chose du texte* corresponds to this discourse. If, as is clear, the colonialist languages *invent* and do not in any sense '*unveil*' Africa, then we must now also reckon with the idea that the anticolonialist languages are not in this respect distinguishable from them: the choice between the 'heart of darkness' and 'negritude' or 'the African personality' cannot be referred to any autochthonous, 'African' ground.

These ideas receive their fullest – but also, I think, their most problematical – elaboration in Mudimbe's celebrated debate with the anthropologist Peter Rigby. In his 1985 study, *Persistent Pastoralists*, Rigby had offered an analysis of the social practice of the Ilparakuyo people of east Africa.[38] (Rigby's status, interestingly, was that of consecrated cultural *insider* to the Ilparakuyo.) Countering Rigby's claims to represent the Ilparakuyo, Mudimbe writes that (and I quote him at length):

I contend that Rigby's text unveils a conceptual space which does not have the stability of the original locus. This does not imply a doubt about the correctness of the translation. On the contrary, I am impressed by the careful way in which his interpretation tests itself against the original locus ... My concern has nothing to do with that, but with what Rigby seems to resist: the best translation is always a reflection, or, more specifically, a metaphoric construct. It can identify with what is prior only figuratively and, in any case, witnesses to a dubious power. Let me specify what I mean. The everyday experience of Ilparakuyo (or Ndebele, Luba, Mande, or whatever) locus articulates itself as being, as text (in the full sense of the word). What a competent translation like Rigby's does is not to apprehend the being-there, not even to unveil it, but to organize a reflection and specify a commentary, a new order of meaning. I do not question the pertinence of specification. The point is to recognize the fact of a jump and, thus, under-stand the power of Rigby, that is, the power of the anthropologist. In reality, his interpretive practice witnesses to a metapower: a capacity of transforming a place into a conceptual space and of moving from this space to the original place ... In effect, Rigby the anthropologist began by terrorizing everybody with his author-ity: he is the only perfect bilingual among his fellow anthropologists and his Ilparakuyo elders, *ilmurran*, and family. And this suggests another dimension of his authority: he is, when he is critical, the only real master of symbolic and conceptual linkages existing between the 'laws of the place' and all interpretive operations that spatialize the being and the body of the Ilparakuyo place. (*Parables and Fables*, p. 171)

What is striking here is that although Mudimbe concedes 'the pertinence of specification' – that is, I take it, the epistemological adequacy of Rigby's representation of Ilparakuyo social practice – this concession counts for very little in his eyes. He is more interested in 'the fact of a jump', that is, in the formal (and unforgoable) gap between concept and object, discourse and *chose du texte*. He construes this gap pre-eminently as the locus of a power differential, such that – despite the fact that he 'gets them right', so to speak – Rigby emerges as a terroriser of the Ilparakuyo merely on the strength of his representation of them. To represent is, then, to dominate. Thus Mudimbe goes on to argue that 'Rigby seems to silence something ... [His] text is interwoven with something like a terror of naming what is out there' (*Parables and Fables*, p. 173). And he explicitly identifies Rigby's project of representation as a colonising enterprise, formally indistinguishable in this respect at least from that of colonialism proper (pp. 177–8).

This argument strikes me as wrong-headed. Mudimbe believes that, for historical reasons, no representation of African culture can be anything other than a commentary upon prior representations; what is at issue in all such representations, therefore, is a reading of a prior text (or texts), rather than an elucidation of *a chose du texte* or a culture, in Raymond Williams's sense of a 'whole way of life'.[39] Rigby clearly disagrees with Mudimbe here. In his rejoinder to Mudimbe's critique of his work (reprinted in Mudimbe's *Parables and Fables*), he reiterates his claim to be able to 're-present' (or 'interpret') Ilparakuyo culture and society (p. 197). He insists that theorists can achieve a 'true dialectic of theory and practice' provided that, in the spirit of intersubjective 'coevality', they devise methods of analysis sensitive to (and capable of minimising) '[t]he inequality, and hence the relation of power, established by both [spatial-ised and temporalised] forms of distancing' (p. 198). If I understand him correctly, Rigby is not claiming here that representation does *not* involve mediation ('the fact of a jump'). Instead, his argument is that not all representations are the same, that some are better than others and, indeed, that some enable the *chose du texte* which constitutes their object to stand revealed as in itself it really is.

I am inclined to agree with Rigby here. Ultimately, I find Mudimbe's critique of Rigby unsatisfactory on two accounts. First, it seems to me that his privileging of the question of the conditions of possibility of the generation of 'truth-effects' over that of representational adequacy is politically disenabling. To maintain that the essential gesture of Rigby's discourse is of a kind with that of colonial ethnography is to dissolve into insignificance its palpable difference from colonial ethnography. It becomes a difference that doesn't make a difference. Mudimbe's critique is one-sided: because of what it brackets, it conveys the impression that between the colonialist discourse and Rigby's commentary – that is, the commentary of the sympathetic and competent translator-interpreter-representer of Ilparakuyo-Maasai culture – there is, at a fundamental level, no important distinction to be drawn.

The second weakness of Mudimbe's presentation follows on directly from the first. As mentioned above, he identifies the 'gap' of ethnographic (or, more generally, social scientific) representation in terms of a power differential. But he then fails absolutely to specify the precise form(s) of power involved. Instead, representational power is conceptualised on the model of colonialist power – on the model, that is to say, of terrorism and dictatorship. It is quite clear that between the logic of practice (Bourdieu's phrase)[40] and the *theory* of that practice – or, better, the representation of it *in theory* – there is an unforgoable gap. The theory of a practice is rarely if ever internal to the actuality of that practice; the theory comes from outside the autonomous, integral, and existentially ineffable universe of the practice itself. In this sense it is true that Rigby 'is the only perfect bilingual among his fellow anthropologists and his Ilparakuyo elders, *ilmurran*, and family', inasmuch as only he is wearing – has required the necessary competence to wear – the two hats of 'theorist' and 'practitioner-participant' at one and the same time. But it does not follow, I think, from the fact that Rigby subjects the practice that he knows (and that he participates in) to the peculiar rigours of theoretical representation, that this activity involves *domination*, still less the terrorisation of others with his authority. And certainly, it does not follow that Rigby's 'intellectual spatialisation' of the 'locus' of Ilparakuyo practice replicates the 'rational madness' of colonialism. Against Mudimbe, I would want to argue that not all forms of objectification are dominative; and that between authority and authoritarianism the question of *application*, that is to say, of material *institution* and social *instantiation*, must be raised.

The line of thinking that I have been analysing through reference to Mudimbe is deeply rooted in postcolonial studies. Thus we find Edward Said insisting, in language very close to Mudimbe's, that

I'm not sure I could define it economically, or neatly for that matter, but certainly representation, or more particularly the *act* of representing (and hence reducing) others, almost always involves violence of some sort to the *subject* of the representation, as well as a contrast between the violence of the act of representing something and the calm exterior of the representation itself, the *image* – verbal, visual, or otherwise – of the subject. Whether you call it a spectacular image, or an exotic image, or a scholarly representation, there is always this paradoxical contrast between the surface, which seems to be in control, and the process which produces it, which inevitably involves some degree of violence, decontextualization, miniaturization, etc. The action or process of representing implies control, it implies accumulation, it implies confinement, it implies a certain kind of estrangement or disorientation on the part of the one representing.[41]

Said does immediately go on, in this 1985 interview, to allow formally for the possibility of a different kind of representation. For he concedes that representations

are a form of human economy, in a way, and necessary to life in society and, in a sense, between societies. So I don't think there is any way of getting away from them – they are as basic as language. What we must eliminate are systems of representation that carry with them the kind of authority which, to my mind, has been repressive because it doesn't permit or make room for interventions on the part of those represented. This is one of the unresolvable problems of anthropology, which is constituted essentially as the discourse of representation of an Other *epistemologically defined as radically inferior* (whether labeled primitive, or backward, or simply Other): the whole science or discourse of anthropology depends upon the silence of this Other. The alternative would be a representational system that was participatory and collaborative, noncoercive, rather than imposed, but as you know, this is not a simple matter. We have no immediate access to the means of producing alternative systems. Perhaps it would be possible through other, less exploitative fields of knowledge. But first we must identify those social-cultural-political formations which would allow for a reduction of authority and increased participation in the production of representations, and proceed from there. (pp. 41–2)

The possibility of another model of representational practice – participatory, collaborative, non-coercive – is mooted here, but effectively placed beyond the horizon, as a merely utopian projection. Where such anthropologists as Rigby and Fabian[42] believe that their discipline is capable of activating and accommodating a 'true dialectic of theory and practice', Said seems to suggest that anthropology is irrecuperably beyond the pale. And not only anthropology, evidently, but also such other 'fields of knowledge' as history, philosophy, sociology, politics, and so on. The 'decolonisation' of these must await the identification of 'social-cultural-political formations which would allow for a reduction of authority and increased participation in the production of representations'.

We should note that Said himself moved decisively away from this way of seeing things as the 1980s unfolded, to adopt a very different standpoint on the question of representation – one openly critical of what he would describe (again in an interview) as 'the general suspicion of representation, the whole problematic of representation' in contemporary theoretical discourse: 'It is assumed that there's a kind of, not so much inauthenticity, but ideological deformation taking place whenever representation is at issue', he argued. 'Thus the notion of the representative intellectual strikes a chord of antipathy because there's assumed to be something constitutively false and deconstructable in it, so that nobody wants to venture into that place.'[43] And he added, pointedly:

I wouldn't want necessarily to leave aside from our discussion the profound effect on all of this of people like Derrida and de Man, who have contributed very much to the disrespect and distrust for the discourse of politics as something by which people live, constitute themselves, fight, die, etc. This kind of suspicion, this hovering on the margins, this infatuation with the undecidable and the ironic, it's all part of this. One can only look at it as a formation of late capitalism in the American academy.[44] (p. 333)

Yet if Said himself moved to dissent from the blanket repudiation of representation itself in contemporary theory, this repudiation has tended to remain a central plank in the postcolonial discussion. Thus we read, in a contemporary commentary by Sam Raditlhalo, that the task 'of claiming agency for marginalized peoples, and describing and analyzing the nature of this agency and subjectivity', which 'has been at the heart of the postcolonial project',

is complicated by two major factors that strike at the root of the very possibility of such a project. The first is the fact that one of the more enduring legacies of the imperialist project was the textual obliteration of the voice of the Other. And then – beyond this erasure – are the even more sophisticated discursive hegemonies that govern the field of knowledge production in colonial and postcolonial societies, hegemonies which ensure that the voice of the Other is always and everywhere subordinated or appropriated by the dominant discourse that controls the sites of utterance.[45]

It is the second of these 'factors' identified by Raditlhalo, with its categorical 'always and everywhere', that I find implausible. Admitting of no exceptions and no corrective, it stands contradicted by what Parry has rightly identified as the 'abundant evidence of native disaffection and dissent under colonial rule, of contestation and struggle against diverse forms of institutional and ideological domination'. For as Parry goes on to point out, not only are '[i]nscriptions and signs of resistance ... discernible in official archives and informal texts, and ... detect[able] in narrativized instances of insurrection and organized political opposition', but '[t]races of popular disobedience can also be recuperated from unwritten symbolic and symptomatic practices which register a rejection or violation of the subject positions assigned by colonialism'.[46]

SUBALTERNITY

All writers everywhere are obliged to think about at least some of the problems involved in representing the life and consciousness of others. (The literary creation of character, among other things, would be impossible in the absence of such reflection.) But the self-conscious counter-discursivity of 'postcolonial' writing has tended to promote among writers in this context a very particular and advanced concern with these problems. In general, the question broached is that articulated by Olanna, in Chimamanda Ngozi Adichie's *Half of a Yellow Sun*, as she tries to understand the feelings of a poor, uneducated village girl for the relatively wealthy and powerful man who has seduced her: 'How much did one know of the true feelings of those who did not have a voice?'[47] The project of reclaiming the history of those who have been un- or under-represented in histories and narratives hitherto (and much 'postcolonial' writing takes this reclamation as its particular burden) obviously involves restoring subjectivity – and hence attributing agency and volition – to people or communities or groups previously figured, for the most part, either (indifferently) as objects or (sympathetically) as pure victims. 'Postcolonial' writing has sought to 'revision' or 'unwrite' prior Eurocentric narratives; but it has also sought to recover and transmit or provide access to modes of life, forms of culture, and ways of thinking that have been obliterated, destabilised, or rendered invisible by the systematic operations of power (global, national, and local) over the course of the past several hundred years. Achebe's desire, in writing *Things Fall Apart*, to demonstrate the cultural depth and integrity of a people denigrated and belittled as 'primitive' in colonial discourse, has already been mentioned;[48] and it is common knowledge also that in the section of his *Canto General* entitled 'The Heights of Machu Picchu', Pablo Neruda set out to give voice, as Jean Franco has written, to 'the nameless men and women who constructed the fortress out of their suffering and who have now no identity except through the poet's re-creation of their saga'.[49]

In Manlio Argueta's *Cuzcatlán* we read of Emiliano and Eusebio, two dirt-poor Salvadoran *campesinos* who meet and befriend one another, that they

recognize one another because they share a common affirmation of poverty and abiding affection ... Their blood is red like that of other men but inspired by something else, something that makes them sensitive to the river, the volcanoes, animals without masters, a future life that exists only in their dreams. Their eyes see into the night; they penetrate the darkness and discover the mystery which holds them in poverty. But they are afraid. There have been five hundred years of terror. They are afraid because they are sensitive. Their eyes see more than the eyes of cats, or jaguars, or pumas. In dreams they see golden hillsides of corn and flowers: pumpkin flowers creeping among the shoots in the fields; bean flowers crawling to the tops of the corn-stalks. (pp. 51–2)

Argueta mixes registers, lexicons, and optics to striking effect here. The formulation, '*they share a common affirmation of poverty and abiding affection*', derives from the universe of social science: its language is analytical, deductive, comparative. But '*Their blood is red like that of other men but inspired by something else, something that makes them sensitive to the river, the volcanoes, animals without masters, a future life that exists only in their dreams*' comes from another discursive universe – that of the poetic imagination – and directs the reader's attention to that which is incomparable and cannot be derived objectively. All blood is red, of course, but that of Emiliano and Eusebio is 'inspired' or given texture by the irreducible particularity of the world in which they live. The logic of determination at play here is not a naturalist one: although the men's outlooks are inevitably shaped and determined by the physical landscape they inhabit, such that they have developed a sensitivity to rivers and volcanoes, they are also governed by an ethical disposition that bespeaks a specific class history. The fact that they are moved by animals without masters testifies both to their own status as members of a land-based peasantry and to their consciousness of themselves as having always been treated like animals; the centuries of their dispossession have led them to believe that the freedom to which they unshakably aspire 'exists only in their dreams'.

In texts like *Cuzcatlán* we encounter a practice of literary representation through which a virtual universe is 'peopled' by characters whose existence in social space and time has been credibly imagined and realised. What is at issue here is not necessarily *realism* but the writer's ability to show us what it feels like to live on a given ground – to show us how a certain socio-natural order is encountered, experienced, lived. The writer's success or failure in this respect is not solely a function of 'authenticity' at the level of content, but also of imagination, dexterity, and telling judgement in the selection and manipulation of the formal resources of fiction. In *Cuzcatlán*, for instance, Argueta frequently moves back and forth from free indirect to indirect style, from individuated to collective focalisation, from dialogue to what in the text itself he calls 'interior voice', from diegetic to extra-diegetic narration, from the register of reportage to that of *testimonio*, from socialist realism to allegory – all in order to render and flesh out the range, specificity, typicality, and generation of the particular thoughts, modes of consciousness, ways of seeing, and structures of feeling of his characters.[50] 'You measure weeks by counting mornings and evenings', one characteristic passage begins, the 'you' standing either as the index of reported speech (someone is saying this to 'you') or as an extrapolated narrative representation of peasant consciousness:

To calculate months you count moons. And you count years from the start of the rainy season. Six months of rain, six months of sun. Invariably May is the first month of rain. The peasant year begins in May. It's a month of happiness, green-corn parties, fruit festivals, green iguanas, and the warbling of the *zensontle* bird. Five hundred years ago they possessed a perfect calendar, and could gauge the movement of the stars and calculate eclipses with precision. It is different now, as if time has been destroyed and everything has regressed. It has all gone to shit. (*Cuzcatlán*, p. 16)

The focalising lens is ever in movement here, first representing 'peasant consciousness' from the 'inside', as it were, then tracking back to describe it externally – 'The peasant year begins in May' – before returning to a standpoint that might be internal, external, or shared between them, and from which a summary judgement issues: 'It has all gone to shit'.

Another, extraordinary, passage shows us the dissemination of ideas in time and space, as experience engenders new structures of consciousness and new concepts, and these in turn modify and structure the terms of experience. The narrative voice is external to what it describes, but is predicated on a deep-seated solidarity with those whose lives and struggles it seeks to represent and champion:

The question about his last name, which he had previously ignored, had opened his eyes as well as what some of his neighbors were already calling consciousness. He needed a shove to be able to comprehend it and they had given it to him. He had had to journey across hundreds of years for that little shove, and he carried those years which his fathers and grandfathers had endured with him. Terrible years. Their vitality used up beneath hurricanes, thunderstorms, and the harsh suns of March and April, just for another piece of tortilla and another grain of salt. And who owned those energies? All this they had endured with the patience and reflection of centuries, he and his fathers and grandfathers. But now a new element had been added: now they came to violate his identity, his nature. People removed from the poor, from their way of being; people unfamiliar with their centuries of slave culture, oppressed culture, but culture nonetheless; the physical oppressors came now to rob them of their only wealth: their integrity. (pp. 243–4)

In postcolonial studies, the question of the representation of popular consciousness (and, more generally, of difference or otherness) has unfortunately been broached mainly with reference to the category of *subalternity*. An extreme and one-sided theorisation has come to provide the general methodological template for the approach to this category: subalternity has more or less been *defined* in terms of unrepresentability. This has neatly closed the circle: popular consciousness devolves to and is understood under the rubric of subalternity, which is understood in turn as being constitutively beyond or outside of representation.

What has come to be considered exemplary is not the work that initially appeared under the imprimatur of 'Subaltern Studies' in the early 1980s, and that was still committed to the enterprise of recovering or uncovering the contents and forms of consciousness of 'the people', those spoken of and for in elite representations, but seldom or never afforded sanctioned or public space to speak of and for themselves: the 'wretched of the earth', in Fanon's famous formula; the 'people without history', in Eric Wolf's.[51] Instead, the version of subalternity that has proved most influential in postcolonial studies is that initially proposed by Gayatri Chakravorty Spivak and glossed and refined since then by a host of other scholars.

Spivak theorises subalternity very austerely in terms of a structured and unforgoable inarticulacy at the elite levels of state and civil society – such that to be positioned as subaltern in any discursive context is to be incapable of representing oneself within that context. Within the elite spheres, '[t]he subaltern cannot speak'.[52] Subaltern practice cannot signify 'as itself' across the divide that separates social elites from those who are not elite. It is, indeed, precisely the irreducible gap between popular practice and its (misrecognising) construal in elite discourse that the term 'subalternity' designates on Spivak's usage of it. The subaltern is the *object* of discourse, never the subject. Whatever is represented as 'subaltern' has always-already been made over: not only translated, but traduced; not only appropriated, but expropriated.

In *Representations of the Intellectual*, by contrast, Edward Said speaks of the intellectual as 'an individual endowed with a faculty for representing, embodying, articulating a message, a view, an attitude, philosophy or opinion to, as well as for, a public', adding that the fundamental responsibility here is always to 'represent all those people and issues that are routinely forgotten or swept under the rug'.[53] Spivak's standpoint does not allow for a practice of representation conceived of in these terms.

Certainly, we can concede that the practice of representation in many 'postcolonial' literary works – including some that are very well known and highly celebrated – is susceptible to deconstruction in Spivak's terms.

It is important to problematise representation and the issues around it where the writer's desire to speak *for* others – to endow 'them' with consciousness and voice – shades over into ventriloquisation, into speaking *instead* of 'them': what starts out as an attempt to speak on behalf of others, or at least about others (in the interests of 'putting them on the map') ends up, paradoxically, as a silencing of 'them' through the writer's own speech. On some occasions, quite clearly, the words that writers put into the mouths of their non-elite characters, the thoughts that they put into their heads, are implausible in situational (and diegetic) terms and are instead conceivable only as the words and thoughts of *writers*, of *intellectuals*. Think, for instance, of the notoriously problematical quality of the central protagonist's consciousness in Ayi Kwei Armah's *The Beautyful Ones are not yet Born*. The mode of thinking attributed to 'the man' in this novel is construable only as that of a radical intellectual. What then rings false is not that, unlike his mentor, 'Teacher', 'the man' is a humble wage-slave, a lowly railway clerk in the dilapidated state sector in Nkrumah's Ghana. (We do, after all, learn of his university experience; and we see that he has self-consciously *chosen* not to live the life of an intellectual.) It is rather that, though supremely isolated in the novel, he is posed as an ideal-typical figure, a sort of 'common man'. This bestows upon Armah's strategy of representation the paradoxical effect of projecting intellectualist conceptions of subjectivity and social being as modal and, indeed, universal, rather than as class-based.[54]

Similar questions might be raised with respect to Vikram Seth's representation of subaltern consciousness in *A Suitable Boy*. In an interesting article comparing Seth's novel, which is set in 1951, with the Hindi novel, *Maila Anchal* (translated into English as *The Soiled Border*), a 1954 work by Phanishwarnath Renu, Angela Atkins has argued that Seth's individualisation of the village labourer Kachheru has the unintended effect of positioning him in terms of the bourgeois paradigm of alienated isolation.[55] Kachheru, Atkins writes, 'is pinned down by passages of extended description about a typified peasant describing his poor accommodation, inadequate diet and back-breaking labour'. She cites a moving passage from the novel, in which the harshness of the work demanded of Kachheru reduces him gradually, over the long hours of a pitiless day, to the condition of a pack-animal. The end of a day that had dawned cool and breezy, and that had seen Kachheru humming 'a bhajan to himself as he [had] walked the bullocks out of the village' is narrated by Seth as follows:

By the time it was late afternoon his dark face was flushed red. His feet, callused and cracked though they were, felt as if they had been boiled. After a short day's work he usually shouldered the plough himself as he drove the cattle back from the fields. But he had no energy to do so today and gave it to the spent cattle to haul. Hardly a coherent thought formed itself in his mind. The metal of his spade, when it touched his shoulder accidentally, made him wince.

   He passed by his own unploughed field with its two mulberry trees and hardly noticed it. Even that small field was not really his own, but it did not strike him to say so – or even think so. His only intention was to place one foot after the other on the path that led back to Debaria. The village lay three-quarters of a mile ahead of him, and it seemed to him that he was walking there through fire. (*A Suitable Boy*, pp. 579–80)

Atkins finds this representation of Kachheru implausible. She complains that he 'is unique among the principal characters of *A Suitable Boy* in having no friends, only a wife and an absent son. He is described as a Chamar, but he is never portrayed with any others of his caste. This is reflected in the description of the village geography that is likewise individualist and sparse'. Atkins's objection is ultimately that, for all his imaginative sympathy, Seth cannot construct a field of vision for the subaltern Kachheru that is not always phenomenologically overshadowed by the field of vision 'inhabited' by the elite characters in the novel. Hence the collective practice of the subaltern classes – which, sociologically and historically speaking, is actually restless and unceasing – finds no representation in the novel. As Atkins puts it, 'the push for change from below, is missing in this novel because the space is too sparsely charactered to allow it to exist'.[56]

   The assumption is widespread among postcolonial critics that the desire to speak *for*, *of*, or even *about* others is always shadowed – and perhaps even overdetermined – by a secretly or latently authoritarian aspiration. Intellectual representation is taken to be a game of high stakes; the danger is thought to rest in the fact that in speaking of or for others (and it is of course our own relative privilege – our schooling, among other things – that has put us in a position to do so and even or especially to *think* of doing so), we might unintentionally and unwittingly find ourselves both objectifying 'them' and superimposing our own elite cognitive maps on 'them' as we do so. The resort, therefore, has been to a consideration of difference under the rubric of *incommensurability*. Critics have supposed that if they work on the strategic assumption that what is 'other' to the representing subject is radically and categorically so, it might be possible to put a spoke in the wheel of any unselfconscious project of representation, at least. Thus Rosalind O'Hanlon, in her contribution to the debate on subaltern studies, suggests that, despite itself, the progressive attempt to recover popular consciousness has invariably ended up misrepresenting 'the people' by transforming them 'into autonomous subject-agents, unitary consciousnesses possessed of their own originary essence, in the manner which we now understand to be the creation, very largely, of Enlightenment humanism's reconstruction of Man'.[57] The progressive conceit, O'Hanlon writes, is that

[t]hrough the restoration of subjectivity and the focus on experience ... a textual space [will be] ... opened up in which subaltern groups may speak for themselves and present their hidden past in their own distinctive voices ... [W]e must ask ourselves whether we are in danger [not only of turning] the silence of the subaltern into speech, but [of making] their words address our own concerns, and [of rendering] their figures in our own self-image. (p. 96)

O'Hanlon speaks here and elsewhere of the 'fundamental alienness' of the subaltern from the representing subject. This is a *definitional* 'otherness' or incommensurability, of course, intended strategically to prevent those who take up the burden of representation from assuming – from their own positions of relative power, relatively untheorised by themselves – that 'the people' are, as it were, 'just like them', only contingently poorer or more disempowered, and that, if these 'people' were to be given the opportunity to do so, they would make the same choices and think the same sorts of thoughts as the representers themselves.

The thesis of incommensurability is given an airing in some very well-known works of the 'postcolonial' corpus: such novels as *Waiting for the Barbarians* and *Foe* by J. M. Coetzee, for instance. There is an interesting moment in Amitav Ghosh's *The Hungry Tide*, in which the Calcutta-born but Seattle-bred marine biologist Piya comes to a realisation about the attitude of Kanai, a man of her own class background, towards the poor and disenfranchised villagers of the Sunderbans. Kanai is a man of substance, educated, cosmopolitan, and urbane, a writer who now runs his own translation company in Delhi. Based temporarily in the fictional small town of Lusibari in the Sundarbans, he and Piya are discussing Moyna and Fokir, two of the local inhabitants with whom they have come into contact. Fokir is a fisherman; Moyna his wife. Moyna is working as a trainee nurse in the Lusibari Hospital, which is administered by Kanai's aunt. She dreams of becoming a full-fledged nurse. Kanai pronounces himself impressed by her enterprise: 'If you consider her circumstances – her caste, her upbringing – it's very remarkable that she's had the forethought to figure out how to get by in today's world. And it isn't just that she wants to get by – she wants to do well; she wants to make a success of her life'.[58] Reflecting on his words, Piya comes to the realisation that

> For Kanai there was a certain reassurance in meeting a woman like Moyna, in such a place as Lusibari; it was as if her very existence were a validation of the choices he had made in his own life. It was important for him to believe that his values were, at bottom, egalitarian, liberal, meritocratic. It reassured him to be able to think, 'What I want for myself is not different from what everybody wants, no matter how rich or poor; everyone who has any drive, any energy, wants to get on in the world – Moyna is the proof.' Piya understood too that this was a looking-glass in which a man like Fokir could never be anything other than a figure glimpsed through a rear-view mirror, a rapidly diminishing presence, a ghost from the perpetual past that was Lusibari. But she guessed also that despite its newness and energy, the country Kanai inhabited was full of these ghosts, these unseen presences whose murmurings could never quite be silenced no matter how loud you spoke. (pp. 219–20)

Piya's conclusion here is that Kanai's ostensibly liberal attribution to subaltern 'others' of values just like his own is in fact an act of symbolic violence. He imposes his own world-picture on 'them', without pausing to think that 'their' world is not simply an attenuated and impoverished mirror of his own but might instead harbour different moral and ideo-logical and aspirational values. Moyna wants to 'get on in the world': he assumes that this means the same for her as for himself, and he regards it therefore as indicative of her realism as well as her intelligence. But by the same token, Fokir's manifest lack of interest in 'getting on in the world' can only be read in terms of backwardness or perversity. The idea that it might implicate a different moral economy is never considered. When Kanai and Fokir are together, they physically inhabit the same place at the same time, obviously; but as Kanai sees the matter, Fokir inhabits this space and time on the verge of extinction; 'development' has consigned people like him to oblivion; he lives on like a spectre: hence Piya's speculation that, to Kanai, Fokir can 'never be anything other than a figure glimpsed through a rear-view mirror'.

Not that, in *The Hungry Tide*, Piya's awareness of this pattern under-lying Kanai's thinking about subaltern others leads her to a different way of thinking herself. On the contrary, the novel is replete with examples of her assuming, quite wrongly in the event, an affinity between Fokir and herself, notwithstanding the fact that she cannot even speak to him, since she has retained no Bengali. (Kanai frequently makes just this point himself in the novel.) Thus she assumes that his deep practical knowledge of the jungles and waterways of the Sunderbans will have as its correlate a form of naturalism compatible with her own differently derived environmentalism; and she is both appalled and confused, accordingly, when Fokir takes an active part in the killing of a tiger that has been trapped in a livestock pen in a local village. Catching sight of him in the crowd of villagers pressing forwards to stab the tiger through the walls of the pen with sharpened bamboo stakes, and about to set the pen alight, she runs to him, 'certain that he would know what to do, that he would find a way to put a stop to what was going on' (p. 295); but his response is to drag her from the scene in order to prevent her from disrupting the course of events.

It is noteworthy that Ghosh does not provide us unmediated access, in *The Hungry Tide*, to Fokir's own thoughts. This obviously allows us to dwell a little longer on the idea that there is an incommensurability – radical alterity – between elite and subaltern cultures, value systems and ways of seeing. Subaltern consciousness is figured consistently as inscrutable; irrecoverable by and inaccessible to any of the novel's elite characters, it is also left unrecovered and unaccessed by the novel itself.

But I wonder whether the narrative, formal, and affective dimensions of *The Hungry Tide* do not cut against and in the end undermine this idea of incommensurability, and of the theoretical anti-humanism that underlies it. Ghosh's self-conscious use here, as elsewhere in his work, of sentimentality and sensationalism (the novel's very title is significant in this respect), of romance and narrative suspense, all point us in a quite different direction, towards the idea not of 'fundamental alienness' but of deep-seated affinity and community, across and athwart the social division of labour.[59]

Brief examination of two moments in the text might help to support this thesis. The first occurs on an occasion when Fokir and Piya are out on the waters together, he to fish for crabs, she to research the behaviour of Orcaella dolphins. Piya is suddenly struck by the almost uncanny mutuality of their respective labours, affects and preoccupations:

It was surprising enough that their jobs had not proved to be utterly incompatible – especially considering that one of the tasks required the input of geostationary satellites while the other depended on bits of shark-bone and broken tile. But that it had proved possible for two such different people to pursue their own ends simultaneously – people who could not exchange a word with each other and had no idea of what was going on in one another's heads – was far more than surprising: it seemed almost miraculous. Nor was she the only one to remark on this: once, when her glance happened accidentally to cross Fokir's, she saw something in his expression that told her that he too was amazed by the seamless intertwining of their pleasures and their purposes. (p. 141)

The impression of mutuality here is centred in Piya's consciousness, to be sure, but Ghosh's formulation makes clear that she is not alone in apprehending it. '[S]he was not the only one to remark on' it, he writes; and it is evident that we are to understand Fokir's silent facial expression as a speech-act whose real meaning is available to Piya – hence the careful synaesthetic wording that has her *seeing* 'something in his expression' that *tells* her 'that he too was amazed by the seamless intertwining of their pleasures and their purposes'.

Piya herself subscribes to a variant of anti-humanism that we might understand as the philosophical reflex of her 'green' politics. Throughout the novel, she evinces a profound mistrust of *language*, repeatedly refer-ring the failure to communicate – to understand what Fokir is thinking or saying, for instance – not (as on the incommensurability thesis) to any supposedly unbridgeable gap between elite and subaltern consciousness, but to an, as it were, *pan-human* predicament. Not merely 'pan-human', indeed, but also *exclusively* human: *Homo sapiens* might be the speaking animal, but Piya's hostility to anthropocentrism leads her to the conviction that language is what divides and separates, not what conduces to commu-nity. Reflecting on the 'serene' sounds that dolphins make to communicate, thus, she sets its uncluttered 'transparency' above the systematic distortions of human intercourse:

She imagined the animals circling drowsily, listening to echoes pinging through the water, painting pictures in three dimensions – images that only they could decode. The thought of experiencing your surroundings in that way never failed to fascinate her: the idea that to 'see' was also to 'speak' to others of your kind, where simply to exist was to communicate.

In contrast, there was the immeasurable distance that separated her from Fokir. What was he thinking about as he stared at the moonlit river? The forest, the crabs? Whatever it was, she would never know: not just because they had no language in common but because that was how it was with human beings, who came equipped, as a species, with the means of shutting each other out. The two of them, Fokir and herself, they could have been boulders or trees for all they knew of each other: and wasn't it better in a way, more honest, that they could not speak? For if you compared it to the ways in which dolphins' echoes mirrored the world, speech was only a bag of tricks that fooled you into believing that you could see through the eyes of another being. (p. 159)

This way of seeing things would hold no appeal to Kanai, of course, who as a translator is presumably disposed to believe in both the expressivity and the communicability of language. And we can surmise that what is true for Kanai is true also, *mutatis mutandis*, for Amitav Ghosh himself. *The Hungry Tide* certainly *plays* with the idea that language is 'only a bag of tricks', and fundamentally anti-mediatory, just as it plays with the ideas of incommensurability and interlinguistic untranslatability. But the suggestions as to the inaccessibility of experience to language are of course precisely *suggestions*, that is to say, themselves based in language. In these terms the novel's commitment to the humanist idea that all experience is communicable is nowhere more evident than when it seems to be proposing that some dimensions of experience are inexpressible through language. Consider, for instance, the climactic scene near the end of the novel in which Fokir and Piya, caught in a typhoon, are forced to seek refuge in the branches of a strong tree. As the eye of the storm passes over them, the fearsome winds begin to change direction, and they are no longer even partly protected by the tree's trunk:

something had changed and it took Piya a moment to register the difference. The wind was now coming at them from the opposite direction. Where she had had the tree trunk to shelter her before, now there was only Fokir's body. Was this why he had been looking for a branch on another tree? Had he known, right from the start that his own body would have to become her shield when the eye had passed? She tried to break free from his grasp, tried to pull him around so that for once, she could be the one who was sheltering him. But his body was unyielding and she could not break free from it, especially now that it had the wind's weight behind it. Their bodies were so close, so finely merged, that she could feel the impact of everything hitting him, she could sense the blows raining down on his back. She could feel the bones of his cheeks as if they had been superimposed on her own; it was as if the storm had given them what life could not; it had fused them together and made them one. (p. 390)

The quoted lines reverse the conclusion of Forster's *A Passage to India*, which had seen Aziz and Fielding being held apart despite their having a language in common, because time and tide would not permit their union:

'Why can't we be friends now?' said the other [Fielding], holding him [Aziz] affectionately. 'It's what I want. It's what you want.'
   But the horses didn't want it – they swerved apart; the earth didn't want it, sending up rocks through which riders must pass single file; the temples, the tank, the jail, the palace, the birds, the carrion, the Guest House, that came into view as they issued from the gap and saw Mau beneath: they didn't want it, they said in their hundred voices, 'No, not yet,' and the sky said, 'No, not there.'[60]

Where Forster's formulation had had the desire of individual human beings for reciprocity and dialogue thwarted by the rigid essentialism of a hostile world – landscape, flora, and fauna as much as built space, institutions, and politics – Ghosh's has nature, in the form of the typhoon, making possible what 'life' (by which we must presumably understand 'social existence') has disallowed. In Ghosh, the opposition between 'individual' and 'society' that is a received legacy of the novel as a bourgeois literary form undergoes modification because it is insistently triangulated by the intervention of what is non-human.

Mahasweta Devi's long story, 'Pterodactyl, Puran Sahay, and Pirtha', explores somewhat similar ground, but heads in a rather different direction. The narrative tells of Puran Sahay, a politically progressive Bihari journalist, who is approached by an old friend of his, Harisharan, currently serving as the Block Development Officer of a district in Madhya Pradesh. Within this district are some tribal villages, one of which is Pirtha, whose inhabitants, desperately poor, lacking all resources, living on inhospitable, effectively uncultivable, land, are at the point of starvation. Despite this, they exhibit little enthusiasm for government or state initiatives offering them aid or relief. Recently, some drawings on the walls of caves around the village have come to light. Whether these engravings are contemporary or prehistoric is uncertain, although one, at least, of a large creature – 'Webbed wings like a bat and a body like a giant iguana. And four legs … A toothless gaping horrible mouth' ('Pterodactyl', p. 102) – has been done by Bikhia, a boy from the village. Harisharan wants Puran to write a report on Pirtha that will call public attention to it – perhaps by discussing the cave drawings – hence affording him the opportunity to bid for greater relief funding. 'My need', as he explains to Puran, 'is to make a big noise in whatever way and put Pirtha on the map of Madhya Pradesh and therefore of India. I don't want heaven. Only what can be done within the administrative framework, what we otherwise can't do, either for want of sympathy, or under pressure of politics and administration. I need help to get that much done' (p. 112).

Puran discovers when he arrives in Pirtha that the village is not merely under intolerable strain from its harsh physical environment, compounded both by mismanagement in the delivery of assistance and exploitation of the villagers by non-tribal labour contractors and money lenders,[61] but seems to be in a state of traumatised mourning. News of Bikhia's engraving has spread through all the tribal villages in the district. In Pirtha itself, the mood is of deep sadness and collective withdrawal from the world, as though in response to a devastating loss. When, accompanied by Harisharan in his official capacity as Block Development

Officer, Puran asks one of the villagers, a man named Shankar, for an explanation of this evident state of crisis, Shankar declaims his response '[a]s if he is singing a saga', leaving Puran to reason to himself that the tribal villagers 'have caught the past in their songs' (p. 119). Shankar's recitation is as follows (I quote at length):

'Once there was forest, hill, river, and us. We had villages, homes, land, ourselves. In our fields we grew rice, kodo, kutki, soma, we lived. Then there was game to hunt. It rained, peacocks danced, we lived. People grew, the community grew, some of us moved to a distance. We asked the earth's permission, we are setting down stakes to build a roof, settling land to grow crops. The Chief of our society told us where we should settle land fit for living. There we built homes, made villages, settled land each for himself. We worshipped the tree that was the spirit of our village. Then we lived, only us.'

Shankar ran in a circle and pointed in all directions ... 'Blessed us. We lived. And now?

Ah misfortune! As ants come before a flood, as white ants fly in teeming swarms before the rains, so did our news reach strangers. Did we make a mistake in our worshipping? Did someone tear a leaf from a tree before it was consecrated, before the new fruit, new leaf, new flower came in the springtime, in the month of Phalgun? Did one of us kill a pregnant doe in the hunt? Did someone insult the elders? The community's rule is to protect orphans, was that rule broken somewhere? I don't know where we became guilty.

Why did the foreigners come? We were kings. Became subjects. Were subjects became slaves. Owed nothing, they made us debtors. Alas, they enslaved and bound us. They named us, as bond slaves ... Our land vanished like dust before a storm, our fields, our homes, all disappeared. The ones who came were not human beings ...' (pp. 119–20)

What Shankar describes here is the cultural annihilation of the tribal peoples of India,[62] who have been subjected to an alien social order, driven off their land and systematically dispossessed of everything that made them who they once were. In *Black Skin, White Masks*, Fanon had attempted to register the extent of the destruction wrought by the clash of civilisations entailed in and by colonialism: 'Overnight the Negro has been given two frames of reference within which he has had to place himself. His metaphysics, or, less pretentiously, his customs and the sources on which they were based, were wiped out because they were in conflict with a civilization that he did not know and that imposed itself on him.'[63] Shankar is describing something similar but even more cataclysmic – more intensive because of much, much longer duration than European colonialism. Puran reads in the *Gazetteer of India* that '*The Austrics form the bedrock of the people*' (p. 114);[64] but it becomes clear that if this metaphor is to be understood as anything more than a reactionary romanticism, it is construable only in the grim sense that what the narrative itself terms 'mainstream' or 'modern' India has been built on the crushed bones – shattered and scattered – of tribal peoples.

Shankar speaks in Hindi – also spoken by Puran and Harisharan – but the experience that he speaks of 'is a million moons old, when they did not speak Hindi'. It occurs to Puran as he listens that 'he doesn't know what language Shankar's people spoke, what they speak. There are no words in their language to explain the daily experience of the tribal in today's India' (p. 118). The circumstances and strictures of the lives that Shankar's people are actually living cannot be represented in their own language, since they exceed and baffle the conceptual horizons of this language. Are we to understand, then, that the reverse is also true: that the cultural inheritance, the wisdom, customs and forms of understanding of 'a million moons' ago, are similarly inexpressible by the Hindi speaker, or inaccessible to 'modern' modes of conceptualising? The problem here is that Shankar's recitation is not only rhetorically evocative and aesthetically moving in its rhythm, tropology, and use of metaphor – the pleasing isocolonic balance of 'Once there was forest, hill, river, and us. We had villages, homes, land, ourselves', for instance; or the use of gradatio in 'We were kings. Became subjects. Were subjects became slaves. Owed nothing, they made us debtors'[65] – but is also exceptionally lucid and expressive.

Ending his recitation, Shankar turns to Harisharan and passionately implores him: 'BDO Sir . . . I say to you in great humility: you can't do anything for us. We became unclean as soon as you entered our lives. No more roads, no more relief – what will you give to a people in exchange for the vanished land, home, field, burial-ground?' (p. 120). Harisharan's response is to point out that Shankar's entreaty places him in an impossible bind. On the one hand, confronted by the hardship in Pirtha, he cannot do nothing. This would be contrary to both his personal ethics and his professional responsibilities as a civil servant. On the other hand, it seems that whatever he might prove capable of doing would be unwelcome to the very people for whom – or so he believes – he would be doing it. As he puts it to Puran, who has asked him what he proposes to do if, as seems quite likely, the villagers refuse to accept the limited assistance that he might be able to provide them:

You too have to understand that a civil servant from today's Madhya Pradesh Civil Service cannot give back to an ancient nation the flowing Pirtha, the spreading forest, fields of grain where the only invaders are deer, peacock, and other birds, festival dancers not watched and photographed by trippers, burial-grounds where others' shovels and spades won't strike. They want recognition of their violated ethno-national identity, their stolen dignity, freedom from slavery ... my power is limited, dear friend. I can fight mightily with various government departments and bring them a little rice, medicine, powdered milk ... (p. 121)

To this point in the narrative, 'Pterodactyl' seems typical of much of Mahasweta's fiction in its concern to document and protest the social conditions under which nomadic and denotified tribes and other subaltern groupings are obliged to eke out a precarious existence throughout India. What, then, takes it into uncharted waters is the authorial decision to render as (diegetically) real the creature that Bikhia draws. Puran initially believes that Bikhia has given pictorial form to the imagined shadow of the tribal ancestors: his speculation is that if the villagers evidently consider themselves 'unclean and in mourning' (p. 140), it must be because they suppose that contemporary conditions in Pirtha have brought pain and distress to their ancestors. But then, one rainy night, 'the soul of the ancestor of Shankar's people, half claw scratching, half floating', comes into Puran's room:

Puran turns to stone, he freezes.
 It rains and rains and rains .... Puran slowly mobilizes his numb still body. He gets up.
 He leaves his bed and stands on the floor. Then he slowly walks toward the *passage*. There is another room at the end of the *passage*. Part of the thatch of the room's roof has blown away. The room is not very large. Lightning flashes in the rain. The eye gets accustomed to it. Filling the floor a dark form sits.
 From the other side of millions of years the soul of the ancestors of Shankar's people looks at Puran, and the glance is so prehistoric that Puran's brain cells, spreading a hundred antennae, understand nothing of that glance. If tonight he'd seen a stone flying with its wings spread, would he have been able to speak to it?
 The creature is breathing, its body is trembling. Puran backs off with measured steps. (p. 141)

Following Spivak's lead, Mahasweta's postcolonialist readers have tended to focus on her delineation of the structural implications of the power differential in relations between elite and subaltern characters.[66] But the direct introduction of the soul of the ancestors into her story[67] changes its focus dramatically, enabling Mahasweta to move beyond this kind of deconstructive exercise to engage boldly with what, in the postcolonial discussion, has tended to be indefinitely deferred: namely, the *content* of subaltern consciousness. Indeed, 'Pterodactyl' offers to represent not merely the content of subaltern consciousness – which, like any situated consciousness, is of course limited, partial, interested (in a word, *ideological*) – but also the reconstructed *truth* that subaltern consciousness only partially represents. The most extraordinary and resonant passages in the story are those in which the narrative reaches out beyond the individual consciousnesses of elite and subaltern characters alike, to articulate a transcendental understanding attributed either to the soul of the ancestors or left unattributed, and therefore appearing as something like a narratorial consciousness. Consider the following paragraphs, for instance, in which Bikhia and Puran are sitting together, jointly observing the embodied soul of the ancestors as, having taken on fleshly form in an unavailing attempt to convey its message to the living generations, it prepares to recede once more into immateriality. First:

Bikhia is witnessing that their ancestors' soul embodied itself and flew in one day, and now it's leaving its form and returning. If it were truly that? Would it have told all the tribals of the burial-grounds in the extinct settlement, lying underneath the *bridges* and paths, the new settlements and fields of grain, that our descendants are disappearing? Their existence is freshly endangered. To survive they must mingle in the mainstream, where their social position will be on the ground floor and their sense of ethnic being will no longer be distinct. Yet there is no liberation for them if they hang on with their teeth to the hillside of Pirtha, their land and their soil have turned to dust and blown away in the wind. Who can catch dust-motes from the wind and compose village, forest, field? Bikhia's eyes are like the still flame of a lamp, he wants to see his fill of the noble death of this noble myth. (p. 180)

Here we see what Bikhia is seeing and thinking, but also what lies beyond his powers of comprehension and understanding. The writing is given its distinctive character by the ceaseless shifting of its representational lens, its swooping in and out of Bikhia's consciousness, its oscillation between situated and transcendental understandings, sometimes even within a single sentence. Thus the opening sentence of the extract presents us with an extradiegetically situated omniscient narrator reporting on what Bikhia is doing and thinking: 'Bikhia is witnessing …' *What* Bikhia is witnessing is then represented in the terms of his own mode of conceptualisation. The very next sentence, however – 'If it were truly that …?' – exceeds and indeed problematises this mode of conceptualisation, moving beyond it to cast doubt not so much on its plausibility as on its *reach*: it seems that some aspects of the incarnation of the soul of the ancestors cannot be accommodated or made sense of in terms of the 'tribal' understanding. The sentence that follows this, in turn, is tremendously complex, beginning with a question that derives from beyond the horizon of 'tribal' understanding – 'Would it have told all the tribals ...?' – but ending once more within the bounds of tribal intelligibility – 'that *our* descendants are disappearing' (emphasis added). Having thus re-entered the circle of tribal intelligibility, the paragraph then departs it again, offering, in a register that we must presume conjoins 'tribal' and 'modern' perspectives, a harsh summary of the prospects for the survival of the tribe: 'Their existence is freshly endangered. To survive they must mingle in the mainstream, where their social position will be on the ground floor and their sense of ethnic being will no longer be distinct.' The only alternative to this debased mode of survival is to seek to withdraw from majoritarian 'India' ('the mainstream'): but this is declared to be too costly an enterprise, and in fact impractical – the land to which the community has now been restricted is arid and unforgiving and will not allow their subsistence. The final sentence of this paragraph then returns us to the optics of its opening, with an extradiegetically situated omniscient narrator observing Bikhia's desire 'to see his fill of the noble death of this noble myth'.

The next paragraph centres on Puran, or rather revolves around him, again swooping between immanent and transcendental axes of focalisation:

Puran is witnessing his own futility. Having seen history from beyond pre-history, continental drift, seasonal changes after much geological turbulence, the advent of the human race, primordial history, the history of the ancient lands, the Middle Ages, the present age, two World Wars, Hiroshima-Nagasaki, holding under its wing this entire history and the current planetary arms race and the terror of nuclear holocaust, it came to give some sharply urgent news. Puran, a modern man, could not read the message in its eyes. Nothing could be known, can be known. One has to leave finally without knowing many things one should definitely have known. Seeing that Puran had understood nothing its eyes were closed since yesterday. The body seemed slowly to sink down, a body crumbling on its four feet, the head on the floor, in front of their eyes the body suddenly begins to tremble steadily. It trembles and trembles, and suddenly the wings open, and they go back in repose, this pain is intolerable to the eye. Bikhia goes on saying something in a soundless mumble, moving his lips. He sways, he mumbles, sways forward and back.

About an hour later Puran says, 'Gone'. (p. 180)

Again, a realist opening, with a situated character and an extradiegetically situated omniscient narrator, gives way to an arrestingly counterintuitive participial clause – 'Having seen history' – whose grammatical subject we must initially suppose to be Puran himself, but that turns out instead to be the soul of the ancestors – 'it came to give some sharply urgent news'. Puran himself could not in fact be the subject of this sentence, because the 'history' to which this subject is said to have borne witness is nothing less than universal history itself – not merely the history that runs, in Adorno's unforgettable phrase, 'from the slingshot to the megaton bomb',[68] but the non-human 'history' of the world before 'the advent of the human race'. The sentence that follows then returns to Puran and measures the limits of his understanding; and this sentence is followed, in turn, by two further sentences – 'Nothing could be known, can be known. One has to leave finally without knowing many things one should definitely have known' – whose attribution is uncertain. Do these sentences register a dawning awareness on Puran's part of the human costs of the socially and historically determined boundedness of his understanding, of the fact, paradoxical though it might sound, that what he knows may be the direct cause of some of what he does not and cannot know? The final sentences of the paragraph are narrated from the standpoint of Puran and Bikhia, who watch the soul of the ancestors in its death throes: Mahasweta's syntax shifts from past to present tense as the creature prepares to depart the material world.

If their encounter with the soul of the ancestors has temporarily brought Puran and Bikhia together, as the sharers of a tremendous secret, then their unity does not survive the creature's demise. In Bikhia's eyes in the aftermath of the creature's death/departure, Puran reads what he takes to be an assertion, or at least an acknowledgement, of the radical incommensurability of their world-views – which assertion Puran himself then comes to acknowledge as an unalterable truth concerning their relationship:

Now Bikhia's eyes explain that this strange situation had made them one but they were never really one. As if in a strange situation of war two people from separate worlds and lives, who do not understand one another's language, were obliged to cross some icy ravine, or to pass an unknown and violent desert, and then complete mutual help became necessary. A time of danger has brought them together. Although their hands were clasped at the end of the episode of danger they realized that they belong to two different worlds. This is not just two classes going back to their separate habitations. (p. 182)

Bikhia and Puran both come to the conclusion that while they can communicate meaningfully with one another, they live in different conceptual (and thence material) worlds, each definitively closed to the other. Their mere ability to speak to one another does not enable the 'fusion of horizons' (*Horizontverschmelzung*) upon which hermeneutic philosophers such as Hans-Georg Gadamer have placed such emphasis.[69]

The key question for us, in these terms, is whether Mahasweta's text itself endorses this conviction, reached by both Bikhia and Puran, that the 'gulf' fixed between elite and subaltern forms of consciousness (p. 140) is not only vast but untranscendable. Certainly, this is the message that Puran himself conveys to Harisharan once he has left Pirtha: 'there is no meeting-point with them', he says, in an explicit assertion of the premise of incommensurability. 'The ways are parallel from the distant past' (pp. 182–3). But Mahasweta's text leads us to suspend judgement on what Puran states here: we read that as he '[looks] at Bikhia's tawny matted hair, freshly shaven face' in the days after their shared encounter with the soul of the ancestors, Puran 'understood that they [the tribal peoples] were being defeated as they were searching in this world for a reason for the ruthless unconcern of government and administration. It was then that the shadow of that bird with its wings spread came back as at once *myth* and analysis' (p. 193). We must ask ourselves what Puran understands in understanding this. When it dawns on him that Bikhia's people are searching for an explanation of their plight, and that this search will inevitably fail, does he not gain a degree of insight into the tribal structure of feeling? How else to explain the fact that it is precisely with this incipient awareness that 'the shadow of that bird with its wings spread' should come back to him, and significantly in the conjoint avatar of myth *and* analysis, of codifying aesthetic representation *and* decoding discursive representation?

Two points can be made here, finally. First, that Puran, recognising the limits of his own culturally determined understanding, is able both to assess the social costs of what this understanding has bracketed or extinguished, and also to glimpse how the centuries-old pattern of marginalisation and destruction might even now begin to be unpicked: 'We built no communication point to establish contact with the tribals', he says to Harisharan:

> Leaving it undiscovered, we have slowly destroyed a continent in the name of civilization.
> There isn't anything at all?
> Nothing at all.
> It is impossible to build it?
> To build it you must love beyond reason for a long time. For a few thousand years we haven't loved them, respected them. Where is the time now, at the last gasp of the century? Parallel ways, their world and our world are different, we have never had a real exchange with them, it could have enriched us. (p. 195)

Second, we must register the space that Mahasweta's text establishes between itself and Puran's consciousness. 'Bikhia has probably understood what the pterodactyl, seeking shelter, had come to say', the text tells us.

'*Puran has not*' (p. 195). The words that follow, and that drive the story towards its conclusion, must be attributed not to Puran but to the narratorial consciousness. They take up Puran's evocation of 'love' – but, placing it within a larger, essentially pan-historical frame, simply and quietly assume the authority to speak of and for Bikhia's people and the tribal ancestors. The text leaves us with the idea that there is a link between the sustainability of human life itself and recovery of the forms of tribal sociality – and that responsibility for establishing this link lies with Puran and, more generally, with 'India' and with 'us' (her presumptive readers). What is said partly echoes what Puran has already said, but with vastly added significance:

Only love, a tremendous, excruciating, explosive love can still dedicate us to this work when the century's sun is in the western sky, otherwise this aggressive civilization will have to pay a terrible price, look at history, the aggressive civilization has destroyed itself in the name of progress, each time.

Love, excruciating love, let that be the first step. Now Puran's amazed heart discovers what love for Pirtha there is in his heart, perhaps he cannot remain a distant spectator anywhere in life.

Pterodactyl's eyes.

Bikhia's eyes.

Oh ancient civilization, the foundation and ground of the civilization of India, oh first sustaining civilization, we are in truth defeated. A continent! We destroyed it undiscovered, as we are destroying the primordial forest, water, living beings, the human. (pp. 195–6)

CHAPTER 4

Frantz Fanon after the 'postcolonial prerogative'

The work of Frantz Fanon served as a central node of focus, discussion, and dispute in the institutionalisation and consolidation of postcolonial studies during the 1980s and 1990s. This much is uncontroversial. Fanon's writings were typically granted a formative, stabilising status in the various readers published during those years, that aimed to set a theoretical and substantive agenda for the field and to provide it with an archive and a canon;[1] and if the best-known surveys, primers, and introductions to the field tended to devote pride of place to individual chapters on Edward W. Said, Gayatri Chakravorty Spivak, and Homi K. Bhabha – the three critics whose publications they typically presented as field-defining – rather than to Fanon, they nevertheless all took time to acknowledge and explore the centrality of Fanon 'beyond' or 'behind' the emergent critical discussion.[2] Scholars in the emergent field looked to Fanon as they looked to no other politico-intellectual active in the decolonising era. There was, to be sure, intermittent – in individual instances, sustained – discussion of such figures as James and Césaire and Senghor, Castro and Guevara, Nehru and Gandhi, Nkrumah, Nyerere, Nasser, and Cabral – even, if much more infrequently, Ho Chi Minh or Mao or Sukarno. But Fanon was the only figure from this era with whose work it was considered *essential* to be familiar. In this respect, Fanon was not first among equals. Instead, he stood alone – sometimes, indeed (and overall, rather too often) as the *only* figure from the decolonising era whose work was known to the aspirant critic.

It was clear from the outset, moreover, that the 'Fanon' that was being construed and constructed within the field was a thinker whose predilections and dispositions were constellated with those of 'post'-theoretical discourse – with 'Theory', as that term was used in the circuits of culture studies across the anglophone academic world during these years. In an influential essay of 1991, Henry Louis Gates, Jr speculated that 'Fanon's current fascination for us has something to do with the convergence of the problematic of colonialism with that of subject-formation. As a psychoanalyst of culture, as a champion of the wretched of the earth, he is an almost irresistible figure for a criticism that sees itself as both oppositional and postmodern'.[3] Gates called for a corrective 're-historicisation' of Fanon. Throughout the 1980s and 1990s a number of other scholars – I among them – were sounding a similar call, urging a more strenuously contextualised and politically discriminating engagement with Fanon and his work.[4] For the most part, however, the 'Fanon' that one encountered in postcolonial studies during those years was a post-structuralist *avant la lettre*: his work was taken to stage a deconstructive critique of 'western' humanism; to propound a colonially and racially inflected variant of Lacan's theory of identity formation; to refuse all notions of fixed identity and all forms of identitarian politics – including those organised under the banners of 'race' and class and nation – in the name of a restless, resolutely anti-essentialist tarrying with the negative. This same general construction of Fanon underpinned most of the defining commentaries on him in the emerging critical literature.[5]

My own sense is that this 'postcolonial' ideologeme of Fanon would have collapsed under the weight of its own myriad and accumulating contradictions soon enough. (Certainly, its radical selectivity and historical implausibility seemed obvious from the outset to most of the scholars who, prior to the advent of postcolonial studies, had researched Fanon's social and intellectual formation and the development of his politics. There is an almost complete disconnect between the previously established and the 'postcolonial' critical literatures on Fanon.)[6] But before it imploded, its residual credibility and prestige were demolished quite spectacularly by the publication, in 2000, of David Macey's magisterial biography, *Frantz Fanon: A Life*.[7]

Macey's study is one of those rare works that breaks open the field into which it intervenes, enforcing in the process a reconfiguration not only of its boundaries but also of its internal arrangements and relations. In what follows, I shall discuss Macey's presentation of Fanon in some detail, before returning to consider some of the directions that research into Fanon's work has taken in the years since the publication of Macey's book. For these are years that have also been marked, of course, by '9/11' and the subsequent invasion and occupation of Iraq as part of the US-orchestrated 'war on terror' – developments that would themselves clearly have mandated a reassessment of Fanon's status and contemporary relevance, even if *Frantz Fanon: A Life* had not been published.

II

Macey begins his book with an account of Fanon's funeral in December 1961 – the 'first and only time in the war of independence they had been waging since November 1954' that the FLN (Front de Libération National) and ALN (Armée de la Libération Nationale) would be 'able to bury one of their own with full honours' in Algerian soil (p. 3). Representing the Provisional Government of the Algerian Republic (GPRA), Belkacem Krim commended Fanon for his general 'commitment to the struggle against [colonialist] oppression' and for his particular commitment to 'our liberation movement'. 'You devoted your life to the cause of freedom, dignity, justice and good', Krim declared in his eulogy. 'Although you are dead, your memory will live on and will always be evoked by the noblest figures of our Revolution' (qtd Macey, *A Life*, pp. 4–5).

Macey proposes that in the years since 1961 the 'meaning' of Fanon has tended to be framed schematically. He identifies two conflicting and incompatible schemas, each in its own way historically determinate.[8] The first of these, to which Fanon himself was a conscious if only partial contributor, was liberationist Third-Worldism. As an ideologeme, this schema corresponded to, and purported to represent, the upsurge of revolutionary anticolonial nationalism in the post-1945 period. The second schema is then that ensuing from the containment and rolling back of insurgent anticolonial nationalism by the imperialist powers since 1975 or so, and also, accordingly, from the assumed obsolescence of the earlier liberationist Third-Worldist ideologeme.

The Third-Worldist Fanon corresponds to the era of insurgent nationalism and liberation struggle. 'The period of ... "revolutionary Algeria"', Macey writes,

represents the high tide of French Third Worldism, and Fanon helped to create that Third Worldism. A generation's disillusionment with the orthodox left, and particularly with the Communist Party coincided with the rise of nationalism in the Third World and gave birth to the belief that the emergence of new states there would create a new humanism or even a new socialism. Algeria, like Cuba, seemed to have a leading role in this process of rebirth. (pp. 20–1)

The Third-Worldist Fanon is the Fanon who writes, in the opening lines of the opening essay of *The Wretched of the Earth*, that decolonisation – 'always a violent phenomenon' – amounts, 'quite simply', to 'the replacing of a certain "species" of men by another "species" of men. Without any period of transition, there is a total, complete, and absolute substitution . . . To tell the truth, the proof of success lies in a whole social structure being changed from the bottom up . . . Decolonization . . . sets out to change the order of the world' (Fanon, *Wretched of the Earth*, p. 35).

This Fanon is disposed, by virtue of his objective situation (to say nothing of his characterological dispositions), to conflate decolonisation with revolution.[9] In his Third-Worldist avatar – which, it is necessary to emphasise, is not the only guise he assumes, not even in his most consistently Third-Worldist texts – Fanon tends to collapse class struggle and national liberation struggle into one another, thus ignoring the specificities and irreducibilities of each.

The weaknesses of Fanon's Third-Worldist formulations were evident from the outset, and – to the degree that they were discussed during his lifetime – they were criticised as such, within the Algerian national movement itself as well as in wider socialist discussions. Yet it was not despite but precisely *because of* his Third-Worldism that Fanon came to be taken up in the years following his death in 1961, as his writings began to find a very particular audience. Not in Algeria, where, as Macey observes, he was and has remained very little read; nor in France; nor in the Caribbean, not even in the francophone territories and not even in his birthplace, Martinique; and nor in sub-Saharan Africa, where, as the novelist Ayi Kwei Armah (Ghanaian by nationality, pan-Africanist by ideological disposition) lamented in an article written in 1969, Fanon was scarcely known at all, whether in anglophone or francophone circles.[10] Instead, in the United States, where the posthumous *Les Damnés de la terre* was first published in English translation as *The Wretched of the Earth* in 1965, and its analysis quickly extrapolated to the then emergent black nationalist and liberationist discourse. (Hence the American Black Cat edition of 1968, whose front cover heralded 'The handbook for the black revolution that is changing the shape of the world', and whose blurb read as follows: 'written in anger, this book by a distinguished Black psychiatrist and leading spokesman of the revolution which won independence for Algeria is no mere diatribe against the white man or the West. It is a brilliant examination of the role of violence in effecting historical change which has served leaders of emerging nations as a veritable handbook of revolutionary practice and social reorganization.')

Macey correctly links the waning of this Third-Worldist Fanon to developments in the wider world. But he is not, I think, quite precise enough in his delineation of what he calls the 'ebb of Third Worldism' (p. 21). Sharper accounts have been presented by Samir Amin, above all in his *Capitalism in the Age of Globalization* and – within postcolonial studies – by such writers as Aijaz Ahmad, Arif Dirlik, and Timothy Brennan.[11] The key point, I take it, is that the containment or recuperation, starting in the 1970s, of the historic challenge from the 'Third World' that had been expressed in the struggle for decolonisation in the post-1945 years must be seen in the light of the global reassertion and consolidation of what Amin calls 'the logic of unilateral capital'. If the crescendo of revolutionary anticolonialism was reached with the defeat of the American forces in Vietnam and the overthrow of fascism in Portugal and of Portuguese colonialism in Guinea-Bissau, Mozambique, and Angola in the mid 1970s, the thirty-five years since then have seen the triumph of neo-liberalism and the reassertion of an imperialist world order, now headquartered in the United States. The misadventures in Iraq and Afghanistan have been but the latest notes to be sounded in this latter cacophony.

It is within this latter phase, of 'globalisation' and the reassertion of imperialism, that the academic field of postcolonial studies has emerged. And it is within postcolonial studies that the second schematic construction of Fanon identified by Macey arose. Since the Third-Worldist mytheme of Fanon was quite manifestly unsuitable to this emerging field's ideological project, it was necessary to construct a new one: a 'postcolonial' Fanon, a Fanon not for or of his own times, but rather for and of 'ours' – where 'we' are taken to be those living in 'post'-time, for whom (around 1975) everything changed, such that in the aftermath 'we' are not only 'post-colonial', but also post-nationalist, post-liberationist, post-Marxist, and post-modern. 'The "post-colonial" Fanon', Macey writes, 'is in many ways an inverted image of the "revolutionary Fanon" of the 1960s':

'Third Worldist' readings largely ignored the Fanon of *Peau noire, masques blancs*, post-colonial readings concentrate almost exclusively on that text and studiously avoid the question of violence. The Third Worldist Fanon was an apocalyptic creature; the post-colonial Fanon worries about identity politics, and often about his own sexual identity, but he is no longer angry. (p. 28)

Macey deplores not only the studied depoliticising (which is to say, *repoliticising*) of Fanon's career, but also the dehistoricising thrust of the postcolonialist scholarship, the crushing selectivity and attenuation of the 'intellectual' or 'theoretical' contexts to which Fanon's thought and writing are related. He argues that

The recent crop of books and articles – and one film – on Fanon . . . construct a Fanon who exists outside time and space and in a purely textual dimension . . . [F]ew of the authors concerned stray far away from the most familiar of his texts and appear to have consulted nothing produced by the FLN. Post-colonial theorists' enthusiasm for Derrida and Lacan tends to blind them to Fanon's debts to Sartre and Merleau-Ponty, not to mention the similarities between his work and that of his contemporaries Albert Memmi and Jean Amrouche. (p. 27)

One of the signal achievements of *Frantz Fanon: A Life*, in these terms, is to put paid, more or less definitively, to arguments that the 'postcolonial' Fanon plausibly registers the thrust and substance of Fanon's actual thought or writing. As Macey remarks, in one of the many asides that he directs tellingly at the theorist whose scholarly production over the course of the past quarter-century has been largely responsible for conjuring the 'postcolonial' Fanon into existence, '[Homi] Bhabha's claim that there is no "master narrative" in *Peau noire* has surely to be countered by the argument that there is most definitely a master narrative at work in *L'An V de la révolution algérienne* and *Les Damnés de la terre*. It is the narrative of the Algerian Revolution. It may be difficult to believe in it at the beginning of a new millennium, but Fanon did believe in it and died for it' (p. 28).

As I have already mentioned, Macey is neither the first nor the only person to argue this case. But his contribution to this still unfolding critique is particularly welcome. To read his study is to recognise that there is no future for the illusion that has been the 'postcolonial' Fanon. Put crudely, Homi Bhabha's Fanon simply cannot be squared either with Fanon's actual writings or with the trajectory of Fanon's own career. The weight and authority of the counter-evidence adduced in Macey's book is sufficient to strip the warrant not only from Bhabha's work on Fanon (at least to the degree that this work is taken to be a commentary *on Fanon* rather than on 'postcoloniality' or the 'globalised' world order), but also from that of the many postcolonial critics who have predicated their own commentaries on Fanon on it. Macey dismisses in passing, in this respect, Isaac Julien's influential film, *Frantz Fanon: Black Skin, White Mask* and Alan Read's edited volume, *The Fact of Blackness: Frantz Fanon and Visual Representation*. But the names of any number of other postcolonial critics of the 1980s and 1990s could be added to this list.

III

To say that Macey's book effectively blows the 'postcolonial' Fanon out of the water is not, of course, to say that it exonerates the earlier schema of the Third-Worldist Fanon. On the contrary: Macey tends, as I have already suggested, to cast the Third-Worldist and the postcolonialist schemas as mirror images of one another. Both appropriate Fanon for their own historically specific projects; both construct him in the image of their own ideological concerns.

What Macey sets out to do instead is to paint a picture of Fanon as a radically singular figure, not a representative one. His study offers both a fine-grained historicisation of its subject (such that we see Fanon constantly in context) and a view on to a quite irreducible life, from which it seems particularly unsound to generalise. After an opening chapter (from which all of my citations thus far have been drawn), metatheoretical in character and entitled 'Forgetting Fanon, Remembering Fanon' (another swipe at Bhabha, whose preface to a 1986 reissue of the English version of *Black Skin, White Masks*, had been entitled 'Remembering Fanon'), Macey gives detailed consideration to Fanon's childhood in Martinique, his wartime experiences, his training as a psychiatrist and subsequent practice in France, his posting to Algeria and – most extensively – his politicisation and revolutionary activism on behalf of the movement for national liberation in Algeria between 1956 and his death in 1961. I will not attempt here to rehearse or even summarise this exposition. Rather, I will highlight certain aspects that, considered together, give insight into the 'line' on Fanon that Macey unfolds over the course of his book.[12]

A good place to start might be with Fanon's anger, to which Macey gives special emphasis, characterising it as the one 'truly Fanonian emotion' (p. 28). He quotes from a January 1945 letter which Fanon wrote to his brother, Joby, from a military hospital in France. (He was in the hospital recovering from wounds he had incurred fighting with the Free French.) The letter is marked by its bitterness of tone: Fanon had come to realise, writes Macey, 'that freedom was not indivisible. He was a black soldier in a white man's army' (p. 103). Specifically, he had learned that his volunteerism on behalf of abstract principles of 'freedom', 'France', 'anti-fascism', counted for nothing in the eyes of the majority of French citizens, for whom he remained a black man, and, as such, unassimilable – indelibly other if not necessarily onto-genetically inferior. In another letter, to his parents, in April 1945, he wrote: 'Nothing here, nothing justifies my sudden decision to defend the interests of farmers who don't give a damn' (p. 104). The 'sudden decision' refers to the impulsive flight he had made from Martinique to Dominica as a 17-year-old in 1943 to sign up to fight with the Free French in the war. Impulsiveness and anger exist side by side in his make-up. His rage is volcanic and abrupt (if, in its *social* dimensions, at least, a response to deeply layered and long-standing injustice: hence massively overdetermined). As he would write in a key sequence in the 1952 *Black Skin, White Masks*,

Where shall I find shelter from now on? I felt an easily identifiable flood mounting out of the countless facets of my being. I was about to be angry. The fire was long since out, and once more the nigger was trembling.

'Look how handsome the Negro is! ...'

'Kiss the handsome Negro's ass, madame!'

Shame flooded her face. At last I was set free from my rumination. At the same time I accomplished two things: I identified my enemies and I made a scene. A grand slam. Now one would be able to laugh. (p. 114)

Macey suggests that to anger and impulsiveness in the Fanonian character we have also to add irrevocability. The decisions Fanon takes are not only made in the blink of an eye, 'spontaneously', as it were, but, once made, are set in stone, irreversible. Thus of his decision to leave France for Algeria in 1953, for instance, Macey writes that it

was taken as suddenly as those that had taken Fanon to Dominica in 1943 and to Lyon in 1946. In an undated letter, he unexpectedly told his brother Joby: 'I'm going to Algeria. You understand: the French have enough psychiatrists to take care of their madmen. I'd rather go to a country where they need me.' Philippe Lucas, a sociologist who knew Fanon in Algeria, reports a conversation with Josie Fanon [Fanon's wife] in which she told him that whilst Fanon settled on Blida after a process of elimination, or in other words because no other post appealed to him, he also had an 'obvious' preference for working in the colonies rather than in the metropolis. Once taken, the decision was, as always, irrevocable. (p. 203)

The characterological features that Macey identifies in Fanon include his explosive rage against injustice, his impulsiveness, the intensity of his ethical disposition, his personal courage, the passion and relentlessness of his intellectual commitments, and the impatience and urgency of his political ones. These are all paradigmatically *modernist* structures of feeling, and it is in precisely these terms– rather than as any kind of postmodernist *avant la lettre* – that Macey situates Fanon in his thought and action. 'In *Peau noire, masques blancs*, Fanon's vocabulary is that of the modernism of the 1940s', he writes at one point (p. 127); and of that book in general, he argues compellingly that

[t]he best way to approach [it] ... is to regard it as an extended exercise in *bricolage*, the term Lévi-Strauss used to describe how myths are assembled from the materials that are to hand; the word literally means 'do it yourself'. *Bricolage* is a good way of describing just what Fanon was doing as he plundered the libraries and bookshops of Lyon and then strode up and down, dictating his text to Josie. The main materials to hand were the phenomenology of Sartre and Merleau-Ponty, the cultural discourse or tradition of negritude, the psychiatry in which Fanon had just trained, and the fragments of psychoanalytic theory he had

absorbed from books. His relationship with his raw materials was never easy – the relationships with negritude and psychoanalysis were particularly fraught – and their synthesis was far from being a smooth one. To describe *Peau noire* as the product of *bricolage* is not to disparage either Fanon or his book. The term quite simply describes what he was doing: using elements of a then modernist philosophy and psychoanalysis to explore and analyse his own situation and experience, even though he had no real academic training as a philosopher and no extensive knowledge of psychoanalysis.[13] (pp. 162–3)

Macey is very persuasive in his explication of the problematic or field of vision of *Black Skin, White Masks*. Like Patrick Taylor, whose *The Narrative of Liberation* he surprisingly appears not to have read, he places particular emphasis on Fanon's phenomenological examination of the experience of racialisation in a colonial world.[14] In passing, he demonstrates how inadequate is the available English translation of Fanon's text, which among other things inexplicably renders the title of the key chapter on 'The Lived Experience [*l'expérience vécue*] of the Black Man' as 'The Fact of Blackness', thereby reifying into an objective and pre-existent social datum precisely the relational and praxiological instance ('race', coming to know oneself as 'black' in a 'white' world) that Fanon sets out to examine. Addressing the Fanonian category of 'lived experience', Macey sketches its derivation from the German *Erlebnis*. This is the term used by Husserl and Heidegger and then drawn into French philosophy by Merleau-Ponty – above all in his *The Phenomenology of Perception*[15] – to designate 'experience' not, as that term is usually understood, as the effect on a subject of events unfolding in the world around it, but rather as a mode of being *in* the world. To 'experience', in this sense, is 'to be in internal communication with the world, the body and other, to be with them rather than alongside them' (Merleau-Ponty, qtd Macey, *A Life*, p. 164). Fanon takes up the category of 'lived experience', in these terms, in order to develop his idea that 'blackness' is not a matter of self-actualisation but of social inscription. As Macey writes,

Fanon speaks of the need to understand the man of colour 'in the dimension of his being-for-others [*pour-autrui*]'. This dimension situates his man of colour in a world in which he never exists in-himself as a monad, but always in a conflict-ridden relationship with others, or the other. He exists to the extent that he is seen and heard by others, to the extent that he *is* for others. So too the white man. Hence the concluding argument that the negro 'is' not (does not exist), and nor 'is' the white man. Trapped in their respective 'whiteness' and 'blackness', they 'are' only insofar as they create one another, though this does not imply any reciprocity. (p. 164)

IV

When Fanon left France to take up a position as *médécin-chef* at the Blida-Joinville psychiatric hospital in Algeria in 1953, he knew very little about Algeria. He had had some professional dealings with North African patients in Lyon. But he spoke no Arabic, had done no specialist reading about the Maghreb, and was more or less completely uninformed about the explosive political situation in Algeria. Certainly, he was disposed to identify with Algerians on the basis of their colonisation by France – there are 'tears to be dried throughout the whole French territory (the metropolis and the French union)', Macey quotes him as writing (p. 203); but he did not move to Algeria out of any sense of political commitment. As Macey observes,

There is no hint that Fanon believed in 1953 that Algeria should be an independent nation. Although he had every sympathy with the people of Algeria, he had no real vision of their future. At this point, his politics consisted of the 'humanist solidarity' that informs *Peau noire, masques blancs* and he was not a member of any political organization or party … Fanon did not go to Algeria armed with any decisive truths or revolutionary doctrines. He did not go there as the apocalyptic prophet of the Third Worldism of *Les Damnés de la terre*. Nothing in his early work anticipates the theses on the cleansing and liberating effects of revolutionary violence with which he would become so closely associated. The Fanon of *Les Damnés de la terre* was a product of Algeria and its war of independence. (pp. 203–4)

Having previously worked both in Lyon and at the celebrated Saint-Alban hospital, Fanon had had some exposure to the most progressive trends then obtaining in French psychiatry. In Algeria, however, he found himself face to face with colonial psychiatry. It was not only that medical practice in Algeria generally was heavily corrupt. It was also, and more importantly, that medicine was 'an integral part of an oppressive system' (p. 217). Many French doctors in Algeria, as Macey explains,

regarded their patients as little better than animals, and described themselves as practising veterinary medicine. Some of Fanon's colleagues in Blida also had lucrative private practices, and did not view their work in the hospital as a full-time commitment. For other doctors working in Algiers, the Blida hospital was no more than a convenient dumping ground for patients whose conditions were such that they could not be effectively – or profitably – treated in the private sector. Fanon accepted that there were decent and humane European doctors working in Algeria, but added 'It is said of them that "They are not like the others."' (pp. 217–18)

The violence of psychiatric practice in Algeria rested on 'doctrinal founda-tions', which, as Fanon was to write in 1956, in his justly famous letter of resignation to the Resident Minister, Governor General of Algeria, consti-tuted 'a daily defiance of an authentically human outlook'.[16] Like medicine more generally, psychiatry as it was practised in Algeria represented an extension – a rationalisation and even a refinement – of colonial thought and administration. Fundamentally racist in its assumptions, the psychiatry of the 'Algiers school' *began* by defining Algerian culture, Maghrebian culture, and Muslim culture in terms of pathology and criminality – which meant, of course, that its subsequent diagnosis of the *expression* of such cultures on the part of individual Algerians, Arabs, and Muslims, as pathological and criminal, was merely tautological. Macey refers to Antoine Porot, the founder of the 'Algiers school', who, in an article published in 1918, had deplored 'the Muslim native's remarkable propen-sity for the passive life, his habitual insouciance about the future, and his childlike credulity and stubbornness' (p. 223). He quotes Porot directly as asserting that it is very difficult to construct a psychology of the Muslim native because 'there is so much mobility, and so many contradictions in a mentality that has developed on such a different level to our own, and which is governed both by the most rudimentary instincts and a sort of religious and fatalistic metaphysics' (p. 223). Other 'Algiers school' psych-iatrists sounded many of the same notes, characterising Algerians in general as 'credulous and suggestible ... prone to outbursts of homicidal rage, fanatical, possessively jealous and fatalistic' (p. 223). Islam itself was directly implicated in 'Algiers school' representations: a 'pathogenic agent', its supposed 'symptoms' included 'fatalism, an obsession with words (the repeated "Allah, Allah"), delusional sadness, the perversion of the sexual instinct (masturbation and pederasty), and auditory hallucinations that provoke sudden outbursts of violence' (p. 221). An influential study pub-lished in 1908 cast Islam as a contagious epidemic, which it was necessary to extirpate root and branch: 'Islam does not bring with it any justification for its existence, because it is *destructive*. It neither creates nor produces anything, and therefore could not survive at all if it could not live parasitic-ally on human groups that do work' (qtd p. 221).

We can note in passing the persistence of these tawdry Orientalist conceptions as to the pathology and incorrigibility of 'Islam' and 'Arab culture', which today are wheeled out by American and European war-mongers eager to justify the terrorism of their own 'war on terrorism'.[17] Fanon, at least, was quick to realise that theories built on a priori assump-tions concerning a 'clash of civilisations', and buttressed by cultural

supremacism, were ideological in the strict sense: that is to say, they served
as a cover or active justification for colonialist or imperialist domination.
Yet although he would come to define psychiatry as an impossibility in a
society steeped, as was the Algeria of the 1950s, in murderous violence,
he did achieve some notable successes in his attempts to render the
provision of psychiatric services at Blida-Joinville compatible with his
broader socialist and humanist ideals. Not that these successes came easy.
On the contrary, they were preceded, and continued to be accompanied,
by signal failures. (Macey's scrupulous account gives the lie to the facile
postcolonialist idyll of Fanon as 'healer/liberator'.) In one of his essays in
The Wretched of the Earth, Fanon was famously to write that

> If the building of a bridge does not enrich the awareness of those who work on it,
> then that bridge ought not to be built and the citizens can go on swimming
> across the river or going by boat. The bridge should not be 'parachuted down'
> from above; it should not be imposed by a *deus ex machina* upon the social scene;
> on the contrary it should come from the muscles and the brains of the citizens.
> (*Wretched of the Earth*, pp. 200–1)

This insight evidently derived, in part at least, from Fanon's own experiences at Blida-Joinville. For at first his attempts to counter what Macey
calls 'the punitive culture of the hospital', and to replace it with a more
receptive and constructively interactive culture, foundered on mutual
incomprehension and mistrust. As Fanon himself wrote, in a 1954 paper
co-authored with his colleague, Jacques Azoulay, 'We were attempting to
create certain institutions, but we forgot that any attempt to do so has to
be preceded by a tenacious, concrete and real investigation into the
organic bases of the native society' (qtd Macey, *A Life*, p. 231). Macey
adds the summary comment that Fanon 'had spontaneously endorsed the
ideology of assimilation by expecting his patients to make the effort to
adapt to a Western culture. He now realized that he had to make the
transition to cultural relativism rather than assuming the superiority of
French culture' (p. 231). Increasingly, Fanon sought to introduce innovations to hospital protocols and procedures in accordance with cultural
norms in the wider Algerian society:

> The gradual process of cultural change began with the creation of that essential
> feature of male social life in North Africa – a Moorish café where patients could
> play dominoes or simply talk while sipping mint tea in a room decorated with
> their own paintings and furnished with both European chairs and tables and the
> traditional floor mats and low tables. Traditional festivals began to be celebrated
> and the local Mufti was invited to come to the hospital twice a month to lead
> Friday prayers. Inviting traditional story-tellers was a successful recognition of

the fact that the local culture was predominantly oral, but it was also a potentially dangerous move on Fanon's part. The colonial authorities had no love of wandering story-tellers who transmitted rumours as well as folk-tales, and such itinerants became objects of great suspicion when the war started. Itinerants carried news and spread rumours; stories could be an incitement to rebellion. Other innovations took Fanon closer still to a major rupture with the hospital authorities. He had discovered that men who could not be persuaded to weave baskets because that was 'women's work' could be persuaded to work in the grounds and to grow vegetables: 'Giving them a spade or a mattock is enough to make them start digging and hoeing.' It was also enough to terrify his European staff: these were the traditional weapons of peasant revolt and they had been used to deadly effect at Sétif; they would be used again to massacre European civilians in the Constantinois in the summer of 1955. (p. 233)

The goal of psychiatry, as Fanon understood it, was reconstitution, disalienation. Psychiatry, as he would put it in his letter of resignation to the Resident Minister, 'is the medical technique that aims to enable man no longer to be a stranger to his environment'.[18] But the longer he worked at Blida-Joinville, the more Fanon was made to see that the conditions of possibility for psychiatric disalienation were definitively lacking in the social universe of Algeria in the mid 1950s. Hence his argument to the Resident Minister that 'the Arab, permanently an alien in his own country, lives in a state of absolute depersonalization' (*Toward the African Revolution*, p. 53). Such a state – which he also termed 'systematized de-humanization' – could not be *psychically* redeemed, since, as he put it, '[t]he social structure existing in Algeria was hostile to any attempt to put the individual back where he belonged' (p. 53). It was impossible to instantiate psychiatry, to give it a tangible and substantive authority – in a word, to make it work – in an environment in which 'the lawlessness, the inequality, the multi-daily murder of man were raised to the status of legislative principles' (p. 53).

v

Fanon's resignation from his position at Blida-Joinville in 1956 (and coincidentally from service in the French colonial state) freed him physically and ethically to dedicate himself to the cause of Algerian liberation. Macey offers a lucid and comprehensive account, both of the course of the war of independence that broke out in November 1954 and that soon thereafter exploded into full-scale revolution, and of Fanon's career during these years, as his own political philosophy radicalised sharply in response to the unfolding events in Algeria and he attempted to contribute his professional and intellectual skills to the revolutionary struggle.

The Fanon who emerges in such works as *L'An V de la Révolution algérienne*[19] and the posthumously published *Les Damnés de la terre* and *Pour la Révolution africaine* (the latter made up substantially of Fanon's writings for the underground FLN organ, *El Moudjahid*) is very much a product of the Algerian revolution. The overarching themes in this work include revolutionary nationalist anticolonialism, violence and counter-violence, popular political mobilisation, the relation between party and people and between proletarian and peasant classes, the role of culture and ideology in the furtherance of the struggle, and the Algerian conflict and its relevance for and relation to 'African' and 'Third World' liberation struggles.

Macey's account is sympathetic but not uncritical. He offers a cogent rebuttal, for instance, of the criticisms of those – such as Jean Daniel, Jean-Marie Domenach, and Hannah Arendt – who have charged Fanon with glorifying violence for its own sake. Quoting from the essay, 'Concerning Violence', in *The Wretched of the Earth* – 'What, in reality, is this violence? . . . It is the colonized masses' intuition that their liberation must come about, and can only come about, through force' – he argues that Fanon's critics have symptomatically misread him:

> In a sense, it is the term 'violence' itself that is so scandalous; had Fanon spoken of 'armed struggle' . . . [his argument] would have been much less contentious . . . Fanon does not 'glorify' violence and in fact rarely describes it in any detail: there are no descriptions of what happens when a bomb explodes in a crowded café and when shards of glass slice into human flesh. The violence Fanon evokes is instrumental and he never dwells or gloats on its effects. In a sense it is almost absurd to criticize Fanon for his advocacy of violence. He did not need to advocate it. The ALN was fighting a war and armies are not normally called upon to justify their violence. By 1961, the violence was everywhere.[20] (*A Life*, p. 475)

Macey suggests, however, that Fanon *is* inclined to generalise unwarrantedly from Algeria to Africa (and the 'Third World') at large, to derive abstract conclusions concerning the necessary course of decolonisation in any context or situation from specific and irreducible Algerian contexts and situations. When Fanon 'insists that a violent liberation struggle leads to a higher or purer form of independence', Macey writes, 'he is thinking of the future independence of Algeria. What he fails to recognize is that, in terms of the decolonization of "French" Africa at least, Algeria was the exception and not the rule' (p. 476).

Now one could argue that while Fanon is certainly right to insist that decolonisation is 'always a violent phenomenon' – 'always', because *colonisation* is always a violent phenomenon; nowhere in the colonial world was independence ever won without tremendous struggle on the part of the colonised – his theories concerning the centrality and, indeed, indispensability of violence in securing decolonisation are more readily applicable to *settler* formations than to 'administrative' colonies. In the former, it almost always proved necessary for the native population to resort to armed struggle to obtain independence; in the latter, independence was often achieved on the basis of 'negotiation' rather than the revolutionary overthrow of the recalcitrant colonial order. Is Fanon's theory then to be understood as grounding or presuming a distinction between decolonisation in settler and administrative colonies, such that the former, because of the revolutionary violence upon which it is predicated, tends to lead to 'a higher or purer form of independence'? The problem here is that if we look at developments *since* independence, there seems little correlation between the level of violence entailed in the liberation struggle and the subsequent success or failure of the revolution. National liberation won on the basis of armed struggle has not necessarily been stronger or more resilient or more deeply sedimented in popular consciousness than liberation secured on the basis of a negotiated transfer of power. (Nor necessarily *weaker* or *less* resilient, of course.) The accumulated examples of, say, Cuba, Nicaragua, Algeria, Vietnam, Zimbabwe, Guinea-Bissau, Mozambique, on the one hand, and India, Tunisia, Jamaica, Ghana, and Senegal, on the other, do not enable a clear-cut pattern to be discerned in this respect.

Macey quotes Francis Jeanson, philosopher, editor of the original French edition of *Peau noire, masques blancs*, subsequently an activist courageously committed to the cause of Algerian liberation, and author of *La Révolution algérienne* (1962), who wrote in 1965 that Fanon 'had a "terrible need" to take the most radical option and to reject any form of action that did not have an immediate influence on the direction of the struggle' (*A Life*, p. 303). This is a damaging assessment, which, if admitted, would certainly go some way towards accounting for the voluntarist tenor of some of Fanon's ideas and formulations. Macey mentions the dreadful mistake over Angola, for instance, where, quite largely at Fanon's insistence, the FLN resolved to lend the weight of its support (as one of the best established and internationally most influential of anticolonial liberation movements) to Roberto Holden's *Frente Nacional de Libertação de Angola*, celebrating both the brutality of FNLA cadres' premature, poorly conceived and ill-prepared assault on Portuguese settlers in 1961 and Holden's refusal, on racial grounds, to merge the FNLA with the mulatto-led *Movimento Popular de Libertação de Angola*, whose popular support and strategic intelligence greatly exceeded that of the FNLA. 'I know Holden is inferior to the MPLA men', Fanon conceded.

'But Holden is ready to begin and they are not. And I am convinced that what is necessary is to begin, and that an Angolan revolutionary movement will be formed in the ensuing struggle' (qtd Macey, *A Life*, p. 391). 'Over-confident and over-optimistic', Macey writes, 'insisting on "beginning now", and convinced that the Algerian model of the uprisings of 1956 could be exported to a country of which they had little concrete knowledge', Fanon and his colleagues in the FLN 'made a disastrous political miscalcu-lation' (p. 392). The Portuguese forces in Angola responded to the FNLA attacks by killing as many as 20,000 Angolans in terroristic reprisals. Moreover, the division within the anticolonial front took years to mend, drastically undermining the effectivity of the resistance.[21]

Fanon's voluntarism derives not from his advocacy of violence, but from what I have elsewhere called his 'messianism' – his tendency to assume the unity and coordinated political will of the masses of the Algerian population in contexts where it could not realistically have been supposed to exist (and where in historical restrospect it can in fact be demonstrated *not* to have existed). Macey speaks in this respect of Fanon's 'idealization' of the Algerian peasantry (*A Life*, pp. 483–4), and suggests illuminatingly that he sometimes 'mistook temporary changes born of extraordinary circumstances for a permanent revolution' (p. 406). Fanon clearly misread the mass recruitment of the Algerian peasantry to the FLN as testifying to their embrace of the FLN's platform. In *The Wretched of the Earth*, thus, he spoke of the 'upward thrust of the people', who had 'decided, in the name of the whole continent, to weigh in strongly against the colonial regime'; and, with reference to Africa at large, he eulogised the 'coordinated effort on the part of two hundred and fifty million men to triumph over stupidity, hunger, and inhumanity at the same time' (p. 164). Such formulations, which seemed implausible even at the time, cannot withstand scrutiny in hindsight. The point is that developments in the immediate postcolonial era cannot be reconciled with Fanon's evoca-tion of a disciplined and progressively unified population coming closer and closer to self-knowledge as the struggle against the French colonial forces intensified. For it seems inconceivable that, having been decisively and world-historically conscientised during the anticolonial struggle (as Fanon claims they had been), Algerians would have permitted themselves to be so easily and so quickly neutralised after decolonisation. The truth would rather seem to be that even when it was fighting under the FLN's leadership, the Algerian peasantry was never fully committed to the secular, socialist vision projected by the movement. (Macey suggests, in fact, that Fanon also tended to gloss over significant and, in the event, portentous divisions within the FLN itself.) Thus Ian Clegg's claim, on the basis of his research into peasant politics and state formation in Algeria in the years following independence in 1962, that

> The involvement of the population of the traditional rural areas in the independence struggle must be clearly separated from their passivity in face of its revolutionary aftermath. The peasants were fighting for what they regarded as their inheritance; a heritage firmly rooted in the Arab, Berber, and Islamic past. Their consciousness was rooted in the values and traditions of this past, and their aim was its re-creation.[22]

Clegg's analysis enables us to account both for the Algerian peasantry's commitment to the struggle for independence, on the one hand, and, on the other, for its lack of concerted militancy in the face of the FLN's (anti-socialist) policies of the years immediately following decolonisation, when '[n]either the peasantry nor the subproletariat played any other than a purely negative role in the events' (Clegg, 'Workers and Managers', p. 239). The general theoretical conclusion to be drawn here has been spelled out, in a different context, by the American academic James C. Scott as follows:

> [Peasant] resistance ... begins ... close to the ground, rooted firmly in the homely but meaningful realities of daily experience ... The *values* resisters are defending are equally near at hand and familiar. Their point of departure is the practices and norms that have proven effective in the past and appear to offer some promise of reducing or reversing the losses they suffer. The *goals* of resistance are as modest as its values. The poor strive to gain work, land, and income; they are not aiming at large historical abstractions such as socialism ... Even when such slogans as 'socialism' take hold among subordinate classes, they are likely to mean something radically different to the rank and file than to the radical intelligentsia.[23]

In this light, Clegg's complaint that Fanon 'lacks a critical and dialectical analysis of the process of the formation of consciousness' ('Workers and Managers', p. 239) rings as plausible and judicious. For Fanon's formulations *are* consistently intellectualist in tone, often phrasing subaltern thought and practice in the elitist-idealist vocabulary of negation, abstract totalisation, and self-actualisation.

VI

In his afterword, Macey recalls his first encounter with Fanon's work. This took place in 1970, during a year that he spent in Paris as part of his undergraduate degree in French. Macey writes that he 'read a lot' that year, and adds significantly that 'It was the beginning of the moment of theory, a time to read Althusser, Lacan and Foucault' (*A Life*, p. 502). We can infer from this description that the 20-year-old Englishman had no sooner discovered Fanon than he forgot him again. For in the light of 'Theory', with its anti-dialectical and anti-humanist emphases and its mistrust of the idea of revolution, Fanon quickly 'began to look naive'. Sophisticated, cool, insistently avant-gardist, 'Theory' duly swept all before it – in the academic circuits of the 'human sciences', at least – junking the past and imagining its own energies and exploits as epoch-making. Was it then only in the 1990s, as the credibility and prestige of this 'moment' was collapsing, that Macey turned again to Fanon? This is what I suspect. For it is hard to imagine that *Frantz Fanon: A Life* would or could have been written if the force had still been with 'Althusser, Lacan and Foucault'.

Writing in 2000 – at the wake of the 'moment of theory' – Macey proposes that the time is now right

to reread Fanon. Not to hear once more the call for violent revolution, but to recapture the quality of the anger that inspired it. Fanon does not speak for the tragic Algeria of today. The themes of Third World solidarity and unity, of a version of Pan-Africanism and of the liberating power of violence have not worn well. For a generation, Fanon was a prophet. He has become a witness to the process of decolonization but, whilst his discussion of racism remains valid, he has little to say about the outcome of that process.

Fanon was angry. His readers should still be angry too. Angry that Algerian immigrants could be treated with such contempt in a police station. Angry at the casual racism that still assumes that the black and North African youths of the suburbs are all criminals or at least potential criminals ... Angry at the cultural alienation that still afflicts the children of Martinique, so beautiful in their smart school uniforms and so convinced that they are just like other French children until someone teaches them otherwise. Angry at what has happened in Algeria. Angry that the wretched of the earth are still with us. Anger does not in itself produce political programmes for change, but it is perhaps the most basic political emotion. Without it, there is no hope. (p. 503)

These are moving lines, but the validity of the central claim that they lodge must, I think, be disputed. The 'wretched of the earth are still with us', Macey says: years after formal decolonisation, the world is still transparently structured in dominance – he mentions hostility towards immigrants and 'casual racism' on one side of the international division of labour; immiseration, 'cultural alienation' and disastrous, cynical misrule on the other. Macey wants us to be as angry about this state of affairs as Fanon had been about the state of affairs by which he had been confronted fifty years ago. Yet he maintains that Fanon has little that is substantive or constructive to contribute to the task of remedying the injustices of today. For he believes that Fanon's ideas and commitments are obsolete. The world has changed fundamentally since Fanon's time.

The suggestion that Fanon 'has little to say about the outcome' of the process of decolonisation seems especially unconvincing, however. Although Macey refers on a number of occasions to 'The Pitfalls of National Consciousness', he does not, I think, pay sufficient attention to this remarkable essay, in which Fanon excoriates a reactionary 'national consciousness' of the *post*-colonial era, concerned to subordinate 'social' to statist 'national' interests. It is clear that Macey is relatively poorly informed about sub-Saharan Africa and the anglophone black Atlantic world.[24] He does not give any space to African(ist) or New World intellectuals who continue to regard Fanon's writings on nationalism and decolonisation as indispensable guides to contemporary politics and culture. I am thinking, for instance, of such writers as Ngugi wa Thiong'o, who urges his readers 'to read two books without which I believe it is impossible to understand what informs African writing, particularly novels written by Africans. They are Frantz Fanon's *The Wretched of the Earth*, mostly the chapter entitled "the pitfalls of national consciousness" and V. I. Lenin's *Imperialism, The Highest Stage of Capitalism*'.[25]

Ngugi's juxtaposition of Fanon and Lenin is especially consequential, I think, since it speaks to Fanon's *contemporary* relevance, disputed by Macey. At least, it does so for those readers for whom the 'moment of theory' looms as a massive wrong turn in the history of ideas – 'one of those awful loops in time', as Raymond Williams once provocatively put it, 'which may, on further analysis, be properly seen as explicitly anti-popular and anti-radical'.[26] Conspicuous by its absence from Macey's final assessment of Fanon is the key category of *imperialism*. The omission serves to situate *Frantz Fanon: A Life* as a paradigm-ending book, not a paradigm-creating one. The paradigm that it ends is that of the 'postcolonial' Fanon, the Fanon read in the light of concerns deriving from the problematic of (post-structuralist) 'Theory' – which, Macey seems to concede in his afterword, have in general been his concerns too. The point is that as a child of this 'moment of theory', postcolonial studies was substantially predicated on the idea that the late twentieth-century world was 'post-imperial'. Hence the claims made (and not only within postcolonial studies, of course) for the epochal character of the restructuring of global social relations since 1968 or 1973, for the revolution wrought by 'globalisation', for the definitive eclipse of nationalism and of liberation struggle, and so on.

Any argument in favour of the 'postcolonial' Fanon must rest on the hypothesis of a radical break between the world order of Fanon's own time – the period of 'Third World' insurgency – and that of today. The mountain of evidence assembled by Macey is sufficient to demolish any suggestion that the 'postcolonial' Fanon corresponds meaningfully to the *actual* Fanon. But because Macey himself subscribes to the view that Fanon's world was so different from ours as to render all aspects of his thought – except for the anger that suffuses it – anachronistic, he leaves the door open for claims on behalf of the 'postcolonial' Fanon. It is a striking irony, for instance, that the critic most centrally implicated in the construction of the 'postcolonial' Fanon that Macey's book so definitively falsifies is able to cite Macey as a resource in the further adumbration of his own views. Homi Bhabha has responded to Macey's book not by ignoring it,[27] but by appropriating it to his own construction. In a 2005 'Foreword' commissioned for a new English translation of *Les Damnés de la terre*, he counterposes the historical moments of 'decolonisation' and 'globalisation', by way of emphasising the definitive obsolescence of Fanon's specific political commitments:

It must seem ironic, even absurd at first, to search for associations and intersections between decolonization and globalization – parallels would be pushing the analogy – when decolonization had the dream of a 'Third World' of free, postcolonial nations firmly on its horizon, whereas globalization gazes at the nation through the back mirror, as it speeds toward the strategic denationalization of state sovereignty. The global aspirations of Third World 'national' thinking belonged to the internationalist traditions of socialism, Marxism, and humanism, whereas the dominant forces of contemporary globalization tend to subscribe to free-market ideas that enshrine ideologies of neoliberal technocratic elitism. And ... while it was the primary purpose of decolonization to repossess land and territoriality in order to ensure the security of national polity and global equity, globalization propagates a world made up of virtual transnational domains and wired communities that live vividly through webs and connectivities 'on line'.[28]

Bhabha's 'Foreword' is not merely an obstinate restatement of the premises of 'postcolonial' Fanonism. In speculating on 'what might be saved from Fanon's ethics and politics of decolonization to help us reflect on globalization in our sense of the term' (p. xi), it attempts to register the pulse of contemporary pressures and imperatives. However, what it has to say in this respect is unconvincing in the extreme. It is not only that Bhabha privileges ethics over politics. It is also that, in the absence of any sustained or concrete analysis of the world-system, his call for 'debt relief and forgiveness', for a universal right to equitable development, sounds hollow. Edward Said's cautionary words in *Humanism and Democratic Criticism* are relevant here: 'In the various contests over justice and human rights that so many of us feel we have joined, there needs to be a component to our engagement that stresses the need for the redistribution of resources and that advocates the theoretical imperative against the huge accumulations of power and capital that so distort human life'.[29] There is nothing in Bhabha's commentary that leads one to believe that the challenge to 'globalisation' that he proposes would also need to be *anti-imperialist*. This ensures that there is not merely a yawning chasm, but active opposition, between the position staked out by Bhabha in his 'Foreword' and that articulated by Fanon in *The Wretched of the Earth*.

A much better overall assessment of Fanon is provided by Immanuel Wallerstein, who has written recently that 'what we have from Fanon is more than passion and more than a blueprint for political action'.[30] Wallerstein differs importantly from Macey – and of course from Bhabha – in identifying the category of imperialism as fundamental to Fanon's work. He believes that it is precisely because anti-imperialism is the wellspring of Fanon's political philosophy that he is able, fifty years after his death, to 'offer ... [us] a brilliant delineation of our collective dilemmas'. Wallerstein specifies three 'themes' in Fanon's work that continue to bear decisively on today's world: 'the use of violence, the assertion of identity and the class struggle' ('Reading Fanon', p. 119). 'We find ourselves, as Fanon expected', he writes,

in the long transition from our existing capitalist world-system to something else. It is a struggle whose outcome is totally uncertain ... Whether we can emerge collectively from this struggle and into a better world-system is in large part dependent on our ability to confront the three dilemmas discussed by Fanon – to confront them, and to deal with them in a way that is simultaneously analytically intelligent, morally committed to the 'disalienation' for which Fanon fought, and politically adequate to the realities we face. (p. 125)

If the grim unfolding of events in Afghanistan and Iraq over the course of the past decade have taught us anything at all, it must surely be that all the millennial post-cold war talk, on both sides of the political ledger, of a 'new world order', was premature. For this vaunted 'new world order' has already turned out not to be so very different, after all, from the 'old world order' of Fanon's time. It is for this reason, I believe, that the example of Fanon's urgent and unrelenting struggle against this order remains of compelling significance. Far from having nothing concrete to say to us today, his work seems, to me, to have lost nothing of its relevance or its urgency. *La lucha continúa*, in the famous words of Fanon's exact contemporary, Che Guevara: the struggle continues.

CHAPTER 5

The battle over Edward Said

Edward Said spoke quite often of the 'politics of interpretation', intending thereby to draw attention both to the 'interestedness' (a term that, as far as I know, he did not use, deriving from the tradition of ideology critique)[1] and to the materiality, or 'worldliness' (very much his word), of ideas and knowledge production. However, the phrase might with justification be applied to his own work, for reading Said has always been a political exercise. Since at least the mid 1970s, there has been intellectually heated and ideologically charged dispute and disagreement over the substance, tendency, and bearing of his work.

One dimension of this conflict has been 'political' in the quite conventional sense, of course, since much of Said's work bore on public affairs and addressed state policy and international relations. As Michael Sprinker noted in introducing a *Critical Reader* on him in 1992,

[Said] has for more than twenty years been the most visible spokesperson for the Palestinian cause in the United States (more recently in Britain as well). As journalist, television pundit, and essayist, he has tirelessly contested the standard caricature of the politically engaged Arab as terrorist, barbarian, maniac. Urbane and charming, he presents a totally different image of Arabs to an Anglophone audience accustomed only to seeing them in the guise of gun-toting kidnappers and hijackers.[2]

Already considerable by 1992, Said's prominence as a dissenting public intellectual expanded exponentially in the decade between that date and his untimely death in 2003. In such publicly oriented writings as *The Politics of Dispossession, Peace and its Discontents* and *The End of the Peace Process*, he inveighed against the appalling and escalating violence of the Israeli state, the blinkered and increasingly dictatorial quality of Yasir Arafat's leadership of the Palestinian national movement, Fatah, and the cynicism and hypocrisy of the American response to these developments.[3] He also wrote, spoke, and campaigned in those years as a resolute opponent of the Gulf War of 1990, of the imperialist sabre-rattling of American and British state ideologists in the post-9/11 period, which duly led to the disastrous and spectacularly misconceived interventions in Afghanistan and Iraq, as a critic of neo-conservatism, and an enemy of all forms of fundamentalism. This principled public stance regularly brought trouble to his door. Behind the frequent media misrepresentations and calumniations of his views could sometimes be glimpsed the hands of puppet-masters in the Israel Lobby and the richly resourced and actively interventionist right-wing think tanks in the United States. On more than one occasion, Said's personal safety and that of his family were threatened.

There is also, however, a politics surrounding the interpretation of Said's *scholarly* work – and it is this more restricted and narrowly defined politics that I want to focus on in this chapter. In the academy, as in the public sphere, Said's readers have argued fiercely with his various philosophical, ideological, theoretical, and methodological allegiances and commitments. Indeed, they have not only argued *with* these allegiances and commitments; they have argued *about* them. In the field of postcolonial studies, in particular, Said has been not just a central participant – putatively the most influential, and certainly the most highly respected figure in the entire field – but also the *subject* of a significant amount of critical debate. One might put it this way: within postcolonial studies, 'Edward Said' is both the name of a particular scholar and also the site of a dispute or battle over meaning, with deep consequences for the field itself.

If we were to begin anywhere but at *Orientalism*, it would be hard to understand what this dispute is all about.[4] For on any long view – that is to say, on any reading of his work overall or in the round – Said's position-taking within the field of postcolonial studies is relatively clear. Consider the following formulation, for instance, from a 1995 essay entitled 'East Isn't East', in which he differentiates sharply between the tendential thrusts of what he calls 'post-modernist' thought and the thought of 'the first generation of post-colonial artists and scholars': 'The earliest studies of the post-colonial', he writes,

were by such distinguished thinkers as Anwar Abdel-Malek, Samir Amin, C. L. R. James; almost all were based on studies of domination and control made from the standpoint of either a completed political independence or an incomplete liberationist project. Yet whereas post-modernism, in one of its most famous programmatic statements (by Jean-François Lyotard), stresses the disappearance of the grand narratives of emancipation and enlightenment, the emphasis behind much of the work done by the first generation of post-colonial artists and scholars is exactly the opposite: the grand narratives remain, even though their implementation and realization are at present in abeyance, deferred, or circumvented. This crucial difference between the urgent historical and political imperatives of post-colonialism and post-modernism's relative detachments makes for altogether different approaches and results. ('East Isn't East', p. 5)

Now it is true that Said doesn't quite nail his own colours to the mast here, inasmuch as he technically leaves open the question of whether the 'crucial difference' that he identifies between 'the urgent historical and political imperatives of post-colonialism' and 'post-modernism's relative detachments' is to be understand as *politically* or as *conjuncturally* motivated. If the latter, then authority would be given to the 'post-modernist' suggestion that the epoch of 'liberationism' is over and that 'the urgent historical and political imperatives of post-colonialism' have simply been rendered obsolete. If we hold the former to be true, however, then the way is open for us to mount an ideological critique of 'post-modernism', on the grounds that its setting aside of the 'urgent imperatives' of 'post-colonialism' betrays its political quietism.

Said's own unstinting practice as a representative of Palestinian aspirations for nation, sovereignty, land, state; his self-conscious identification with the 'first generation' 'post-colonialists' (Fanon, Césaire, Antonius, Faiz, Eqbal Ahmad, for instance, in addition to Abdel-Malek, Amin, and James, who are mentioned in the passage just cited); his unambiguous espousal and championing of the 'grand narratives' of humanism, enlightenment, emancipation – all these make clear which side of the ledger he would choose to place himself. In 'East Isn't East', accordingly, we wait for the other shoe to drop – for Said to make it clear that the 'crucial difference' between ('first generation') 'post-colonialism' and 'post-modernism' is precisely replicated in the relation between that 'first generation' 'post-colonialism' and the form of 'postcolonialism' prevailing in the institutionalised academic field of 'postcolonial studies' (perhaps we should call this 'second-generation postcolonialism'?), for the simple reason that the practitioners of the latter are themselves nearly all to be classed (on Said's own definition) as 'post-modernists' – the 'post-' in 'postcolonialism' being, to use the title of one of Kwame Anthony Appiah's best-known essays, very much the 'post-' in 'postmodernism'.

We wait in vain, however. Perhaps it is just for reasons of politeness that Said scruples at making his views about postcolonial studies explicit? But the truth is a little more intricate than this, I think. To unpack it, we have to return to *Orientalism*. Specifically, we have to return to the fact that this book, by some distance the most celebrated and influential that Said would ever write, appeared at the end of the 1970s in a United States in which, as Timothy Brennan has put it, there was discernible 'a shift of depressing and far-reaching dimensions in which a newly emboldened far right-wing began to permeate government and the popular sphere, and where a social democratic common sense was pushed to the margins as a lunatic fringe' (*Wars of Position*, p. 100). It was in and against this increasingly chill sociological climate that, within the walls of the academy – and more particularly within departments of literature – 'post-' theory rose to prominence and began, indeed, to command the heights.[5] If the rise of 'post-' theory seemed irresistible, this had something to do with its heady, not to say delirious, insistence on the radical novelty as well as the novel radicalism of its principles and procedures, which seemed to offer what the old, presumptively discredited 'modern' systems of thought – all of them, left, right, and centre – evidently could not: a counter-narrative to the 'new world order' of such as Reagan and Thatcher, a different basis for counter-action.

Orientalism was enthusiastically received, in this context, as a work of the new formation; and it was as such that it quickly assumed a canonical status that it has never subsequently lost, as the foundational text of the emergent disciplinary enterprise of postcolonial studies. The latter came into being and consolidated itself during the 1980s in a relation of supplementarity to 'post-' theory, whose key insights and assumptions – among which we might list hostility towards totality and systematic analysis; aversion to dialectics; critique of realism and adoption instead of epistemological conventionalism or constructivism; anti-foundationalism; anti-humanism; refusal of struggle-based models of politics in favour of models that privilege 'difference', 'ambivalence', 'complexity', and 'complicity'; repudiation of Marxism, usually taking the form not of a cold war anti-Marxism but of an avant-gardist 'post-Marxism' – it echoed and, indeed, amplified. Thus such prominent figures in the new field as Homi K. Bhabha, Leela Gandhi, Walter Mignolo, Sara Suleri, and Robert Young all wrote at length to condemn as naive or, worse, tacitly authoritarian, any commitment to universalism, metanarrative, enlightenment, social emancipation, or revolution. Postcolonial studies also brought to 'post-' theory at large certain specifically derived emphases, among the more consequential of which were a disavowal of all forms of nationalism and a corresponding exaltation of migrancy, liminality, hybridity, and multiculturality.

Inasmuch as Said's own commitments to humanism, enlightenment, and what Jürgen Habermas has influentially dubbed 'the philosophical discourse of modernity'[6] never wavered, there was always a disjuncture between his work and the assumptions of most of his postcolonialist (and, more generally, his 'post-' theoretical) readers and interlocutors. This disjuncture is starkly apparent in such late works as the posthumously published *Humanism and Democratic Criticism*; but it is manifest in all of Said's major writings from *The World, the Text and the Critic* to *Culture and Imperialism* and beyond, as well as in many of the occasional essays on such figures as Eqbal Ahmad, Mahmoud Darwish, and C. L. R. James. These also make clear that Said's politics were emphatically liberationist and *nationalitarian* (though never narrowly nationalist) in character.[7]

The disjuncture between Said and his 'post-' theoretical readers is discernable in *Orientalism* also. But the problem here is that *Orientalism* is at the same time postcolonial studies' foundation text, ubiquitously taken to have set the template for the field – at the very least, to have formulated the critique of Eurocentrism as its essential gesture. The work is conventionally and, indeed – and however paradoxical this might sound at first – *correctly* cited as indispensable to the emergence of the very 'post-modernist' form of 'postcolonial studies' to which Said himself was staunchly opposed. We have therefore to reckon (to put it in Bourdieusian terms) with a gap between Said's *position-taking* in the writing of *Orientalism*, and the *position* that this text came to occupy within the field of postcolonial studies.

In a thought-provoking and important revisionist commentary, Timothy Brennan grasps the nettle of this paradox and contends that *Orientalism* is simply two texts at once: the book that Said wrote and the book that his 'post-' theoretical interlocutors read and appropriated. If *Orientalism* is Said's most *read* text, it is also his most *misread* text. Brennan's argument is that *Orientalism*'s deep commitment to historical understanding and its attempt – above all in its final chapter – to offer up the concept of 'Orientalism' as allegorically resonant to the present by 'compar[ing] the scholarly machinery of nineteenth-century humanists and twentieth-century media intellectuals', have been symptomatically and systematically misconstrued by postcolonialists, who have been inclined to interpret the work as performing a genealogical critique of the colonising propensities of 'western' culture and knowledge production as such (*Wars of Position*, p. 113).

'A good deal of postcolonial studies drew on *Orientalism* without being true to it', Brennan writes (*Wars of Position*, p. 115). It is an intriguing argument. Correctly noting that the paramount conceptual and methodological resource in what he calls 'the postcolonial tendency' (p. 102) has been the work of Michel Foucault, he proposes that while it was unquestionably *Orientalism* that brought Foucault into the postcolonial discussion in the first instance, the text in question here was not the *Orientalism* that Said wrote, but rather the *Orientalism* that the book's postcolonialist readers 'produced', as it were, in the margins or between the lines of what Said *actually* wrote: 'the major source of Foucault's influence on postcolonial studies has been ... Said's *Orientalism*, although an *Orientalism* that Said did not write' (p. 103). Brennan focuses particularly, therefore, on the fact that Said's book was initially received as an extended (if, on some critical accounts, a flawed and somewhat irritatingly inconsistent) application of Foucauldian theory. To a significant degree, it has continued to be so received. Certainly, it is possible to draw a more or less straight and unbroken line from such early critiques of *Orientalism* as James Clifford's[8] – which awarded Said high marks for being a Foucauldian but went on to complain that he wasn't quite a good or rigorous enough one – to such more recent commentators as Valerie Kennedy – who insists that *Orientalism* is 'unimaginable without Foucault's concepts of discourse and of discursive formations, his discussions of the relationships between power and knowledge, and his view that representations are always influenced by the systems of power in which they are located', but who then immediately goes on to note reprovingly that there are 'major inconsistencies in Said's use of Foucault's concept of discourse' in the book.[9]

I agree with the general thrust of Brennan's argument: that in its presumptions and conceptual disposition, *Orientalism* is not to be understood as 'Foucauldian'. Yet it seems to me that in correctly opposing the 'postcolonialist' reading of *Orientalism* as a text that 'play[s] ... itself out as an epochal skirmish over Foucauldian power/knowledge' (*Wars of Position*, p. 102), Brennan bends the stick too far in the opposite direction. His counter-suggestion, that the reference to Foucault in *Orientalism* is skin-deep only, 'part of a patented eclectic amalgam in which the concepts of discursive network, hegemony, the homologies of Lucien Goldmann, and cultural materialism all mix' (p. 111), is surely overstated – and not only because, as it happens, Goldmann is conspicuous by his absence from *Orientalism*, and the concept of 'discourse' is much more thickly elaborated in the book, and more central to it, than any other concept, 'hegemony' included. The fact is that Foucault's work provides a central point of departure, and of reference, for Said in *Orientalism*.[10]

William Hart gets the balance here right, I believe, when he observes, with respect to Said's use of Foucault's *The Archaeology of Knowledge*, for example, that while '[o]nly traces of [its] rich conceptual scheme ... are evident in *Orientalism*', these traces

are very rich indeed. Said refers frequently (though his language is not always explicit) to the Western *archive*, the Oriental as an *object* of discourse, Orientalist scholarship as an *enunciative modality*, Oriental despotism and irrationality as *conceptual formations*. He also refers to the *strategic choices* that produce, on different spatial planes, incompatible objects, authoritative subject positions, and concepts. More important than any discrete element for Said is Foucault's general category of discourse. As he [himself] says ... Orientalism cannot be understood without the category discourse, without the systematic discipline that it presupposed and the distinctive relation between the exercise of power and the production of forms of knowledge (power/knowledge) that it represents.[11]

This is not to weaken the force of Brennan's suggestion that '*Orientalism* was, among other things, an attempt to arrest – or at least redirect – the drift of Euro-theory in the American university' (*Wars of Position*, p. 120) – although Brennan's recognition that this attempt *failed* is necessary also: the 'allegorical resonance for the present' of Said's 'historicist project ... was ... lost on an audience that saw primarily race in large letters, or the Arab-Israeli conflict in costume, or an urbane Afrocentricity in Arab garb – an Occidentalism, as some of his critics put it' (p. 120). Nor is it to give warrant to the multifarious scholarship – I have already cited the work of Clifford and Kennedy, although scores of other examples could equally be adduced here – that finds *Orientalism* wanting not because of any supposed weaknesses in the argument it puts forth, but for *programmatic* reasons – that is, because it falls short of Foucauldian orthodoxy. As Hart points out in his suggestive analysis, many commentaries on *Orientalism* tend to accord Foucault's key concepts and ideas the status of scripture, such that Said's heterodox use of them is understood and frowned upon as heretical (*Religious Effects*, p. 68). Nothing could be more inimical to Said's own deep-set commitment to secular criticism (and perhaps to Foucault's own intellectual practice also) than this reprobation of him as an idolater in the cathedral of St Michel.[12]

In an interesting critical comment on *Culture and Imperialism* (which he believes 'does not measure up to other books in [Said's] oeuvre'), Brennan writes that Said's 'assessments of theory' in this work 'take on a[n] ... almost uncritical ... resonance, as if compelled to pay homage to the hegemony of the times, particularly evident in the decade of the 1990s' (*Wars of Position*, pp. 101–2). I myself would make a structurally similar argument, but with respect to Said's treatment of Foucault in *Orientalism*, not to his 'assessments of theory' in *Culture and Imperialism* (which I value more highly than Brennan does, evidently): my own sense is that Said had recourse to a Foucauldian problematic in this work for the very obvious and immediate reason that the French theorist's name was beginning to be on everybody's lips at the time: for many theoretically inclined, politically progressive scholars, 'Foucault' was fast becoming *the* gold standard of theoretical currency. My suggestion is that in *Orientalism*, Said attempted to talk the Foucauldian talk – even though he had no intention of walking the Foucauldian walk – because he hoped through this means to reach his prospective readership, to make the greatest possible impact on their judgements and sensibilities.

The deployment of the Foucauldian category of 'discourse' in *Orientalism* is surely to be read in the light of the intense contemporary theoretical discussion of such notions as 'ideology', 'subjectivity' and 'consciousness'. Louis Althusser's hugely influential structuralist reformulation of the Marxist theory of ideology in his essay, 'Ideology and Ideological State Apparatuses' had already jettisoned the critical thrust of the concept and dispensed with its implicit linkage to 'ideas' on the grounds that the construal of 'ideology' in these terms – even as a *system* of ideas – failed to register the materiality of all social practice (including thought). The critical assault on Althusser's reformulation, in turn, by any number of post-structuralist, anti-essentialist and anti-humanist 'post-Althusserians', including, notably, Foucault himself, then proceeded to 'out-Althusser' Althusser, laying siege to such notions as 'consciousness', 'belief', and especially 'truth', which had 'survived' (Althusser's own term) his intervention, and quickly reaching a point from which not only Althusser's reformulation but the concept of 'ideology' as a whole came to seem not merely limited but altogether untenable – tied to idealist or empiricist notions of scientificity and truth. A consensus had formed on this assessment in the avant-gardist circuits of radical critical theory by the mid 1970s. The Foucauldian category of 'discourse' – dispersed and subjectless, institutional, inextricably material in its 'expression', and ineluctably linked to power – was proposed as one corrective substitute for this now discarded concept of 'ideology'; and it was in just these terms that Said reached for it in *Orientalism*.[13]

One of the very first moves that Said makes in his book, accordingly, is to insist that Orientalism is not an 'ideology' in the sense of a structure of lies or of myths which, were the truth about them to be told, would simply blow away ... [W]hat we must respect and try to grasp is the sheer knitted-together strength of Orientalist discourse, its very close ties to the enabling socio-economic and political institutions, and its redoubtable durability ... Orientalism ... is not an airy European fantasy about the Orient, but a created body of theory and practice in which, for many generations, there has been a considerable material investment. (*Orientalism*, p. 6)

The stipulation here is not merely along the lines of the Althusserian specification that we understand 'ideology' properly only if we conceive it as having a material existence. On the one hand, Said holds no brief for Marxism; on the other, he clearly follows Foucault, rather than Althusser, in regarding the apparent idealist entailments of the concept of 'ideology' as an irredeemable liability. As he put it in an interview that appeared in the post-structuralist theoretical journal *Diacritics* in 1976, when he was busy writing *Orientalism*,

The focus of interest in Orientalism for me has been the partnership between a discursive and archival textuality and worldly power, one as an index and refraction of the other. As a systematic discourse Orientalism is written knowledge, but because it is in the world and directly about the world, it is *more* than knowledge: it is *power* since, so far as the Oriental is concerned, Orientalism is the operative and effective knowledge by which he was delivered textually to the West, occupied by the West, milked by the West for his resources, humanly quashed by the West.[14]

Discourse analysis is seen to be indispensable inasmuch as the task is not only to register the link between 'language' (including thought) and material institutions, but to suggest that 'language' must be understood as always already materially inscribed, that is to say, as always already institutionalised. Orientalism, as Said would come to put it in his celebrated work,

is, rather than expresses, a certain *will* or *intention* to understand, in some cases to control, manipulate, even to incorporate, what is a manifestly different (or alternative and novel) world; it is, above all, a discourse that is by no means in direct, corresponding relationship with political power in the raw, but rather is produced and exists in an uneven exchange with various kinds of power, shaped to a degree by the exchange with power political ... power intellectual ... power cultural ... power moral. (*Orientalism*, p. 12)

It is interesting to contrast Said here with Raymond Williams – a decade older than Said and, at this moment in time, certainly, less inclined than he to be buffeted by topical winds blowing through the groves of

Academe. Williams never found 'ideology' a particularly serviceable or useful concept either. But since he was also utterly unimpressed by post-structuralism, and never looked twice at Foucault, he was never drawn to the purportedly corrective category of 'discourse'. Instead, having developed his own home-spun notions of 'culture' and 'structure of feeling' in his early works, his later full engagement with Marxist and materialist theory in the 1960s and 1970s led him to the Gramscian concept of 'hegemony', which, he suggested in *Marxism and Literature*, goes beyond both 'culture' and 'ideology' 'in its insistence on relating the "whole social process" to specific distributions of power and influence' (p. 108). 'What is decisive', Williams wrote, 'is not only the conscious system of ideas and beliefs, but the whole lived social process as practically organized by specific and dominant meanings and values' (p. 109). The differentiation between 'ideology' and 'hegemony' in *Marxism and Literature* is worth quoting at length. The latter is distinct from 'ideology', Williams wrote,

in its refusal to equate consciousness with the articulate formal system which can be and ordinarily is abstracted as 'ideology'. It of course does not exclude the articulate and formal meanings values and beliefs which a dominant class develops and propagates. But it does not equate these with consciousness, or rather it does not reduce consciousness to them. Instead it sees the relations of domination and subordination, in their forms as practical consciousness, as in effect a saturation of the whole process of living – not only of political and economic activity, nor only of manifest social activity, but of the whole substance of lived identities and relationships, to such a depth that the pressures and limits of what can ultimately be seen as a specific economic, political, and cultural system seem to most of us the pressures and limits of simple experience and common sense. Hegemony is then not only the articulate upper level of 'ideology', nor are its forms of control only those ordinarily seen as 'manipulation' or 'indoctrination'. It is a whole body of practices and expectations, over the whole of living: our senses and assignments of energy, our shaping perceptions of ourselves and our world. It is a lived system of meanings and values – constitutive and constituting – which as they are experienced as practices appear as reciprocally confirming. It thus constitutes a sense of reality for most people in the society, a sense of absolute because experienced reality beyond which it is very difficult for most members of the society to move, in most areas of their lives. It is, that is to say, in the strongest sense a 'culture', but a culture which has also to be seen as the lived dominance and subordination of particular classes. (pp. 109–10)

Now Said, too, is a close reader of Gramsci. Although he keeps his distance from the specifically Marxist axis of Gramsci's writing – such that there is, for instance, no engagement with class (class struggle, class consciousness, class relations) in *Orientalism*[15] – the concept of hegemony is of considerable importance to his work also.[16] But Said's deployment of 'discourse' lacks, in general, the suppleness, plasticity, and reflexivity of Williams's theorising. The long passage from *Marxism and Literature* just cited is governed by a solidaristic and activist notion of human sociality, evident both in its reference and its language, in what it says and in how it says it: 'lived identities', 'shaping', making and self-making, experience, 'constitutive and constituting' 'meanings and values', 'people in the society', 'ourselves and our world'. Said's *humanist* sentiments gesture in this direction as well. But because in *Orientalism* these are channelled through the Foucauldian category of 'discourse', whose massive and thoroughgoing *anti-humanism* is among its most striking features, they struggle to find expression there. What emerges instead is a certain incoherence, an imprecision, in the overarching conception of *Orientalism*, not to be found in any other text by Said. *Orientalism* is, in this respect, in its methodological aspect, at least, atypical of Said's work as a whole.

This imprecision clearly derives from the unresolved juxtaposition in *Orientalism* of incompatible problematics. Clifford's recognition of this discordance had provided the basis of his early discussion of *Orientalism*, of course – except that, as a card-carrying Foucauldian himself, he had chosen to criticise Said's humanism (residual, as it must have seemed to him) and had urged Said to follow Foucault more closely in breaking decisively with this legacy. In his subsequent reconsiderations of *Orientalism*, Said occasionally picked up this suggestion that the theoretical entailments of an anti-humanism deriving from Foucault and his own humanism were irreconcilable, but without seeming ever to concede that the implications of this for the coherence of his celebrated study might be substantial. In *Humanism and Democratic Criticism*, for example, he discusses Clifford's critique, noting that it turned on the inconsistency between 'my avowed and unmistakable humanistic bias and the antihumanism of my subject and my approach to it' (p. 8). Said acknowledges that he 'particularly stressed and drew on' Foucauldian theory in *Orientalism*; and he concedes that Foucault's work 'largely disposed of humanism's essentializing and totalizing modes'. But he disputes Clifford's suggestion that there is therefore 'something fundamentally discordant' in his own use of Foucault and 'post-' theory more generally in his text: 'Although I was one of the first critics to engage with and discuss French theory in the American university ... I somehow remained unaffected by that theory's ideological antihumanism, mainly,

I think, because I did not (and still do not) see in humanism only the kind of totalizing and essentializing trends that Clifford identified' (*Humanism*, p. 10).

This is a very peculiar and, it has to be said, uncompelling defence. It amounts basically to saying that he was able to use Foucault's work 'neutrally' or purely 'technically', because he took no account of its underlying premises, discriminations, intentions, or thrusts. Surely, though, the relationship between Foucauldian *method* and Foucauldian *philosophy* is more integrally connected than this attempted justification would make it sound? One might have supposed that, precisely *because* Said believed Foucault's critique of humanism to be profoundly misconceived, it would have been wiser for him to subject Foucault's methods as well as his substantive claims to critique.[17]

Certainly, in the writing that followed the publication of *Orientalism*, Said turned increasingly strongly against Foucault. In an interview published in 1993, he argued that he had 'gotten what there was to be gotten out of Foucault by about the time *Discipline and Punish* appeared, in the mid-1970s'.[18] He came to realise, he says, that

> Despite the fact that he seemed to be a theorist of power, obviously, and kept referring to resistance, he was really the *scribe* of power. He was really writing about the victory of power. I found very little in his work, especially after the second half of *Discipline and Punish*, to help in resisting the kinds of administrative and disciplinary pressures that he described so well in the first part. So I completely lost interest in his work. The later stuff on the subject I just found very weak and, to my way of thinking, uninteresting. ('*Orientalism* and After', p. 214)

This severe assessment is a feature of Said's commentary on Foucault from the early 1980s onwards – although it is necessary to contest his own retrospective dating of his turn against Foucault to the pre-*Orientalism* period. As Paul Armstrong has argued in suggesting that there is a contradiction between the conceptual and methodological thrusts of *Orientalism* and *Culture and Imperialism*, Said showed a tendency in his later writings to 'recast' the former text 'in the image of his later views'.[19]

In Said's own view, the greatest liability of his reliance on Foucault in *Orientalism* was that, inasmuch as it directed him to a focused examination of the intricate systematicity of imperialist 'discourse', it prevented him from grappling with the response to imperialism, and indeed the active resistance to it, of the people upon whom it was imposed. As he pointed out in an interview with Gauri Viswanathan in 1996, in *Orientalism*

I think I was very limited in what I was trying to do, that is to say, I was trying to look at the way in which a certain view of the Orient was created and accompanied, or perhaps was used to subordinate the Orient during the period of imperialism beginning with the conquest of Egypt by Napoleon. And that's all I was trying to do. I had *nothing* to say about what the Orient was *really* like. I said *nothing* about the possibility of resistance to it. That's a fair criticism, because one of the things that I think Foucault is very wrong about is that he always writes from the point of view of power ... And I think that always struck me as wrong, and my attitude to power, in *Orientalism* and elsewhere, has always been deeply suspicious and hostile. It took me another ten years to actually make that more explicit in *Culture and Imperialism*, where I was very interested not only in talking about the *formation* of imperialism, but also of *resistances* to it, and the fact that imperialism *could* be overthrown and *was* – as a result of resistance and decolonization and nationalism.[20]

One takes Said's point here. But it seems to me that it is not so much the fact that, in *Orientalism*, he has 'nothing to say about what the Orient was really like' that is the problem. Rather, the problem – deriving, again, from the incompatibility between 'Foucauldian' and 'humanist' problematics – is that he tends to hesitate in the text between realist and conventionalist epistemologies, thus leaving it unclear as to whether he is willing to concede the externality of 'the Orient' to Orientalist 'discourse', or whether, in accordance with 'post-' theoretical premises generally, he believes that it is to be understood as a discursive construction 'all the way down'. The problem is signalled on the very first page of *Orientalism*, where the suggestion that the Orient is 'almost a European invention' (p. 1) promotes the conventionalist understanding at the same time as it limits or even undermines it through the qualifier, 'almost'.

Most of Said's postcolonialist readers have tended to assume that his commitment to an anti-essentialist critical practice derives from a conventionalist epistemology. Even Hussein, for instance, who does not subscribe to the general wisdom that *Orientalism* is a Foucauldian text, maintains that '[o]n the whole ... Said finds Foucault's critique of realist and idealist epistemology powerfully compelling' (*Edward Said*, p. 136). Ashcroft and Ahluwalia, similarly, position Said as a conventionalist, although they do register a countervailing tendency in *Orientalism* also. Acknowledging the text's 'tendency to impute a real world behind the structures of signification that represent the world', they argue that 'this is something Said continually denies. He says time and again that there is, for instance, no "real" Orient, obscured by the misrepresentations of Orientalism'.[21] It is this latter asseveration that Ashcroft and Ahluwalia take to be finally decisive in *Orientalism*.

My own view is the opposite of theirs. No sooner has Said introduced 'Foucault's notion of a discourse' at the beginning of his text, than he moves to insist that 'it would be wrong to conclude that the Orient was *essentially* an idea, or a creation with no corresponding reality … There were – and are – cultures and nations whose location is in the East, and their lives, histories, and customs have a brute reality obviously greater than anything that could be said about them in the West' (*Orientalism*, p. 5). He quite obviously believes both that there is an 'East', with its own 'brute reality', and that it is systematically misrepresented in Orientalist discourse. But what he then goes on to say is that his book will be concerned less with this question of misrepresentation – that is, with 'the correspondence between Orientalism and Orient' – than with 'the internal consistency of Orientalism and its ideas about the Orient'.

Here again, however, we must be careful in correcting the conventional wisdom not to bend the stick too far in the other direction. If it would be incorrect to construe the epistemology of *Orientalism* as conventionalist, it would be equally wrong to pretend that it was uncomplicatedly or unambiguously realist either. Hesitation between the two optics is the truth here; and, again, the incompatibilities between them cannot be rationalised away as though they were generative or enabling contraries – although this is how Said often seemed to *want* to represent them when asked to reflect on his achievement in *Orientalism*. In a 1999 interview with Moustafa Bayoumi and Andrew Rubin, for instance, he mused that '[i]n *Orientalism*, I begin with a notion that interpretation is misinterpretation, that there is no such thing as the correct interpretation'.[22] One can certainly find evidence to support the suggestion that this is indeed the point from which Said *did* begin in *Orientalism*, although it is hard to reconcile this conventionalist premise with the idea that the reality of 'lives, histories and customs' in the 'East' has been misrepresented in Orientalist discourse. If one believes that all 'interpretation is misinterpretation', it is difficult for one to speak of 'truth' in interpretation at all. Certainly the idea that 'interpretation is misinterpretation' cannot easily be reconciled with the kinds of observation that Said would make routinely in his later work. In *Representations of the Intellectual*, for example, he argues that the goal of the intellectual is to 'speak the truth' and that the 'intellectual meaning of a situation is arrived at by comparing the known and available facts with a norm, also known and available' (*Representations*, p. 99). To be sure, he adds that '[t]his is not an easy task, since documentation, research, probings are required in order to get beyond the usually piecemeal, fragmentary and necessarily flawed way in which information is presented'. But he concludes that, despite this, 'in most cases it is possible, I believe, to ascertain whether in fact a massacre was committed or an official cover-up produced. The first imperative is to find out what occurred and then why, not as isolated events but as part of an unfolding history' (p. 99). As I understand it, 'finding out what occurred', or 'speaking the truth' cannot plausibly be deemed 'misinterpretation' – as it would seem that they are, at least some of the time, in *Orientalism*. Samir Amin has written, in a critique of Said's work, that 'Orientalist' thinking 'merits reproach for the simple reason that it produced false judgements'.[23] It is only in *Orientalism* that Said might have been disposed to disagree with him.

Concerning the theory of knowledge in *Orientalism*, I am persuaded by Neil Larsen, who notes the forced juxtaposition of 'humanist' and 'post-structuralist' problematics in the text – he refers to the irreconcilability of Said's citations of Nietzsche and his proclamations of 'the discursive construction of truth', on the one hand, with his denunciations of various nineteenth-century Orientalists, on the other – and goes on, very suggest-ively, to suggest a link between *Orientalism* and Gayatri Chakravorty Spivak's almost equally influential essay, 'Can the Subaltern Speak?'[24] This latter text, Larsen writes, 'executes a Derridean move on Said's Foucaultian reading of colonialism as "discursive practice." The latter now becomes a "social text," an englobing, systemic presence of Western imperialism that obviates *Orientalism*'s vacillation – ideological misrepresentation or "power/knowledge" construct? – on the question of discursive truth content. "Imperialism," as understood by Spivak, does not merely monopolize the power to represent its "other"; all such representations have (always) already fallen under the aegis of the Western "Subject"' ('Imperialism', pp. 46–7).

Whatever might be said about *Orientalism*, it is clear that in all of his work from the time of *The World, the Text, and the Critic* onwards, Said wrote from premises and on behalf of principles quite different from those generally prevailing in postcolonial studies. A window on to his wider views is to be found in his important commentaries on the social role of intellectuals. In these, Said emerges quite unambiguously as a left-wing critical humanist. In his Reith Lectures of 1993, subsequently pub-lished as *Representations of the Intellectual*, he defines the intellectual as

an individual endowed with a faculty for representing, embodying, articulating a message, a view, an attitude, philosophy or opinion to, as well as for, a public. And this role has an edge to it, and cannot be played without a sense of being someone whose place it is publicly to raise embarrassing questions, to confront orthodoxy and dogma (rather than to produce them), to be someone who cannot easily be co-opted by governments or corporations, and whose *raison d'être* is to represent all those people and issues that are routinely forgotten or swept under the rug. The intellectual does so on the basis of universal principles: that all human beings are entitled to expect decent standards of behavior concerning freedom and justice from worldly powers or nations, and that deliberate or inadvertent violations of these standards need to be testified and fought against courageously. (*Representations*, pp. 11–12)

He adds, a couple of paragraphs later, that

in the end it is the intellectual as a representative figure that matters – someone who visibly represents a standpoint of some kind, and someone who makes articulate representations to his or her public despite all sorts of barriers. My argument is that intellectuals are individuals with a vocation for the art of representing, whether that is talking, writing, teaching, appearing on television. And that vocation is important to the extent that it is publicly recognizable and involves both commitment and risk, boldness and vulnerability. (pp. 12–13)

The emphases here are explicit, and noteworthy: individuality, autonomy, independence, secularity, universality; the commitment to speak on behalf of those who need or request representation coupled with the aptitude for and acquisition of the 'art of representing' – eloquence and articulacy, passion and courage, skill in argument and persuasion.

   Particularly suggestive in Said's representation of the intellectual, in my view, is his identification of what might be *specific* to intellectual work, that is, his grasp of what it is that intellectuals do that might be both socially valuable and also not within the remit of any other group of social agents – not because intellectuals are cleverer than other people, still less because they are morally better than other people, but because they have been socially endowed with the resources, the status, the symbolic and social capital, to do this particular kind of work.[25] In a 1990 essay, 'Figures, Configurations, Transfigurations', Said speaks movingly of the centrality of writers to the struggle against imperialism throughout the twentieth century: literature, he writes, 'played a crucial role in the establishment of a national cultural heritage, in the reinstatement of native idioms, in the re-imagining and re-figuring of local histories, geographies, communities. As such … literature not only mobilised active resistance to incursions from the outside, but also contributed massively as the shaper, creator, agent of illumination within the realm of the colonised.'[26] In *Representations of the Intellectual*, he moves to distinguish, still further, between the work of the writer or artist and the work of the intellectual more properly and narrowly conceived. 'In dark times', he writes, an intellectual is very often looked to by members of his or her nationality to represent, speak out for, and testify to the sufferings of that nationality ... To this terribly important task of representing the collective suffering of your own people, testifying to its travails, reasserting its enduring presence, reinforcing its memory, there must be added something else, which only an intellectual, I believe, has the obligation to fulfill. After all, many novelists, painters, and poets, like Manzoni, Picasso, or Neruda, have embodied the historical experience of their people in aesthetic works, which in turn become recognized as great masterpieces. For the intellectual the task, I believe, is explicitly to universalize the crisis, to give greater human scope to what a particular race or nation suffered, to associate that experience with the sufferings of others ... This does not at all mean a loss in historical specificity, but rather it guards against the possibility that a lesson learned about oppression in one place will be forgotten or violated in another place or time. (*Representations*, pp. 43–4)

Said's appeal here to the category of the *universal* in defining the specificity of intellectual work is tremendously important. 'Universalism', as he grasps it, is no woolly abstraction. It derives, rather, from the kind of engaged (and, indeed, *enraged*!) citizenship that he has elsewhere termed 'worldly': an active searching out and public presentation of connections, contrasts and alternatives that shade necessarily and ineluctably into the framing and articulation of political demands. In his essay, 'For a Corporatism of the Intellectual', Pierre Bourdieu has written that to speak 'with the ambition to be universal' is precisely what makes intellectual practice *intellectual* practice.[27] Said would agree with that; and he would agree, also, with what Bourdieu writes in another of his many essays on the responsibility of intellectuals and the nature of intellectual work:

The spokesman's problem is to offer a language that enables the individuals concerned to universalize their experiences without thereby effectively excluding them from the expression of their own experience, which amounts to dispossessing them ... [T]he work ... consists precisely in transforming the personal, individual misfortune ('I've been made redundant') into a particular case of a more general social relation ('you've been made redundant because ...').[28]

Universalism is in these terms both the goal of intellectual practice and its formal condition of possibility. We could say, in fact – continuing for the moment to use Bourdieu as a foil for Said – that intellectuals' specific struggle 'to universalize the conditions of access to the universal'[29] comes into focus as a sort of political correlative of the objective interest that they are disposed to have – in their capacity *as intellectuals* – in 'grasping particularity in generality, and generality in particularity'.[30] There is no contradiction between intellectuals' demands for autonomy and their functioning as representatives of the aspirations of others. As Bourdieu puts it: 'I think that the intellectual has the privilege of being placed in conditions that enable him to strive to understand his generic and specific conditions. In so doing, he can hope to free himself (in part at least) and to offer others the means of liberation.'[31]

I cite Bourdieu here not only to draw attention to some key similarities between his understanding of the social role of intellectuals and Said's. I also want to use Bourdieu's ideas as a way of pinpointing some potential weaknesses in Said's account. Take, for instance, the distinct whiff of modernist nostalgia – metropolitanism, exile not as deracination but as a *willed principle*, metaphorically construed – that sometimes emanates from Said's pen. I think that he is considerably too much given to such pronouncements as that the intellectual life is 'a lonely condition, yes, but it is always a better one than a gregarious tolerance for the way things are' (*Representations*, p. xviii) – pronouncements that, in general, suggest a suspiciously self-justifying romanticisation of the intellectual vocation.

It is not, of course, that Said is in any sense blind to what George Lamming has famously dubbed 'the pleasures of exile'.[32] Noting that 'the intellectual as exile tends to be happy with the idea of unhappiness' (*Representations*, p. 53), Said explicitly rebukes the Adornian understanding with which in other respects he very closely aligns himself. Above all, he says, it is important not to forget that the metaphorical construal of intellectualism as exile bespeaks a condition of *privilege*:

What Adorno doesn't speak about are indeed the pleasures of exile, those different arrangements of living and eccentric angles of vision that it can sometimes afford, which enliven the intellectual's vocation, without perhaps alleviating every last anxiety or feeling of bitter solitude. So while it is true to say that exile is the condition that characterizes the intellectual as someone who stands as a marginal figure outside the comforts of privilege, power, being-at-homeness ... it is also very important to stress that the condition carries with it certain rewards and, yes, even privileges. (*Representations*, p. 59)

Nor, by the same token, can Said be accused of smuggling in a defence of elitism under cover of his championing of 'loneliness'. Bourdieu situates intellectuals in structural terms as 'a dominated fraction of the dominant class. They are dominant, in so far as they hold the power and privileges conferred by the possession of cultural capital ... but writers and artists are dominated in their relations with those who hold political and economic power'.[33] He notes that this rather tenuous position – within the sphere of the dominant, but on its margins, at its least privileged and least valorised edge – *can* have the effect of disposing intellectuals to align themselves, to throw in their lot, with the dominated sectors of society at large. The intellectuals who take this step, who 'put their power at the service of the dominated in the social field taken as a whole' (p. 146), will certainly experience the hostility of the members of the dominant class with whom they share *filiations* but not *affiliations*; but this will be balanced, presumably, by what they gain on the basis of their activism: the sense that they are a part of a vast progressive historical movement implicating, and drawing upon, the energies and resources of 'the people' at large. The 'loneliness' of the intellectual registers dominant society's ostracism of the dissident. It is compensated for by affiliative ties of political participation, solidarity, and community.

It is precisely at this point, however, that Said baulks. On the one hand, he wears his dissidence courageously, almost as a badge of honour. He is utterly disdainful of the accommodated intellectual, 'aligned with institutions and deriv[ing] power from those institutions' (*Representations*, p. 67). Moreover, he feels that *especially* in times like the present, 'when the struggle on behalf of underrepresented and disadvantaged groups seems so unfairly weighted against them' (p. xvii), it is necessary for intellectuals to commit themselves to a representative practice, on the model of what he terms 'defensive nationalism' (p. 40). Yet on the other hand, he inveighs repeatedly *against* solidarity: not merely on the temperamental grounds (which in any event merely defer the question) that he has never been 'a joiner or party member by nature' (p. 107), but because he believes that solidarity makes it impossible to exercise independent judgement. 'Never solidarity before criticism' (p. 32) is his celebrated slogan. Said says important things about the dangers of orthodoxy and hero worship, and about the pitfalls of headlong commitment. He also has in mind the sorry history of the suppression of criticism and dissent by states, parties, and movements, left and right, throughout the blood-drenched twentieth century. Even so, I find it strange that he seems not even to entertain the idea that criticism and solidarity might coexist. When he writes that 'there is inestimable value to what an intellectual does to ensure the community's survival during periods of extreme national emergency', he is immediately driven, as though by political reflex, to add that 'loyalty to the group's fight for survival cannot draw in the intellectual so far as to narcotize the critical sense, or reduce its imperatives, which are always to go beyond survival to questions of political liberation, to critiques of the leadership, to presenting alternatives that are too often marginalized or pushed aside as irrelevant to the main battle at hand' (p. 41). One concedes the point, of course, that the 'critical sense' should not be 'narcotized' through 'loyalty'. But in some of Said's writings, the gap between 'loyalty' and 'narcotization' seems so narrow as to disappear altogether, and with it the possibility of solidaristic critical practice.

Two other features of Said's account of the social role of the intellectual that I find troubling can also be traced to his intermittent tendency to romanticise the uncommitted, exilic, individual vocation of intellectualism. The first of these centres on the celebrated idea of 'speaking truth to power'. One might simply juxtapose this slogan with Noam Chomsky's or Arundhati Roy's insistence that 'speaking truth to power' is *not* what they do. As Roy puts it, in an interview with David Barsamian, 'Isn't there a flaw in the logic of that phrase – speak truth to power? It assumes that power doesn't know the truth. But power knows the truth just as well, if not better, than the powerless know the truth. Enron knows what it's doing. We don't have to tell it what it's doing. We have to tell other people what Enron is doing.'[34] Also very much to the point is Roy's rejoinder to Barsamian's question about critical journalism: oughtn't it to be the role of journalists 'to comfort the afflicted and afflict the comfortable?' he asks. Her answer: 'I don't think that people in power become uneasy and uncomfortable. But you can annoy and provoke them. People who are powerful are not people who have subtle feelings like uneasiness. They got there because of a certain capacity for ruthlessness. I don't even consider their feelings when I write. I don't write for them' (p. 67).

Naturally, when Said evokes the idea of 'speaking truth to power', he does not have in mind that intellectuals should direct their discourse towards the powerful – in other words, that they should restrict themselves to 'internal' protestation and critique. On the contrary, 'speaking truth to power', as he understands it, presumably means speaking truth *in the face of power* – not quite regardless of, but despite the dangers involved in so doing. As he puts it, '[s]peaking the truth to power is no Panglossian idealism: it is carefully weighing the alternatives, picking the right one, and then intelligently representing it where it can do the most good and cause the right change' (*Representations*, p. 102). Yet there is a sense in which Said's model of intellectual practice, precisely because of its Adornian concerns with propriety, amateurism, and outsiderism, is brought within the compass of Roy's criticism after all. The conviction that 'there is a special duty to address the constituted and authorized powers of one's own society, which are accountable to its citizenry' (p. 98) seems questionable to me: I understand it as reflecting, again, an unwarranted suspicion of solidaristic intellectualism and, beyond that, arguably, of an unambiguously antagonistic or struggle-based conception of cultural politics.[35]

The second problem is related to this first. When Said talks about the need for the intellectual to be autonomous in his or her thought and actions, not to be beholden to anyone or any power or institution, he tends somewhat, I think, to de-realise the practice of intellectualism, to imagine that it is less materially implicated than it actually is. We can concede, I think, that what he calls 'amateurism' – 'choosing the risks and uncertain results of the public sphere – a lecture or a book or an article in wide and unrestricted circulation' is to be preferred over 'the insider space controlled by experts and professionals' (*Representations*, p. 87). But the 'public sphere' is not quite as evenly or readily accessible as Said's formulation makes it out to be. It is not for nothing, after all, that Bourdieu speaks of the 'power relations which are imposed on all the agents entering the field [of cultural production] – and which weigh with a particular brutality on the new entrants' ('Intellectual Field', p. 141). It is as though Said has for a moment forgotten about the dialectics of privilege.[36]

The criticisms I am drawing here derive, obviously, from a leftist standpoint substantially compatible with Said's own, but differently articulated or accented than his. My feeling is that it is in the context of a debate between what we might call *aligned* and *non-aligned* leftisms that Said's work is likely to prove most energising and illuminating in the years to come. For a brief moment in the mid 1990s it already looked as though it might be possible for a debate about Said to be joined in postcolonial studies between left critics and left champions of his. That potential discussion never really got off the ground, partly because of the peculiarly personal and *ad hominem* quality of the critique of Said that Aijaz Ahmad published in 1992, and that had the effect of poisoning the atmosphere within which the debate might have been conducted.[37] As a result, the fraught relation between Said and Marxism has still to be explored in depth, especially by Marxist scholars. A start has been made in recent writings by Parry, especially, but we still await a fully-fledged Marxist critique of Said's work. Perhaps the time is propitious, now, for this long-deferred debate to be joined in earnest?

Notes

INTRODUCTION: THE POLITICAL UNCONSCIOUS OF
POSTCOLONIAL STUDIES

1 See for instance N. Lazarus, 'Is a Counterculture of Modernity a Theory of Modernity?', *Diaspora: A Journal of Transnational Studies*, 4.3 (1996), pp. 323–39; *Nationalism and Cultural Practice in the Postcolonial World* (Cambridge University Press, 1999); 'Postcolonial Studies after the Invasion of Iraq', *New Formations*, 59 (2006), pp. 10–22; N. Lazarus and R. Varma, 'Marxism and Postcolonial Studies' in J. Bidet and S. Kouvelakis (eds), *The Critical Companion to Contemporary Marxism* (Leiden: Brill, 2008), pp. 309–31. I use the term 'world-system', following Wallerstein and Brandel, to indicate a bounded social universe whose functioning is more or less autonomous, more or less integrated. A 'world-system', in these terms, is not coextensive with the 'world' as such, and is hence not a 'world system' except in the unique instance of capitalism, whose historical unprecedentedness consists precisely in the fact that it is a world-system that is also a world system.

2 Benita Parry, for instance, observes that '[t]he institutionalization of postcolonial studies took place at a time when the linguistic turn was in the ascendant within philosophy and literary theory, and at the moment when cultural studies was in the process of turning its back on its materialist beginnings ... The stage was then set for the reign of theoretical tendencies which Edward Said, among others, has deplored for permitting intellectuals "an astonishing sense of weightlessness with regard to the gravity of history". In the realm of postcolonial studies, where premises affording analytical priority to formations of discourse and signifying processes were already to the fore, discussion of the internal structures of texts, enunciations, and sign systems became detached from a concurrent examination of social and experiential contexts, situations, and circumstances.' 'The Institutionalization of Postcolonial Studies' in N. Lazarus (ed.), *The Cambridge Companion to Postcolonial Literary Studies* (Cambridge University Press, 2004), p. 74. Parry's citation from Said is from *Culture and Imperialism* (London: Chatto and Windus, 1993), pp. 366–7.

3 E. Hobsbawm, *The Age of Extremes: A History of the World, 1914–1991* (New York: Pantheon Books, 1994).

4 R. Brenner, *The Economics of Global Turbulence: The Advanced Capitalist Economies from Long Boom to Long Downturn* (London and New York: Verso, 2006).

5 S. Amin, *Capitalism in the Age of Globalization: The Management of Contemporary Society* (London: Zed Books, 1997), p. 95. See also N. Lazarus, 'Introducing Postcolonial Studies' and 'The Global Dispensation since 1945' in N. Lazarus (ed.), *The Cambridge Companion to Postcolonial Literary Studies* (Cambridge University Press, 2004), pp. 1–16 and 19–40, from which I have drawn selectively in the pages that follow.

6 For discussion of the political and economic dimensions, see, among others, G. Arrighi, *The Long Twentieth-Century: Money, Power, and the Origins of Our Times* (London and New York: Verso, 1994); E. A. Brett, *The World Economy since the War: The Politics of Uneven Development* (Houndmills: Macmillan, 1985); Hobsbawm, *Age of Extremes*; T. Szentes, *The Transformation of the World Economy: New Directions and New Interests* (London: Zed Books, 1988); G. Therborn, *European Modernity and Beyond: The Trajectory of European Societies 1945–2000* (London: Sage, 1996).

7 C. Leys, *The Rise and Fall of Development Theory* (Nairobi: East African Publishing House; Bloomington: Indiana University Press; London: James Currey, 1996), p. 193.

8 J. Habermas, 'Learning from Catastrophe? A Look Back at the Short Twentieth Century' in *The Postnational Constellation: Political Essays*, trans. M. Pensky (Oxford: Polity, 2001), p. 48.

9 B. Davidson, *The Black Man's Burden: Africa and the Curse of the Nation-State* (New York: Times Books, 1992), p. 196.

10 Compare the comments of the Zimbabwean novelist Chenjerai Hove, reflecting, in a 2007 interview, on the 'permanence' of the changes wrought by the national liberation struggle in his country, notwithstanding the brutality of the subsequent years of misrule and dictatorship under Robert Mugabe: 'You'll find that in my writing, I always use the liberation struggle as a back-drop because it gave us a new conscience. Who bore the brunt of the war? It was the peasants, the villagers. When I was a teacher in Bikita [District] during that time, we had nothing. I saw people killing their last goat, their last chicken to feed the guerrillas. And I saw that they had hope. They were not going to despair. They knew that the only permanent thing left was hope. That is why when I think of the future, I see permanence. What we fought for will never be taken away by anybody. Dictatorships, tyrannies, they are transient: they come and pass. I understand that and I will go through that.' 'Dictatorships are Transient', interview with Ranka Primorac, *Journal of Commonwealth Literature*, 43.1 (2008), p. 146.

11 For discussion of the achievements and legacies of anti-colonial nationalism and of political decolonisation in the sub-Saharan African context, see P. T. Zeleza, 'The Historic and Humanistic Agendas of African Nationalism: A Reassessment' in T. Falola and S. Hassan (eds), *Power and Nationalism in Modern Africa: Essays in Honor of the Memory of the Late Professor Don Ohadike*

(Durham, NC: Carolina Academic Press, 2008), pp. 37–53; and P. T. Zeleza, 'What Happened to the African Renaissance? The Challenges of Development in the Twenty-First Century', *Comparative Studies of South Asia, Africa and the Middle East*, 29.2 (2009), pp. 160ff.

12 In a nice turn of phrase, Peter Hitchcock speaks of 'the kinds of rulers … who turned the principle of sovereignty into their own self-image'. 'Post-colonial Failure and the Politics of the Nation', *South Atlantic Quarterly*, 106.4 (2007), p. 739. He refers explicitly here to Siad Barre, whose dictatorship in Somalia stretched from 1969 to 1991.

13 N. Larsen, 'Imperialism, Colonialism, Postcolonialism' in H. Schwartz and S. Ray (eds), *A Companion to Postcolonial Studies* (Oxford: Blackwell, 2005), p. 33. The reference is to the historic conference in 1955, at which leaders of the decolonising world (among them Nehru of India, Nasser of Egypt and Sukarno of the host country Indonesia, with Tito of Yugoslavia 'as the sole European interloper and Zhou-En-Lai [of China] the somewhat anxiously tolerated guest of honor') had launched the Non-aligned Movement.

14 J. Larrain, *Identity and Modernity in Latin America* (Oxford: Polity, 2000), p. 16.

15 N. Mailer, *The Naked and the Dead* (London; Flamingo, 1993 [1949]), p. 327.

16 See W. Blum, *Killing Hope: US Military and CIA Interventions since World War II* (London: Zed Books, 2003); N. Chomsky, *The Chomsky Reader*, ed. James Peck (New York: Pantheon, 1987), pp. 203–405; N. Chomsky, *Deterring Democracy* (New York: Hill and Wang, 1992).

17 T. Brennan, *At Home in the World: Cosmopolitanism Now* (Cambridge, MA: Harvard University Press, 1997), p. 33.

18 F. Fanon, *The Wretched of the Earth*, trans. C. Farrington (New York: Grove Press, 1968 [1961]), p. 164.

19 P. Wilkin, 'New Myths for the South: Globalization and the Conflict between Private Power and Freedom' in C. Thomas and P. Wilkin (eds), *Globalization and the South* (London: Macmillan; New York: St Martin's Press, 1997), p. 24.

20 W. Tabb, 'Globalization is *an* Issue, the Power of Capital is *the* Issue', *Monthly Review*, 49.2 (1997), p. 20.

21 For further commentary, see P. Bourdieu, *Firing Back: Against the Tyranny of the Market* 2, trans. L. Wacquant (London: Verso, 2003); P. Gowan, *The Global Gamble: Washington's Faustian Bid for World Dominance* (London and New York: Verso, 1999); and the essays in A. Saad-Filho (ed.), *Anti-Capitalism: A Marxist Introduction* (London: Pluto, 2003).

22 See the accounts in Z. Bauman, *Globalization: The Human Consequences* (New York: Columbia University Press, 1998); P. Bourdieu, *Acts of Resistance: Against the New Myths of our Time*, trans. R. Nice (Oxford: Polity, 1998); J. Brecher and T. Costello, *Global Village or Global Pillage: Economic Reconstruction from the Bottom Up* (Boston, MA: South End Press, 1994); A. Cockburn, *The Golden Age is in us: Journeys and Encounters 1987–1994* (London and New York: Verso, 1997); G. Duménil and D. Lévy, *Capital*

Resurgent: Roots of the Neoliberal Revolution, trans. D. Jeffers (Cambridge, MA: Harvard University Press, 2004); D. Harvey, *A Brief History of Neoliberalism* (Oxford University Press, 2005); H-P. Martin and H. Schumann, *The Global Trap: Globalization and the Assault on Prosperity and Democracy*, trans. P. Camiller (London and New York: Zed Books, 1997); K. Moody, *Workers in a Lean World: Unions in the International Economy* (London and New York: Verso, 1997); W. Tabb, *The Amoral Elephant: Globalization and the Struggle for Justice in the Twenty-First Century* (New York: Monthly Review Press, 2001).

23 J. Saul, *Millennial Africa: Capitalism, Socialism, Democracy* (Trenton and Asmara: Africa World Press, 2001), p. 23.

24 R. N. Gwynne and C. Kay, 'Latin America Transformed: Changing Paradigms, Debates and Alternatives' in R. N. Gwynne and C. Kay (eds), *Latin America Transformed: Globalization and Modernity* (London: Edward Arnold, 1999), p. 6.

25 For further commentary, see Zeleza, 'African Renaissance'.

26 H. K. Bhabha, *The Location of Culture* (London and New York: Routledge, 1994).

27 In the context of African literature, to give just one example, the first issue of the influential periodical, *African Literature Today*, was published in 1968, and the first issue of what is still the field's flagship journal, *Research in African Literatures*, appeared in 1970.

28 H. Alavi, 'The State in Post-Colonial Societies', *New Left Review*, 74 (1972), pp. 59–81; J. S. Saul, 'The State in Post-Colonial Societies: Tanzania' in R. Miliband and J. Saville (eds), *The Socialist Register* (New York: Monthly Review Press; London: Merlin Press, 1974), pp. 349–72, reprinted in J. S. Saul, *The State and Revolution in Eastern Africa* (New York and London: Monthly Review Press, 1979), pp. 167–99.

29 For a late example of such usage, see my own *Resistance in Postcolonial African Fiction* (New Haven, CT: Yale University Press, 1990).

30 A. Ahmad, 'The Politics of Literary Postcoloniality', *Race & Class*, 36.3 (1995), p. 1.

31 E. W. Said, 'East isn't East', *Times Literary Supplement*, 4792 (1995), p. 5.

32 A. Dirlik, 'The Postcolonial Aura: Third World Criticism in the Age of Global Capitalism', *Critical Inquiry*, 20 (1994), p. 352.

33 It is noteworthy that Dirlik makes no mention of Marxism in his diagnosis here of the contemporary 'crisis of progress' – which 'crisis' he sees as imposing upon us the burden of rethinking 'the structure of the globe'. Some scholars on the left, of course, were never much persuaded by 'three worlds theory' in the first place, and always preferred to conceptualise 'modernity' through reference to a capitalist *world-system*. For these theorists, Dirlik's 'crisis of progress' might be taken precisely to *confirm* their understanding of 'the structure of the globe', rather than to enjoin them to 'question' or rethink it. See also the discussion in Dirlik's *After the Revolution: Waking to Global Capitalism* (Hanover, VA: Wesleyan University Press, 1994).

34 In this respect, as Timothy Brennan has suggested, postcolonial studies can be regarded as a cousin of globalisation theory as well as a child of post-structuralism. 'From Development to Globalization: Postcolonial Studies and Globalization Theory' in N. Lazarus (ed.), *The Cambridge Companion to Postcolonial Literary Studies* (Cambridge University Press, 2004), pp. 120–38.

35 Cf. F. Jameson, *The Political Unconscious: Narrative as a Socially Symbolic Act* (Ithaca, NY: Cornell University Press, 1981).

36 See for example N. Lazarus, 'Doubting the New World Order: Marxism and Postmodernist Social Theory', *differences: A Journal of Feminist Cultural Studies*, 3.3 (1991), pp. 94–138; 'Transnationalism and the Alleged Death of the Nation-State' in Keith Ansell-Pearson, Benita Parry, and Judith Squires (eds), *Cultural Readings of Imperialism: Edward Said and the Gravity of History* (London: Lawrence and Wishart, 1997), pp. 28–48; 'Charting Globalization', *Race & Class*, 40.2 (1999), pp. 91–109; N. Lazarus, A. Arnove, S. Evans, and A. Menke, 'The Necessity of Universalism', *differences: A Journal of Feminist Cultural Studies*, 7.1 (1995), pp. 75–145.

37 D. Harvey, *The New Imperialism* (Oxford University Press, 2003), pp. 189–99.

38 N. Smith, 'After the American *Lebensraum*: "Empire", Empire and Globalization', *Interventions*, 5.2 (2003), pp. 263.

39 Cf. Edward Said, who commented in an interview in 2003 that '[t]errorism has become a sort of screen created since the end of the Cold War by policymakers in Washington as well as a whole group of people like Samuel Huntington and Steven Emerson, who have their meal ticket in that pursuit. It is fabricated to keep the population afraid, insecure, and to justify what the United States wishes to do globally . . . [T]he whole history of terrorism has a pedigree in the policies of imperialists. The French used the word terrorism for everything that the Algerians did to resist the French occupation, which began in 1830 and didn't end until 1962. The British used it in Burma, in Malaysia, the same idea. Terrorism is anything that stands in the face of what "we" want to do.' E.W. Said, *Culture and Resistance: Conversations with Edward W. Said* (Cambridge: South End Press, 2003), p. 89. See also J. B. Foster, 'Imperial America and War', *Monthly Review*, 55.1 (2003), pp. 1–10, and C. Johnson, *The Sorrows of Empire* (New York: Henry Holt, 2004).

40 S. Ray, 'Postscript: Popular Perceptions of Postcolonial Studies after 9/11' in H. Schwartz and S. Ray, *A Companion to Postcolonial Studies* (Oxford: Blackwell, 2005), p. 583. See also P. Ahluwalia, who congratulates postcolonial theorists on 'hav[ing] been at the forefront of breaking down imperial binaries' ('Afterlines of Post-Colonialism: Reflections on Theory post-9/11', *Postcolonial Studies*, 10.3 [2007], p. 267), but has nothing to say about imperialist violence even in an essay devoted explicitly to 'reflecting' 'on theory post-9/11'.

41 A. Loomba, S. Kaul, M. Bunzl, A. Burton, and J. Esty, 'Beyond What? An Introduction' in A. Loomba *et al.* (eds), *Postcolonial Studies and Beyond* (Durham, MD: Duke University Press, 2004), p. 1.

42 In the interests of full disclosure, I should state that my own essay, 'The Politics of Postcolonial Modernism' – an early version of the first part of what is now presented as Chapter 2, below – appears in this volume, pp. 423–38.

43 J. Schell, 'Letter from Ground Zero', *Nation*, 5 May 2003, p. 8.

44 R. Williams, *The Politics of Modernism: Against the New Conformists* (London and New York: Verso, 1990), p. 35.

45 F. Jameson, 'Third-World Literature in the Era of Multinational Capitalism', *Social Text*, 15 (1986), p. 69.

1 THE POLITICS OF POSTCOLONIAL MODERNISM

1 The phrase appears in Homi Bhabha's essay, 'The Postcolonial and the Postmodern: The Question of Agency' (*Location of Culture*, p. 173).

2 The symptomaticity of this particular hostility in contemporary critical theory overall has been well glossed by Fredric Jameson, who suggests that 'hostility to the concept of "totalization" would ... seem to be most plausibly decoded as a systematic repudiation of notions and ideals of praxis as such, or of the collective project'. *Postmodernism, or, The Cultural Logic of Late Capitalism* (Durham, NC: Duke University Press, 1995), p. 333.

3 See for instance Ahmad, *In Theory* and 'Literary Postcoloniality'; T. Brennan, *At Home* and *Wars of Position: The Cultural Politics of Left and Right* (New York: Columbia University Press, 2006); L. Chrisman, *Postcolonial Contraventions: Cultural Readings of Race, Imperialism and Transnationalism* (Manchester University Press, 2003); Dirlik, 'Postcolonial Aura' and 'Is there History after Eurocentrism? Globalism, Postcolonialism, and the Disavowal of History', *Cultural Critique*, 42 (1999), pp. 1–34; B. Jeyifo, 'The Nature of Things: Arrested Decolonization and Critical Theory', *Research in African Literatures*, 21.1 (1990), pp. 33–48; N. Larsen, *Determinations: Essays on Theory, Narrative and Nation in the Americas* (London and New York: Verso (2001) and 'Imperialism'; B. Parry, 'Directions and Dead Ends in Postcolonial Studies' in D. T. Goldberg and A. Quayson (eds), *Relocating Postcolonialism* (Oxford: Blackwell, 2002), pp. 66–81, *Postcolonial Studies: A Materialist Critique* (London and New York: Routledge, 2004) and 'Institutionalization of Postcolonial Studies'; E. San Juan, Jr, *Hegemony and Strategies of Transgression: Essays in Cultural Studies and Comparative Literature* (Albany: State University of New York Press, 1995) and *Beyond Postcolonial Theory* (New York: St Martin's Press, 1998). See also the essays by Brennan, Larsen, Parry, and San Juan, Jr in C. Bartolovich and N. Lazarus (eds), *Marxism, Modernity and Postcolonial Studies* (Cambridge University Press, 2002).

4 See for instance S. Gikandi, *Ngugi wa Thiong'o* (Cambridge University Press, 2000); 'Cultural Translation and the African Self: A (Post)Colonial Case Study', *Interventions*, 3.3 (2001), pp. 355–75; 'Theory, Literature and Moral Considerations', *Research in African Literatures*, 32.4 (2001), pp. 1–18; P. Gopal, *Literary Radicalism in India: Gender, Nation, and the Transition*

to Independence (London and New York: Routledge, 2005); N. Harrison, *Postcolonial Criticism: History, Theory and the Work of Fiction* (Oxford: Polity, 2003); P. C. Hogan, *Colonialism and Cultural Identity: Crises of Tradition in the Anglophone Literatures of India, Africa, and the Caribbean* (Albany: State University of New York Press, 2000); G. Huggan, *The Post-Colonial Exotic: Marketing the Margins* (London and New York: Routledge, 2001); D. Murphy, 'De-Centring French Studies: Towards a Postcolonial Theory of Francophone Cultures', *French Cultural Studies*, 38 (2002), pp. 165–85; S. Shankar, 'Midnight's Orphans, or, A Postcolonialism Worth its Name', *Cultural Critique*, 56 (2004), pp. 64–95; K. Sole, 'South Africa Passes the Posts', *Alternation*, 4.1 (1997), pp. 116–51; 'Political Fiction, Representation and the Canon: The Case of Mtutuzeli Matshoba', *English in Africa*, 28.2 (2001), pp. 101–22; 'The Witness of Poetry: Economic Calculation, Civil Society and the Limits of the Everyday in Post-Liberation South Africa', *New Formations*, 45 (2002), pp. 24–53.

5 Salman Rushdie, *Midnight's Children* (London: Jonathan Cape, 1981); *Shame* (New York: Alfred A. Knopf, 1983); *The Satanic Verses* (London: Viking, 1988).

6 A *locus classicus* of this sort of approach to Rushdie is to be found in Bhabha's essay, 'How Newness Enters the World: Postmodern Space, Postcolonial Times and the Trials of Cultural Translation' (*Location of Culture*, pp. 212–35). But see also C. Cundy, *Salman Rushdie* (Manchester University Press, 1996); A. Mufti, 'Reading the Rushdie Affair: "Islam", Cultural Politics, Form' in M. Keith Booker (ed.), *Critical Essays on Salman Rushdie* (New York: G. K. Hall, 1999), pp. 51–77; and J. C. Sanga, *Salman Rushdie's Postcolonial Metaphors: Migration, Translation, Hybridity and Globalization* (Westport, CT: Greenwood Press, 2001). A notable exception to such readings is T. Brennan, *Salman Rushdie and the Third World: Myths of the Nation* (Houndmills: Macmillan, 1989), in fact the first book-length study of Rushdie to have been published, which to this day stands almost alone in the critical literature in its attempt to *situate* the mode of representation in Rushdie and not simply to abstract it as an epistemology. The general point that I am making here has also been made forcefully by Gopal in *Literary Radicalism in India*, her book about the All-India Progressive Writers' Association. Gopal writes that 'the canonisation of a handful of authors, most prominently Salman Rushdie and Gabriel García Márquez' in post-colonial studies 'has allowed for a talismanic reiteration of privileged conceptual categories such as "hybridity" and "ambivalence". Even when an unambiguously liberationist and realist author such as Mahasweta Devi is brought to metropolitan academic attention by a distinguished theorist such as Gayatri Spivak (making for a salutary consideration of non-Anglophone texts), she must first be made fit for refined theoretical company. Her text must be "[reconstellated] to draw out its use", a process that entails undoing the distinction between history and fiction' (p. 3). See A. Ben-Yishai, 'The Dialectic of Shame: Representation in the Metanarrative of Salman Rushdie's

Shame', *Modern Fiction Studies*, 48.1 (2002), pp. 194–215 for an interesting 'negative dialectical' reading of *Shame* in explicit opposition to the 'decon-structive' commentaries on Rushdie of such theorists as Bhabha, Cundy, and Mufti.

7 I insert the scare quotes around the 'postcolonial' of '"postcolonial" literature' by way of emphasising that this is a problematical category. *Postcolonial studies* is an institutionalised field of academic specialisation. However, few of the literary writers whose work might be said to fall within the purview of this field would situate themselves as 'postcolonial' writers. See, for instance, T. Vijay Kumar's interview with Amitav Ghosh, in which the novelist explains his dislike of the term 'postcolonial' in description of his work. A. Ghosh, '"Postcolonial" Describes you as Negative', *Interventions*, 9.1 (2007), p. 105.

8 The term derives, of course, from Benedict Anderson's seminal text, *Imagined Communities: Reflections on the Origins and Spread of Nationalism* (London and New York: Verso, 1991 [1983]), although one needs to add that, in the postcolonial discussion, Anderson's own materialist premises are very largely disregarded.

9 Ben Okri, *The Famished Road* (London: Vintage, 1992 [1991]); Amitav Ghosh, *The Shadow Lines* (London: Viking, 1990).

10 See also G. Jusdanis, 'World Literature: the Unbearable Lightness of Think-ing Globally', *Diaspora*, 12.1 (2003), pp. 103–30. Jusdanis writes that 'Critics point to the self-consciousness of contemporary works of world literature; in other words, to novels that either are consciously prepared for the global market or are attentive to and thematize this market … To be sure, today's writers understand global literary fashions, the intricacies of the transnational book trade, and the current obsession with exoticism in the West. They may write with these in mind' (p. 118). Like Huggan in *The Post-Colonial Exotic*, Jusdanis views Arundhati Roy's *The God of Small Things* as 'emblematic' of such works. I note in passing my disagreement with this judgement, which tends, I think, to dissolve the difference between Roy's novel and the exoticised image of it projected by its 'new cosmopolitan *readers*'. These ideas are developed suggestively in S. Brouillette, *Postcolonial Writers in the Global Literary Marketplace* (London: Palgrave, 2007).

11 F. Jussawalla and R.W. Dasenbrock (eds), *Interviews with Writers of the Postcolonial World* (Jackson and London: University Press of Mississippi, 1992), p. 14.

12 Jussawalla's and Dasenbrock's conceptualisation of the status and tendency of these new traditions of writing has much in common with Wlad Godzich's theorisation of 'Emergent Literature in the Field of Comparative Literature' in *The Culture of Literacy* (Cambridge, MA: Harvard University Press, 1994), pp. 274–92. See also G. C. Spivak, *Death of a Discipline* (New York: Columbia University Press, 2003), which also argues for a new literary comparativism.

13 A far more sensitive approach to Ghose's work is to be found in Brouillette's *Postcolonial Writers in the Global Literary Marketplace*. Brouillette suggests

that Ghose 'goes to considerable lengths to distance himself from the cosmopolitan function of postcolonial literature, as sanctioned by the Anglo-
American market, and uses his novel (*The Triple Mirror of the Self* [London:
Bloomsbury, 1992]) to stage his rejection of the role of Third World writer
and the expectation that he will act as an interpreter of an authenticated
location' (p. 147). She subsequently adds: 'Ghose's tendency to focus on an
aesthetic tradition and literary impetus should be read as an attempt to
distinguish himself from this market niche and its usual legitimations. His
repeated insistence in his critical non-fiction that writers should espouse no
particular "-ism" popular with a current audience, while evidently combat-
ively dedicated to a troubled aesthetic ideology, takes on a different valence
when read in this light. It can be interpreted as an explicit and rather pained
reaction to his own racialization at the hands of his critical public' (p. 153).
See also C. Kanaganayakam, *Structures of Negation: The Writings of Zulfikar
Ghose* (University of Toronto Press, 1993), which also helps to pull Ghose
away from a 'postcolonialist' reception.

14 J. M. Coetzee, *Waiting for the Barbarians* (Harmondsworth: Penguin, 1982
[1980]); *Foe* (Johannesburg: Ravan Press, 1986); T. Ben Jelloun, *The Sand
Child*, trans. Alan Sheridan (San Diego, New York, London: Harcourt,
Brace, Jovanovich, 1987 [1985]); N. Farah, *Maps* (New York: Pantheon,
1986).

15 The Anglocentrism of postcolonial studies as an institutionalised form of
scholarship has often been deplored by scholars who work with French- or
Spanish-language materials. See for instance F. Coronil, 'Latin American
Postcolonial Studies and Global Decolonization' in N. Lazarus (ed.), *The
Cambridge Companion to Postcolonial Literary Studies* (Cambridge University
Press, 2004), pp. 221–40; D. Murphy, 'Beyond Anglophone Imperialism?',
New Formations, 59 (2006), pp. 132–43; and the various 'Opinion Pieces' in
the inaugural issue of *Francophone Postcolonial Studies*, 1.1 (2003).

16 Williams, *Politics of Modernism*, p. 33.

17 P. Bourdieu, *The Rules of Art: Genesis and Structure of the Literary Field*, trans.
S. Emanuel (Stanford University Press, 1996 [1992]), p. 224.

18 I consider this issue in greater detail in 'Modernism and African Literature' in
Mark Wollaeger (ed.), *Global Modernisms* (Oxford University Press, 2011).

19 S. Gikandi, 'The Short Century: On Modernism and Nationalism', *New
Formations*, 51 (2004), p. 19.

20 With Adorno, of course, almost the opposite is true. His treatment of
modernism dwells only on its aspect as critique and tends to ignore the large
volume of modernist work, from vorticism to futurism, Pound to Jünger to
Marinetti, that actively aligned itself with fascism.

21 T. W. Adorno, 'Commitment', trans. S. W. Nicholsen, in *Notes to Literature*,
vol. II, ed. R. Tiedemann (New York: Columbia University Press, 1992
[1962]), p. 90.

22 I am referring here to the wording in a second English translation of
Adorno's 'Commitment' essay. F. McDonagh translates the sentence we

are considering as follows: 'he over whom Kafka's wheels have passed, has lost forever both any peace with the world and any chance of consoling himself with the judgement that the way of the world is bad'. T. W. Adorno, 'Commitment', in A. Arato and E. Gebhardt (eds), *The Essential Frankfurt School Reader* (New York: Continuum, 1983), p. 315. Adorno's German original had read as follows: 'Wen einmal Kafkas Räder überfuhren, dem ist der Friede mit der Welt ebenso verloren wie die Möglichkeit, bei dem Urteil sich zu bescheiden, der Weltlauf sei schlecht: das bestätigende Moment ist weggeätzt, das der resignierten Feststellung von der Übermacht des Bösen innewohnt.' 'Engagement' in *Noten zur Literatur. Gesammelte Schriften*, vol. XI (Frankfurt on Main: Suhrkamp, 1974), p. 426.

23 In *A Singular Modernity: Essay on the Ontology of the Present* (London and New York, 2002), Jameson distinguishes between the initial 'modernism' of the 'classical' or 'high' modernist artists themselves and the subsequent 'ideology of modernism' – 'a belated product, and essentially an invention and an innovation of the years following World War II' (p. 164); indeed, 'an *American* invention' (p. 165, emphasis added) – which came to represent 'modernism', but on the basis of an attenuated and highly selective construction of it. This formulation does, in principle, allow for the possibility of a modernist writing after the canonisation of modernism, though it is striking that Jameson prefers to instance *postmodernism* here instead. Thus, of the modernist 'canon' as 'the late modernists have selected and rewritten it in their image', he writes that '[i]ts "greatness" and timeless permanence is the very sign of its historical impermanence; and it is with this late modernism that postmodernism attempts radically to break, imagining that it is thereby breaking with classical modernism, or even modernity, in general and as such' (p. 210). For an interesting and incisive critique of Jameson on modernism and postmodernism, inspired by Adorno, see R. Spencer, 'Fredric Jameson and the Ends of Art', unpublished Ph.D. thesis, University of Warwick, 2004.

24 G. García Márquez, *One Hundred Years of Solitude*, trans. G. Rabassa (New York: Harper and Row, 1970 [1967]); S. H. Manto, 'Toba Tek Singh' (1955), in *Kingdom's End and Other Stories*, trans. K. Hasan (New Delhi: Penguin Books, 1989), pp. 11–18.

25 In *J. M. Coetzee and the Ethics of Reading: Literature in the Event* (University of Chicago Press, 2005), Derek Attridge insists on the continuing ethically subversive value of modernist writing – which he privileges over 'postmodernist' cultural forms. But he defines this subversiveness as a feature of modernism in its anti-realist dimensions only, thus ratifying modernism's own bias (shared by postmodernism, ironically) against 'classical realism'. This restriction strikes me as both unwarranted and unnecessary. See also B. May, 'Reading Coetzee, Eventually', *Comparative Literature*, 48.4 (2007), pp. 629–38, for a discussion of Attridge's argument.

26 A. Roy, *The God of Small Things* (New York: Random House, 1997), p. 219. It would also have been possible to cite here the final line from Derek

Walcott's poem, 'Sea Grapes', in *Collected Poems 1948–1984* (New York: Farrar, Straus, and Giroux, 1990), p. 297: 'The classics can console. But not enough'. As Robert Spencer has pointed out to me, the idea enunciated in this line might be regarded as the counterpoint or dialectical corollary of the notion of 'disconsolation'. The point is not that culture does not console, but that the consolation it brings retains a critical purchase. In consoling us, 'the classics' do not reconcile us to life; they console us while fuelling our anger, leaving us, in fact, unreconciled. In responding to an earlier version of this chapter, Jed Esty suggested that since my central interest lies in identifying the *critical* thrust of 'postcolonial' literature, I ought to counterpose the notion of writing as disconsolation with a top-down, 'official' notion of writing as *consolation*, in analogy with Herbert Marcuse's notion of 'affirmative culture'. This is a very challenging suggestion. Marcuse distinguishes affirmative culture from culture as critique. The former corresponds in a sense to the dominant ideology of culture in bourgeois society: on the one hand, culture is celebrated as a transcendent realm of beauty, truth, and humane values which is 'essentially different from the factual world of the daily struggle for existence'; on the other hand, it is deemed at the same time to be 'realizable by every individual for himself "from within", without any transformation of the state of fact'. 'The Affirmative Character of Culture' (1937), in *Negations: Essays in Critical Theory*, trans. J. J. Shapiro (Harmondsworth: Penguin, 1968), p. 95. Affirmative culture therefore 'affirms' or 'consoles' without in any sense challenging the structures in the 'state of fact' (the 'real world') that make it necessary to project transcendence of it in the first instance. It might be possible to mobilise this Marcusean opposition between 'critical' and 'affirmative' culture in postcolonial literary studies. There is certainly a strain of criticism in the field – linked, most notably, to the liberal problematics of multiculturalism and cultural feminism – whose understanding of culture is 'affirmative' in the Marcusean sense. Hence, for instance, the numerous commentaries on Bessie Head's *A Question of Power* (London: Heinemann, 1974) that premise themselves unreflexively on the 'gesture of belonging' with which this novel ends; or the – again unreflexive – celebration of the motif of assimilation in Bharati Mukherjee's novels that, as the blurb on my copy of *Jasmine* (New York: Fawcett Crest, 1991 [1989]) has it, teach us 'what it is to become an American'.

27 K. Ishiguro, *The Unconsoled* (London: Faber and Faber, 1995).

28 K. Ishiguro, *A Pale View of Hills* (London: Faber and Faber, 1982); *An Artist of the Floating World* (London: Faber and Faber, 1986); *The Remains of the Day* (London: Faber and Faber, 1989).

29 The reference is of course to Walter Benjamin's 'Theses on the Philosophy of History' (1940) in *Illuminations*, trans. H. Zohn (New York: Schocken, 1969), p. 263.

30 This is a point that is touched on by Barry Lewis in *Kazuo Ishiguro* (Manchester University Press, 2000). Lewis proposes both that 'dignity . . . is what Ishiguro's novels are "about"' and also that 'they are equally about

displacement, which is the removal of dignity'. 'Or perhaps', he reasons further, 'dignity and displacement and storytelling are just different ways of saying that the books address what Ishiguro calls the "scariest arena in life, which is the emotional arena". Emotion: a simple noun – with tentacles. Yet in Ishiguro's fictions, the heart is where the home is' (p. 146). See also W. C. Sim, 'Kazuo Ishiguro', *Review of Contemporary Fiction*, 25.1 (2005), pp. 80–115; *Globalization and Dislocation in the Novels of Kazuo Ishiguro* (Lewiston, Queenstown, Lampeter: Edwin Mellen Press, 2006); *Kazuo Ishiguro* (London and New York: Routledge, 2009).

31 G. Pearce, 'Margins and Modernism: Ireland and the Formation of Modern Literature', unpublished Ph.D. thesis, Monash University, 2002.

32 In *The Caribbean Postcolonial: Social Equality, Post/Nationalism, and Cultural Hybridity* (New York: St Martin's Press; London: Palgrave, 2003), Shalini Puri proposes that we construe Bhabha's writings under the generic sign of the manifesto rather than of criticism. Viewed thus, they are able to emerge as utopian texts, exemplifying an 'intense nostalgia for the poetic word'. This argument is suggestive with respect to the theoretical work of such writers as Glissant and Walcott – and it is with these writers, and with Caribbean discourse in general, that Puri is centrally concerned in her book – but I am less convinced as to its applicability to Bhabha, not least because in his case, unlike in those of Glissant and Walcott, there is no creditable accompanying work in poetry, drama, or fiction.

33 I was born into a large peasant family: father, four wives and about twenty-eight children. I also belonged, as we all did in those days, to a wider extended family and to the community as a whole.
   We spoke Gikuyu as we worked in the fields. We spoke Gikuyu in and outside the home. I can vividly recall those evenings of story-telling around the fireside. It was mostly the grown-ups telling the children but everybody was interested and involved ... We ... learnt to value words for their meaning and nuances. Language was not a mere string of words. It had a suggestive power well beyond the immediate and lexical meaning ... the language, through images and symbols, gave us a view of the world ... The home and the field were then our pre-primary school but what is important, for this discussion, is that the language of our evening teach-ins, and the language of our immediate and wider community, and the language of our work in the fields were one.
   And then I went to school, a colonial school, and this harmony was broken. The language of my education was no longer the language of my culture' ...
   Ngugi wa Thiong'o, *Decolonising the Mind: The Politics of Language in African Literature* (London: James Currey; Nairobi, Portsmouth NH: Heinemann; Harare: Zimbabwe Publishing House, 1987), pp. 10–11.

34 Ngugi wa Thiong'o, *Petals of Blood* (London: Heinemann, 1977); *Devil on the Cross*, trans. Ngugi wa Thiong'o (London: Heinemann, 1982 [1980]); *Matigari*, trans. Wangui wa Goro (London: Heinemann, 1989 [1987]); *Wizard of the Crow*, trans. Ngugi wa Thiong'o (London: Harvill Secker, 2006).

35 N. Sahgal, *Prison and Chocolate Cake* (New Delhi: HarperCollins, 1953); *This Time of Morning* (London: Victor Gollancz, 1965); *A Time to be Happy*

(New Delhi: Sterling Publishers, 1975); *Rich Like Us* (W. W. Norton, 1986 [1985]); *Mistaken Identity* (New York: New Directions, 1988); *Lesser Breeds* (New Delhi: HarperCollins, 2003). See P. Jani, *Decentering Rushdie: Cosmopolitanism and the Indian Novel in English* (Columbus: Ohio State University Press, 2010) for a penetrating and sensitive examination of the ideological positions occupied by Sahgal over the course of her career.

36   T. Mo, *Renegade or Halo²* (London: Paddleless Press, 1999), p. 10.

37   S. Huntington, *The Clash of Civilizations and the Remaking of World Order* (London: Touchstone, 1998).

38   I would, however, resist the suggestion that what I am calling for here is a 'sociology of literature' rather than 'literary criticism' proper. What is at issue is not 'form' versus 'content' or 'text' versus 'context'. The point is well made by Roberto Schwarz in his suggestion that '[literary] forms are the abstract of specific social relationships'. *Misplaced Ideas: Essays on Brazilian Culture* (London and New York: Verso, 1992), p. 53. Schwarz adds: 'that is how … the difficult process of transformation of social questions into properly literary ones – ones that deal with internal logic and not with origins – is realized'. See also the discussion in Williams's essay, 'Literature and Sociology' in *Problems in Materialism and Culture: Selected Essays* (London: Verso, 1980), esp. pp. 22–5.

39   In a discussion of the relationship between 'theory' and 'literature' in the African context, S. Gikandi has argued, in similar vein, that 'the narrative of human beings, rather than subjects, which recent African writing has foregrounded, seems at odds with some of the major claims of poststructural theory' ('Theory, Literature', p. 4). Just the opposite is claimed by Mpalive-Hangson Msiska, in the context of a discussion of Chinua Achebe's *Things Fall Apart* – '*Things Fall Apart*: A Resource for Cultural Theory', *Interventions*, 11.2 (2009), pp. 171–5. Msiska contends that 'Postcolonial critical practice is the veritable offspring of postcolonial textual creative practice. Postcolonial writing as paradigmatically expressed in Achebe's novel, accounts for this theoretical practice's distinctive ideological lineaments and moral geography. What I am saying here is that as postcolonial critics, the texts we study have given us our critical ethical moorings as well as the fundamental categories which inform our critical analysis … the particularity of our practice arises out of the dynamic interaction with these texts' (p. 172). The untenability of this claim is already partially attested to by the fact that Achebe's novel has actually been comparatively little discussed by 'postcolonial' critics, as distinct from critics of 'African literature', for whom it has been central. The truth is that there is no congruity but rather a vast gap between the world-view that one encounters in Achebe's work and the 'ideological lineaments and moral geography' encountered in postcolonial theory.

40   I derive my terms here, of course, from E. W. Said's *The World, the Text, and the Critic* (Cambridge, MA: Harvard University Press, 1983).

41   B. Parry, 'Countercurrents and Tensions in Said's Critical Practice' in Adel Iskandar and Hakem Rustom (eds), *Edward Said: A Legacy of Emancipation and Representation* (Berkeley: University of California Press, 2010), p. 508.

42 K. Marx, *Capital: A Critique of Political Economy*, vol. I, 2nd edn, trans. B. Fowkes (Harmondsworth: Penguin, 1990 [1873]), p. 125.

43 I. Wallerstein, *Historical Capitalism* with *Capitalist Civilization* (London and New York: Verso, 1996), pp. 11–43; S. Labou Tansi, *The Antipeople*, trans. J. A. Underwood (London and New York: Marion Boyars, 1988 [1983]), p. 28.

44 T. Sivanandan, '"Lies of our own Making": The Post-Colonial Nation-State in the Writings of Ngugi wa Thiong'o, V. S. Naipaul and Salman Rushdie', unpublished MA dissertation, University of Essex, 1993, p. 15.

45 The *Rosales Saga* is made up of *The Sampsons* (New York: Modern Library, 2000), comprising two novels, *The Pretenders* (1962) and *Mass* (1982); *Tree* (Manila: Solidaridad, 1978, but originally serialised a decade earlier); *My Brother, My Executioner* (Quezon City: New Day, 1979 [1973]); and *Po-on* (*Dusk*) (New York: Modern Library, 1998 [1984]).

46 A. Munif, *Cities of Salt*, trans. P. Theroux (New York: Vintage, 1989 [1984]); C. Fuentes, *The Years with Laura Díaz*, trans. A. Mac Adam (New York: Farrar, Straus, and Giroux, 2000 [1999]); E. Lovelace, *Salt* (London and Boston: Faber and Faber, 1996).

47 P. Anderson, 'Modernity and Revolution', *New Left Review*, 144 (1984), p. 101. In this sense, the famous passages from the *Communist Manifesto* that seem to evoke a transformation that is as abrupt as it is total, are potentially misleading: 'All fixed, fast-frozen relations, with their train of ancient prejudices and opinions are swept aside, all new-formed ones become antiquated before they can ossify. All that is solid melts into air', etc. K. Marx and F. Engels, *Manifesto of the Communist Party* (Beijing: Foreign Languages Press, 1988 [1848]), p. 38. But just as readings of such passages in the *Manifesto* as being infused with enthusiasm for capitalism typically 'forget' that the writings of Marx and Engels are notable also for recording and protesting the violence of expropriation, the systematised misery and servitude that the imposition of capitalist social relations visited on populations everywhere, so too it is necessary to insist that the authors were well aware of the fact that the 'capitalist revolution' was not a once and for all event, but rather a sprawling, erratic and bloody historical process.

48 L. Trotsky, *History of the Russian Revolution*, vol. I, trans. M. Eastman (London: Sphere Books, 1967 [1932–3]), p. 432.

49 Lu Hsun, 'A Madman's Diary' [1918] in *Selected Stories of Lu Hsun*, trans. Yang Hsien-yi and Gladys Yang (Peking: Foreign Languages Press, 1978; O. Sembène, *Xala*, trans. Clive Wake (London: Heinemann, 1976 [1974].

50 F. Jameson, 'On Magic Realism in Film', *Critical Inquiry*, 12 (1986), p. 311. Cf. also the argument in the concluding section of his book on postmodernism that modernism itself must be seen as 'uniquely corresponding to an uneven moment of social development', in which there is a 'peculiar overlap of future and past', such that 'the resistance of archaic feudal structures to irresistible modernizing tendencies' is evident (*Postmodernism*, pp. 307, 309). Jameson illustrates this argument through reference to Kafka's *The Trial*,

focusing on the juxtaposition in the novel of a thoroughly modernised economic order and an older, indeed archaic, legal bureaucracy and political order deriving from the Austro-Hungarian Empire.

51 He adds that comparative analysis of this kind 'would necessarily include such features as the interrelationship of social classes, the role of intellectuals, the dynamics of language and writing, the configuration of traditional forms, the relationship to western influences, the development of urban experience and money, and so forth'.

52 Faiz Ahmed Faiz, *The Rebel's Silhouette: Selected Poems*, trans. Agha Shahid Ali (Amherst: University of Massachusetts Press, 1995), p. 5.

53 A more literal translation of the lines quoted would read as follows: 'The dark, dreadful mysteries of countless centuries / have been woven into brocades and silks / here and there bodies being sold in narrow streets and bazaars / smeared with dust, bathed in blood / The gaze returns to this as well, what is to be done? / Your beauty is still heart-rending, what is to be done?' I thank Shafaq Afraz, a former MA student of mine at Warwick, for providing me with this rendition.

54 The result is to align the poem at this point with the *Communist Manifesto's* heady asseveration: 'The history of all hitherto existing society is the history of class struggles' (p. 32).

55 Mahasweta Devi, 'Pterodactyl, Puran Sahay, and Pirtha' in *Imaginary Maps: Three Stories by Mahasweta Devi*, trans. G. C. Spivak (New York and London: Routledge, 1995), p. 97.

56 Mahasweta Devi, 'Paddy Seeds' (1979) in K. Bardhan (ed.), *Of Women, Outcastes, Peasants, and Rebels*, trans. K. Bardhan (Berkeley: University of California Press, 1990), pp. 168–9. Mahasweta's narrative links this razing of Tamadi village to the burning of the Khandava forest in the *Mahabharata*. 'In some places, a few Rajputs or Brahmans or Kayasthas, and more than a few Bhumihars or Jadavs or Kurmis, may be as poor as the untouchables. Sometimes they may be even poorer. But they are not thrown into the fire so readily, with such impunity. The god of fire must have to this day remained partial to the meat of the untouchable, ever since the time of the burning of the Khandava forest, which gave him the taste for roasted flesh of the dark-skinned dwellers of the forest' (p. 169). In her reading of 'Paddy Seeds', Jennifer Wenzel attributes these ideas to Dulan himself, rather than to the narrative voice: 'for Dulan, the trappings of modern democracy have failed to resolve the ancient conflict symbolized in the charred remains of the Khandava forest'. 'Epic Struggles over India's Forests in Mahasweta Devi's Short Fiction', *Alif: Journal of Comparative Poetics*, 18 (1998), p. 138. Whether we accept this reading or not, it appears that Wenzel has mistaken the narrative sequence that leads up to the razing of Tamadi village. She writes: 'When in Mahasweta's story "Paddy Seeds", a rivalry between two cousins, both Rajput landlords, results in the burning to the ground of an entire low caste village'. In fact, Lachman Singh burns Tamadi village to the ground not in the playing out of a rivalry with his cousin, but in order to punish Karan Dusad

for his presumption in asking Madanlal of the *Harijan Sewa Sangha* to advocate on his behalf for higher wages – and to set an example, in doing so, to all those eking out an existence on his land.

57 Cf. S. Banerjee: 'To describe [the] … relentless struggle between the oppressed and the oppressors, the powerful and the powerless, at the various levels of our society, Mahasweta Devi has developed a unique style that combines stinging wit with a note of pathos. When she touches this note in her stories, it never degenerates into the melodrama that is the usual staple of most bestsellers by today's Bengali authors. Instead, it gains force from the contrast with the tone of unemotional cynicism with which she narrates the events or describes the characters.' 'Translator's Note', Mahasweta Devi, *Bait: Four Stories* (Calcutta: Seagull Books, 2004), p. xxi.

58 The routine nature of this violence is further attested to by the sheer ubiquity of its appearance in Mahasweta's work: in her story 'Douloti the Bountiful', for instance, we read of Bono Nagesia, who builds a house with money that he has saved, only to have it burnt down by the landlord: 'Munabar Singh Chandela got some men to surround the place and burn Bono's house. They trussed up Bono like a pig and carried him hanging to Munabar's office. It was quite dark. Munabar's face couldn't be seen. But Bono could feel that even at the sight of Munabar's face no compassion would come. Nor the thought that Munabar was some mother's darling' ('Douloti the Bountiful' in *Imaginary Maps: Three Stories by Mahasweta Devi*, trans. G. C. Spivak (New York and London: Routledge, 1995), p. 28). Bono is subsequently forced by Munabar to sign a document indenturing himself to the landlord. Contemplating this development, Bono's neighbour Bhuneswar thinks to himself: 'What's there to weep for? Has the master never burnt down a new house put up by a poor Nagesia before this? Did a poor Nagesia never become a bondslave before this? It had happened before, and would happen again. It would go on in this way for as long as my lord the Sun would rise from the Eastern Hills and set in the Western Hills' (pp. 28–9).

59 In addition to the stories already discussed, see especially 'Pterodactyl, Puran Sahay, and Pirtha', in which the inability of the journalist, Puran, to represent the knowledge, forms of consciousness and custom of the Adivasi community of Pirtha in Madhya Pradesh is central to the narrative; 'Operation? – Bashai Tudu' (1978) in *Bashai Tudu*, trans. S. Bandyopadhyay (Calcutta: Thema, 1990), pp. 1–148; and *Mother of 1084*, trans. S. Bandyopadhyay (Calcutta: Seagull, 2001 [1973]). The latter two are formally and stylistically very different works centred on the Naxalite uprising. See Chapter 3, below, for further commentary on 'Pterodactyl, Puran Sahay, and Pirtha'.

60 R. Mistry, *A Fine Balance* (New York: Vintage International, 1997 [1995]).

61 M. R. Anand, *Untouchable* (Harmondsworth: Penguin, 1986 [1935]) and *Coolie* (Harmondsworth: Penguin, 1993 [1936]); P. Renu, *The Soiled Border*, trans. I. Junghare (Delhi: Chanakya Publications, 1991 [1954]); G. Mohanty, *Paraja*, trans. B. K. Das (Oxford University Press, 1989 [1945]); B. Bhattacharya,

So Many Hungers! (London: Victor Gollancz, 1947) and *A Goddess Named Gold* (New Delhi: Arnold-Heinemann, 1984 [1960]). I ask my readers' indulgence for the fact that here, and elsewhere in this chapter, I resort occasionally to a mere listing of titles. I recognise that is stylistically cumbersome and might come across as being pretentious. But I have not been able to think of another way of making the point, central to my argument in general, that the themes and motifs I am discussing are pervasive across the full range of 'postcolonial' literature.

62 Vikram Seth, *A Suitable Boy* (London: Phoenix, 1994), p. 1131.

63 Cf. Mahasweta, 'Pterodactyl, Puran Sahay, and Pirtha': 'The same person, at the same time, banishes poverty in Constitution and Proclamation, creates poverty, protests in art-films' (p. 140).

64 M. Argueta, *One Day of Life*, trans. B. Brow (New York: Aventura, 1983 [1980]) and *Cuzcatlán*, trans. C. Hensen (London: Chatto and Windus, 1987); Shahnon Ahmad, *No Harvest but a Thorn*, trans. A. Amin (Kuala Lumpur: Oxford University Press, 1972 [1966]) and *Rope of Ash*, trans. H. Aveling (Kuala Lumpur: Oxford University Press, 1979 [1965]); A. R. al-Sharqawi, *Egyptian Earth*, trans. Desmond Stewart (London: Al Saqi Books, 1994 [1954]); C. Hove, *Bones* (London: Heinemann, 1990 [1988]); Jia Pingwa, *Turbulence*, trans. H. Goldblatt (New York: Grove Press, 1991 [1987]).

65 See for example S. Basu, *Selected Stories*, vol. I, trans. S. Banerjee (Calcutta: Thema, 2003); R. de Boissière, *Crown Jewel* (London, Picador, 1981 [1952]); C. Fuentes, *Where the Air is Clear*, trans. S. Hileman (New York: Farrar, Straus, and Giroux, 1960 [1958]); R. Heath, *A Man Come Home* (Port of Spain: Longman, 1974); F. Iyayi, *Violence* (Harlow: Longman, 1987 [1979]) and *The Contract* (Harlow: Longman, 1982); Lao She, *Rickshaw*, trans. J. M. James (Honolulu: University Press of Hawaii, 1979 [1937]); N. Mahfouz, *Midaq Alley*, trans. T. Le Gassick (Washington: Three Continents Press, 1981 [1947]), *The Cairo Trilogy: Palace Walk*, trans. W. M. Hutchins and O. E. Kenny (London: Doubleday, 1991 [1956]), *Palace of Desire*, trans. W. M. Hutchins, L. M. and O. E. Kenny (London: Doubleday, 1991 [1957]) and *Sugar Street*, trans. W. M. Hutchins and A. B. Samaan (London: Black Swan, 1994 [1957]); O. Sembène, *God's Bits of Wood*, trans. F. Price (London: Heinemann, 1976 [1960]), *Xala* and *The Money Order*, trans. C. Wake (London: Heinemann, 1977 [1965]).

66 See for example C. Bulosan, *America is in the Heart* (Seattle: University of Washington Press, 1990 [1946]); J. Kincaid, *Lucy* (New York: Plume, 1991 [1990]); T. Mo, *Brownout on Breadfruit Boulevard* (London: Paddleless Press, 1995) and *Renegade or Halo²*; S. Selvon, *The Lonely Londoners* (London: Longman, 1985 [1956]), *The Housing Lark* (Washington, DC: Three Continents Press, 1990 [1965]) and *Moses Ascending* (London: Heinemann, 1984 [1975]).

67 Nirala, *A Season on the Earth: Selected Poems of Nirala*, trans. D. Rubin (Oxford University Press, 2003), p. 39.

68 The specific object of Bourdieu's analysis is the French literary field at the end of the nineteenth century; but while much of what he says pertains to this particular context only, the broad structural dynamics that he identifies are arguably of wider applicability. See P. Bourdieu, *The Field of Cultural Production: Essays on Art and Literature* (New York: Columbia University Press, 1993) and also 'The Intellectual Field: A World Apart' (1985) in *In Other Words: Essays Towards a Reflexive Sociology*, trans. M. Adamson (Stanford University Press, 1990), where he argues that '[t]he fields of cultural production occupy a dominated position in the field of power ... Or, to retranslate this into a more common (but inadequate) language, I could say that artists and writers, and more generally intellectuals, are a dominated fraction of the dominant class' (pp. 144–5). He adds that '[t]his contradictory position of dominant-dominated, of dominated among the dominant or, to make use of the homology with the political field, of the left wing of the right wing, explains the ambiguity of the positions they adopt, an ambiguity which is linked to this precariously balanced position' (p. 145). Individual cultural producers may, in terms of this schema, place the specific power that they hold 'at the service of the dominant. They may also, in the logic of their struggle within the field of power, put their power at the service of the dominated in the social field taken as a whole' (p. 146). In 'postcolonial' contexts, it is the latter gesture that is the more common.

69 This point is developed further in Chapter 3, below.

70 E. Mphahlele, *The African Image*, rev. edn (New York and Washington, DC: Praeger, 1974), p. 77; W. Soyinka, 'The Writer in a Modern African State' (1967) in *Art, Dialogue and Outrage: Essays on Literature and Culture* (London: Methuen, 1993), p. 20.

71 Lu Hsun, 'The True Story of Ah Q' (1921) in *Selected Stories of Lu Hsun*, trans. Yang Hsien-yi and G. Yang (Peking: Foreign Languages Press, 1971), p. 67.

72 T. W. Adorno, *Minima Moralia: Reflections from Damaged Life*, trans. E. F. N. Jephcott (London: Verso, 1978 [1951]), p. 28.

73 D. Rubin, 'Nirala and the Renaissance of Hindi Poetry', *Journal of Asian Studies*, 31.1 (1971), p. 121.

74 I. Sant, 'Household Fires' [1975], trans. V. Dharwadker, in V. Dharwadker and A. K. Ramanujan (eds), *The Oxford Anthology of Modern Indian Poetry* (Oxford University Press, 1995), pp. 48–9.

75 A comparison might be drawn in this respect between Hsiang Tzu in Lao She's novel and Munoo in Mulk Raj Anand's *Coolie*, published just one year earlier in 1937.

76 A. Laâbi, 'Writing requires more than one hand' (1993) in *The World's Embrace: Selected Poems*, trans. A. George, E. Makward, V. Reinking, and P. Joris (San Francisco: City Lights Books, 2003), p. 99.

77 A. K. Armah, *Fragments* (London: Heinemann, 1979 [1970]; B. Okri, *Dangerous Love* (London: Phoenix, 1996).

78 B. Bose, *Selected Poems*, trans. K. K. Dyson (Oxford University Press, 2003), p. 24.

79 Thus Nizar Qabbani, for example:

> Friends!
> What is poetry if it does not declare mutiny?
> If it does not topple tyrants?
> What is poetry if it does not stir up volcanoes where we need them?
> And what is poetry if it cannot dislodge the crown
> Worn by the powerful kings of this world?
>
> 'A Very Secret Report from Fist Country' in *On Entering the Sea: The Erotic and Other Poetry of Nizar Qabbani*, trans. L. Jayyusi and S. Elmusa (New York: Interlink Books, 1996), p. 119.

80 In the contemporary circuits of 'second generation' postmodernist theory, indeed, the work associated with such figures as Giorgio Agamben, Michael Hardt and Antonio Negri, Paolo Virno, and Jean-Luc Nancy, this 'early' postmodernist provocation is given a further twist: it seems that not only is all social practice 'writing', but the most significant forms of value are now immaterial. For succinct materialist critiques of this hyperidealist discourse, see the special issue of *South Atlantic Quarterly*, 108.2 (2009), devoted to the topic of 'Intellectual Labor', and especially T. Brennan, 'Intellectual Labor', pp. 395–415 and K. Ganguly, 'Introduction: After Resignation and Against Conformity', pp. 239–47.

81 T. Eagleton, *Ideology: An Introduction* (London: Verso, 1991), p. 219. Eagleton continues: 'Why should we want to *call* a building a "menu", just because in some structuralist fashion we might examine it along those lines? … The category of discourse is inflated to the point where it imperializes the whole world, eliding the distinction between thought and material reality' (p. 219). Similarly, I am suggesting, the category of 'writing' is inflated in postmodernist and poststructuralist literary theory to the point where it imperialises the whole world, eliding the distinction between *literary* production and other kinds of work.

82 An important critical work is U. P. Mukherjee's recent study, *Postcolonial Environments: Nature, Culture and the Contemporary South Asian Novel in English* (Houndmills: Palgrave Macmillan, 2010). See also G. Huggan and H. Tiffin, 'Green Postcolonialism', *Interventions*, 9.1 (2009), pp. 1–11.

83 R. Williams, *The Country and the City* (Oxford University Press, 1973), p. 2.

84 Cf. C. Craig, *Out of History: Narrative Paradigms in Scottish and English Culture* (Edinburgh: Polygon, 1996). Craig's critique focuses on the unportability of Williams's analysis to the specifically peripheralised Scottish context.

85 J. Graham, *Land and Nationalism in Fictions from Southern Africa: Culture, Politics, and Self-Representation* (London and New York: Routledge, 2009).

86 T. Mofolo, *Chaka*, trans. D. P. Kunene (London: Heinemann, 1981 [1925, first English translation, 1931]), pp. 1–2.

87 J. Bernabé, P. Chamoiseau and R. Confiant, *Éloge de la créolité: In Praise of Creoleness*, trans. M. B. Taleb-Khyar (Baltimore, MD: Johns Hopkins University Press, 1990), p. 76.

88 P. Chamoiseau, *Texaco*, trans. R.-M. Réjouis and V. Vinokurov (New York: Vintage, 1998 [1992]), p. 184.

89 Marie-Sophie explains that the term '*noutéka*' was coined by her father as 'a kind of magical *we*', a solidaristic and trans-individual consciousness of community developed and secured against enormous odds: 'He loaded it with the meaning of one fate for many, invented the *we* that would prey on his mind in his last years' (pp. 122–3).

90 D. Harvey, *Consciousness and the Urban Experience* (Baltimore, MD: Johns Hopkins University Press, 1985); M. Berman, *All that is Solid Melts into Air: The Experience of Modernity* (London: Verso, 1983).

91 R. Williams, 'The Welsh Industrial Novel' in *Problems in Materialism and Culture: Selected Essays* (London: Verso, 1980), p. 214.

92 Cf. Priyamvada Gopal, who writes of *A Fine Balance* that it 'explores the issue of how ... cataclysmic historical events unfold in insistently personal terms. The grand sweep of communal violence, caste oppression, patriarchy, agrarian politics, economic exploitation, and urban migration all make their presence felt through small, but powerful, individual stories of loss, despair, pain, small victories, quiet resistance, and the occasional triumph. The making and breaking of families, friendships, and small communities are unique affairs deriving from specific encounters and dynamics, yet they are inexorably shaped by forces and histories that extend well beyond them.' *The Indian English Novel: Nation, History, and Narration* (Oxford University Press, 2009), p. 122.

93 D. M. Diop, 'The Vultures' (1956) in *Hammer Blows*, trans. Simon Mpondo and Frank Jones (London: Heinemann, 1975), p. 5.

94 M. Carter, 'I come from the Nigger Yard' (1954) in *Poems of Succession* (London and Port of Spain: New Beacon Books, 1977), p. 38.

95 A. Césaire, *Notebook of a Return to the Native Land* (1939) in *The Collected Poetry of Aimé Césaire*, trans. C. Eshleman and A. Smith (Berkeley: University of California Press, 1983), pp. 43–85. See the interesting discussion of what she calls the 'Césaire Effect' in M. Rosello, 'The "Césaire Effect", or How to Cultivate One's Nation', *Research in African Literatures*, 32.4 (2001), pp. 77–91.

96 A. Césaire, *Ferrements* (1960) in *Collected Poetry of Aimé Césaire*, pp. 260–357.

97 A. A. Neto, 'Here I Stand' (1960) in *Sacred Hope*, trans. M. Holness (Dar es Salaam: Tanzania Publishing House, 1974).

98 B. S. al-Sayyab, 'Rain Song' [1960], trans, L. Jayyusi and C. Middleton in S. K. Jayyusi (ed.), *Modern Arabic Poetry* (New York: Columbia University Press, 1987), pp. 429–30.

99 The concept of 'resistance literature' is interestingly deployed in B. Harlow, *Resistance Literature* (New York and London: Methuen, 1987). See also B. Harlow, *After Lives: Legacies of Revolutionary Writing* (London and New York: Verso, 1996).

100 M. Darwish, 'Poem of the Land', trans. L. Jayyusi and C. Middleton in S. K. Jayyusi (ed.), *Anthology of Modern Palestinian Literature* (New York: Columbia University Press, 1992), p. 146.

101 A. Loomba, *Colonialism/Postcolonialism* (London and New York: Routledge, 1998).

102 An exception that might be said to prove the rule is provided by the example of Singapore, in which a strongly accented statist nationalism in the aftermath of decolonisation is used to rationalise a profound, and indeed ruthless, transformation of the independent nation. See J. K. Watson, 'The Way Ahead: The Politics and Poetics of Singapore's Developmental Landscape', *Contemporary Literature*, 49.4 (2008), pp. 683–711. Watson discusses the statist discourse of Lee Kuan Yew's government itself; but his essay is particularly insightful in its examination of the poetry of Edwin Thumboo, which provides a celebratory 'monumentalisation' of statist modernisation, and in the contrast that it establishes between Thumboo's verse and that of Arthur Yap. See also R. B. H. Goh, 'Imagining the Nation: The Role of Singapore Poetry in English in "Emergent Nationalism"', *Journal of Commonwealth Literature*, 41.2 (2006), pp. 21–41; and R. S. Patke, *Postcolonial Poetry in English* (Oxford University Press, 2006).

103 E. W. Said in an interview with J. Wicke and M. Sprinker in M. Sprinker (ed.), *Edward Said: A Critical Reader* (Oxford: Blackwell, 1992), p. 236. Predicating himself explicitly on Fanon's 'The Pitfalls of National Consciousness', Said speaks of the widespread failure of the political elites in the newly independent states, in the years following decolonisation, to transform 'national consciousness into political and social consciousness' (p. 236); see also E. W. Said, *Reflections on Exile and Other Literary and Cultural Essays* (London: Granta, 2001), pp. 377–8.

104 A. Roy, 'Fascism's Firm Footprint in India', *Nation*, 275.10 (2002), p. 18.

105 S. Khilnani, *The Idea of India* (Harmondsworth: Penguin, 1998), p. 9.

106 A. K. Armah, *The Beautyful Ones are not yet Born* (London: Heinemann, 1981 [1968]), p. 63.

107 T. Simatei, 'Colonial Violence, Postcolonial Violations: Violence, Landscape, and Memory in Kenyan Fiction', *Research in African Literatures*, 36.2 (2005), p. 91.

108 The mention of Fanon here is overdetermined, since postcolonial Algeria might be cited as a particular instance of this 'state-enforced amnesia' – or, as the historian Benjamin Stora calls it, 'fabricated forgetting'. *Algeria, 1820–2000: A Brief History*, trans. J. M. Todd (Ithaca, NY: Cornell University Press, 2001), p. 190. See also R. Vallury, who, glossing Stora's commentary on Chadli Bendjedid's presidency of 1979–1992, speaks of the Algerian state's wilful 'manufacturing [of] a unanimist national (and revolutionary) history that delegitimizes linguistic and cultural plurality in Algeria'. 'Walking the Tightrope between Memory and History: Metaphor in Tahar Djaout's *L'Invention du désert*', *Novel*, 41.2–3 (2008), p. 329.

109 W. Soyinka, 'Elegy for a Nation' in *Samarkand, and Other Markets I have Known* (London: Methuen, 2002), p. 68. In an interesting commentary, Neil ten Kortenaar has suggested, with reference to Soyinka's *Season of Anomy* (London: Rex Collings, 1973) and Achebe's *Anthills of the Savannah* (London: Heinemann, 1987), that neither can be described as 'nationalist' in the strict sense, since nationalism 'posits a congruity between cultural identity (the nation) and political identity (the state), and with no readers do the characters in Soyinka's and Achebe's novels share a political identity'. Both are deeply committed to the idea of *citizenship*, nevertheless: 'Soyinka's and Achebe's fictive nations are inhabited by resolutely political animals who are willing to sacrifice all other aspects of their lives (and indeed their very lives) to their duty as citizens. Soyinka has recently written that Nigeria has no existence except as a "duty" … but that importunate summons means that Nigeria is of pressing concern.' Neil ten Kortenaar, 'Fictive States and the State of Fiction in Africa', *Comparative Literature*, 52.3 (2000), p. 239. The quotation is from *The Open Sore of a Continent: A Personal Narrative of the Nigerian Crisis* (Oxford University Press, 1996), where Soyinka writes: 'for the moment, I am able to claim that I accept Nigeria as a duty that is all. I accept Nigeria as a responsibility, without sentiment. I accept that entity, Nigeria, as a space into which I happen to have been born, and therefore a space within which I am bound to collaborate with fellow occupants in the pursuit of justice and ethical life, to establish a guaranteed access for all to the resources it produces, and to thwart every tendency in any group to act against that determined common denominator of a rational social existence' (p. 133). See also I. Szeman, who, also focusing on Soyinka and Achebe, argues that, '[t]hrough all the events of Biafra and all the coups, countercoups, and endlessly proclaimed democratic transition programs, they have remained vocal supporters of the Nigerian *nation*, believing that it is above all else the nation that provides a political form that will enable a renewed postcolonial polity to exist. For each writer, the issue of the nation figures prominently in their understanding of the necessity and the form that African writing takes; for both writers, African literature must be *nationalist* literature before it can be anything else.' *Zones of Instability: Literature, Postcolonialism, and the Nation* (Baltimore, MD: Johns Hopkins University Press, 2003), p. 118.

110 See the discussion in S. Nair, 'Diasporic Roots: Imagining a Nation in Earl Lovelace's *Salt*', *South Atlantic Quarterly*, 100.1 (2001), pp. 259–85.

111 E. Adnan, *Sitt Marie Rose*, trans. G. Kleege (Sausalito, CA: Post-Apollo Press, 1982 [1978]); Argueta, *Cuzcatlán*; Chamoiseau, *Texaco*; Z. Edgell, *In Times Like These* (Oxford: Heinemann, 1991); José, *My Brother, My Executioner*; E. Khoury, *Gate of the Sun*, trans. H. Davies (New York: Picador, 2006 [1998]); Lovelace, *Salt*; Pepetela, *Yaka*, trans. M. Holness (Oxford: Heinemann, 1996 [1984]); Pramoedya Ananta Toer, *The Buru Quartet*,

trans. M. Lane (Harmondsworth: Penguin, 1990, 1992), comprising *This Earth of Mankind* (1980), *Child of all Nations* (1980), *Footsteps* (1980), and *House of Glass* (1988); S. Ramirez, *To Bury our Fathers*, trans. N. Caistor (London and New York: Readers International, 1984 [1977]); M. Rui, *Yes, Comrade!*, trans. R. W. Sousa (Minneapolis: University of Minnesota Press, 1993 [1977]); A. Sivanandan *When Memory Dies* (London: Arcadia Books, 1997); E. van Heerden, *The Long Silence of Mario Salviati*, trans. C. Knox (London: Sceptre, 2003); Y. Vera, *Nehanda* (Toronto: TSAR Publications, 1994 [1993]); Rushdie, *Midnight's Children* and *The Moor's Last Sigh* (London: Vintage, 1996).

112 See for instance K. Swaminathan, *Water!*, trans. S. Shankar (Calcutta: Seagull, 2001 [1980]); Ngugi wa Thiong'o and Ngugi wa Mirii, *I Will Marry When I Want* (London: Heinemann, 1982 [1980]); W. Soyinka, *A Dance of the Forests* (Oxford University Press, 1963), *Kongi's Harvest* (Oxford University Press, 1967), *A Play of Giants* (London: Methuen, 1984); and Agha Shahid Ali, *The Country without a Post Office* (New York and London: W. W. Norton, 1998); E. K. Brathwaite, *The Arrivants: A New World Trilogy* (Oxford University Press, 1973), comprising *Rights of Passage* (1967), *Masks* (1968), and *Islands* (1969); E. Cardenal, *From Nicaragua with Love: Poems 1979–1986*, trans. J. Cohen (San Francisco: City Lights Books, 1986) and *Flights of Victory*, trans. M. Zimmerman (Willimantic, CT: Curbstone Press, 1988); M. Darwish, *Memory for Forgetfulness: August, Beirut, 1982*, trans. I. Muhawi (Berkeley: University of California Press, 1995 [1986]), *Unfortunately, it was Paradise*, trans. M. Akash and C. Forché with S. Antoon and A. El-Zein (Berkeley: University of California Press, 2003); M. Darwish, S. al-Qasim, and Adonis, *Victims of a Map: A Bilingual Anthology of Arabic Poetry*, trans. A. al-Udhari (London: Al Saqi Books, 1984); N. Guillén, *Man-Making Words: Selected Poems of Nicolás Guillén*, trans. R. Márquez and D. A. McMurray (Amherst: University of Massachusetts Press, 1972); S. Sepamla, *Hurry Up To It!* (Johannesburg: Ad. Donker, 1975); and Wong Phui Nam, *Ways of Exile: Poems from the First Decade* (London: Skoob Books, 1993).

113 Agha Shahid Ali, *Rooms are Never Finished* (New York and London: W. W. Norton, 2003 [2002]; A. Desai, *Clear Light of Day* (Harmondsworth: Penguin, 1980); Mo Yan, *Red Sorghum*, trans. H. Goldblatt (London: Arrow Books, 2003 [1988]); A. K. Ramanujan, *Relations* (Oxford University Press, 1971).

114 In the case of *A Suitable Boy*, one might speak of a mimicking of the 'gap' between the time of writing and the time of setting of George Eliot's *Middlemarch*, and self-consciously to the same effect: realising the past is in fact a way of narrating the coming of the present; not only to what degree things have changed between then and now, but also how much has been lost, the hopes, aspirations, and promises that have not been redeemed. Between setting and writing are the Emergency, economic 'liberalisation' and the rise to hegemony of the ideology of Hindutva.

115 E. W. Said, Foreword to E. Khoury, *Little Mountain*, trans. M. Tabet (Minneapolis: University of Minnesota Press, 1989), p. xii.

116 Mahfouz, *Cairo Trilogy*, comprising *Palace Walk*, *Palace of Desire*, and *Sugar Street*; and N. Mahfouz, *Adrift on the Nile*, trans. F. Liardet (New York: Doubleday, 1993 [1966]). Cf. also in this context Said's comment that 'there's a certain relaxation in the idea of Cairo – at least the way I've gradually grasped it – which makes it possible for all manner of identities to exist unhurriedly within this whole. The idea is an indistinct one but you can actually experience it. All kinds of histories, narratives, and presences intersect, coexist in what I suggest is a "natural" way. For me that defines the pleasurably urban – not Paris, the vigorously planned city as an Imperial Center, nor London, with its carefully displayed monumentality, but rather a city providing a relaxed interchange between various incomplete, partially destroyed histories that still exist and partially do not, competed over, contested, but somehow existing in this rather, in my view, fascinating way. Cairo has come to symbolize for me, therefore, a much more attractive form of the way in which we can look at history, not necessarily to look at it as something neatly manageable by categories or by the inclusiveness of systems and totalizing processes, but rather through the inventory that can be reconstructed. Cairo requires a certain effort of reconstruction.' Interview with Wicke and Sprinker, pp. 223–4.

117 G. Kanafani, *Men in the Sun*, trans. H. Kilpatrick (Washington, DC: Three Continents Press, 1988 [1962]).

118 G. Kanafani, *All That's Left to You*, trans. M. Jayyusi and J. Reed (Austin: University of Texas Press, 1990 [1966]).

119 E. Habiby, *The Secret Life of Saeed, the Ill-Fated Pessoptimist*, trans. S. K. Jayyusi and T. Le Gassick (London and New York: Readers International, 1985 [1974]).

120 Jameson offers a spirited critique of this tendency in his controversial essay 'Third-World Literature in the Era of Multinational Capitalism', which I discuss in detail in Chapter 2, below. Roberto Schwarz, similarly, demonstrates that the conceptualisation of developments in Latin American culture exclusively in relation to presumptively prior developments in European culture cannot but have as its consequence the understanding of them as parasitic. 'We Brazilians and other Latin Americans constantly experience the artificial, inauthentic and imitative nature of our cultural life', he writes in the opening sentence of his important essay, 'Brazilian Culture: Nationalism by Elimination' (*Misplaced Ideas*, p. 1).

121 See, for instance, G. Gaylard, *After Colonialism: African Postmodernism and Magical Realism* (Johannesburg: Wits University Press, 2005).

122 K. Laing, *Search Sweet Country* (London: Heinemann, 1986), *Woman of the Aeroplanes* (London: Heinemann, 1988); S. Labou Tansi, *The Seven Solitudes of Lorsa Lopez*, trans. C. Wake (London: Heinemann, 1995 [1985]); M. Couto, *Voices Made Night*, trans. D. Brookshaw (London: Heinemann, 1990 [1986]), *Every Man is a Race*, trans. D. Brookshaw

(London: Heinemann, 1994 [1989, 1990]), *The Last Flight of the Flamingo*, trans. D. Brookshaw (London: Serpent's Tail, 2004 [2000]); I. Vladislavic, *Propaganda by Monuments and Other Stories* (Cape Town and Johannesburg: David Philip, 1996), *The Restless Supermarket* (Cape Town and Johannesburg: David Philip, 2001), *The Exploded View* (Johannesburg: Random House, 2004). An important challenge to this 'pomo-postcolonialist' construction of 'magical realism' is provided by Christopher Warnes, who writes in *Magical Realism and the Postcolonial Novel: Between Faith and Irreverence* that the 'overhasty alignment of magical realist with post-structuralist thinking obstructs the recognition of that strand in magical realist writing which does not seek as much to deconstruct as to explore and affirm. In Asturias, Okri, and to a lesser degree Carpentier, the novel is the vehicle for transmitting cultural codes and an expanded world-view different from that which prevails in the secular West' (Basingstoke: Palgrave, 2009, p. 152). This formulation opens on to a conception of a body of literature whose juxtaposition or concatenation of registers and epistemes might indeed be thought of under the rubric of 'magical realism', but only if that rubric is itself then understood in terms of the idea of combined and uneven development. '[M]agical realism of this kind', as Warnes puts it, 'may represent an attempt to supplement, extend or overwhelm causality with the terms of participation ... [It] seeks to reclaim what has been lost: knowledge, values, traditions, ways of seeing, beliefs. In this model, the horizons of the causal paradigm are extended to include events and possibilities that would ordinarily be circumscribed' (p. 12).

123 P. Lenta, '"Everyday Abnormality": Crime and In/security in Ivan Vladislavic's *Portrait with Keys*', *Journal of Commonwealth Literature*, 44.1 (2009), pp. 117–33.

124 For interesting commentary on Vladislavic in this context, see C. Charos, '"The End of an Error": Transition and "Post-apartheid Play" in Ivan Vladislavic's *The Restless Supermarket*', *Safundi: The Journal of South African and American Studies*, 9.1 (2008), pp. 23–38; S. Graham, 'Memory, Memorialization, and the Transformation of Johannesburg: Ivan Vladislavic's *The Restless Supermarket* and *Propaganda by Monuments*', *Modern Fiction Studies*, 53.1 (2007), pp. 70–96; C. Warnes, 'The Making and Unmaking of History in Ivan Vladislavic's *Propaganda by Monuments and Other Stories*', *Modern Fiction Studies*, 46.1 (2000), pp. 67–89; and E. Young, '"Or is it just the angle?": Rivalling Realist Representation in Ivan Vladislavic's *Propaganda by Monuments and Other Stories*', *English Academy Review*, 18 (2001), pp. 38–45.

125 I. Vladislavic, 'When my Hands Burst into Flames' in *Missing Persons* (Cape Town and Johannesburg: David Philip, 1996), p. 99.

126 N. Gordimer, 'Living in the Interregnum' in S. Clingman (ed.), *The Essential Gesture: Writing, Politics and Places* (New York: Alfred A. Knopf, 1988), pp. 261–84.

127 A. Dangor, *Kafka's Curse. A Novella and Three Other Stories* (Cape Town: Kwela Books, 1997).

128 Z. Mda, *Ways of Dying* (Oxford University Press, 2002 [1995]).

129 I had originally written this sentence in the autumn of 2002. However, in the light of the subsequent disclosures concerning the torture of Iraqi prisoners by US military personnel in Abu Ghraib prison and the humiliating treatment inflicted upon detainees in Guantánamo Bay, one would have to say that van Heerden's sentence is not so 'unthinkable'.

130 E. van Heerden, 'My Cuban' in *Mad Dog and Other Stories*, trans. C. Knox (Cape Town and Johannesburg: David Philip, 1992 [1983]), p. 74.

131 See also, in this context, Breyten Breytenbach's extraordinary poem, 'Please don't feed the animals', which, like 'My Cuban', attempts to render the absolutism and fanaticism of apartheid reason:

> I am Germanic
> I am cruel
> I am white
> I steal from the primordial forest of myths
> and sagas
> and stand called upon and resolute
> and predestined
> upright
> on the plains of this chaotic continent
> listen
> > 'Please don't feed the animals' (1970), in *In Africa even the Flies are Happy: Selected Poems and Prose 1964–1977*, trans. D. Hirson (London: John Calder, 1978), p. 49.

132 Cf. Jennifer Wenzel's interesting suggestion that, if we are going to use the idea of 'magical realism' to discuss Okri, we would do better to term it 'petro-magic-realism', a rubric that would enable us to think about 'how Okri manages the pressures of a particular political ecology within a particular literary idiom'. 'Petro-Magic-Realism: Toward a Political Ecology of Nigerian Literature', *Postcolonial Studies*, 9.4 (2006), p. 457. Discussing Okri's short story, 'What the Tapster Saw', in *Stars of the New Curfew* (Harmondsworth: Penguin, 1988), pp. 183–94, Wenzel goes on to link her thesis with Fredric Jameson's understanding of 'magical realism' as a formal registration of combined and uneven development: '[Okri's] tale of the palm-wine tapster's nightmarish experience in Delta Oil Company territory thematises the conflict between established and emergent modes of production (here between artisanal palm-wine tapping and capital-intensive petroleum drilling that Fredric Jameson posits as constitutive of magical realism. Yet because "What the Tapster Saw" emphasises the phantasmagoric aspects of petroleum extraction, the marvellous reality represented in this narrative has a decidedly modern source, even if it is described in a fantastic idiom with a venerable literary history. Petro-magic is in no way a vestige of tradition or pre-capitalism ... The modernity of Okri's petro-magic-realism

obstructs the consumption of magical realist texts as nostalgic encounters with an exotic yet vanishing world ... "What the Tapster Saw" implicates metropolitan consumers of magical realism and petroleum products not in modernisation's inevitable disenchantment of vestigial tradition, but rather in petro-modernity's phantasmagoric ravagements of societies and lifeworlds. In this sense, petro-magic is the future' (pp. 457–8).

133 'Memory studies' has typically entered the postcolonial critical literature quite differently, in the form of applied trauma theory or under the sign of the Kunderan notion that 'the struggle of man against power is the struggle of memory against forgetting'. Illuminating though the work thus produced has been in many respects, it is vulnerable to criticism on the grounds that it is individualistic. It is prone to valorise 'memory' as private experience, and to set it off against public or (especially) statist history or memorialisation, whose organisation of remembrance is understood inevitably to involve, and at the same time, organised or mandatory *forgetting*. What often gets lost in this skirmishing between (private) memory and (public) history is the achievement – the actuality and often the instantiation – of memory as a trans-individual modality, collective and collectivist, and as such potentially capable of routing or refuting top-down (statist) History on its own terrain.

134 K. N. Daruwalla, *Collected Poems 1970–2005* (New Delhi: Penguin, 2006), p. 140.

135 B. King, 'K. N. Daruwalla's Poetry – 1: Parsi Bard of North India', *Journal of Postcolonial Writing*, 45.1 (2009), p. 103.

136 W. Soyinka, 'Exit Left, Monster, Victim in Pursuit (Death of a Tyrant)' in *Mandela's Earth and Other Poems* (London: Methuen, 1990 [1989]); 'Vain Ransom' in *Samarkand and Other Markets I Have Known*.

137 Qabbani, *On Entering the Sea*.

138 F. M. Chipasula, *Nightwatcher, Nightsong* (Peterborough: Paul Green, 1986); A. Dorfman, *In Case of Fire in a Foreign Land: New and Collected Poems from Two Languages*, trans. E. Grossman and A. Dorfmann (Durham, NC: Duke University Press, 2002); C. Alegría, *Woman of the River*, trans. D. J. Flakoll (University of Pittsburgh Press, 1989); Kim Chiha, *Heart's Agony: Selected Poems of Chiha Kim*, trans. W.-C. Kim and J. Han (New York: White Pine Press, 1998).

139 N. Farah, *Variations on the Theme of an African Dictatorship*, comprising *Sweet and Sour Milk* (London: Allison and Busby, 1979), *Sardines* (London: Allison and Busby, 1981), and *Close Sesame* (London: Allison and Busby, 1983); M. Beti, *Perpetua and the Habit of Unhappiness*, trans. J. Reed and C. Wake (London: Heinemann, 1978 [1974]), *Remember Ruben*, trans. G. Moore (London: Heinemann, 1987 [1974]), and *Lament for an African Pol*, trans. R. Bjornson (Washington, DC: Three Continents Press, 1985 [1979]); A. Carpentier, *Reasons of State*, trans. F. Partridge (London: Victor Gollancz, 1976 [1974]); G. García Márquez, *The Autumn of the Patriarch*, trans. G. Rabassa (New York: Avon Books,

1977 [1975]); A. Roa Bastos, *I the Supreme*, trans. H. Lane (London: Faber and Faber, 1987 [1974]).

140 L. Valenzuela, *The Lizard's Tale*, trans. G. Rabassa (London: Serpent's Tale, 1987 [1983]).

141 Dai Houying, *Stones of the Wall*, trans. F. Wood (London: Sceptre, 1987 [1981]); Bei Dao, *Waves*, trans. B. S. McDougall and S. T. Cooke (New York: New Directions, 1986).

142 Adonis, 'A Mirror for the Executioner' in Darwish, al-Qasim, and Adonis, *Victims of a Map*, pp. 88–9; A. Djebar, *Algerian White: A Narrative*, trans. D. Kelley and M. de Jager (New York: Seven Stories Press, 2000). In this context, see Hafid Gafaïti, 'Culture and Violence: the Algerian Intelligentsia between Two Political Illegitimacies', *Parallax*, 4.2 (1998), pp. 71–7. Gafaïti argues that 'meditation on the fate of writers, journalists and intellectuals in recent Algerian history and the analysis of the status of culture from the 1954 Revolution to the present show that, often, the intellectual has been singled out as the object of sacrifice of an apparently structural hatred of culture' (p. 71).

143 Bei Dao, 'An End of a Beginning' in *The August Sleepwalker*, trans. B. S. McDougall (London: Anvil Press Poetry, 1988), p. 65.

144 A. Laâbi, *Rue du retour*, trans. J. Kaye (London and Columbia, LA: Readers International, 1989 [1982]); Ngugi wa Thiong'o, *Detained: A Writer's Prison Diary* (London: Heinemann, 1981); A. Partnoy, *The Little School*, trans. A. Partnoy et al. (London: Virago, 1988 [1981]); Pramoedya Ananta Toer, *The Mute's Soliloquy: A Memoir*, trans. W. Samuels (New York: Hyperion East, 1999); G. Ramos, *Prison Memoirs*, trans. T. Colchie (New York: Evans, 1974 [1953]). We might note here the late appearance, in the Heinemann African Writers Series (now sadly defunct), of a volume entitled *Gathering Seaweed: African Prison Writing*, edited by Jack Mapanje (Oxford: Heinemann, 2002), featuring contributions both from significant political figures (Kaunda, Oginga Odinga, Nkrumah, Kenyatta, Biko, Mandela, Neto) and important writers (Mapanje himself, Laâbi, Cronin, Mnthali, Brutus, Craveirinha, Soyinka, Cheney-Coker, Ngugi, Breytenbach, Djabali, Jacinto, and others). The structural organisation of this volume, with its sectional headings – 'Origins', 'Arrest, Detention and Prison', 'Torture', 'Survival', 'The Release' – stands as an implicit rebuke of the disavowal of struggle and organised resistance in postcolonial studies. As Mapanje puts it in his introduction, 'This anthology is unique not only as an indictment of the brutality of European imperialism, colonialism and neocolonialism, apartheid and African dictatorship; but it is also an indelible record of the origins, growth and maturity of the struggle for the restitution of human dignity and integrity, justice and peace on the African continent' (pp. xiii–xiv).

145 There is, of course, a sizeable *sociological* literature dealing with questions of state and nation, nationalism and violence in the postcolonial era. In the African context, see for instance, J. Alexander, J. McGregor, and T. Ranger,

Violence and Memory: One Hundred Years in the 'Dark Forests' of Matabele-land (Oxford: James Currey, 2000); P. Chabal, *Power in Africa: An Essay in Political Interpretation* (New York: St Martin's Press, 1994); P. Chabal and J-P. Daloz, *Africa Works: Disorder as Political Instrument* (Oxford: James Currey, 1999); Davidson, *Black Man's Burden*; J-F. Bayart, *The State in Africa: The Politics of the Belly*, trans. M. Harper, C. Harrison, and E. Harrison (London and New York: Longman, 1993); M. Mamdani, *Citizen and Subject: Contemporary Africa and the Legacy of Late Colonialism* (London: James Currey; Kampala: Fountain Publishers; Cape Town: David Philip, 1996); M. Mamdani, *When Victims Become Killers: Colonialism, Nativism and the Genocide in Rwanda* (Oxford: James Currey, 2001). Some of this work has found a readership among scholars in postcolonial *literary* studies. By far the most influential author in this respect, however, has been Achille Mbembe, whose work has received an adulatory welcome in postcolonial studies. See especially 'The Banality of Power and the Aesthetics of Vulgarity', *Public Culture*, 4.2 (1992), pp. 1–30, and *On the Postcolony* (Berkeley: University of California Press, 2001). I do not find Mbembe's work either convincing or congenial. Much of it strikes me, indeed, as incoherent. A pointed critique of Mbembe's scholarship is to be found in J. Weate, 'Achille Mbembe and the Postcolony: Going beyond the Text', *Research in African Literatures*, 34.4 (2003), pp. 27–41, and 'Postcolonial Theory on the Brink: A Critique of Achille Mbembe's *On the Postcolony*', *African Identities*, 1.1 (2003), pp. 1–18. See also the sharp commentaries by Gilroy and Guyer in a special issue of the journal *Public Culture* devoted to Mbembe's work: P. Gilroy, 'Towards a Critique of Consumer Imperialism', *Public Culture*, 14.3 (2002), pp. 489–91; J. Guyer, 'Contemplating Uncertainty', *Public Culture*, 14.3 (2002), pp. 599–602. A good example of the use to which Mbembe's work is being put in contemporary postcolonial studies is to be found in Asha Varadharajan's 'Afterword: The Phenomenology of Violence and the Politics of Becoming', *Comparative Studies of South Asia, Africa and the Middle East*, 28.1 (2008), pp. 124–41, which seems to me both to de-actualise 'violence' and to render its determinants moot or undecidable. The Mbembe-inspired questions that guide Varadharajan's enquiry – 'What does the subject of violence reveal about identity and subject formation? How do extremity and divestiture mark the self-possessed humanist subject with their taint? Could violence be the harbinger of a new "politics of becoming"' (p. 125) – do not seem to me promissory of any decisive new opening in postcolonial studies.

146 See for instance the discussion of the representation of state violence in the fiction of Roy and Rushdie, in Y. Siddiqi, *Anxieties of Empire and the Fiction of Intrigue* (New York: Columbia University Press, 2008), pp. 67–91; and the special issue of *Contemporary Literature*, 49.4 (2008), edited by Matthew Hart and Jim Hansen, devoted to the topic of 'Contemporary Literature and the State'.

147 E. Boehmer, 'Beside the West: Postcolonial Women Writers, the Nation, and the Globalised World', *African Identities*, 2.2 (2004), p. 186.

148 Y. Vera, *The Stone Virgins* (Harare: Weaver Press, 2002).

149 R. Primorac, *The Place of Tears: The Novel and Politics in Modern Zimbabwe* (London: I. B. Tauris, 2006), pp. 3–4. See also S. Chan, 'The Memory of Violence: Trauma in the Writings of Alexander Kanengoni and Yvonne Vera and the Idea of Unreconciled Citizenship', *Third World Quarterly*, 26.2 (2005), pp. 369–82; Graham, *Land and Nationalism*; R. Primorac, 'The Poetics of State Terror in Twenty-First Century Zimbabwe', *Interventions*, 9.3 (2007), pp. 435–51; R. Muponde and R. Primorac (eds), *Versions of Zimbabwe: New Approaches to Literature and Culture* (Harare: Weaver Press, 2005). A recent essay by M. T. Vambe, however, displays feet of clay: 'Changing Nationalist Politics in African Fiction', *African Identities*, 6.3 (2008), pp. 227–39. Like other contemporary critics, Vambe is concerned to register the critique of statist nationalist discourse in contemporary Zimbabwean literature. 'In contrast to official images of guerrillas as "comrades", "freedom fighters", "liberators", "combatants", and "war veterans"', he writes, 'Zimbabwean writers are contesting this narrow "patriotic" definition of the guerrillas … Black writers in independent Zimbabwe believe that their works can bring out other patterns of meanings and produce a different truth about the image of the guerrillas' (p. 228). However, this argument is rendered nugatory by Vambe's decision to submit – without remainder, as it were – the Zimbabwean material before him to the strictures of the received postcolonialist theory of nationalism. This ensures that no 'other patterns of meanings' or 'different truths' emerge from his reading: there is a deconstruction of the official, statist discourse, to be sure; but nothing substantive enough to be extrapolated to a 'pattern of meaning' or a 'truth' is posited. Another consequence of the generally undiscriminating and imprecise critique of nationalism in the essay is that Dambudzo Marechera's politics are conflated with those of Chenjarai Hove, with both authors being strapped unhelpfully (and implausibly) to the mast of deconstruction. For interesting new work on state and nation in African literatures beyond the Zimbabwean case, see also A. Gagiano, 'Surveying the Contours of "a Country in Exile": Nuruddin Farah's Somalia', *African Identities*, 4.2 (2006), pp. 251–68; Hitchcock, 'Postcolonial Failure'; J. Marx, 'Failed-State Fiction', *Contemporary Literature*, 49.4 (2008), pp. 597–633.

150 The concept of 'structure of feeling' derives, obviously, from Raymond Williams's early work, where he used it extensively in thinking about the problem of the *specificity* of a given culture or formation. In *The Long Revolution* (London: Hogarth Press, 1992 [1961]), for example, he wrote that 'in one sense … [the] structure of feeling is the culture of a period: it is the particular living result of all the elements in the general organization' (p. 48). In *Marxism and Literature* (Oxford University Press, 1977) he returned to the concept, offering the following formal definition: 'The term is difficult, but "feeling" is chosen to emphasize a distinction from more formal

concepts of "world-view" or "ideology". It is not only that we must go beyond formally held and systematic beliefs, though of course we have always to include them. It is that we are concerned with meanings and values as they are actively lived and felt, and the relations between these and formal or systematic beliefs and acted and justified experiences. An alternative definition would be structures of *experience*: in one sense the better and wider word, but with the difficulty that one of its senses has that past tense which is the most important obstacle to recognition of the area of social experience which is being defined. We are talking about characteristic elements of impulse, restraint, and tone; specifically affective elements of consciousness and relationships: not feeling against thought, but thought as felt and feeling as thought: practical consciousness of a present kind, in a living and interrelating continuity. We are then defining these elements as a "structure": as a set, with specific internal relations, at once interlocking and in tension. Yet we are also defining a social experience which is still *in process*, often indeed not yet recognized as social but taken to be private, idiosyncratic, and even isolating, but which in analysis (though rarely otherwise) has its emergent, connecting, and dominant characteristics, indeed its specific hierarchies' (p. 132). 'Structure of feeling' is also closely related to the Bourdieusian concepts of 'habitus' and 'logic of practice'. See P. Bourdieu, *The Logic of Practice*, trans. R. Nice (Stanford University Press, 1990 [1980]), esp. pp. 52–79; *Field of Cultural Production*, pp. 64–72, 161–75; and P. Bourdieu and L. J. D. Wacquant, *An Invitation to Reflexive Sociology* (University of Chicago Press, 1992), pp. 115–40.

151 C. Noland, 'Red Front/Black Front: Aimé Césaire and the Affaire Aragon', *Diacritics*, 36.1 (2006), p. 83.

152 See for instance V. Y. Mudimbe, *The Invention of Africa: Gnosis, Philosophy, and the Order of Knowledge* (Bloomington: Indiana University Press; London: James Currey, 1988), where *la chose du texte* is spoken of as 'that which is out there in the African traditions, insistent and discrete, determining the traditions yet independent from them' (p. 183). See also the discussion of Mudimbe in Chapter 3, below.

153 T. Salih, *Season of Migration to the North*, trans. D. Johnson-Davies (London: Heinemann, 1978 [1969]), pp. 1–2.

154 M. A. Asturias, *Men of Maize*, trans. G. Martin (London: Verso, 1988 [1949]); Mohanty, *Paraja*; N.V.M. Gonzalez, *A Season of Grace* (Manila: Benipayo Press, 1956).

155 L. Nkosi, *Tasks and Masks: Themes and Styles of African Literature* (London: Longman, 1981), p. 100; B. Head, *When Rain Clouds Gather* (New York: Simon and Schuster, 1969).

156 L. Moss, 'Can Rohinton Mistry's Realism Rescue the Novel?' in R. Smith (ed.), *Postcolonizing the Commonwealth: Studies in Literature and Culture* (Waterloo, IA: Wilfred Laurier University Press, 2000), p. 158. Jusdanis makes a related point in a more general discussion of the relation between 'world literature' and the 'global culture industry'. Focusing on the Turkish

writer Orhan Pamuk, he follows critic Güneli Gün in arguing that Pamuk's lionisation in the Euro-American literary world has a lot to do with the fact that he writes in a 'postcolonialist' idiom. Above all, Pamuk 'has incorporated two characteristics that Third world writing must have to succeed in the West: cleverness and fantasy. Interestingly, these two traits are outside the concerns of [the] mainstream realist tradition of Turkish literature, specifically the so-called Village Novel. Although they deal with exotic themes, these novels are not sufficiently international for translation into Western languages. In other words, their depiction of peasant life through traditional, transparent prose is not what international readers want today' ('World Literature', p. 119).

157 See also D. Head, *The Cambridge Introduction to Modern British Fiction, 1950–2000* (Cambridge University Press, 2002). Focusing on the general valorisation of 'experimental' or anti-realist writing in the postcolonial and 'Black British' discussions, Head argues that a 'productive cultural hybridity is commonly (and erroneously) perceived to go hand-in-glove with overtly experimental forms. In such a view, you either have a startlingly innovative style *and* rapturous presentation of multicultural energies, or you have neither.' He adds that this 'easy equation between experiment and cultural hybridity can imply a simple opposition between experiment and tradition that is inappropriate, with traditional realism coming to embody a reactionary conservatism' (p. 172). See also Parry, 'Directions and Dead Ends in Postcolonial Studies', pp. 66–81; and E. P. Sorensen, 'Postcolonial Melancholia', *Paragraph*, 30.2 (2007), pp. 65–81. For a very well thought out discussion of the *formal* entailments of 'cultural hybridity' in these contexts, see A. Cormack, 'Migration and the Politics of Narrative Form: Realism and the Postcolonial Subject in *Brick Lane*', *Contemporary Literature*, 47.4 (2006), pp. 695–721.

158 In 'The Welsh Industrial Novel', Raymond Williams had distinguished 'the industrial novel' – and, more generally, 'the realist and the naturalist novel' – from all other forms of writing, on the grounds that it was 'predicated on the distinctive assumption – I say assumption, though if I were not being academic I would say, more shortly, the distinctive truth – that the lives of individuals, however intensely and personally realized, are not just influenced but in certain crucial ways formed by general social relations'. In the realist and naturalist novel, Williams wrote, '[labour], and its characteristic places and communities, are not just a new background: a new "setting" for a story. In the true industrial novel they are seen as formative. Social relations are not assumed, are not static, are not conventions within which the tale of a marriage or an inheritance or an adventure can go its own way. The working society – actual work, actual relations, an actual and visibly altered place – is in the industrial novel central: not because, or not necessarily because, the writer is "more interested in sociology than in people" – which is what a degraded establishment criticism would have us believe – but because in these working communities it is a trivial fantasy to

suppose that these general and pressing conditions are for long or even at all separable from the immediate and the personal. The abstracted categories of "social" and "personal" are here, in these specific human conditions – the conditions, moreover, of the great majority of human beings – interfused and inextricable though not always indistinguishable. The privileged distances of another kind of fiction, where people can "live simply as human beings", beyond the pressures and interruptions and accidents of society, are in another world or more specifically in another class. Here, in the world of the industrial novel – as indeed in the best rural fiction; in Hardy for example – work is pressing and formative, and the most general social relations are directly experienced within the most personal' (pp. 221–2). My suggestion here is that what Williams here identifies as a 'distinctive truth' about realist and naturalist fiction is more widely and diversely registered – across all genres and forms of writing – in the context of 'postcolonial' literature.

159 E. Glissant, 'November' (1954) in *Black Salt*, trans. B. Wing (Ann Arbor: University of Michigan Press, 1998), p. 22.
160 B. Wing, 'Introduction' to Glissant, *Black Salt*, pp. 5–6.
161 D. Walcott, 'Islands' (1962) in *Collected Poems 1948–1984*.
162 M. Merleau-Ponty, 'Eye and Mind' (1962), trans. C. Dallery, in *Phenomenology, Language and Sociology: Selected Essays* (London: Heinemann, 1974), p. 280.
163 Jibanananda Das, *Naked Lonely Hand*, trans. J. Winter (London: Anvil Press Poetry, 2003 [1957]), p. 27.
164 J. Winter, 'Introduction' to Jibananda, *Naked Lonely Hand*, p. 12.

2 FREDRIC JAMESON ON 'THIRD-WORLD LITERATURE': A DEFENCE

1 Compare E. Cazdyn, 'Anti-Anti: Utopia, Globalization, Jameson', *Modern Language Quarterly*, 68.2 (2007): 'Jameson's interventions always seem to hit us with the left hand, from an unexpected place that pushes us sideways into formerly unthinkable realms' (p. 331).
2 F. Jameson, *Marxism and Form: Twentieth-Century Dialectical Theories of Literature* (Princeton University Press, 1971).
3 T. Eagleton, *Walter Benjamin or Towards a Revolutionary Criticism* (London: New Left Books, 1981), p. xii.
4 F. Jameson, *The Prison-House of Language: A Critical Account of Structuralism and Russian Formalism* (Princeton University Press, 1972).
5 Jameson has himself commented obliquely on the vagaries of his readership. In the 'Secondary Elaborations' that bring his magisterial book on postmodernism to a conclusion, he notes that 'a book I published years ago on structuralism elicited letters, some of which addressed me as a "foremost" spokesperson for structuralism, while the others appealed to me as an "eminent" critic and opponent of that movement. I was really neither of

those things, but I have to conclude that I must have been "neither" in some relatively complicated way that it seemed hard for people to grasp' (*Postmodernism*, p. 297). See also I. Buchanan, 'Reading Jameson Dogmatically', *Historical Materialism*, 10.3 (2002), pp. 223–43.

6 P. Anderson, *The Origins of Postmodernity* (London and New York: Verso, 1998), p. 66.

7 This line of criticism is of course indebted to Pierre Bourdieu. See, for instance *Field of Cultural Production*, pp. 29–73.

8 F. Jameson, 'Postmodernism, or, The Cultural Logic of Late Capitalism', *New Left Review*, 146 (1984), pp. 59–92.

9 Jameson, 'Third-World Literature in the Era of Multinational Capitalism', p. 69.

10 A. Ahmad, 'Jameson's Rhetoric of Otherness and the "National Allegory"', *Social Text*, 17 (1987), pp. 3–26; *In Theory: Classes, Nations, Literatures* (London and New York: Verso, 1992), pp. 95–122.

11 The *locus classicus* of colonialist discourse in this respect is probably the text that has come to be known as 'Macaulay's Minute' – Thomas Babington Macaulay's 1835 contribution to the debate then raging over the goals and content of colonial education in India. Macaulay wrote: 'I have no knowledge of either Sanscrit or Arabic. But I have done what I could to form a correct estimate of their value. I have read translations of the most celebrated Arabic and Sanscrit works. I have conversed, both here and at home, with men distinguished by their proficiency in the Eastern tongues. I am quite ready to take the oriental learning at the valuation of the orientalists themselves. I have never found one among them who could deny that a single shelf of a good European library was worth the whole native literature of India and Arabia.' 'Thomas Babington Macaulay on Education for India' in P. D. Curtin (ed.), *Imperialism* (London: Harper and Row, 1971), p. 182.

12 F. Jameson, 'Foreword' in R. F. Retamar, *Caliban and Other Essays*, trans. E. Baker (Minneapolis: University of Minnesota Press, 1989), pp. vii–xii.

13 Jameson, 'Third-World Literature', p. 67; Ahmad, *In Theory*, p. 98.

14 See, for instance, M. Prasad, 'On the Question of a Theory of (Third World) Literature', *Social Text*, 31/32 (1992), pp. 57–83; Larsen, *Determinations*; I. Buchanan, 'National Allegory Today: A Return to Jameson', *New Formations*, 51 (2003), pp. 66–79; J. McGonegal, 'Postcolonial Metacritique: Jameson, Allegory and the Always-Already-Read Third World Text', *Interventions*, 7.2 (2005), pp. 251–65; and Vallury, 'Walking the Tightrope'. See also the commentaries in G. Kapur, 'Globalization and Culture: Navigating the Void' in F. Jameson and M. Miyoshi (eds), *The Cultures of Globalization* (Durham, NC: Duke University Press, 1998), pp. 191–217; A. Quayson, *Postcolonialism: Theory, Practice or Process?* (Cambridge: Polity, 2000), pp. 76–102; and I. Szeman, 'Who's Afraid of National Allegory?', *South Atlantic Quarterly*, 100.3 (2001), pp. 803–27.

15 F. Buell, *National Culture and the New Global System* (Baltimore, MD: Johns Hopkins University Press, 1994), p. 286.

16 S. Suleri, *The Rhetoric of English India* (University of Chicago Press, 1992), p. 13.

17 Compare Buell: 'Jameson sought to transport the concept of radical difference out of Orientalism and into political economy, and to make it a reflection of power relations rather than primordial cultures.' Criticising him for his cultural essentialism, Buell adds that Jameson 'discern[s] in heterogeneous evidence a single, buried pattern … making it representative of a whole culture, thereby valorizing the notion of cultural wholes' (*National Culture*, p. 279).

18 R. M. George, *The Politics of Home: Postcolonial Relocations and Twentieth-Century Fiction* (Cambridge University Press, 1996), pp. 102–13; J. Fabian, *Time and the Other: How Anthropology Makes its Object* (New York: Columbia University Press, 1983).

19 C. L. Miller, *Blank Darkness: Africanist Discourse in French* (University of Chicago Press, 1985), pp. 169–83.

20 G. C. Spivak, *A Critique of Postcolonial Reason: Toward a History of the Vanishing Present* (Cambridge, MA: Harvard University Press, 1999), pp. 109–10. In an interview in 2001, Spivak claims never to have read Ahmad's *In Theory*. She is 'intellectually sensitive', she says: 'sometimes I keep myself from reading things that I have heard a good deal of, seen a lot of quotation from and so I say to myself "put this in the background for now. There is a lot of stuff to look at. You should carry on so that you don't get into a defensive mode".' 'Mapping the Present: Interview with Gayatri Spivak', conducted by M. Yegenoglu and M. Mutman, *New Formations*, 45 (2001), pp. 17–18. In *A Critique of Postcolonial Reason*, however – published *before* this interview – she twice cites *In Theory*, not generally but in detail (pp. 41n, 273n). We must assume that the subsequent claim not to have read Ahmad's book is meant as a provocation.

21 Compare Nicholas Brown, *Utopian Generations: The Political Horizon of Twentieth-Century Literature* (Princeton University Press, 2005), who writes: 'What is unfortunate is that an entirely salutary and productive reading within the micropolitics of the North American academy at the moment of the self-definition of postcolonial studies played directly into the macropolitics of the cold war: the description of Marxism (which, surely we do not need to be reminded, was appropriated by countless anticolonial struggles) as an intrinsically reductive and totalizing-totalitarian colonizer in its own right' (p. 9). Brown's commentary on Jameson's essay in *Utopian Generations* is very curious, however. While freely conceding his indebtedness to Jameson's work generally, he argues that his book 'is devoted in part to undoing the damage done to the reputation of the dialectic for postcolonial criticism' by Jameson's essay (p. 7). He immediately cites the 'infamous suggestion' that 'all third-world texts are necessarily … to be read as … *national allegories*' and proposes that Ahmad's 'canonical critique of this position is astute and unassailable on many counts. Jameson's essay contains several bad, positivist

reasons for reading literature produced on the periphery of capitalism as national allegory, and indeed substantial parts of the essay ... are indefensible' (pp. 7–8). Yet in the paragraphs that follow, Brown produces not a compelling critique but a compelling *defence* of Jameson's argument, which he cogently links to the broader working through of the idea of allegory that Jameson had developed in *The Political Unconscious.*

22 See, in addition to the essays already cited, S. López, 'Peripheral Glances: Adorno's *Aesthetic Theory* in Brazil' in M. Pensky (ed.), *Globalizing Critical Theory* (New York: Rowman and Littlefield, 2005), pp. 241–52.

23 See K. A. Appiah, 'Is the Post- in Postmodernism the Post- in Postcolonial?', *Critical Inquiry,* 17 (1991), pp. 336–57; and Dirlik, 'Postcolonial Aura'.

24 G. C. Spivak, 'Theory in the Margin: Coetzee's *Foe* Reading Defoe's *Crusoe/ Roxana*' in J. Arac and B. Johnson (eds), *Consequences of Theory* (Baltimore, MD: Johns Hopkins University Press, 1990), p. 172. See also Spivak, *Outside in the Teaching Machine* (London and New York: Routledge, 1993), pp. 60–1. Actually, the 'scandal' here is that – notwithstanding her own professed politics, which one might have thought were distinctly closer to those of Parry than to those of Bhabha or JanMohamed – Spivak insists on calling 'postcolonials' 'resistant' merely because they are postcolonials, rather than because they have demonstrated any active disposition to resist anything. This, of course, was precisely what Parry had been trying to argue in the critique to which Spivak took such strident exception.

25 In this context see Buchanan, who cannily observes that in objecting to Jameson's allegedly 'alterist' discourse, Ahmad actually contradicts his own premise concerning the incoherence and absolute untenability of the notion of the 'third world'. Citing the passage in which Ahmad complains that, as he was reading Jameson, he was brought up against the uncomfortable realisation that 'what was being theorised was, among many other things, myself', Buchanan argues that '[i]f the notion of the third world holds no meaning for him [Ahmad], if in fact it doesn't exist, then how come he so readily identifies himself with it? By the same token, if he isn't Jameson's civilisational Other, why take such pains to prove otherwise? My point is that if the term "third world" does not somehow claim Ahmad as one of its own, if it doesn't interpellate him, then he could not take it so personally, his objections would have to be of a different, more objective stripe. His attempt to repudiate the existence of the third world is, in this respect, peculiarly and indeed literally self-defeating: it would deny the very thing he relies on as his authority to speak in so wounded a tone, namely his status as an intellectual from a third world country' ('National Allegory', p. 76).

26 Again, see Buchanan, who argues that Ahmad 'misreads Jameson's essay in two ways: he does not take any notice of its context and therefore fails to catch the inflection of Jameson's rhetoric – he doesn't hear either who Jameson is speaking to or who Jameson is speaking for; he reduces a dialectical argument to a positivist assertion and, in a high dudgeon, lampoons it' ('National Allegory', p. 67).

27 Compare Buchanan, who writes as follows: '[Jameson] paints a picture of a certain kind of reader, formed in the image of the field, sharing their faith in "great books" and their suspicion of the "non-canonical", who feels they cannot enjoy third world literature. To this reader he says, yes, it is true, the third world novel "will not offer the satisfactions of Proust or Joyce" and it may even strike you as a little crude or rudimentary, stuck as it sometimes is in a realist mode western authors have already left behind. But, he goes on to argue, this perception should not be accepted at face value, it needs to be historicised in itself because it is symptomatic of "our imprisonment in the present of postmodernism and calls for the reinvention of the radical difference of *our own* cultural past and its now seemingly old-fashioned situations and novelties" ... Confronting this almost automatic distaste for third world writing requires we examine both the "humanly impoverishing" demands the canon places on our sympathies ... and the visceral fear many of us in the more affluent parts of the world have of the genuinely impoverished conditions of some aspects of third world existence. But we also have to conquer the embarrassed feeling of incompetence that third world writing seems to induce when it deals with issues and ideas outside our sphere of experience' ('National Allegory', pp. 67–8).

28 Again contra Ahmad, such allegorisation ought not to be confused with the advocacy of *nationalism*. As Buchanan points out, 'nowhere in Jameson's paper does he state that Third World writers are only or can only be nationalists. What he does say is that Third World writers are obsessively concerned with the "national situation" – nationalism would be but one part of this vastly more complex problem ... [Ahmad] attributes a position to Jameson his textual evidence does not and cannot support – in effect, he moves "too quickly" from "national allegory" to "nationalism", which he says is "the necessary, exclusively desirable ideology" underpinning Jameson's paper as a whole. In so doing, he skips over the problematic of the "national situation" and of course much else besides. Yet even to put it like that is already to move "too quickly" ourselves because as Jameson theorises it, "national allegory" is not a meditation on this problem per se, rather it uses it as the particular solution to a more general problem of representation' ('National Allegory', p. 71).

29 Larsen, *Determinations*, p. 19.

30 'History itself as one long nightmare', as Jameson himself puts it in the penultimate paragraph of *The Political Unconscious* (p. 299).

31 F. Jameson, 'Modernism and Imperialism' in T. Eagleton, F. Jameson, and E. W. Said, *Nationalism, Colonialism and Literature* (Minneapolis: University of Minnesota Press, 1990), p. 44. Cf. also the following, later in the same essay: 'The traces of imperialism can ... be detected in Western modernism, and are indeed constitutive of it; but we must not look for them in the obvious places, in content or in representation. Save in the special case of Irish literature, and of Joyce, they will be detected spatially, as formal symptoms, within the structure of First World modernist texts themselves' (p. 64).

32 F. Jameson, 'Notes on Globalization as a Philosophical Issue' in F. Jameson and M. Miyoshi (eds), *The Cultures of Globalization* (Durham, NC: Duke University Press, 1998), p. 58.

33 L. Althusser, 'Ideology and Ideological State Apparatuses (Notes Towards an Investigation)' (1970) in *Lenin and Philosophy and Other Essays*, trans. B. Brewster (New York and London: Monthly Review Press, 1971), p. 162.

34 P. Smith, *Millennial Dreams: Contemporary Culture and Capital in the North* (London and New York: Verso, 1997), p. 25.

35 It is well known that the 'Third-World Literature' essay was conceived as a supplement to this 1984 'Postmodernism' essay.

36 In addition to the works variously cited above, see for instance the essay 'Culture and Finance Capital' in *The Cultural Turn: Selected Writings on the Postmodern, 1983–1998* (London and New York: Verso, 1998), pp. 136–61.

3 'a figure glimpsed in a rear-view mirror': the question of representation in 'postcolonial' fiction

1 Literally hundreds of studies could be cited here: among the best known and most influential of these are R. Ballaster, *Fabulous Orients: Fictions of the East in England 1662–1785* (Oxford University Press, 2005); P. Brantlinger, *Rule of Darkness: British Literature and Imperialism, 1830–1914* (Ithaca, NY: Cornell University Press, 1988); E. Cheyfitz, *The Poetics of Imperialism: Translation and Colonization from* The Tempest *to* Tarzan (Oxford University Press, 1991); R. Edmond, *Representing the South Pacific: Colonial Discourse from Cook to Gauguin* (Cambridge University Press, 1997); C. Hall, *Civilising Subjects: Metropole and Colony in the English Imagination 1830–1867* (Cambridge: Polity, 2002); P. Hulme, *Colonial Encounters: Europe and the Native Caribbean, 1492–1797* (London, Methuen, 1992); K. Jayawardene, *The White Woman's Other Burden: Western Women and South Asia during British Colonial Rule* (London: Routledge, 1995); R. Kabbani, *Imperial Fictions: Europe's Myths of Orient* (London: Pandora, 1994 [1986]); A. Loomba, *Shakespeare, Race, and Colonialism* (Oxford University Press, 2002); L. Lowe, *Critical Terrains: French and British Orientalisms* (Ithaca and London: Cornell University Press, 1991); A. McClintock, *Imperial Leather: Race, Gender and Sexuality in the Colonial Contest* (New York and London: Routledge, 1995); Miller, *Blank Darkness*; S. Mills, *Discourses of Difference: An Analysis of Women's Travel Writing and Colonialism* (London and New York: Routledge, 1991); M. L. Pratt, *Imperial Eyes: Travel Writing and Transculturation* (New York and London: Routledge, 1992); T. Richards, *The Imperial Archive: Knowledge and the Fantasy of Empire* (New York and London: Verso, 1993); N. Thomas, *Colonialism and Culture* (Oxford: Polity, 1994); G. Viswanathan, *Masks of Conquest: Literary Study and British Rule in India* (New York: Columbia University Press, 1989); M. Wood, *Blind Memory: Visual Representation of Slavery in England and America 1780–1865* (Manchester University Press, 2000); R. Young, *Colonial Desire: Hybridity in Theory, Culture and Race* (London: Routledge, 1995). See also the

recent studies by S. Deckard, *Paradise Discourse, Imperialism, and Globalization: Exploited Eden* (London: Routledge, 2009); H. Waters, *Racism on the Victorian Stage: Representation of Slavery and the Black Character* (Cambridge University Press, 2007); and R. Weaver-Hightower, *Empire Islands: Castaways, Cannibals, and Fantasies of Conquest* (Minneapolis: University of Minnesota Press, 2007).

2 A. Césaire, *Discourse on Colonialism*, trans. J. Pinkham (New York: Monthly Review Press, 1972 [1955]), pp. 21–2.

3 The signature text here is B. Ashcroft, G. Griffiths and H. Tiffin, *The Empire Writes Back: Theory and Practice in Post-Colonial Literatures* (London and New York: Routledge, 1989).

4 B. Davidson, *Let Freedom Come: Africa in Modern History* (Boston and Toronto: Little, Brown, 1978), p. 155.

5 D. P. Kunene, 'Introduction' in Mofolo, *Chaka*, p. xii.

6 A. Gérard, *Four African Literatures* (Berkeley: University of California Press, 1971), p. 119.

7 I derive this phrase from Bernabé, Chamoiseau and Confiant, who propose that, 'More than anyone else, the writer's vocation is to identify what, in our daily lives, determines the patterns and structure of the imaginary. To perceive our existence is to perceive us in the context of our history, of our daily lives, of our reality. It is also able to perceive our virtualities' (*Éloge*, p. 100).

8 Boehmer makes this point also, although she focuses on an earlier moment of what she calls 'anti-imperialist nationalist resistance'. During the years following the First World War, she writes, 'the monopoly on imperial writing was broken': 'culture – in the form of reinterpreted history, religious revivals, elegiac and nostalgic poetry – developed into an important front for nationalist mobilization. To this end literary conventions and discourses inherited from the colonizer were appropriated, translated, decentred, and hybridized in ways which we now name postcolonial but were in fact at the time anti-colonial, often opportunistic, tactical, and *ad hoc*, and which formed an important means of self-expression. Though very gradually at first, given imperial constraints, colonized writers began to come into their own. Starting before the Great War but especially during decades following, writers like Rabindranath Tagore (India), Claude McKay (Jamaica), Raja Rao (India), and Solomon Plaatje (South Africa) took up the Western genres of the novel and short story to articulate their own perceptions of cultural space and experience.' *Colonial and Postcolonial Literature* (Oxford University Press, 1995), p. 100. For discussion of Plaatje in this context, see L. Chrisman, *Rereading the Imperial Romance: British Imperialism and South African Resistance in Haggard, Schreiner, and Plaatje* (Oxford University Press, 2000), pp. 163–208.

9 C. Achebe, *Morning Yet on Creation Day: Essays* (London: Heinemann, 1977 [1975]), p. 45.

10 C. Achebe, *Things Fall Apart* (London: Heinemann, 1983 [1958]); *Arrow of God* (London: Heinemann, 1975 [1964]).

11 E. Coundouriatis, *Claiming History: Colonialism, Ethnography, and the Novel* (New York: Columbia University Press, 1999), p. 38.

12 Compare the discussion of Achebe's *Things Fall Apart* in S. Newell, *West African Literatures: Ways of Reading* (Oxford University Press, 2006), pp. 85–100.

13 A. Djebar, *Fantasia: An Algerian Cavalcade*, trans. D.S. Blair (Portsmouth, NH: Heinemann, 1993 [1985]), p. 6.

14 I derive the phrase from the title of André Brink's novel, *The Other Side of Silence* (London: Secker and Warburg, 2002), which deals with the violence of colonial regulation in German South-West Africa (today's Nambia). Brink's novel has its source in a late nineteenth-century scheme to import hundreds of poor German women to the colony to serve as sexual partners and servants to men stationed there. Brink, of course, had himself derived his novel's title from a resonant passage in George Eliot's *Middlemarch* (New York: Signet, 1981 [1872]): 'That element of tragedy which lies in the very fact of frequency has not yet wrought itself into the coarse emotion of mankind, and perhaps our frames could hardly bear much of it. If we had a keen vision and feeling of all ordinary human life, it would be like hearing the grass grow and the squirrel's heart beat, and we should die of that roar which lies on the other side of silence. As it is, the quickest of us walk about well wadded with stupidity' (p. 191).

15 The question of how *Fantasia* ought to be classified generically has been the subject of much debate. As Nicholas Harrison writes, the text, first published in French in 1985, is 'at once more historical and more personal' than Djebar's preceding novel, *Women of Algiers in their Apartment*, which had initially appeared five years earlier. *Fantasia* 'is often discussed by its author and critics as a work of autobiography. The cover of the original French edition is stamped with the word "roman" (novel), but the decision to apply this label was apparently made not by Djebar but by publishers nervous about how the public would respond to a work of uncertain generic affiliations; indeed, Djebar recalls that she had trouble finding anyone willing to publish it at all ... *Fantasia* intercuts scenes from Djebar's own life and Algeria's past, and from both oral and written history. Revisiting colonial-era documents and placing them in a new context, Djebar pieces together scenes from the colonial encounter, underscoring its violence and, still more explicitly ... the stake of representations within it.' *Postcolonial Criticism*, pp. 128–9.

16 C.-R. Ageron, *Modern Algeria: A History from 1830 to the Present*, trans. M. Brett (Trenton, NJ: Africa World Press, 1991 [1964]), p. 20.

17 A comparison could be drawn here with Malek Alloula's *The Colonial Harem*, trans. M. Godzich and W. Godzich (Minneapolis: University of Minnesota Press, 1986 [1981]), which offers a reading of the postcards, ostensibly of Algerian women, that were mass produced during the early decades of the twentieth century and posted, in their hundreds of thousands, to recipients in France by colonial French settlers, soldiers, functionaries, and

casual travellers in Algeria. 'History knows of no other society in which women have been photographed on such a large scale to be delivered to public view', Alloula writes. 'Behind this image of Algerian women, probably reproduced in the millions, there is visible the broad outline of one of the figures of the colonial perception of the native. This figure can be essentially defined as the practice of a right of (over)sight that the colonizer arrogates to himself and that is the bearer of a multiform violence. The postcard fully partakes in such violence; it extended its effects; it is its accomplished expression, no less efficient for being symbolic ... To track, then, through the colonial representations of Algerian women – the figures of a phantasm – is to attempt a double operation: first, to uncover the nature and the meaning of the colonialist gaze; then, to subvert the stereotype that is so tenaciously attached to the bodies of women' (p. 5). Cf. also in this context Djebar's own long engagement with Eugène Delacroix's canonical 1834 painting, *Les Femmes d'Alger dans leur appartement*, as evidenced most notably in her own *Women of Algiers in their Apartment*, trans. M. de Jager (Charlottesville and London: Caraf Books, 1999 [1980]).

18 R. Guha, *Dominance without Hegemony: History and Power in Colonial India* (Cambridge, MA and London: Harvard University Press, 1997), p. 1.

19 Among these sweeping conclusions, two might be mentioned here. The first, associated most significantly with the work of Partha Chatterjee, is that anti-colonial nationalism is exclusively a 'derivative discourse', whose 'thematic' or underlying framework 'accepts and adopts the same essentialist conception based on the distinction between "the East" and "the West", the same typology created by a transcendent studying subject, and hence the same "objectifying" procedures of knowledge constructed in the post-Enlightenment age of Western science'. P. Chatterjee, *Nationalist Thought and the Colonial World: A Derivative Discourse* (Minneapolis: University of Minnesota Press, 1993 [1986]), p. 38). For my critique of this emphasis in Chatterjee's work, see *Nationalism and Cultural Practice*, esp. pp. 128–33. The second sweeping conclusion, stemming especially from deconstructive scholarship on the archive – see J. Derrida, *Archive Fever: A Freudian Impression*, trans. E. Prenowitz (University of Chicago Press, 1996) – is that because our access to historical events is always discursively mediated, such 'events' must be viewed as effects of archivisation or the discourse of history. The error here is the standard conventionalist one of inferring from the fact that we cannot give a 'theory-independent' description of a thing, that there are no 'theory independent' things. For a recent example of this error in postcolonial studies, see E. Byrne, *Homi K. Bhabha* (Houndmills: Palgrave Macmillan, 2009), who proceeds from the warranted observation that 'the archive and the processes of archivisation are far from being neutral transparent cata-loguers of actual events, or truths', to the unwarranted inference that 'the archive and the processes of archivisation' therefore 'produce those events and decide what *constitutes* an event' (p. 53). A decisive critique of epistemological conventionalism is to be found in the work of Roy Bhaskar. See *Reclaiming*

Reality: A Critical Introduction to Contemporary Philosophy (London: Verso, 1989), and *Philosophy and the Idea of Freedom* (London: Blackwell, 1990); see also A. Collier, *Critical Realism: An Introduction to Roy Bhaskar's Philosophy* (London: Verso, 1994).

20 Le Duan, *The Vietnamese Revolution: Fundamental Problems, Essential Tasks* (Hanoi: Foreign Languages Publishing House, 1973), p. 11. Or – remaining within the context of this particular theatre of conflict – consider Ho Chi Minh, who surveys French colonialism in Annam (Vietnam) and concludes that 'behind a mask of democracy, French imperialism has transplanted in Annam the whole cursed medieval regime, including the salt tax … [T]he Annamese peasant is crucified on the bayonet of capitalist civilization and on the Cross of prostituted Christianity'. *On Revolution: Selected Writings, 1920–66* (New York: Signet, 1967), p. 38.

21 G. Mbeki, *South Africa: The Peasants' Revolt* (Harmondsworth: Penguin, 1964), pp. 16–17.

22 Thus Kortenaar, for example, who – discussing Nkiru Uwechia Nzegwu's sharp critique of Chinua Achebe's representation of 'traditional patriarchy' in *Things Fall Apart* – suggests that he does not mean 'to pit Nzegwu against Achebe in order to uncover the truth of the past'. Rather, he wants to propose 'that the most valuable lesson Nzegwu teaches scholars of Achebe is that *Things Fall Apart* is not an account of the past. Nzegwu's idealised and very attractive account reminds us that she and Achebe both invent the past they need for the sake of the future they want. With Nzegwu beside us, we can read *Things Fall Apart* not as an historical reconstruction but as a product of the moment in which it was written. The historical document Achebe produced testifies not to 1900, when the novel is approximately set, but to 1958, on the eve of Nigerian independence.' N. ten Kortenaar, '*Things Fall Apart* in History', *Interventions*, 11.2 (2009), p. 168. It does not seem to occur to Kortenaar that Achebe's novel might be read *simultaneously* as politically contingent 'invention' *and* as historical reconstruction. Certainly, his suggestion that the novel 'testifies' *only* to 1958, and not to 1900, seems too strong.

23 P. Bourdieu and H. Haacke, *Free Exchange* (Stanford University Press, 1995 [1994]), pp. 23, 28.

24 Multatuli [E. D. Dekker], *Max Havelaar, or, The Coffee Auctions of the Dutch Trading Company*, trans. R. Edwards (Amherst: University of Massachusetts Press, 1982 [1860]), p. 278.

25 For contemporary commentary on *Max Havelaar*, see A. M. Feenberg, '*Max Havelaar*: An Anti-Imperialist Novel', *MLN*, 112.5 (1997), pp. 817–35, and 'The Book that Killed Colonialism', a short testimonial by the great Indonesian writer, Pramoedya Ananta Toer: *New York Times Magazine*, 18 April 1999, pp. 112–14.

26 The phrase derives from E. Shohat and R. Stam, *Unthinking Eurocentrism: Multiculturalism and the Media* (London: Routledge, 1994).

27 V. Y. Mudimbe, *The Idea of Africa* (Bloomington and Indianapolis: Indiana University Press; London: James Currey, 1994), p. xv.

28 V. Y. Mudimbe, *Parables and Fables: Exegesis, Textuality, and Politics in Central Africa* (Madison: University of Wisconsin Press, 1991), p. xi.

29 V. Y. Mudimbe, *The Rift*, trans. M. de Jager (Minneapolis: University of Minnesota Press, 1993 [1979]), p. 13.

30 D. Chakrabarty, *Provincializing Europe: Postcolonial Thought and Historical Difference* (Princeton University Press, 2000).

31 Adorno, *Minima Moralia*, p. 192.

32 See also the description of Ann Hammond: 'When she saw me, she saw a dark twilight like a false dawn. Unlike me, she yearned for tropical climes, cruel suns, purple horizons. In her eyes I was a symbol of all her hankerings' (Salih, *Season of Migration from the North*, p. 30).

33 A. K. Armah, *Why Are We So Blest?* (London: Heinemann, 1974 [1972]), p. 115.

34 K. Harrow, *Thresholds of Change in African Literature: The Emergence of a Tradition* (Portsmouth, NH: Heinemann; London: James Currey, 1994), p. 210.

35 See also his recent essay on narratives of the genocide in Rwanda: K. Harrow, '"Ancient Tribal Warfare": Foundational Fantasies of Ethnicity and History', *Research in African Literatures*, 36.2 (2005), pp. 34–45.

36 V. Y. Mudimbe, *Before the Birth of the Moon*, trans. M. de Jager (New York: Simon and Schuster, 1989 [1976]), p. 68.

37 For commentary on cannibalism in colonial discourse, see the essays in F. Barker, P. Hulme, and M. Iversen (eds), *Cannibalism and the Colonial World* (Cambridge University Press, 1998).

38 P. Rigby, *Persistent Pastoralists: Nomadic Societies in Transition* (London: Zed Books, 1985).

39 Williams, *Marxism and Literature*, p. 13.

40 Bourdieu, *Logic of Practice*.

41 E. W. Said, 'In the Shadow of the West', interview with J. Crary and P. Mariani (1985), in G. Viswanathan (ed.), *Power, Politics and Culture: Interviews with Edward W. Said* (London: Bloomsbury, 2004), pp. 40–1.

42 See the essays collected in J. Fabian, *Anthropology with an Attitude: Critical Essays* (Stanford University Press, 2001).

43 E. W. Said, 'American Intellectuals and Middle East Politics', interview with B. Robbins (1998), in Viswanathan (ed.), *Power, Politics and Culture*, p. 333.

44 For discussion of the shifts and movements in Said's thought from *Orientalism* onwards, see Chapter 5, below.

45 S. Raditlhalo, 'Rewriting Modernity', *Safundi: The Journal of South African and American Studies*, 9.2 (2008), p. 225.

46 Parry, *Postcolonial Studies*, p. 38.

47 C. N. Adichie, *Half of a Yellow Sun* (London: Fourth Estate, 2006), p. 250.

48 Commenting on the famous concluding lines of Achebe's novel, in which the last word is given to the British District Commissioner, who thinks that he might devote a paragraph to the story of Okonkwo and the village of Umuofia in the book he is in the process of writing on colonial governance – and

for which he has already chosen the title of *The Pacification of the Primitive Tribes of the Lower Niger* – Simon Gikandi observes that 'The District Commissioner writes to compress the history of Umuofia into a general text of colonization; Achebe writes to liberate his people from that text and to inscribe the values and ideological claims of Igbo culture in the language and form that sought to repress it. The ultimate irony of his novel is that although the Commissioner has the final word in the fictional text, Achebe – the African writer who has appropriated a Western narrative practice – writes the colonizer's words and hence commemorates an African culture which the colonizer thought he had written out of existence.' *Reading Chinua Achebe: Language and Ideology in Fiction* (London: James Currey; Portsmouth, NH and Nairobi: Heinemann, 1991), p. 50.

49 J. Franco, *The Modern Culture of Latin America: Society and the Artist*, rev. edn (Harmondsworth: Penguin, 1970), p. 175; P. Neruda, *Canto General*, trans. J. Schmitt (Berkeley: University of California Press, 2000 [1950]).

50 For informed and illuminating discussions of 'the narrative strategies of Cuzcatlán', see A. Astvaldsson, 'Toward a New Humanism: Narrative Voice, Narrative Structure and Narrative Strategy in Manlio Argueta's *Cuzcatlán, donde bate la mar del sur*', *Bulletin of Hispanic Studies*, 77 (2000), pp. 603–15; K. Oloff, 'Modernity and the Novel in the Expanded Caribbean: Wilson Harris, Patrick Chamoiseau, and Carlos Fuentes', unpublished Ph.D. thesis, University of Warwick, 2007, pp. 115–37.

51 E. R. Wolf, *Europe and the People without History* (Berkeley: University of California Press, 1982). The literature on the historiographic project of Subaltern Studies is by now extensive. Subtitled *Writings in South Asian History and Society*, the first volume of *Subaltern Studies*, edited by Ranajit Guha, was published by Oxford University Press, India, in 1982. Further volumes in the series have appeared regularly since then. Guha and Spivak co-edited *Selected Subaltern Studies* (Oxford University Press, 1988); a collection intended for the western readership that had by then begun to register the significance of the project. (The foreword to this volume was written by Edward Said.) Guha has subsequently edited another volume of essays from the journal: *A Subaltern Studies Reader, 1986–1995* (Minneapolis: University of Minnesota Press, 1997). Monographs and collections of essays by the scholars centrally associated with *Subaltern Studies* – among them Guha himself, Partha Chatterjee, Gyanendra Pandey, Dipesh Chakrabarty, and Gyan Prakash – are now widely available throughout the anglophone world. Starting in the late 1980s and developing increasing authority and critical mass since then, critiques have emerged of the methodology, epistemology, and politics underpinning *Subaltern Studies*, and especially of the intellectual path the project has followed in recent years – a path that has, in general, taken *Subaltern Studies* from a form of 'history from below' to deconstructive metahistory. A sampling of these critiques can be found in V. Chaturvedi (ed.), *Mapping Subaltern Studies and the Postcolonial* (London and New York: Verso, 2000), a volume that even-handedly presents the debates between the subalternists and their critics. See especially the

chapters by Rosalind O'Hanlon, C. A. Bayly, Tom Brass, Rosalind O'Hanlon and David Washbrook, and Sumit Sarkar, and the review of the Chaturvedi volume by Pranav Jani in *Historical Materialism*, 11.3 (2003), pp. 81–97. See also A. Vanaik, *The Furies of Indian Communalism: Religion, Modernity and Secularization* (London and New York: Verso, 1997), esp. pp. 180–92; and V. Kaiwar, 'Towards Orientalism and Nativism: The Impasse of Subaltern Studies', *Historical Materialism*, 12.2 (2004), pp. 189–247. An assessment of the achievements and weaknesses of the *Subaltern Studies* project is provided in P. Gopal, 'Reading Subaltern History' in Lazarus (ed.), *Cambridge Companion*, pp. 139–61. See S. Sarkar, 'The Return of Labour to South-Asian History', *Historical Materialism*, 12.3 (2004), pp. 285–313 for an assessment of contemporary labour history in India beyond the problematic of *Subaltern Studies*.

52 G. C. Spivak, 'Can the Subaltern Speak?' in C. Nelson and L. Grossberg (eds), *Marxism and the Interpretation of Culture* (Urbana: University of Illinois Press, 1988), p. 308.

53 E. W. Said, *Representations of the Intellectual* (London: Vintage, 1994), p. 11.

54 One is here reminded, in a certain respect, of Georg Lukács's notion of 'imputed consciousness [*zugerechnetes Bewusstsein*]' – the consciousness that members of the proletariat *would* have if they were thinking the thoughts 'appropriate' and 'rational' to their 'particular typical position[s] in the process of production', that is, viewed from the objectively derivable standpoint of totality. *History and Class Consciousness: Studies in Marxist Dialectics*, trans. R. Livingstone (London: Merlin, 1971 [1923]), p. 51. But Lukács's point is precisely that there is a categorical gap between this 'imputed' consciousness and the 'empirical' consciousness of actual workers; moreover, that this gap cannot be closed by an act of will, but only through the collective, revolutionary practice of the proletariat. In these terms, Armah's characterisation of 'the man' is susceptible to the charge of theoreticism.

55 A. Atkins, 'Land as Legislative Space in Vikram Seth's *A Suitable Boy* and Phanishwarnath Renu's *Maila Anchal*', *SOAS Literary Review*, 3 (2001); Renu, *The Soiled Border*.

56 Altogether harsher critiques of *A Suitable Boy* are to be found in P. Casanova, *The World Republic of Letters*, trans. M. B. DeBevoise (Cambridge, MA: Harvard University Press, 2004 [1999]), who dismisses the novel as a 'neo-colonial saga ... adopt[ing] all the familiar devices of exoticism' (p. 171; see also pp. 121–2); and F. Orsini, 'India in the Mirror of World Fiction' in C. Prendergast (ed.), *Debating World Literature* (London and New York: Verso, 2004), who denounces what she sees as the novel's pandering to a western audience, as it 'painfully explain[s] to the foreigners what Indian trains and mud-thatched huts look like' (p. 331).

57 R. O'Hanlon, 'Recovering the Subject: Subaltern Studies and Histories of Resistance in Colonial South Asia' in Chaturvedi (ed.), *Mapping Subaltern Studies*, pp. 80–1.

58 A. Ghosh, *The Hungry Tide* (London: HarperCollins, 2005 [2004]), p. 219.

59 This is an argument also made in T. Tomsky, 'Amitav Ghosh's Anxious Witnessing and the Ethics of Action in *The Hungry Tide*', *Journal of Commonwealth Literature*, 44.1 (2009), pp. 53–65, through reference to humanism, affect and the Saidian concept of 'anxious witnessing'. For a more general critique of the idea of incommensurability prevailing in postcolonial and 'transnational' cultural studies, see Zhang Longxi, *Unexpected Affinities: Reading Across Cultures* (University of Toronto Press, 2007).

60 E. M. Forster, *A Passage to India* (San Diego, New York, London: Harcourt, Brace, Jovanovich, 1984 [1924]), p. 322.

61 Mahasweta's identification of mismanagement, corruption and exploitation sounds a theme common to much radical Bengali (and Indian) writing in the contexts (post-1975) of 'liberalisation' and 'globalisation'. Cf. Bani Basu's *The Enemy Within*, trans. J. Datta (Hyderabad: Orient Longman, 2002 [1991]), in which we read that 'On the surface it appears as though the villages of this area are prospering. It is said they are getting three harvests these days. The banks have given generous loans. The government has arranged to distribute fertilisers and high quality seeds. But are the one-time landless labourers or tenant farmers, benefiting by all this? Is the prosperity really shared by them? It is said that three lakh acres of land were distributed by the Left Front government during its second term. But are we sure that the proprietors are not making illegal use of this under assumed names? There is some flaw in any social welfare programme initiated by the government, because of which corruption can enter without hindrance' (p. 6).

62 In an author's note appended to the story, Mahasweta emphasises her self-conscious use of national and social allegory in 'Pterodactyl': 'Madhya Pradesh' in the story is meant to stand in for 'India', the tribal village for 'the entire tribal society' (p. 196).

63 F. Fanon, *Black Skin, White Masks*, trans. C. L. Markmann (New York: Grove Press, 1967 [1952]), p. 110.

64 'Pterodactyl' is translated by Gayatri Chakravorty Spivak, who chooses to italicise all words and phrases originally in English in Mahasweta's text. Mahasweta herself is on record as regarding Spivak as the best of her English translators. 'Gayatri does not distort, not even one word. And what she does not understand, she always asks me and we work in close collaboration. That's how it's done. Her translation is the most faithful.' 'Speaking with Mahasweta Devi: Mahasweta Devi interviewed by Gabrielle Collu', *Journal of Commonwealth Literature*, 33.2 (1998), p. 143. But see M. Salgado, who deplores the tendentiousness of Spivak's method of translation. Concerning Spivak's decision to italicise all English words, for instance, she writes that it 'effectively wipes out … exegetical variation by polarizing subtle linguistic registers to create a totalized representation of cultural difference and linguistic disjunction, thereby promoting the contestational and oppositional nature of Mahasweta's work.' 'Tribal Stories, Scribal Worlds: Mahasweta Devi and the Unreliable Translator', *Journal of Commonwealth Literature*, 35.1 (2000), p. 135.

65 I thank my colleague Peter Mack for identifying the rhetorical figures of gradatio and isocolon for me.

66 Mahasweta's work provides a limited warrant for the deconstructive bent of this scholarship, which has tended to cluster around the sorts of question that I listed at the beginning of this chapter, concerning the different conditions of possibility (and relatively impossibility) of social signification for agents located at different points in the social spectrum. For example, 'Pterodactyl' provides us with a rigorous and exact representation of the intricate mechanics and hierarchies governing the transactions and intercourse of individual characters, agencies, institutions, languages, and discourses – as when the ideologically progressive civil servant Harisharan and his friend, the journalist Puran Sahay, are engaged in politically mandated discussion with the tribal villager Shankar and the Sarpanch, who is himself a tribal though comparatively well off and who, by virtue of his status, has 'changed class long ago' (p. 116). It is worthy of note that Mahasweta introduces the Sarpanch through reference to his relative prosperity: 'In his fortlike house with high earth walls you can see a separate enclosure for water-buffalo, a granary for corn. Cots in the courtyard. One of his sons is a messenger in the Electricity Office and another has passed an exam to become a clerk in the Post and Telegraph Department' (p. 115). A question raised in the text itself, concerning the social implications of the Sarpanch's circumstances, is not finally diegetically attributable: it seems not to be sited in Puran's consciousness, but to exist rather as narratorial commentary: 'when the tribal gets a little education, gains a little safety and moves from his class, does he go up or down? Does the lower middle class or the middle class accept him as a member? If even one percent of the tribals gets a house, a motorcycle, a job, some land, do they enter the well-to-do middle class or the rural kulak class? No, the main point is that he is not of the destitute tribal community, and not of the class which is his in the adjacent community. Is that why he has to empathize with his poor tribal community in troubled times? Why did the Sarpanch first say "tribals" and then "we"? A many-leveled problem. It is improper to pass quick judgment from a safe distance' (p. 116).

67 The creature is not, of course, a pterodactyl, since the flighted reptiles of the order *Pterosauria* have been extinct since the end of the Cretaceous Period, around 65 million years ago. The narrative suggestion, however, is that it is presumably easier for the 'modern' consciousness to rest with the absurd suggestion that the creature is an extant pterodactyl than with the idea – diegetically framed as true – that it is the embodied form of the soul of the ancestors of the inhabitants of Pirtha.

68 T. W. Adorno, *Negative Dialectics*, trans. E. B. Ashton (New York: Continuum, 1997 [1966]), p. 320.

69 H.-G. Gadamer, *Truth and Method*, trans. W. Glen-Doepel (London: Sheed and Ward, 1979 [1960]).

4 FRANTZ FANON AFTER THE 'POSTCOLONIAL PREROGATIVE'

1 See for example B. Ashcroft, G. Griffiths, and H. Tiffin (eds), *The Post-Colonial Studies Reader* (London and New York: Routledge, 1995); G. Castle (ed.), *Postcolonial Discourses: An Anthology* (Oxford: Blackwell, 2001); P. Williams and L. Chrisman (eds), *Colonial Discourse and Post-Colonial Theory: A Reader* (Hemel Hempstead: Harvester Wheatsheaf, 1993).

2 See for example P. Childs and P. Williams, *An Introduction to Post-Colonial Theory* (London: Prentice Hall, 1997); L. Gandhi, *Postcolonial Theory: An Introduction* (Edinburgh University Press, 1998); J. McLeod, *Beginning Postcolonialism* (Manchester University Press, 2000); B. Moore-Gilbert, *Postcolonial Theory: Contexts, Practices, Politics* (London and New York: Verso, 1997). Loomba, *Colonialism/Postcolonialism* and R. J. C. Young, *Postcolonialism: An Historical Introduction* (Cambridge: Blackwell, 2001) are exceptional in being theme-driven in their focus, rather than centred on individual writers and critics.

3 H. L. Gates, Jr, 'Critical Fanonism', *Critical Inquiry*, 17.3 (1991), p. 458.

4 See for instance N. C. Gibson, 'Fanon and the Pitfalls of Cultural Studies' in A. C. Alessandrini (ed.), *Frantz Fanon: Critical Perspectives* (London and New York: Routledge, 1999), pp. 99–125; L. R. Gordon, 'Black Skins Masked: Finding Fanon in Isaac Julien's *Frantz Fanon: Black Skin, White Mask*', *differences: A Journal of Feminist Cultural Studies*, 8.3 (1996), pp. 148–58; Lazarus, *Nationalism and Cultural Practice*; B. Parry, 'Signs of our Times: A Discussion of Homi Bhabha's *The Location of Culture*', *Third Text*, 28/29 (1994), pp. 5–24; Robinson, 'Appropriation of Frantz Fanon', pp. 79–91; E. San Juan, Jr, 'Fanon: An Intervention into Cultural Studies' in Alessandrini (ed.), *Frantz Fanon*, pp. 126–45; A. Sekyi-Otu, *Fanon's Dialectic of Experience* (Cambridge, MA: Harvard University Press, 1996). Said's discussion of Fanon in *Culture and Imperialism* (esp. pp. 323–32) also needs to be cited in this context.

5 See H. K. Bhabha, 'Foreword: Remembering Fanon: Self, Psyche and the Colonial Condition' in F. Fanon, *Black Skin, White Masks*, trans. C. L. Markmann (London: Pluto, 1986 [1952]), pp. vii–xxvi., and *The Location of Culture*, most notably, but also R. Chow, 'The Politics of Admittance: Female Sexual Agency, Miscegenation, and the Formation of Community in Frantz Fanon' in *Ethics after Idealism: Theory-Culture-Ethnicity-Reading* (Bloomington: Indiana University Press, 1998), pp. 55–73; D. Fuss, 'Interior Colonies: Frantz Fanon and the Politics of Identification' in *Identification Papers: Readings on Psychoanalysis, Sexuality and Culture* (New York and London: Routledge, 1995), pp. 141–72; S. Hall, 'The After-Life of Frantz Fanon: Why Fanon? Why Now? Why *Black Skin, White Masks?*' in A. Read (ed.), *The Fact of Blackness: Frantz Fanon and Visual Representation* (London: Institute of Contemporary Arts; Seattle: Bay Press, 1996), pp. 12–37; K. Mercer, 'Decolonisation and Disappointment: Reading Fanon's Sexual Politics' in Read (ed.), *Fact of Blackness*, pp. 114–31; J. Mowitt, 'Algerian Nation: Fanon's

Fetish', *Cultural Critique*, 22 (1992), pp. 165–86, and 'Breaking up Fanon's Voice' in Alessandrini (ed.), *Frantz Fanon*, pp. 89–98; F. Vergès, 'Chains of Madness, Chains of Colonialism: Fanon and Freedom' in Read (ed.), *Fact of Blackness*, pp. 46–75; and R. J. C. Young, *White Mythologies: Writing History and the West* (London: Routledge, 1990).

6 The previously established critical literature would include H. A. Bulhan, *Frantz Fanon and the Psychology of Oppression* (New York: Plenum Press, 1985); D. Caute, *Frantz Fanon* (New York: Viking, 1970); P. Geismar, *Frantz Fanon* (New York: Grove Press, 1969); I. Gendzier, *Frantz Fanon: A Critical Study* (New York: Grove Press, 1973); E. Hansen, *Frantz Fanon: Social and Political Thought* (Columbus: Ohio State University Press, 1977); L. A. Jinadu, *Fanon: In Search of the African Revolution* (London: Kegan Paul, 1986); J. McCulloch, *Black Soul, White Artifact: Fanon's Critical Psychology and Social Theory* (Cambridge University Press, 1983); B. M. Perinbam, *Holy Violence: The Revolutionary Thought of Frantz Fanon* (Washington, DC: Three Continents Press, 1983); and R. Zahar, *Frantz Fanon: Colonialism and Alienation* (New York: Monthly Review Press, 1974). Little if any of this body of work finds mention in the 'postcolonial' discussion of Fanon.

7 D. Macey, *Frantz Fanon: A Life* (London: Granta, 2000).

8 Compare L. R. Gordon, T. D. Sharpley-Whiting and R. T. White (eds), *Fanon: A Critical Reader* (Oxford: Blackwell, 1996), pp. 5–8, which offers a five-stage schema of Fanon scholarship. See also the discussion in A. C. Alessandrini, 'Introduction: Fanon Studies, Cultural Studies, Cultural Politics' in Alessandrini (ed.), *Frantz Fanon*, pp. 5–6.

9 This is an argument I have tried to make in some of my own writings on Fanon over the years. See for instance, *Resistance in Postcolonial African Fiction*, pp. 27–45 and *Nationalism and Cultural Practice*, pp. 76–105.

10 See A. K. Armah, 'Fanon: The Awakener', *Negro Digest*, 18.12 (1969), pp. 4–9, 29–43.

11 Ahmad, *In Theory*; Dirlik, 'Postcolonial Aura'; Brennan, *At Home*. See also the account presented in Chapter 1 above.

12 Macey's commentary ought to be read alongside other recent work that shares his interest in situating Fanon historically and comparatively, rather than abstractly as the sole precursive representative of 'postcolonial' intellectualism. From within francophone postcolonial studies, for instance, has latterly come work identifying the thrust and contours of Fanon's thought through reference to his intellectual formation within a specifically French colonial order and discursive universe. See for instance Harrison, *Postcolonial Criticism*, pp. 151–64; P. Williams, '"Faire peau neuve": Césaire, Fanon, Memmi, Sartre and Senghor' in C. Forsdick and D. Murphy (eds), *Francophone Postcolonial Studies: A Critical Introduction* (London: Edward Arnold, 2003), pp. 181–91; M. A. Majumdar, *Postcoloniality: The French Dimension* (New York and Oxford: Berghahn Books, 2007): esp. pp. 119–24. Paget Henry's discussion in *Caliban's Reason: Introducing Afro-Caribbean Philosophy* (New York and London:

Routledge, 2000), meanwhile, is attentive not to the francophone but to the specifically Caribbean dimensions of Fanon's intellectual formation.

13 Compare A. C. Alessandrini, who writes that Fanon's work 'is an attempt to stretch certain modernist metanarratives from within; in fact, the inability to stand outside such metanarratives, or to claim to be uncontaminated by them, is central to Fanon's arguments. Fighting a battle against universalism from within, Fanon works to adapt and stretch such tools as Marxism, existentialism, Hegelianism, and psychoanalysis to fit his needs. The tortured *écriture* and melding of genres in *Black Skin, White Masks* and the way in which *The Wretched of the Earth* teems with multiple themes, voices, and methodologies attest to this struggle.' 'Humanism in Question: Fanon and Said' in Schwarz and Ray (eds), *Companion to Postcolonial Studies*, p. 434. See also Ewa Plonowska Ziarek's introduction to a special issue of the journal *parallax*, in which she speaks of the need for 'a much more complex and interdisciplinary interpretation of Fanon's critical engagements with the multiple philosophical and political traditions of modernity and their critiques, ranging from Hegelianism, Marxism, phenomenology to psychoanalysis, from the Negritude movement to the African and Afro-Caribbean philosophies.' 'Introduction: Fanon's Counterculture of Modernity', *parallax*, 8.2 (2002), pp. 1–2.

14 P. Taylor, *The Narrative of Liberation: Perspectives on Afro-Caribbean Literature, Culture, and Politics* (Ithaca, NY: Cornell University Press, 1989). See also in this context Bulhan, *Frantz Fanon*; Gordon, *Fanon and the Crisis*; Sekyi-Otu, *Fanon's Dialectic*.

15 M. Merleau-Ponty, *Phenomenology of Perception*, trans. C. Smith (London: Routledge, 1999 [1945]).

16 F. Fanon, *Toward the African Revolution*, trans. H. Chevalier (New York: Grove Press, 1969 [1964]), p. 52.

17 Concerning the latter, cf. Edward W. Said's comments, in interview with David Barsamian: 'I would also want to add that some of the things that powers like Britain, the United States, and France have done against lesser people, like bombing them from the air, where the bomber cannot be reached by essentially defenseless people, are also inexcusable. This is what the Israelis are doing in the West Bank and Gaza, using F-16s to attack Palestinian homes, which are completely undefended ... I think that too has the structure of terror. It's meant to impose fear, it's indiscriminate, and there is no chance for any response. It is pure destruction for the sake of destruction and terrorizing people.' *Culture and Resistance: Conversations with Edward W. Said* (Cambridge, MA: South End Press, 2003), p. 113.

18 Fanon, *Toward the African Revolution*, p. 53. This understanding of the goal of psychiatry, as Macey correctly points out, is fundamentally at odds with the tenets of Lacanian psychoanalysis, from which Fanon 'departs ... by referring to the need to strengthen the ego – which Lacan regarded as the capital sin of American ego-psychology. Fanon consistently described mental illness as a form of alienation from the world and as a loss of existential freedom. As a

therapist, his goal was to "consciousnessize" (*conscienciser*) his patient's conflicts so as to establish a new and more positive relationship with the external world. Fanon always stresses the sociogenic aspects of symptomatology: symptoms did not, in this view, originate from the personal unconscious or repressed sexual impulses so much as from a distorted dialectic between the ego and the world and from the internalization of social conflicts' (p. 323).

19 Translated into English as *Studies in a Dying Colonialism*, trans. H. Chevalier (Harmondsworth: Penguin, 1970 [1959]).

20 This rebuttal also tells against the American academic Christopher L. Miller, who has given a more recent airing to the argument that Fanon glorifies violence. 'For Fanon', Miller has written, 'violence has a transcendental power to liberate and cure the psychological ills of the colonized; violence "illuminates", "deintoxicates", and "unifies the people"'. *Theories of Africans: Francophone Literature and Anthropology in Africa* (University of Chicago Press, 1990), p. 49. Macey cites Miller's study, but surprisingly fails to subject it to criticism. For a critique of Miller, see Lazarus, *Nationalism and Cultural Practice*, pp. 82–8, 97–103.

21 For further commentary on these developments, see B. Davidson, *In the Eye of the Storm: Angola's People* (Harmondsworth: Penguin, 1975), on which Macey draws, and R. Gibson, *African Liberation Movements: Contemporary Struggles Against White Minority Rule* (Oxford University Press, 1972), pp. 197–242. See also A. Cherki, *Frantz Fanon: A Portrait*, trans. N. Benabid (Ithaca, NY: Cornell University Press, 2006); Gibson, 'Fanon and the Pitfalls'; and A. Stafford, 'Frantz Fanon, Atlantic Theorist; or, Decolonization and Nation State in Postcolonial Theory' in C. Forsdick and D. Murphy (eds), *Francophone Postcolonial Studies: A Critical Introduction* (London: Edward Arnold, 2003), pp. 166–77, in all of whom the individual focus on Fanon opens on to a rigorously comparative – and, through this means, critical – analysis of Fanon's revolutionary and anti-imperialist theory and practice, in relation to the theory and practice of other politico-intellectuals – from Che Guevara and Vo Nguyen Giap to Gérard Chaliand and Mohamed Harbi.

22 I. Clegg, 'Workers and Managers in Algeria' in R. Cohen, P. C. W. Gutkind, and P. Brazier (eds), *Peasants and Proletarians: The Struggles of Third World Workers* (New York: Monthly Review Press, 1979), p. 239.

23 J. C. Scott, *Weapons of the Weak: Everyday Forms of Peasant Resistance* (New Haven, CT: Yale University Press, 1985), pp. 348–9.

24 Hence, presumably, the consistent misspelling of names that plague his study in this particular respect: of George Lamming, Alain Locke, Tom Mboya, Moise Tshombe, and Peter Worsley, among others.

25 Ngugi wa Thiong'o, *Decolonising the Mind*, p. 63.

26 Williams, *Politics of Modernism*, p. 170.

27 This had been his favoured mode of 'dealing' with the materialist critique of his work during the 1980s and 1990s: 'dealing' with it, that is to say, through the simple expedient of not dealing with it.

28 H. K. Bhabha, 'Foreword: Framing Fanon', F. Fanon, *The Wretched of the Earth*, trans. R. Philcox (New York: Grove Press, 2005), p. xi.

29 E. W. Said, *Humanism and Democratic Criticism* (New York: Columbia University Press, 2004), p. 142.

30 I. Wallerstein, 'Reading Fanon in the 21st Century', *New Left Review*, 57 (2009), p. 124.

5 THE BATTLE OVER EDWARD SAID

1 See for example J. Habermas, *Knowledge and Human Interests*, trans. J. J. Shapiro (London: Heinemann, 1978 [1968]).

2 M. Sprinker, 'Introduction' in M. Sprinker (ed.), *Edward Said: A Critical Reader* (Oxford: Blackwell, 1992), p. 2.

3 E. W. Said, *The Politics of Dispossession: the Struggle for Palestinian Self-Determination, 1969–1994* (New York: Pantheon Books, 1994); *Peace and its Discontents: Essays on Palestine in the Middle East Peace Process* (New York: Vintage, 1995); *The End of the Peace Process: Oslo and After*, 2nd edn (London: Granta, 2002).

4 E. W. Said, *Orientalism* (New York: Vintage, 1979 [1978]).

5 I use 'post-' theory rather than the term 'post-modern' theory, preferred by Said. The formation includes, I think, a variety of initiatives not especially marked by an emphasis on 'modernity': post-structuralism, Lacanian psychoanalysis, deconstruction, semiotics, the Foucault-derived projects of genealogy and archaeology, etc.

6 J. Habermas, *The Philosophical Discourse of Modernity: Twelve Lectures*, trans. F. Lawrence (Cambridge, MA: MIT Press, 1987 [1985]).

7 I derive the term 'nationalitarian' from Anouar Abdel-Malek: '[The] nationalitarian phenomenon … has as its object, beyond the clearing of the national territory, the independence and sovereignty of the national state, uprooting in depth the positions of the ex-colonial power – the reconquest of the power of decision in all domains of national life … Historically, fundamentally, the struggle is for national liberation, the instrument of that reconquest of identity which … lies at the heart of everything.' *Nation and Revolution*, trans. M. Gonzalez (Albany: State University of New York Press, 1981), p. 13. In an important essay, 'Nationalism, Human Rights, and Interpretation', *Raritan*, 12.3 (1993), Said wrote that 'what has not received as much notice as it should have from historians of Third World nationalism is that a clear if paradoxical antinationalist theme emerges in the writings of a fair number of nationalists who are wholehearted supporters of the national movement itself' (p. 41). Said mentions Tagore, Césaire, Fanon, Shibley Shumayil, Rashid Rida, Abdel Rahman al-Bazzaz, Qunstantin Zurayk, Taha Hussayn, and W. E. B. Du Bois. My sense is that this identification of nationalists who criticise nationalism while continuing to support the national movement wholeheartedly accurately describes Said's position also.

8 J. Clifford, 'On *Orientalism*' in *The Predicament of Culture: Twentieth-Century Ethnography, Literature, and Art* (Cambridge, MA: Harvard University Press), pp. 255–76.

9 V. Kennedy, *Edward Said: A Critical Introduction* (Oxford: Polity, 2000), pp. 25, 27.

10 It is quite true that in *The World, the Text, and the Critic*, Said would come to take up a critical distance from Foucault that would be maintained for the remainder of his career. But Brennan makes too much of this, I think, arguing not only that '*The World, the Text, and the Critic* is tightly bound up with *Orientalism*, and has a special relationship to it' (*Wars of Position*, p. 95) – which can readily be conceded – but effectively that the lens on Foucault is *identical* in the two works.

11 W. D. Hart, *Edward Said and the Religious Effects of Culture* (Cambridge University Press, 2000), p. 70.

12 Compare Hart: 'Clifford's assertions may be true. But how would we know? He gives us no reason to take what he says as true aside from merely asserting that it is. If this assertion relies on claims that Foucault makes, what is the status of those claims? Are we to take them on faith? Only if Foucault is taken as the *inspired author* (how ironic is that?) of sacred texts can assertions such as Clifford's be made so dogmatically. For surely the point of *Orientalism* is to revise Foucault's notion of discourse, methodologically, in light of the empirical evidence' (*Religious Effects*, p. 69).

13 See the discussion in Loomba, *Colonialism/Postcolonialism*, pp. 32ff. Childs and Williams correctly point out that Said's failure to make much use of the concept of ideology is 'simultaneously surprising (given its explanatory/analytical potential), and understandable (given the influence of Foucault – who also avoided it – at this period, as well as Said's own complicated relationship to Marxism)' (*An Introduction*, p. 102).

14 E. W. Said, 'Beginnings' (1976) in Viswanathan (ed.), *Power, Politics and Culture*, p. 26.

15 In a curious formulation, Arif Dirlik argues that this changes in Said's later work, when his 'recognition of the importance of class-related questions to the project of liberation draws on the legacy of Marxism in earlier national liberation movements'. 'Placing Edward Said: Space Time and the Travelling Theorist' in B. Ashcroft and H. Kadhim (eds), *Edward Said and the Post-Colonial* (Huntington, NY: Nova Science Publishers, 2001), p. 19. Dirlik immediately qualifies this observation, however: 'in spite of his references to the fundamentally economic and political nature of imperialism and colonialism, [Said's] … attention to the question of class is restricted to its implications for national struggles, divorced from class analysis in the critique of capitalism, and the internationalism that motivated earlier national liberation theorists who perceived in the struggle for national liberation a struggle both for the nation – and against a capitalism which was viewed, rightly or wrongly, as the ultimate source of colonialism. The project of "liberation", as distinct from "independence", was in fact premised on just such an internationalism that

drove Canadian (Norman Bethune) and Arab-American (George Hatem) doctors to fight in the Chinese Revolution, or for a brief time rendered Guangzhou (Canton) in South China into the "headquarters" of world revolution' (pp. 19–20). I find this formulation curious inasmuch as several of the discriminations upon which it is premised strike me as being contestable. Contra Dirlik, I would suggest that even in his later work, Said does *not* 'draw ... on the legacy of Marxism in earlier national liberation movements'; instead, he tends to *bracket* their Marxism and to draw on their *liberationism*. Nor does Said make very much at all of 'the fundamentally economic ... nature of imperialism and colonialism'. As I have suggested elsewhere in this book, he seems to me to pay scant regard to this aspect, preferring to emphasise the cultural and political effects of imperialism and of the challenge to it. Partly for this very reason, he is precisely and sensitively attuned to what Dirlik suggests that he ignores: internationalism, and the 'project of "liberation", as distinct from independence"'.

16 Although not as important, as he pointed out in an interview conducted in 1993, as 'the idea that everything, including civil society to begin with but really the whole world, is organized according to geography ... [The] *Prison Notebooks* are a kind of map of modernity. They're not a history of modernity, but his notes really try to *place* everything, like a military map; I mean that there was always some struggle going on over territory. I think that is his single, most powerful idea.' 'Culture and Imperialism' (1993), interview with J. A. Buttigieg and P. A. Bové in Viswanathan (ed.), *Power, Politics and Culture*, p. 195. The importance of Gramsci to Said's project in *Orientalism* is persuasively explored in Brennan, *Wars of Position* and A. A. Hussein, *Edward Said: Criticism and Society* (London and New York: Verso, 2002).

17 Hussein attempts to defend Said here, arguing that 'at its metacritical or infrastructural level, Said's intellectual project is guided, often explicitly but sometimes as a presumed backcloth, by what could best be described as "a technique of trouble" (to use Said's own Blackmurrian metaphor for Michel Foucault's methodology). Marked by both eccentricity and difficulty, this technique of extremes involves an activated confrontation between agonist dialectic and archaeology/genealogy' (*Edward Said*, p. 4). My own sense, however, is that Said's mobilisation of dialectics is very much less assured and less prominent in *Orientalism* than is his deployment of 'archaeology/genealogy'. Moreover, Hussein fails to take into consideration the degree to which the two 'approaches' or 'methods' are irreconcilable and work to undermine one another.

18 E. W. Said, '*Orientalism* and After' (1993), interview with A. Beezer and P. Osborne in Viswanathan (ed.), *Power, Politics and Culture*, p. 214.

19 P. B. Armstrong, 'Being "out of place": Edward W. Said and the Contradictions of Cultural Differences', *Modern Language Quarterly*, 64.1 (2003), p. 99.

20 E. W. Said, 'Language, History and the Production of Knowledge', interview with G. Viswanathan in Viswanathan (ed.), *Power, Politics and Culture*, p. 268.

21 B. Ashcroft and P. Ahluwalia, *Edward Said: The Paradox of Identity* (London and New York: Routledge, 1999), p. 4.

22 E. W. Said, 'An Interview with Edward W. Said' in M. Bayoumi and A. Rubin (eds), *The Edward Said Reader* (London: Granta, 2000), p. 423.

23 S. Amin, *Eurocentrism*, trans. R. Moore (New York: Monthly Review Press, 1989), p. 101.

24 Larsen, 'Imperialism', pp. 46–7. Cf. T. Cochran, 'The Matter of Language' in P. A. Bové (ed.), *Edward Said and the Work of the Critic: Speaking Truth to Power* (Durham, NC: Duke University Press, 2000), who insists on the 'extreme importance' of Nietzsche's essay, 'On Truth and Lie in the Extramoral Sense' for 'Said's work and for contemporary critical thought generally' (p. 92).

25 In *Humanism and Democratic Criticism*, Said lists time and relative freedom from the specific burdens of commodity production as among the more important such resources – for university-based scholars and intellectuals, at least: 'University humanists are in an exceptionally privileged position in which to do their work, but it is not simply as academic professionals or experts that their advantage lies. Rather, the academy – with its devotion to reflection, research, Socratic teaching and some measure of sceptical detachment – allows one freedom from the deadlines, the obligations to an importunate and exigent employer, and the pressures to produce on a regular basis, that afflict so many experts in our policy-think-tank riddled age. Not the least valuable thing about the reflection and thoughts that takes place in a university is that one has time to do it' (pp. 71–2).

26 E. W. Said, 'Figures, Configurations, Transfigurations', *Race & Class*, 32.1 (1990), pp. 1–2.

27 Bourdieu, *Field of Cultural Production*, p. 344.

28 P. Bourdieu, 'Are Intellectuals out of Play?' (1978) in *Sociology in Question*, trans. R. Nice (London, Thousand Oaks, CA, New Delhi: Sage, 1993), p. 38.

29 P. Bourdieu, *On Television*, trans. P. P. Ferguson (New York: New Press, 1998 [1996]), p. 66.

30 Bourdieu, 'Intellectual Field', p. 141.

31 P. Bourdieu, 'How can "Free-Floating Intellectuals" be set Free?' (1980) in *Sociology in Question*, p. 44.

32 G. Lamming, *The Pleasures of Exile* (London: Michael Joseph, 1960).

33 Bourdieu, 'Intellectual Field', p. 145.

34 A. Roy, *The Checkbook and the Cruise Missile: Conversations with Arundhati Roy*, interviews by D. Barsamian (Cambridge, MA: South End Press, 2004), p. 68.

35 This is a point made by Parry in 'Countercurrents'.

36 Compare S. Collini, *Absent Minds: Intellectuals in Britain* (Oxford University Press, 2006), who argues, with respect to *Representations of the Intellectual*, that it 'does not really confront let alone resolve, the ... tensions between lonely individuality and axiomatic solidarity, in part because it never rises to a sufficiently analytical level. It is, in every sense, a romantic picture,

concentrating on the talent and good faith of the isolated individual in his heroic struggle with the oppressive power of the conventional, the official, the established' (p. 428). The latter sentence here is glib: Said was never remotely concerned to combat 'the conventional, the official, the established' as such. His interest lay rather in contesting arbitrary power and in identifying the destruction it wrought. Collini goes on to label Said's 'romantic' portrayal of the intellectual vocation 'culpable', 'both in its damaging under-description of the actual social and institutional position of intellectuals in any period and society (and here the observation by some of his critics that Said himself held a well-funded named chair at one of the most prestigious American universities becomes potentially more than just a cheap jibe), and in its neglect of the enabling role of cultural tradition and intellectual community. This exaggerated individualism (remarkable in a self-described "radical" critic) prevents him from taking the measure even of topics he himself introduces, such as professionalization and specialization' (pp. 428–9). The asides here are waspish, and introduce poison to the meat of Collini's critique. One begins to suspect that the criticism of the Parr Professor of English and Comparative Literature at Columbia University by the Professor of Intellectual History and English Literature at Cambridge University is not without a taint of personal animus. The suggestion that while 'Said implicitly represents himself as resisting the glamour and seductiveness of official patronage ... he succumbs to a more insidious kind of glamour, that of being the champion of the wretched of the earth' (p. 428), is simply tendentious.

37 See Ahmad, *In Theory*, pp. 159–219. For left-wing rejoinders to Ahmad's critique of Said, see B. Parry, 'A Critique Mishandled', *Social Text*, 35 (1993), pp. 121–33; N. Larsen, 'Postcolonialism's Unsaid', *Minnesota Review*, 45–6 (1996), pp. 285–90; N. Lazarus, 'Postcolonialism and the Dilemma of Nationalism: Aijaz Ahmad's Critique of Third-Worldism', *Diaspora: A Journal of Transnational Studies*, 2.3 (1993), pp. 373–400; M. Sprinker, 'The National Question: Said, Ahmad, Jameson', *Public Culture*, 6.1 (1993), pp. 3–29.

Works cited

PRIMARY

Achebe, Chinua, *Arrow of God* (London: Heinemann, 1975 [1964]).
  Things Fall Apart (London: Heinemann, 1983 [1958]).
  Anthills of the Savannah (London: Heinemann, 1987).
Adichie, Chimamanda Ngozi, *Half of a Yellow Sun* (London: Fourth Estate, 2006).
Adnan, Etel, *Sitt Marie Rose*, trans. Georgina Kleege (Sausalito, CA: Post-Apollo Press, 1982 [1978]).
Adonis, 'A Mirror for the Executioner' in Mahmud Darwish, Samih al-Qasim, and Adonis, *Victims of a Map: A Bilingual Anthology of Arabic Poetry*, trans. Abdullah al-Udhari (London: Al Saqi Books, 1984), pp. 88–9.
Alegría, Claribel, *Woman of the River*, trans. D. J. Flakoll (University of Pittsburgh Press, 1989).
Ali, Agha Shahid, *The Country without a Post Office* (New York and London: W. W. Norton, 1998 [1997]).
  Rooms are Never Finished (New York and London: W. W. Norton, 2003 [2002]).
Anand, Mulk Raj, *Untouchable* (Harmondsworth: Penguin, 1986 [1935]).
  Coolie (Harmondsworth: Penguin, 1993 [1936]).
Argueta, Manlio, *One Day of Life*, trans. Bill Brow (New York: Aventura, 1983 [1980]).
  Cuzcatlán, trans. Clark Hansen (London: Chatto and Windus, 1987).
Armah, Ayi Kwei, *Why Are We So Blest?* (London: Heinemann, 1974 [1972]).
  Fragments (London: Heinemann, 1979 [1970]).
  The Beautyful Ones are not yet Born (London: Heinemann, 1981 [1968]).
Asturias, Miguel Angel, *Men of Maize*, trans. Gerald Martin (London: Verso, 1988 [1949]).
Basu, Bani, *The Enemy Within*, trans. Jayanti Datta (Hyderabad: Orient Longman, 2002 [1991]).
Basu, Samaresh, *Selected Stories*, vol. 1, trans. Sumanta Banerjee (Calcutta: Thema, 2003).
Bei Dao, *Waves*, trans. Bonnie S. McDougall and Susette Ternent Cooke (New York: New Directions, 1986).

260

The August Sleepwalker, trans. Bonnie S. McDougall (London: Anvil Press Poetry, 1988).

Ben Jelloun, Tahar, *The Sand Child*, trans. Alan Sheridan (San Diego, New York, London: Harcourt, Brace, Jovanovich, 1987 [1985]).

Beti, Mongo, *Perpetua and the Habit of Unhappiness*, trans. John Reed and Clive Wake (London: Heinemann, 1978 [1974]).

  Lament for an African Pol, trans. Richard Bjornson (Washington, DC: Three Continents Press, 1985 [1979]).

  Remember Ruben, trans. Gerald Moore (London: Heinemann, 1987 [1974]).

Bhattacharya, Bhabani, *So Many Hungers!* (London: Victor Gollancz, 1947).

  A Goddess Named Gold (New Delhi: Arnold-Heinemann, 1984 [1960]).

Boissière, Ralph de, *Crown Jewel* (London: Picador, 1981 [1952]).

Bose, Buddhadeva, *Selected Poems*, trans. Ketaki Kushari Dyson (Oxford University Press, 2003).

Brathwaite, Edward Kamau, *The Arrivants: A New World Trilogy*, comprising *Rights of Passage* (1967), *Masks* (1968), and *Islands* (1969) (Oxford University Press, 1973).

Breytenbach, Breyten, 'Please don't feed the animals' (1970) in *In Africa even the Flies are Happy: Selected Poems and Prose 1964–1977*, trans. Denis Hirson (London: John Calder, 1978), pp. 48–51.

Brink, André, *The Other Side of Silence* (London: Secker and Warburg, 2002).

Bulosan, Carlos, *America is in the Heart* (Seattle: University of Washington Press, 1990 [1946]).

Cardenal, Ernesto, *From Nicaragua with Love: Poems, 1979–1986*, trans. Jonathan Cohen (San Francisco: City Lights Books, 1986).

  Flights of Victory, trans. Marc Zimmerman (Willimantic, CT: Curbstone Press, 1988).

Carpentier, Alejo, *Reasons of State*, trans. Frances Partridge (London: Victor Gollancz, 1976 [1974]).

Carter, Martin, 'I come from the Nigger Yard' (1954) in *Poems of Succession* (London and Port of Spain: New Beacon Books, 1977), pp. 38–40.

Césaire, Aimé, *Notebook of a Return to the Native Land* (1939) and *Ferrements* (1960) in *The Collected Poetry of Aimé Césaire*, trans. Clayton Eshleman and Annette Smith (Berkeley: University of California Press, 1983), pp. 43–85; 260–357.

Chamoiseau, Patrick, *Texaco*, trans. Rose-Myriam Réjouis and Val Vinokurov (New York: Vintage, 1998 [1992]).

Chipasula, Frank M., *Nightwatcher, Nightsong* (Peterborough: Paul Green, 1986).

Coetzee, J. M., *Waiting for the Barbarians* (Harmondsworth: Penguin, 1982 [1980]).

  Foe (Johannesburg: Ravan Press, 1986).

Couto, Mia, *Voices Made Night*, trans. David Brookshaw (London: Heinemann, 1990 [1986]).

  Every Man is a Race, trans. David Brookshaw (London: Heinemann, 1994 [1989, 1990]).

The Last Flight of the Flamingo, trans. David Brookshaw (London: Serpent's Tail, 2004 [2000]).

Dai Houying, *Stones of the Wall*, trans. Frances Wood (London: Sceptre, 1987 [1981]).

Dangor, Achmat, *Kafka's Curse. A Novella and Three Other Stories* (Cape Town: Kwela Books, 1997).

Daruwalla, Keki N., *Collected Poems 1970–2005* (New Delhi: Penguin, 2006).

Darwish, Mahmoud, 'Poem of the Land', trans. Lena Jayyusi and Christopher Middleton, in Salma Khadra Jayyusi (ed.), *Anthology of Modern Palestinian Literature* (New York: Columbia University Press, 1992), pp. 145–51.

  Memory for Forgetfulness. August, Beirut, 1982, trans. Ibrahim Muhawi (Berkeley: University of California Press, 1995 [1986]).

  Unfortunately, it was Paradise: Selected Poems, trans. and ed. Munir Akash and Carolyn Forché with Sinan Antoon and Amira El-Zein (Berkeley: University of California Press, 2003).

Darwish, Mahmoud, Samih al-Qasim, and Adonis, *Victims of a Map: A Bilingual Anthology of Arabic Poetry*, trans. Abdullah al-Udhari (London: Al Saqi Books, 1984).

Desai, Anita, *Clear Light of Day* (Harmondsworth: Penguin, 1980).

Diop, David Mandessi, 'The Vultures' (1956) in *Hammer Blows*, trans. and ed. Simon Mpondo and Frank Jones (London: Heinemann, 1975), pp. 4–5.

Djebar, Assia, *Fantasia: An Algerian Cavalcade*, trans. Dorothy S. Blair (Portsmouth, NH: Heinemann, 1993 [1985]).

  Women of Algiers in their Apartment, trans. Marjolijn de Jager (Charlottesville and London: Caraf Books, 1999 [1980]).

  Algerian White: A Narrative, trans. David Kelley and Marjolijn de Jager (New York: Seven Stories Press, 2000).

Dorfman, Ariel, *In Case of Fire in a Foreign Land: New and Collected Poems from Two Languages*, trans. Edith Grossman and Ariel Dorfman (Durham, NC: Duke University Press, 2002).

Edgell, Zee, *In Times Like These* (Oxford: Heinemann, 1991).

Eliot, George, *Middlemarch: A Study of Provincial Life* (New York: Signet, 1981 [1872]).

Faiz Ahmed Faiz, *The Rebel's Silhouette: Selected Poems*, rev. edn, trans. Agha Shahid Ali (Amherst: University of Massachusetts Press, 1995).

Farah, Nuruddin, *Sweet and Sour Milk* (London: Allison and Busby, 1979).

  Sardines (London: Allison and Busby, 1981).

  Close Sesame (London: Allison and Busby, 1983).

  Maps (New York: Pantheon, 1986).

Forster, E. M., *A Passage to India* (San Diego, New York, London: Harcourt, Brace, Jovanovich, 1984 [1924]).

Fuentes, Carlos, *Where the Air is Clear*, trans. Sam Hileman (New York: Farrar, Straus, and Giroux, 1960 [1958].

  The Years with Laura Díaz, trans. Alfred Mac Adam (New York: Farrar, Straus, and Giroux, 2000 [1999]).

García Márquez, Gabriel, *One Hundred Years of Solitude*, trans. Gregory Rabassa (New York: Harper and Row, 1970 [1967]).

    The Autumn of the Patriarch, trans. Gregory Rabassa (New York: Avon Books, 1977 [1975]).

Ghose, Zulfikar, *The Triple Mirror of the Self* (London: Bloomsbury, 1992).

Ghosh, Amitav, *The Shadow Lines* (London: Viking, 1990 [1988]).

    The Hungry Tide (London: HarperCollins, 2005 [2004]).

Glissant, Édouard, *Black Salt*, trans. Betsy Wing (Ann Arbor: The University of Michigan Press, 1998).

Goh Poh Seng, *If We Dream Too Long* (Singapore: Island Press, 1972).

Gonzalez, N. V. M., *A Season of Grace* (Manila: Benipayo Press, 1956).

Guillén, Nicolás, *Man-Making Words: Selected Poems of Nicolás Guillén*, trans. Robert Márquez and David Arthur McMurray (Amherst: University of Massachusetts Press, 1972).

Habiby, Emile, *The Secret Life of Saeed, the Ill-Fated Pessoptimist*, trans. Salma Khadra Jayyusi and Trevor Le Gassick (London and New York: Readers International, 1985 [1974]).

Head, Bessie, *When Rain Clouds Gather* (New York: Simon and Schuster, 1969).

    A Question of Power (London: Heinemann, 1974).

Heath, Roy, *A Man Come Home* (Port of Spain: Longman, 1974).

Hove, Chenjerai, *Bones* (London: Heinemann, 1990 [1988]).

Ishiguro, Kazuo, *A Pale View of Hills* (London: Faber and Faber, 1982).

    An Artist of the Floating World (London: Faber and Faber, 1986).

    The Remains of the Day (London: Faber and Faber, 1989).

    The Unconsoled (London: Faber and Faber, 1995).

Iyayi, Festus, *The Contract* (Harlow: Longman, 1982).

    Violence (Harlow: Longman, 1987 [1979]).

Jia Pingwa, *Turbulence*, trans. Howard Goldblatt (New York: Grove Press, 1991 [1987]).

Jibanananda Das, *Naked Lonely Hand*, trans. Joe Winter (London: Anvil Press Poetry, 2003).

José, F. Sionil, *Tree* (Manila: Solidaridad, 1978).

    My Brother, My Executioner (Quezon City: New Day, 1979 [1973]).

    Dusk (New York: Modern Library, 1998).

    The Sampsons, comprising *The Pretenders* (1962) and *Mass* (1982) (New York: Modern Library, 2000).

Kanafani, Ghassan, *Men in the Sun*, trans. Hilary Kilpatrick (Washington, DC: Three Continents Press, 1988 [1962]).

    All That's Left to You, trans. May Jayyusi and Jeremy Reed (Austin: University of Texas Press, 1990 [1962]).

Khoury, Elias, *Little Mountain*, trans. Maia Tabet (Minneapolis: University of Minnesota Press, 1989 [1977].

    Gate of the Sun, trans. Humphrey Davies (New York: Picador, 2006 [1998]).

Kim Chiha, *Heart's Agony: Selected Poems of Chiha Kim*, trans. Won-Chung Kim and James Han (New York: White Pine Press, 1998).

Kincaid, Jamaica, *Lucy* (New York: Plume, 1991 [1990]).
Laâbi, Abdellatif, *Rue du retour*, trans. Jacqueline Kaye (London and Columbia, LA: Readers International, 1989 [1982]).
  'Writing requires more than one hand' (1993) in *The World's Embrace: Selected Poems*, trans. Anne George, Edris Makward, Victor Reinking, and Pierre Joris (San Francisco: City Lights Books, 2003), pp. 98–9.
Labou Tansi, Sony, *The Antipeople*, trans. J. A. Underwood (London and New York: Marion Boyars, 1988 [1983]).
  The Seven Solitudes of Lorsa Lopez, trans. Clive Wake (London: Heinemann, 1995 [1985]).
Laing, Kojo, *Search Sweet Country* (London: Heinemann, 1986).
  Woman of the Aeroplanes (London: Heinemann, 1988).
Lao She, *Rickshaw*, trans. Jean M. James (Honolulu: University Press of Hawaii, 1979 [1937]).
Lovelace, Earl, *Salt* (London and Boston: Faber and Faber, 1996).
Lu Hsun, 'A Madman's Diary' (1918) and 'The True Story of Ah Q' (1921) in *Selected Stories of Lu Hsun*, trans. Yang Hsien-yi and Gladys Yang (Peking: Foreign Languages Press, 1978), pp. 7–18; 65–112.
Mahasweta Devi, 'Operation? – Bashai Tudu' (1978), in *Bashai Tudu*, trans. Samik Bandyopadhyay (Calcutta: Thema, 1990), pp. 1–148.
  'Paddy Seeds' (1979), in Kalpana Bardhan (ed.), *Of Women, Outcastes, Peasants, and Rebels*, trans. Kalpana Bardhan (Berkeley: University of California Press, 1990), pp. 158–84.
  'Douloti the Bountiful' in *Imaginary Maps: Three Stories by Mahasweta Devi*, trans. Gayatri Chakravorty Spivak (New York and London: Routledge, 1995), pp. 19–93.
  'Pterodactyl, Puran Sahay, and Pirtha' in *Imaginary Maps: Three Stories by Mahasweta Devi*, trans. Gayatri Chakravorty Spivak (New York and London: Routledge, 1995), pp. 95–196.
  Mother of 1084, trans. Samik Bandyopadhyay (Calcutta: Seagull Books, 2001 [1973]).
Mahfouz, Naguib, *Midaq Alley*, trans. Trevor Le Gassick (Washington, DC: Three Continents Press, 1981 [1947]).
  Palace Walk, trans. William Maynard Hutchins and Olive E. Kenny (London: Doubleday, 1991 [1956]).
  Palace of Desire, trans. William Maynard Hutchins, Lorne M. Kenny, and Olive E. Kenny (London: Doubleday, 1991 [1957]).
  Sugar Street, trans. William Maynard Hutchins and Angele Botros Samaan (London: Black Swan, 1994 [1957]).
  Adrift on the Nile, trans. Frances Liardet (New York: Doubleday, 1993 [1966]).
Mailer, Norman, *The Naked and the Dead* (London: Flamingo, 1993 [1949]).
Manto, Saadat Hasan, 'Toba Tek Singh' (1955) in *Kingdom's End and Other Stories*, trans. Khalid Hasan (New Delhi: Penguin, 1989), pp. 11–18.
Mapanje, Jack (ed.), *Gathering Seaweed: African Prison Writing* (London: Heinemann, 2002).

Mda, Zakes, *Ways of Dying* (Oxford University Press, 2002 [1995]).

Mistry, Rohinton, *A Fine Balance* (New York: Vintage International, 1997 [1995]).

Mo, Timothy, *Brownout on Breadfruit Boulevard* (London: Paddleless Press, 1995).
  Renegade or Halo² (London: Paddleless Press, 1999).

Mo Yan, *Red Sorghum*, trans. Howard Goldblatt (London: Arrow Books, 2003 [1988]).

Mofolo, Thomas, *Chaka*, trans. Daniel P. Kunene (London: Heinemann, 1981 [1925]).

Mohanty, Gopinath, *Paraja*, trans. Bikram K. Das (Oxford University Press, 1989 [1945]).

Mudimbe, V. Y., *Before the Birth of the Moon*, trans. Marjolijn de Jager (New York: Simon and Schuster, 1989 [1976]).
  The Rift, trans. Marjolijn de Jager (Minneapolis: University of Minnesota Press, 1993 [1979]).

Mukherjee, Bharati, *Jasmine* (New York: Fawcett Crest, 1991 [1989]).

Multatuli [Edouard Douwes Dekker], *Max Havelaar, or, The Coffee Auctions of the Dutch Trading Company*, trans. Roy Edwards (Amherst: University of Massachusetts Press, 1982 [1860]).

Munif, Abdelrahman, *Cities of Salt*, trans. Peter Theroux (New York: Vintage, 1989 [1984]).

Neruda, Pablo, *Canto General*, trans. Jack Schmitt (Berkeley: University of California Press, 2000 [1950]).

Neto, Agostinho, *Sacred Hope*, trans. Marga Holness (Dar es Salaam: Tanzania Publishing House, 1974).

Ngugi wa Thiong'o, *Petals of Blood* (London: Heinemann, 1977).
  Detained: A Writer's Prison Diary (London: Heinemann, 1981).
  Devil on the Cross, trans. Ngugi wa Thiong'o (London: Heinemann, 1982 [1980]).
  A Grain of Wheat (London: Heinemann, 1986 [1967]).
  Matigari, trans. Wangui wa Goro (London: Heinemann, 1989 [1987]).
  Wizard of the Crow, trans. Ngugi wa Thiong'o (London: Harvill Secker, 2006).

Ngugi wa Thiong'o and Ngugi wa Mirii, *I Will Marry When I Want* (London: Heinemann, 1982 [1980]).

Nirala, *A Season on the Earth: Selected Poems of Nirala*, trans. David Rubin (Oxford University Press, 2003).

Okri, Ben, 'What the Tapster Saw' in *Stars of the New Curfew* (Harmondsworth: Penguin, 1988), pp. 183–94.
  The Famished Road (London: Vintage, 1992 [1991]).
  Dangerous Love (London: Phoenix, 1996).

Partnoy, Alicia, *The Little School*, trans. Alicia Partnoy *et al.* (London: Virago, 1988 [1981]).

Pepetela, *Yaka*, trans. Margaret Holness (Oxford: Heinemann, 1996 [1984]).

Pramoedya Ananta Toer, *The Buru Quartet*, trans. Max Lane (Harmondsworth: Penguin, 1990, 1990, 1990, 1992), comprising *This Earth of Mankind* (1980), *Child of all Nations* (1980), *Footsteps* (1980), and *House of Glass* (1988).

The Mute's Soliloquy: A Memoir, trans. Willem Samuels (New York: Hyperion East, 1989).

Qabbani, Nizar, *On Entering the Sea: The Erotic and Other Poetry of Nizar Qabbani*, trans. Lena Jayyusi and Sharif Elmusa, with Jack Collom, Diana Der Hovanessian, John Heath-Stubbs, W. S. Merwin, Christopher Middleton, Naomi Shihab Nye, and Jeremy Reed (New York: Interlink Books, 1996).

Ramanujan, A. K., *Relations* (Oxford University Press, 1971).

Ramirez, Sergio, *To Bury our Fathers*, trans. Nick Caistor (London and New York: Readers International, 1984 [1977]).

Ramos, Graciliano, *Prison Memoirs*, trans. Thomas Colchie (New York: Evans, 1974 [1953]).

Renu, Phanishwarnath, *The Soiled Border*, trans. Indira Junghare (Delhi: Chanakya Publications, 1991 [1954]).

Roa Bastos, Augusto, *I the Supreme*, trans. Helen Lane (London: Faber and Faber, 1987 [1974]).

Roy, Arundhati, *The God of Small Things* (New York: Random House, 1997).

Rui, Manuel, *Yes, Comrade!*, trans. Ronald W. Sousa (Minneapolis: University of Minnesota Press, 1993 [1977]).

Rushdie, Salman, *Midnight's Children* (London: Jonathan Cape, 1981).
  Shame (New York: Alfred A. Knopf, 1983).
  The Satanic Verses (London: Viking, 1988).
  The Moor's Last Sigh (London: Vintage, 1996).

Sahgal, Nayantara, *Prison and Chocolate Cake* (New Delhi: HarperCollins, 1953).
  This Time of Morning (London: Victor Gollancz, 1965).
  A Time to be Happy (New Delhi: Sterling Publishers, 1975).
  Rich Like Us (New York: W. W. Norton, 1986 [1985]).
  Mistaken Identity (New York: New Directions, 1988).
  Lesser Breeds (New Delhi: HarperCollins, 2003).

Salih, Tayeb, *Season of Migration to the North*, trans. Denys Johnson-Davies (London: Heinemann, 1978 [1969]).

Sant, Indira, 'Household Fires' (1975), trans. Vinay Dharwadker, in Vinay Dharwadker and A. K. Ramanujan (eds), *The Oxford Anthology of Modern Indian Poetry* (Delhi: Oxford University Press, 1995), pp. 48–9.

Sayyab, Badr Shakir al-, 'Rain Song' (1960), trans. Lena Jayyusi and Christopher Middleton, in Salma Khadra Jayyusi (ed.), *Modern Arabic Poetry* (New York: Columbia University Press, 1987), pp. 427–30.

Selvon, Samuel, *Moses Ascending* (London: Heinemann, 1984 [1975]).
  The Lonely Londoners (London: Longman, 1985 [1956]).
  The Housing Lark (Washington, DC: Three Continents Press, 1990 [1965]).

Sembène, Ousmane, *God's Bits of Wood*, trans. Francis Price (London: Heinemann, 1976 [1960]).
  Xala, trans. Clive Wake (London: Heinemann, 1976 [1974]).
  The Money Order with White Genesis, trans. Clive Wake (London: Heinemann, 1977 [1965]).

Sepamla, Sipho, *Hurry Up To It!* (Johannesburg: Ad. Donker, 1975).

Seth, Vikram, *A Suitable Boy* (London: Phoenix, 1994).

Shahnon Ahmad, *No Harvest but a Thorn*, trans. Adibah Amin (Kuala Lumpur: Oxford University Press, 1972 [1966]).

 Rope of Ash, trans. Harry Aveling (Kuala Lumpur: Oxford University Press, 1979 [1965]).

Sharqawi, Abdel Rahman al-, *Egyptian Earth*, trans. Desmond Stewart (London: Al Saqi Books, 1994 [1954]).

Sivanandan, A., *When Memory Dies* (London: Arcadia Books, 1997).

Soyinka, Wole, *A Dance of the Forests* (Oxford University Press, 1963).

 Kongi's Harvest (Oxford University Press, 1967).

 Season of Anomy (London: Rex Collings, 1973).

 A Play of Giants (London: Methuen, 1984).

 Mandela's Earth and Other Poems (London: Methuen, 1990 [1989]).

 The Open Sore of a Continent: A Personal Narrative of the Nigerian Crisis (Oxford University Press, 1996).

 Samarkand, and Other Markets I have Known (London: Methuen, 2002).

Swaminathan, Komal, *Water!*, trans. S. Shankar (Calcutta: Seagull, 2001 [1980]).

Valenzuela, Luisa, *The Lizard's Tale*, trans. Gregory Rabassa (London: Serpent's Tail, 1987 [1983]).

Van Heerden, Etienne, 'My Cuban' in *Mad Dog and Other Stories*, trans. Catherine Knox (Cape Town and Johannesburg: David Philip, 1992 [1983]), pp. 74–83.

 The Long Silence of Mario Salviati, trans. Catherine Knox (London: Sceptre, 2003).

Vera, Yvonne, *Nehanda* (Toronto: TSAR Publications, 1994 [1993]).

 The Stone Virgins (Harare: Weaver Press, 2002).

Vladislavic, Ivan, 'When my Hands Burst into Flames' in *Missing Persons* (Cape Town and Johannesburg: David Philip, 1989), pp. 99–103.

 Propaganda by Monuments and Other Stories (Cape Town and Johannesburg: David Philip, 1996).

 The Restless Supermarket (Cape Town and Johannesburg: David Philip, 2001).

 The Exploded View (Johannesburg: Random House, 2004).

Walcott, Derek, *Collected Poems 1948–1984* (New York: Farrar, Straus, and Giroux, 1990).

Wong Phui Nam, *Ways of Exile: Poems from the First Decade* (London: Skoob Books, 1993).

SECONDARY

Abdel-Malek, Anouar, *Nation and Revolution*, trans. Mike Gonzalez (Albany: State University of New York Press, 1981).

Achebe, Chinua, *Morning Yet on Creation Day: Essays* (London: Heinemann, 1977 [1975]).

Adorno, Theodor W., 'Engagement' (1962) in *Noten zur Literatur, Gesammelte Schriften*, vol. XI (Frankfurt-on-Main: Suhrkamp, 1974), pp. 409–30.

Minima Moralia: Reflections from Damaged Life, trans. E. F. N. Jephcott (London: Verso, 1978 [1951]).

'Commitment' (1962), trans. Francis McDonagh in Andrew Arato and Eike Gebhardt (eds), *The Essential Frankfurt School Reader* (New York: Continuum, 1983), pp. 300–18.

'Commitment' (1962), trans. Shierry Weber Nicholsen in Rolf Tiedemann (ed.), *Notes to Literature*, vol. II (New York: Columbia University Press, 1992), pp. 76–94.

Negative Dialectics, trans. E. B. Ashton (New York: Continuum, 1997 [1966]).

Ageron, Charles-Robert, *Modern Algeria: A History from 1830 to the Present*, trans. Michael Brett (Trenton, NJ: Africa World Press, 1991 [1964]).

Ahluwalia, Pal, 'Afterlives of Post-Colonialism: Reflections on Theory post-9/11', *Postcolonial Studies*, 10.3 (2007), pp. 257–70.

Ahmad, Aijaz, 'Jameson's Rhetoric of Otherness and the "National Allegory"', *Social Text*, 17 (1987), pp. 3–26.

In Theory: Classes, Nations, Literatures (London: Verso, 1992).

'The Politics of Literary Postcoloniality', *Race & Class*, 36.3 (1995), pp. 1–20.

Alavi, Hamza, 'The State in Post-Colonial Societies', *New Left Review*, 74 (1972), pp. 59–81.

Alessandrini, Anthony C., 'Introduction: Fanon Studies, Cultural Studies, Cultural Politics' in Anthony C. Alessandrini (ed.), *Frantz Fanon: Critical Perspectives* (London and New York: Routledge, 1999), pp. 1–17.

'Humanism in Question: Fanon and Said' in Henry Schwarz and Sangeeta Ray (eds), *A Companion to Postcolonial Studies* (Oxford: Blackwell, 2005), pp. 431–50.

Alexander, Jocelyn, JoAnn McGregor, and Terence Ranger, *Violence and Memory: One Hundred Years in the 'Dark Forests' of Matabeleland* (Oxford: James Currey, 2000).

Alloula, Malek, *The Colonial Harem*, trans. Myrna Godzich and Wlad Godzich (Minneapolis: University of Minnesota Press, 1986 [1981]).

Althusser, Louis, 'Ideology and Ideological State Apparatuses (Notes Towards an Investigation)' (1970) in *Lenin and Philosophy and Other Essays*, trans. Ben Brewster (New York and London: Monthly Review Press, 1971), pp. 127–86.

Amin, Samir, *Eurocentrism*, trans. Russell Moore (New York: Monthly Review Press, 1989).

Capitalism in the Age of Globalization: The Management of Contemporary Society (London: Zed Books, 1997).

Anderson, Benedict, *Imagined Communities: Reflections on the Origins and Spread of Nationalism*, rev. edn (London and New York: Verso, 1991).

Anderson, Perry, 'Modernity and Revolution', *New Left Review*, 144 (1984), pp. 96–113.

The Origins of Postmodernity (London and New York: Verso, 1998).

Appiah, Kwame Anthony, 'Is the Post- in Postmodernism the Post- in Postcolonial?', *Critical Inquiry*, 17 (1991), pp. 336–57.

Armah, Ayi Kwei, 'Fanon: The Awakener', *Negro Digest*, 18.12 (1969), pp. 4–9; 29–43.

Armstrong, Paul B., 'Being "out of place": Edward W. Said and the Contradictions of Cultural Differences', *Modern Language Quarterly*, 64.1 (2003), pp. 97–121.

Arrighi, Giovanni, *The Long Twentieth Century: Money, Power, and the Origins of our Times* (London and New York: Verso, 1994).

Ashcroft, Bill and Pal Ahluwalia, *Edward Said: The Paradox of Identity* (London and New York: Routledge, 1999).

Ashcroft, Bill, Gareth Griffiths, and Helen Tiffin, *The Empire Writes Back: Theory and Practice in Post-Colonial Literatures* (London and New York: Routledge, 1989).

The Post-Colonial Studies Reader (London and New York: Routledge, 1995).

Astvaldsson, Astvaldur, 'Toward a New Humanism: Narrative Voice, Narrative Structure and Narrative Strategy in Manlio Argueta's *Cuzcatlán, donde bate la mar del sur*', *Bulletin of Hispanic Studies*, 77 (2000), pp. 603–15.

Atkins, Angela, 'Land as Legislative Space in Vikram Seth's *A Suitable Boy* and Phanishwarnath Renu's *Maila Anchal*', *SOAS Literary Review*, 3 (2001), available at www.soas.ac.uk/soaslit/

Attridge, Derek, *J. M. Coetzee and the Ethics of Reading: Literature in the Event* (University of Chicago Press, 2005).

Ballaster, Rosalind, *Fabulous Orients: Fictions of the East in England 1662–1785* (Oxford University Press, 2005).

Banerjee, Sumanta, 'Translator's Note' in Mahasweta Devi, *Bait: Four Stories* (Calcutta: Seagull Books, 2004), pp. vii–xxii.

Barker, Francis, Peter Hulme, and Margaret Iversen (eds), *Cannibalism and the Colonial World* (Cambridge University Press, 1998).

Bartolovich, Crystal and Neil Lazarus (eds), *Marxism, Modernity and Postcolonial Studies* (Cambridge University Press, 2002).

Bauman, Zygmunt, *Globalization: The Human Consequences* (New York: Columbia University Press, 1998).

Bayart, Jean-François, *The State in Africa: The Politics of the Belly*, trans. Mary Harper and Christopher and Elizabeth Harrison (London and New York: Longman, 1993).

Bayly, C. A., 'Rallying Around the Subaltern' in Vinayak Chaturvedi (ed.), *Mapping Subaltern Studies and the Postcolonial* (London and New York: Verso, 2000), pp. 116–26; first published *Journal of Peasant Studies*, **16.**1 (1988), pp. 110–20.

Benjamin, Walter, 'Theses on the Philosophy of History' (1940; first published 1950) in Hannah Arendt (ed.), *Illuminations*, trans. Harry Zohn (New York: Schocken, 1969), pp. 253–64.

Ben-Yishai, Ayelet, 'The Dialectic of Shame: Representation in the Metanarrative of Salman Rushdie's *Shame*', *Modern Fiction Studies*, 48.1 (2002), pp. 194–215.

Berman, Marshall, *All that is Solid melts into Air: The Experience of Modernity* (London: Verso, 1983).

Bernabé, Jean, Patrick Chamoiseau and Raphael Confiant, *Éloge de la créolité: In Praise of Creoleness*, trans. Mohamed B. Taleb-Khyar (Baltimore, MD: Johns Hopkins University Press, 1990).

Bhabha, Homi K., 'Foreword: Remembering Fanon: Self, Psyche and the Colonial Condition' in Frantz Fanon, *Black Skin, White Masks*, trans. Charles Lam Markmann (London: Pluto, 1986 [1952]), pp. vii–xxvi.

The Location of Culture (London and New York: Routledge, 1994).

'Foreword: Framing Fanon' in Frantz Fanon, *The Wretched of the Earth*, trans. Richard Philcox (New York: Grove Press, 2005), pp. vii–xli.

Bhaskar, Roy, *Reclaiming Reality: A Critical Introduction to Contemporary Philosophy* (London: Verso, 1989).

Philosophy and the Idea of Freedom (London: Blackwell, 1990).

Blum, William, *Killing Hope: US Military and CIA Interventions since World War II* (London: Zed Books, 2003).

Boehmer, Elleke, *Colonial and Postcolonial Literature* (Oxford University Press, 1995).

'Beside the West: Postcolonial Women Writers, the Nation, and the Globalised World', *African Identities*, 2.2 (2004), pp. 173–88.

Bourdieu, Pierre, *The Logic of Practice*, trans. Richard Nice (Stanford University Press, 1990 [1980]).

'The Intellectual Field: A World Apart' (1985), in *In Other Words: Essays Towards a Reflexive Sociology*, trans. Matthew Adamson (Stanford University Press, 1990), pp. 140–9.

The Field of Cultural Production: Essays on Art and Literature (New York: Columbia University Press, 1993).

'Are Intellectuals out of Play?' (1978) in *Sociology in Question*, trans. Richard Nice (London, Thousand Oaks, CA, New Delhi: Sage, 1993), pp. 36–40.

'How can "Free-Floating Intellectuals" be set Free?' (1980) in *Sociology in Question*, trans. Richard Nice (London, Thousand Oaks, CA, New Delhi: Sage, 1993), pp. 41–8.

The Rules of Art: Genesis and Structure of the Literary Field, trans. Susan Emanuel (Stanford University Press, 1996 [1992]).

On Television, trans. Priscilla Parkhurst Ferguson (New York: New Press, 1998 [1996]).

Acts of Resistance: Against the New Myths of our Time, trans. Richard Nice (Oxford: Polity, 1998).

Firing Back: Against the Tyranny of the Market 2, trans. Loïc Wacquant (London: Verso, 2003).

Bourdieu, Pierre and Hans Haacke, *Free Exchange* (Stanford University Press, 1995 [1994]).

Bourdieu, Pierre and Loïc J. D. Wacquant, *An Invitation to Reflexive Sociology* (University of Chicago Press, 1992).

Brantlinger, Patrick, *Rule of Darkness: British Literature and Imperialism, 1830–1914* (Ithaca, NY: Cornell University Press, 1988).

Brass, Tom, 'Moral Economists, Subalterns, New Social Movements and the (Re-)Emergence of a (Post-)Modernized (Middle) Peasant', in Vinayak

Chaturvedi (ed.), *Mapping Subaltern Studies and the Postcolonial* (London and New York: Verso, 2000), pp. 127–62; first published *Journal of Peasant Studies,* 18.2 (1991), pp. 173–205.

Braudel, Fernand, *Civilization and Capitalism 15th–18th Century,* 3 vols, trans. Sian Reynolds (New York: Harper and Row, 1981).

Brecher, Jeremy and Tim Costello, *Global Village or Global Pillage: Economic Reconstruction from the Bottom Up* (Boston, MA: South End Press, 1994).

Brennan, Timothy, *Salman Rushdie and the Third World: Myths of the Nation* (Houndmills: Macmillan, 1989).

   At Home in the World: Cosmopolitanism Now (Cambridge, MA: Harvard University Press, 1997).

   'From Development to Globalization: Postcolonial Studies and Globalization Theory' in Neil Lazarus (ed.), *The Cambridge Companion to Postcolonial Literary Studies* (Cambridge University Press, 2004), pp. 120–38.

   Wars of Position: The Cultural Politics of Left and Right (New York: Columbia University Press, 2006).

   'Intellectual Labor', *South Atlantic Quarterly,* 108.2 (2009), pp. 395–415.

Brenner, Robert, *The Economics of Global Turbulence: The Advanced Capitalist Economies from Long Boom to Long Downturn* (London and New York: Verso, 2006).

Brett, E. A., *The World Economy since the War: The Politics of Uneven Development* (Houndmills: Macmillan, 1985).

Brouillette, Sarah, *Postcolonial Writers in the Global Literary Marketplace* (London: Palgrave, 2007).

Brown, Nicholas, *Utopian Generations: The Political Horizon of Twentieth-Century Literature* (Princeton University Press, 2005).

Buchanan, Ian, 'Reading Jameson Dogmatically', *Historical Materialism,* 10.3 (2002), pp. 223–43.

   'National Allegory Today: A Return to Jameson', *New Formations,* 51 (2003), pp. 66–79.

Buell, Frederick, *National Culture and the New Global System* (Baltimore, MD: Johns Hopkins University Press, 1994).

Bulhan, Hussein Abdilahi, *Frantz Fanon and the Psychology of Oppression* (New York: Plenum Press, 1985).

Byrne, Eleanor, *Homi K. Bhabha* (Houndmills: Palgrave Macmillan, 2009).

Cairns, C., *Out of History: Narrative Paradigms in Scottish and English Culture* (Edinburgh: Polygon, 1996).

Casanova, Pascale, *The World Republic of Letters,* trans. M. B. DeBevoise (Cambridge, MA: Harvard University Press, 2004 [1999]).

Castle, Gregory (ed.), *Postcolonial Discourses: An Anthology* (Oxford: Blackwell, 2001).

Caute, David, *Frantz Fanon* (New York: Viking, 1970).

Cazdyn, Eric, 'Anti-Anti: Utopia, Globalization, Jameson', *Modern Language Quarterly,* 68.2 (2007), pp. 331–43.

Césaire, Aimé, *Discourse on Colonialism,* trans. Joan Pinkham (New York: Monthly Review Press, 1972 [1955]).

Chabal, Patrick, *Power in Africa: An Essay in Political Interpretation* (New York: St Martin's Press, 1994).

Chabal, Patrick and Jean-Pascal Daloz, *Africa Works: Disorder as Political Instrument* (Oxford: James Currey, 1999).

Chakrabarty, Dipesh, *Provincializing Europe: Postcolonial Thought and Historical Difference* (Princeton University Press, 2000).

Chan, Stephen, 'The Memory of Violence: Trauma in the Writings of Alexander Kanengoni and Yvonne Vera and the Idea of Unreconciled Citizenship', *Third World Quarterly*, 26.2 (2005), pp. 369–82.

Charos, Caitlin, '"The End of an Error": Transition and "Post-Apartheid Play" in Ivan Vladislavic's *The Restless Supermarket*', *Safundi: The Journal of South African and American Studies*, 9.1 (2008), pp. 23–38.

Chatterjee, Partha, *Nationalist Thought and the Colonial World: A Derivative Discourse* (Minneapolis: University of Minnesota Press, 1993 [1996]).

Chaturvedi, Vinayak (ed.), *Mapping Subaltern Studies and the Postcolonial* (London and New York: Verso, 2000).

Cherki, Alice, *Frantz Fanon: A Portrait*, trans. Nadia Benabid (Ithaca, NY: Cornell University Press, 2006).

Cheyfitz, Eric, *The Poetics of Imperialism: Translation and Colonization from* The Tempest *to* Tarzan (Oxford University Press, 1991).

Childs, Peter and Patrick Williams, *An Introduction to Post-Colonial Theory* (London: Prentice Hall, 1997).

Chomsky, Noam, *The Chomsky Reader*, ed. James Peck (New York: Pantheon, 1987).

Deterring Democracy (New York: Hill and Wang, 1992).

Chow, Rey, 'The Politics of Admittance: Female Sexual Agency, Miscegenation, and the Formation of Community in Frantz Fanon' in *Ethics after Idealism: Theory–Culture–Ethnicity–Reading* (Bloomington: Indiana University Press, 1998), pp. 55–73.

Chrisman, Laura, *Rereading the Imperial Romance: British Imperialism and South African Resistance in Haggard, Schreiner, and Plaatje* (Oxford University Press, 2000).

Postcolonial Contraventions: Cultural Readings of Race, Imperialism and Transnationalism (Manchester University Press, 2003).

Clegg, Ian, 'Workers and Managers in Algeria' in Robin Cohen, Peter C. W. Gutkind, and Phyllis Brazier (eds), *Peasants and Proletarians: The Struggles of Third World Workers* (New York: Monthly Review Press, 1979), pp. 223–47.

Clifford, James, 'On *Orientalism*' in *The Predicament of Culture: Twentieth-Century Ethnography, Literature, and Art* (Cambridge, MA: Harvard University Press, 1988), pp. 255–76.

Cochran, Terry, 'The Matter of Language' in Paul A. Bové (ed.), *Edward Said and the Work of the Critic: Speaking Truth to Power* (Durham, NC: Duke University Press, 2000), pp. 78–96.

Cockburn, Alexander, *The Golden Age is in us: Journeys and Encounters 1987–1994* (London and New York: Verso, 1997).

Collier, Andrew, *Critical Realism: An Introduction to Roy Bhaskar's Philosophy* (London: Verso, 1994).

Collini, Stefan, *Absent Minds: Intellectuals in Britain* (Oxford University Press, 2006).

Cormack, Alistair, 'Migration and the Politics of Narrative Form: Realism and the Postcolonial Subject in *Brick Lane*', *Contemporary Literature*, 47.4 (2006), pp. 695–721.

Coronil, Fernando, 'Latin American Postcolonial Studies and Global Decolonization' in Neil Lazarus (ed.), *The Cambridge Companion to Postcolonial Literary Studies* (Cambridge University Press, 2004), pp. 221–40.

Coundouriotis, Eleni, *Claiming History: Colonialism, Ethnography, and the Novel* (New York: Columbia University Press, 1999).

Craig, Cairns, *Out of History: Narrative Paradigms in Scottish and English Culture* (Edinburgh: Polygon, 1996).

Cundy, Catherine, *Salman Rushdie* (Manchester University Press, 1996).

Davidson, Basil, *In the Eye of the Storm: Angola's People* (Harmondsworth: Penguin, 1975).

   Let Freedom Come: Africa in Modern History (Boston and Toronto: Little, Brown, 1978).

   The Black Man's Burden: Africa and the Curse of the Nation-State (New York: Times Books, 1992).

Deckard, Sharae, *Paradise Discourse, Imperialism, and Globalization: Exploited Eden* (London: Routledge, 2009).

Derrida, Jacques, *Archive Fever: A Freudian Impression*, trans. Eric Prenowitz (University of Chicago Press, 1996).

Dirlik, Arif, *After the Revolution: Waking to Global Capitalism* (Hanover, VA: Wesleyan University Press, 1994).

   'The Postcolonial Aura: Third World Criticism in the Age of Global Capitalism', *Critical Inquiry*, 20 (1994), pp. 328–56.

   'Is there History after Eurocentrism? Globalism, Postcolonialism, and the Disavowal of History', *Cultural Critique*, 42 (1999), pp. 1–34.

   'Placing Edward Said: Space Time and the Travelling Theorist' in Bill Ashcroft and Hussein Kadhim (eds), *Edward Said and the Post-Colonial* (Huntington, NY: Nova Science Publishers, 2001), pp. 1–29.

Duménil, Gérard and Dominique Lévy, *Capital Resurgent: Roots of the Neoliberal Revolution*, trans. Derek Jeffers (Cambridge, MD: Harvard University Press, 2004).

Eagleton, Terry, *Walter Benjamin or Towards a Revolutionary Criticism* (London: New Left Books, 1981).

   Ideology: An Introduction (London: Verso, 1991).

Edmond, Rod, *Representing the South Pacific: Colonial Discourse from Cook to Gauguin* (Cambridge University Press, 1997).

Fabian, Johannes, *Time and the Other: How Anthropology Makes its Object* (New York: Columbia University Press, 1983).

   Anthropology with an Attitude: Critical Essays (Stanford University Press, 2001).

Fanon, Frantz, *Black Skin, White Masks*, trans. Charles Lam Markmann (New York: Grove Press, 1967 [1952]).
  The Wretched of the Earth, trans. Constance Farrington (New York: Grove Press, 1968 [1961]).
  Toward the African Revolution, trans. Haakon Chevalier (New York: Grove Press, 1969 [1964]).
  Studies in a Dying Colonialism, trans. Haakon Chevalier (Harmondsworth: Penguin, 1970 [1959]).
Feenberg, Anne-Marie, '*Max Havelaar*: An Anti-Imperialist Novel', *MLN*, 112.5 (1997), pp. 817–35.
Foster, John Bellamy, 'Imperial America and War', *Monthly Review*, 55.1 (2003), pp. 1–10.
Franco, Jean, *The Modern Culture of Latin America: Society and the Artist*, rev. edn (Harmondsworth: Penguin, 1970).
Francophone Postcolonial Studies, inaugural issue, **1**.1 (2003).
Fuss, Diana, 'Interior Colonies: Frantz Fanon and the Politics of Identification' in *Identification Papers: Readings on Psychoanalysis, Sexuality and Culture* (New York and London: Routledge, 1995), pp. 141–72.
Gadamer, Hans-Georg, *Truth and Method*, trans. William Glen-Doepel (translation edited by John Cumming and Garrett Barden) (London: Sheed and Ward, 1979 [1960]).
Gafaïti, Hafid, 'Culture and Violence: the Algerian Intelligentsia between Two Political Illegitimacies', *Parallax*, 4.2 (1998), pp. 71–7.
Gagiano, Annie, 'Surveying the Contours of "a Country in Exile": Nuruddin Farah's Somalia', *African Identities*, 4.2 (2006), pp. 251–68.
Gandhi, Leela, *Postcolonial Theory: An Introduction* (Edinburgh University Press, 1998).
Ganguly, Keya, 'Introduction: After Resignation and Against Conformity', *South Atlantic Quarterly*, 108.2 (2009), pp. 239–47.
Gates, Henry Louis, Jr, 'Critical Fanonism', *Critical Inquiry*, 17.3 (1991), pp. 457–70.
Gaylard, Gerald, *After Colonialism: African Postmodernism and Magical Realism* (Johannesburg: Wits University Press, 2005).
Geismar, Peter, *Frantz Fanon* (New York: Grove Press, 1969).
Gendzier, Irene, *Frantz Fanon: A Critical Study* (New York: Grove Press, 1973).
George, Rosemary Marangoly, *The Politics of Home: Postcolonial Relocations and Twentieth-Century Fiction* (Cambridge University Press, 1996).
Gérard, Albert, *Four African Literatures* (Berkeley: University of California Press, 1971).
Ghosh, Amitav, '"Postcolonial" Describes you as a Negative', interview with T. Vijay Kumar, *Interventions*, 9.1 (2007), pp. 99–105.
Gibson, Nigel C., 'Fanon and the Pitfalls of Cultural Studies' in Anthony C. Alessandrini (ed.), *Frantz Fanon: Critical Perspectives* (London and New York: Routledge, 1999), pp. 99–125.
  Fanon: The Postcolonial Imagination (Oxford: Polity, 2003).

Gibson, Richard, *African Liberation Movements: Contemporary Struggles Against White Minority Rule* (Oxford University Press, 1972).

Gikandi, Simon, *Reading Chinua Achebe: Language and Ideology in Fiction* (London: James Currey; Portsmouth NH and Nairobi: Heinemann, 1991).

Ngugi wa Thiong'o (Cambridge University Press, 2000).

'Cultural Translation and the African Self: A (Post)Colonial Case Study', *Interventions*, 3.3 (2001), pp. 355–75.

'Theory, Literature and Moral Considerations', *Research in African Literatures*, 32.4 (2001), pp. 1–18.

'The Short Century: On Modernism and Nationalism', *New Formations*, 51 (2004), pp. 10–25.

Gilroy, Paul, 'Towards a Critique of Consumer Imperialism', *Public Culture*, 14.3 (2002), pp. 589–91.

Godzich, Wlad, 'Emergent Literature in the Field of Comparative Literature' in *The Culture of Literacy* (Cambridge, MA: Harvard University Press, 1994), pp. 274–92.

Goh, Robbie B.H., 'Imagining the Nation: The Role of Singapore Poetry in English in "Emergent Nationalism"', *Journal of Commonwealth Literature*, 41.2 (2006), pp. 21–41.

Gopal, Priyamvada, 'Reading Subaltern History' in Neil Lazarus (ed.), *The Cambridge Companion to Postcolonial Literary Studies* (Cambridge University Press, 2004), pp. 139–61.

Literary Radicalism in India: Gender, Nation and the Transition to Independence (London and New York: Routledge, 2005).

The Indian English Novel: Nation, History, and Narration (Oxford University Press, 2009).

Gordimer, Nadine, 'Living in the Interregnum' in Stephen Clingman (ed.), *The Essential Gesture: Writing, Politics and Places* (New York: Alfred A. Knopf, 1988), pp. 261–84.

Gordon, Lewis R., *Fanon and the Crisis of European Man: An Essay on Philosophy and the Human Sciences* (New York: Routledge, 1995).

'Black Skins Masked: Finding Fanon in Isaac Julien's *Frantz Fanon: Black Skin, White Mask*', *differences: A Journal of Feminist Cultural Studies*, 8.3 (1996), pp. 148–58.

Gordon, Lewis R., T. Denean Sharpley-Whiting, and Renee T. White (eds), *Fanon: A Critical Reader* (Oxford: Blackwell, 1996).

Gowan, Peter, *The Global Gamble: Washington's Faustian Bid for World Dominance* (London and New York: Verso, 1999).

Graham, James, *Land and Nationalism in Fictions from Southern Africa: Culture, Politics, and Self-Representation* (London and New York: Routledge, 2009).

Graham, Shane, 'Memory, Memorialization, and the Transformation of Johannesburg: Ivan Vladislavic's *The Restless Supermarket* and *Propaganda by Monuments*', *Modern Fiction Studies*, 53.1 (2007), pp. 70–96.

Guha, Ranajit, *Dominance without Hegemony: History and Power in Colonial India* (Cambridge, MA: Harvard University Press, 1997).

Guha, Ranajit (ed.), *A Subaltern Studies Reader, 1986–1995* (Minneapolis: University of Minnesota Press, 1997).

Guha, Ranajit and Gayatri Chakravorty Spivak (eds), *Selected Subaltern Studies* (Oxford University Press, 1988).

Guyer, Jane, 'Contemplating Uncertainty', *Public Culture*, 14.3 (2002), pp. 599–602.

Gwynne, Robert N. and Cristóbal Kay, 'Latin America Transformed: Changing Paradigms, Debates and Alternatives' in Robert N. Gwynne and Cristóbal Kay (eds), *Latin America Transformed: Globalization and Modernity* (London: Edward Arnold, 1999), pp. 2–30.

Habermas, Jürgen, *Knowledge and Human Interests*, trans. Jeremy J. Shapiro (London: Heinemann, 1978 [1968]).
  The Philosophical Discourse of Modernity: Twelve Lectures, trans. Frederick Lawrence (Cambridge, MA: MIT Press, 1987 [1985]).
  'Learning from Catastrophe? A Look Back at the Short Twentieth Century' in *The Postnational Constellation: Political Essays*, trans. and ed. Max Pensky (Oxford: Polity, 2001), pp. 38–57.

Hall, Catherine, *Civilising Subjects: Metropole and Colony in the English Imagination 1830–1867* (Cambridge: Polity, 2002).

Hall, Stuart, 'The After-Life of Frantz Fanon: Why Fanon? Why Now? Why *Black Skin, White Masks*?' in Alan Read (ed.), *The Fact of Blackness: Frantz Fanon and Visual Representation* (London: Institute of Contemporary Arts; Seattle: Bay Press, 1996), pp. 12–37.

Hansen, Emmanuel, *Frantz Fanon: Social and Political Thought* (Columbus: Ohio State University Press, 1977).

Harlow, Barbara, *Resistance Literature* (New York and London: Methuen, 1987).
  After Lives: Legacies of Revolutionary Writing (London and New York: Verso, 1996).

Harrison, Nicholas, *Postcolonial Criticism: History, Theory and the Work of Fiction* (Oxford: Polity, 2003).

Harrow, Kenneth W., *Thresholds of Change in African Literature: The Emergence of a Tradition* (Portsmouth, NH: Heinemann; London: James Currey, 1994).
  '"Ancient Tribal Warfare": Foundational Fantasies of Ethnicity and History', *Research in African Literatures*, 36.2 (2005), pp. 34–45.

Hart, William D., *Edward Said and the Religious Effects of Culture* (Cambridge University Press, 2000).

Harvey, David, *Consciousness and the Urban Experience* (Baltimore, MD: Johns Hopkins University Press, 1985).
  The New Imperialism (Oxford University Press, 2003).
  A Brief History of Neoliberalism (Oxford University Press, 2005).

Head, Dominic, *The Cambridge Introduction to Modern British Fiction, 1950–2000* (Cambridge University Press, 2002).

Henry, Paget, *Caliban's Reason: Introducing Afro-Caribbean Philosophy* (New York and London: Routledge, 2000).

Hitchcock, Peter, 'Postcolonial Failure and the Politics of Nation', *South Atlantic Quarterly*, 106.4 (2007), pp. 727–52.

Ho Chi Minh, *On Revolution: Selected Writings, 1920–66* (New York: Signet, 1967).

Hobsbawm, Eric, *The Age of Extremes: A History of the World, 1914–1991* (New York: Pantheon Books, 1994).

Hogan, Patrick Colm, *Colonialism and Cultural Identity: Crises of Tradition in the Anglophone Literatures of India, Africa, and the Caribbean* (Albany: State University of New York Press, 2000).

Hove, Chenjarai, 'Dictatorships are Transient', interview with Ranka Primorac, *Journal of Commonwealth Literature*, 43.1 (2008), pp. 135–46.

Huggan, Graham, *The Post-Colonial Exotic: Marketing the Margins* (London and New York: Routledge, 2001).

Huggan, Graham and Helen Tiffin, 'Green Postcolonialism', *Interventions*, 9.1 (2007), pp. 1–11.

Hulme, Peter, *Colonial Encounters: Europe and the Native Caribbean, 1492–1797* (London: Methuen, 1992).

Huntington, Samuel, *The Clash of Civilizations and the Remaking of World Order* (London: Touchstone, 1998).

Hussein, Abdirahman A. *Edward Said: Criticism and Society* (London and New York: Verso, 2002).

Jameson, Fredric, *Marxism and Form: Twentieth-Century Dialectical Theories of Literature* (Princeton University Press, 1971).

The Prison-House of Language: A Critical Account of Structuralism and Russian Formalism (Princeton University Press, 1972).

The Political Unconscious: Narrative as a Socially Symbolic Act (Ithaca, NY: Cornell University Press, 1981).

'Postmodernism, or, The Cultural Logic of Late Capitalism', *New Left Review*, 146 (1984), pp. 59–92.

'Third-World Literature in the Era of Multinational Capitalism', *Social Text*, 15 (1986), pp. 65–88.

'On Magic Realism in Film', *Critical Inquiry*, 12 (1986), pp. 301–25.

'Foreword' in Roberto Fernández Retamar, *Caliban and Other Essays*, trans. Edward Baker (Minneapolis: University of Minnesota Press, 1989), pp. vii–xii.

'Modernism and Imperialism' in Terry Eagleton, Fredric Jameson and Edward W. Said, *Nationalism, Colonialism and Literature* (Minneapolis: University of Minnesota Press, 1990), pp. 43–66.

Postmodernism, or, The Cultural Logic of Late Capitalism (Durham, NC: Duke University Press, 1995).

'Notes on Globalization as a Philosophical Issue' in Fredric Jameson and Masao Miyoshi (eds), *The Cultures of Globalization* (Durham, NC: Duke University Press, 1998), pp. 54–77.

'Culture and Finance Capital' in *The Cultural Turn: Selected Writings on the Postmodern, 1983–1998* (London and New York: Verso, 1998), pp. 136–61.

A Singular Modernity: Essay on the Ontology of the Present (London and New York: Verso, 2002).

Jani, Pranav, review of Vinayak Chaturvedi, *Mapping Subaltern Studies and the Postcolonial, Historical Materialism*, 11.3 (2003), pp. 271–88.

Decentering Rushdie: Cosmopolitanism and the Indian Novel in English (Columbus: Ohio State University Press, 2010).

Jayawardene, Kumari, *The White Woman's Other Burden: Western Women and South Asia during British Colonial Rule* (London: Routledge, 1995).

Jeyifo, Biodun, 'The Nature of Things: Arrested Decolonization and Critical Theory', *Research in African Literatures*, 21.1 (1990), pp. 33–48.

Jinadu, L. Adele, *Fanon: In Search of the African Revolution* (London: Kegan Paul, 1986).

Johnson, Chalmers, *The Sorrows of Empire* (New York: Henry Holt, 2004).

Jusdanis, Gregory, 'World Literature: The Unbearable Lightness of Thinking Globally', *Diaspora*, 12.1 (2003), pp. 103–30.

Jussawalla, Feroza and Reed Way Dasenbrock (eds), *Interviews with Writers of the Postcolonial World* (Jackson and London: University Press of Mississippi, 1992).

Kabbani, Rana, *Imperial Fictions: Europe's Myths of Orient* (London: Pandora, 1994 [1986]).

Kaiwar, Vasant, 'Towards Orientalism and Nativism: The Impasse of Subaltern Studies', *Historical Materialism*, 12.2 (2004), pp. 189–247.

Kanaganayakam, Chelva, *Structures of Negation: The Writings of Zulfikar Ghose* (University of Toronto Press, 1993).

Kapur, Geeta, 'Globalization and Culture: Navigating the Void' in Fredric Jameson and Masao Miyoshi (eds), *The Cultures of Globalization* (Durham, NC: Duke University Press, 1998), pp. 191–217.

Kennedy, Valerie, *Edward Said: A Critical Introduction* (Oxford: Polity, 2000).

Khilnani, Sunil, *The Idea of India* (Harmondsworth: Penguin, 1998).

King, Bruce, 'K. N. Daruwalla's Poetry – 1: Parsi Bard of North India', *Journal of Postcolonial Writing*, 45.1 (2009), pp. 97–106.

Kortenaar, Neil ten, 'Fictive States and the State of Fiction in Africa', *Comparative Literature*, 52.3 (2000), pp. 228–45.

'*Things Fall Apart* in History', *Interventions*, 11.2 (2009), pp. 166–70.

Kunene, Daniel P., 'Introduction' in Thomas Mofolo, *Chaka* (London: Heinemann, 1981), pp. xii–xxiii.

Lamming, George, *The Pleasures of Exile* (London: Michael Joseph, 1960).

Larrain, Jorge, *Identity and Modernity in Latin America* (Oxford: Polity, 2000).

Larsen, Neil, 'Postcolonialism's Unsaid', *Minnesota Review*, 45–6 (1996), pp. 285–90.

Determinations: Essays on Theory, Narrative and Nation in the Americas (New York and London: Verso, 2001).

'Imperialism, Colonialism, Postcolonialism' in Henry Schwarz and Sangeeta Ray (eds), *A Companion to Postcolonial Studies* (Oxford: Blackwell, 2005), pp. 23–52.

Lazarus, Neil, *Resistance in Postcolonial African Fiction* (New Haven, CT: Yale University Press, 1990).

'Doubting the New World Order: Marxism and Postmodernist Social Theory', *differences: A Journal of Feminist Cultural Studies*, 3.3 (1991), pp. 94–138.

'Postcolonialism and the Dilemma of Nationalism: Aijaz Ahmad's Critique of Third-Worldism', *Diaspora: A Journal of Transnational Studies*, 2.3 (1993), pp. 373–400.

'Is a Counterculture of Modernity a Theory of Modernity?', *Diaspora: A Journal of Transnational Studies*, 4.3 (1996), pp. 323–39.

'Transnationalism and the Alleged Death of the Nation-State' in Keith Ansell-Pearson, Benita Parry, and Judith Squires (eds), *Cultural Readings of Imperialism: Edward Said and the Gravity of History* (London: Lawrence and Wishart, 1997), pp. 28–48.

Nationalism and Cultural Practice in the Postcolonial World (Cambridge University Press, 1999).

'Charting Globalization', *Race & Class*, 40.2–3 (1999), pp. 91–109.

'Introducing Postcolonial Studies' in Neil Lazarus (ed.), *The Cambridge Companion to Postcolonial Literary Studies* (Cambridge University Press, 2004), pp. 1–16.

'The Global Dispensation since 1945' in Neil Lazarus (ed.), *The Cambridge Companion to Postcolonial Literary Studies* (Cambridge University Press, 2004), pp. 19–40.

'The Politics of Postcolonial Modernism' in Ania Loomba, Suvir Kaul, Matti Bunzl, Antoinette Burton, and Jed Esty (eds), *Postcolonial Studies and Beyond* (Durham, NC: Duke University Press, 2004), pp. 423–38.

'Postcolonial Studies after the Invasion of Iraq', *New Formations*, 59 (2006), pp. 10–22.

'Modernism and African Literature' in Mark Wollaeger (ed.), *Global Modernisms* (Oxford University Press, 2011).

Lazarus, Neil and Rashmi Varma, 'Marxism and Postcolonial Studies' in Jacques Bidet and Stathis Kouvelakis (eds), *The Critical Companion to Contemporary Marxism* (Leiden: Brill, 2008), pp. 309–31.

Lazarus, Neil, Anthony Arnove, Steven Evans, and Anne Menke, 'The Necessity of Universalism', *differences: A Journal of Feminist Cultural Studies*, 7.1 (1995), pp. 75–145.

Le Duan, *The Vietnamese Revolution: Fundamental Problems, Essential Tasks* (Hanoi: Foreign Languages Publishing House, 1973).

Lenta, Patrick, '"Everyday Abnormality": Crime and In/security in Ivan Vladislavic's *Portrait with Keys*', *Journal of Commonwealth Literature*, 44.1 (2009), pp. 117–33.

Lewis, Barry, *Kazuo Ishiguro* (Manchester University Press, 2000).

Leys, Colin, *The Rise and Fall of Development Theory* (Nairobi: East African Publishing House; Bloomington: Indiana University Press; London: James Currey, 1996).

Loomba, Ania, *Colonialism/Postcolonialism* (London and New York: Routledge, 1998).

Shakespeare, Race, and Colonialism (Oxford University Press, 2002).

Loomba, Ania, Suvir Kaul, Matti Bunzl, Antoinette Burton, and Jed Esty, 'Beyond What? An Introduction' in Ania Loomba, Suvir Kaul, Matti Bunzl, Antoinette Burton, and Jed Esty (eds), *Postcolonial Studies and Beyond* (Durham, MD: Duke University Press, 2004), pp. 1–38.

López, Silvia, 'Peripheral Glances: Adorno's *Aesthetic Theory* in Brazil' in Max Pensky (ed.), *Globalizing Critical Theory* (New York: Rowman and Littlefield, 2005), pp. 241–52.

Lowe, Lisa, *Critical Terrains: French and British Orientalisms* (Ithaca, NY: Cornell University Press, 1991).

Lukács, Georgy, *History and Class Consciousness: Studies in Marxist Dialectics*, trans. Rodney Livingstone (London: Merlin, 1971 [1923]).

Macaulay, Thomas Babington, 'Thomas Babington Macaulay on Education for India' (1835) in Philip D. Curtin (ed.), *Imperialism* (London: Harper and Row, 1971), pp. 178–91.

Macey, David, *Frantz Fanon: A Life* (London: Granta, 2000).

Mahasweta Devi, 'Speaking with Mahasweta Devi: Mahasweta Devi Interviewed by Gabrielle Collu', *Journal of Commonwealth Literature*, 33.2 (1998), pp. 143–8.

Majumdar, Margaret A., *Postcoloniality: The French Dimension* (New York and Oxford: Berghahn Books, 2007).

Mamdani, Mahmood, *Citizen and Subject: Contemporary Africa and the Legacy of Late Colonialism* (London: James Currey; Kampala: Fountain Publishers; Cape Town: David Philip, 1996).

  When Victims Become Killers: Colonialism, Nativism and the Genocide in Rwanda (Oxford: James Currey, 2001).

Marcuse, Herbert, 'The Affirmative Character of Culture' (1937) in *Negations: Essays in Critical Theory*, trans. Jeremy J. Shapiro (Harmondsworth: Penguin, 1968), pp. 88–133.

Martin, Hans-Peter and Harald Schumann, *The Global Trap: Globalization and the Assault on Prosperity and Democracy*, trans. Patrick Camiller (Pretoria: HRSC/RGN; Leichhardt, NSW: Pluto Press; Bangkok: White Lotus; London and New York: Zed Books, 1997).

Marx, John, 'Failed-State Fiction', *Contemporary Literature*, 49.4 (2008), pp. 597–633.

Marx, Karl, *Capital: A Critique of Political Economy*, vol. I, 2nd edn, trans. B. Fowkes (Harmondsworth: Penguin, 1990 [1873]).

Marx, Karl and Friedrich Engels, *Manifesto of the Communist Party* (Beijing: Foreign Languages Press, 1988 [1848]).

May, Brian, 'Reading Coetzee, Eventually', *Comparative Literature*, 48.4 (2007), pp. 629–38.

Mbeki, Govan, *South Africa: The Peasants' Revolt* (Harmondsworth: Penguin, 1964).

Mbembe, Achille, 'The Banality of Power and the Aesthetics of Vulgarity', *Public Culture*, 4.2 (1992), pp. 1–30.

On the Postcolony (Berkeley: University of California Press, 2001).

McClintock, Anne, *Imperial Leather: Race, Gender and Sexuality in the Colonial Contest* (New York and London: Routledge, 1995).

McCulloch, Jock, *Black Soul, White Artifact: Fanon's Clinical Psychology and Social Theory* (Cambridge University Press, 1983).

McGonegal, Julie, 'Postcolonial Metacritique: Jameson, Allegory and the Always-Already-Read Third World Text', *Interventions*, 7.2 (2005), pp. 251–65.

McLeod, John, *Beginning Postcolonialism* (Manchester University Press, 2000).

Mercer, Kobena, 'Decolonisation and Disappointment: Reading Fanon's Sexual Politics' in Alan Read (ed.), *The Fact of Blackness: Frantz Fanon and Visual Representation* (London: Institute of Contemporary Arts; Seattle: Bay Press, 1996), pp. 114–31.

Merleau-Ponty, Maurice, 'Eye and Mind' (1962), trans. Carleton Dallery, in *Phenomenology, Language and Sociology: Selected Essays* (London: Heinemann, 1974), pp. 280–311.

Phenomenology of Perception, trans. Colin Smith (London: Routledge, 1999 [1945]).

Miller, Christopher L., *Blank Darkness: Africanist Discourse in French* (University of Chicago Press, 1985).

Theories of Africans: Francophone Literature and Anthropology in Africa (University of Chicago Press, 1990).

Mills, Sara, *Discourses of Difference: An Analysis of Women's Travel Writing and Colonialism* (London and New York: Routledge, 1991).

Moody, Kim, *Workers in a Lean World: Unions in the International Economy* (London and New York: Verso, 1997).

Moore-Gilbert, Bart, *Postcolonial Theory: Contexts, Practices, Politics* (London and New York: Verso, 1997).

Moss, Laura, 'Can Rohinton Mistry's Realism Rescue the Novel?' in Rowland Smith (ed.), *Postcolonizing the Commonwealth: Studies in Literature and Culture* (Waterloo, IA: Wilfred Laurier University Press, 2000), pp. 157–65.

Mowitt, John, 'Algerian Nation: Fanon's Fetish', *Cultural Critique*, 22 (1992), pp. 165–86.

'Breaking up Fanon's Voice' in Anthony C. Alessandrini (ed.), *Frantz Fanon: Critical Perspectives* (London and New York: Routledge, 1999), pp. 89–98.

Mphahlele, Ezekiel, *The African Image*, rev. edn (New York and Washington, DC: Praeger, 1974).

Msiska, Mpalive-Hangson, '*Things Fall Apart*: A Resource for Cultural Theory', *Interventions*, 11.2 (2009), pp. 171–5.

Mudimbe, V. Y., *The Invention of Africa: Gnosis, Philosophy, and the Order of Knowledge* (Bloomington: Indiana University Press; London: James Currey, 1988).

Parables and Fables: Exegesis, Textuality, and Politics in Central Africa (Madison: University of Wisconsin Press, 1991).

The Idea of Africa (Bloomington: Indiana University Press; London: James Currey, 1994).

Mufti, Aamir, 'Reading the Rushdie Affair: "Islam", Cultural Politics, Form' in M. Keith Booker (ed.), *Critical Essays on Salman Rushdie* (New York: G. K. Hall, 1999), pp. 51–77.

Mukherjee, Upamanyu Pablo, *Postcolonial Environments: Nature, Culture and the Contemporary South Asian Novel in English* (Houndmills: Palgrave Macmillan, 2010).

Muponde, Robert and Ranka Primorac (eds), *Versions of Zimbabwe: New Approaches to Literature and Culture* (Harare: Weaver Press, 2005).

Murphy, David, 'De-Centring French Studies: Towards a Postcolonial Theory of Francophone Cultures', *French Cultural Studies*, 38 (2002), pp. 165–85.

'Beyond Anglophone Imperialism?', *New Formations*, 59 (2006), pp. 132–43.

Nair, Supriya, 'Diasporic Roots: Imagining a Nation in Earl Lovelace's *Salt*', *South Atlantic Quarterly*, 100.1 (2001), pp. 259–85.

Newell, Stephanie, *West African Literatures: Ways of Reading* (Oxford University Press, 2006).

Ngugi wa Thiong'o, *Decolonising the Mind: The Politics of Language in African Literature* (London: James Currey; Nairobi, Portsmouth NH: Heinemann; Harare: Zimbabwe Publishing House, 1987).

Nkosi, Lewis, *Tasks and Masks: Themes and Styles of African Literature* (London: Longman, 1981).

Noland, Carrie, 'Red Front/Black Front: Aimé Césaire and the Affaire Aragon', *Diacritics*, 36.1 (2006), pp. 64–84.

O'Hanlon, Rosalind, 'Recovering the Subject: *Subaltern Studies* and Histories of Resistance in Colonial South Asia' in Vinayak Chaturvedi (ed.), *Mapping Subaltern Studies and the Postcolonial* (London and New York: Verso, 2000), pp. 72–115; first published *Modern Asian Studies*, 22.1 (1988), pp. 189–224.

O'Hanlon, Rosalind and David Washbrook, 'After Orientalism: Culture, Criticism and Politics in the Third World' in Vinayak Chaturvedi (ed.), *Mapping Subaltern Studies and the Postcolonial* (London and New York: Verso, 2000), pp. 191–219; first published *Comparative Studies in Society and History*, 32.1 (1992), pp. 141–67.

Oloff, Kerstin Dagmar, 'Modernity and the Novel in the Expanded Caribbean: Wilson Harris, Patrick Chamoiseau and Carlos Fuentes', unpublished Ph.D. thesis, University of Warwick, 2007.

Orsini, Francesca, 'India in the Mirror of World Fiction' in Christopher Prendergast (ed.), *Debating World Literature* (London and New York: Verso, 2004), pp. 319–33; first published *New Left Review*, 13 (2002), pp. 75–88.

Parry, Benita, 'A Critique Mishandled', *Social Text*, 35 (1993), pp. 121–33.

'Signs of our Times: A Discussion of Homi Bhabha's *The Location of Culture*', *Third Text*, 28/29 (1994), pp. 5–24.

'Directions and Dead Ends in Postcolonial Studies' in David Theo Goldberg and Ato Quayson (eds.), *Relocating Postcolonialism* (Oxford: Blackwell, 2002), pp. 66–81.

Postcolonial Studies: A Materialist Critique (London and New York: Routledge, 2004).

'The Institutionalization of Postcolonial Studies' in Neil Lazarus (ed.), *The Cambridge Companion to Postcolonial Literary Studies* (Cambridge University Press, 2004), pp. 66–80.

'Countercurrents and Tensions in Said's Critical Practice' in Adel Iskandar and Hakem Rustom (eds), *Edward Said: A Legacy of Emancipation and Representation* (Berkeley: University of California Press, 2010), pp. 499–512.

Patke, Rajeev S., *Postcolonial Poetry in English* (Oxford University Press, 2006).

Pearce, Gary, 'Margins and Modernism: Ireland and the Formation of Modern Literature', unpublished Ph.D. thesis, Monash University, 2002.

Perinbam, B. Marie, *Holy Violence: The Revolutionary Thought of Frantz Fanon* (Washington, DC: Three Continents Press, 1983).

Pramoedya Ananta Toer, 'The Book that Killed Colonialism', *New York Times Magazine*, 18 April 1999, pp. 112–14.

Prasad, Madhava, 'On the Question of a Theory of (Third World) Literature', *Social Text*, 31/32 (1992), pp. 57–83.

Pratt, Mary Louise, *Imperial Eyes: Travel Writing and Transculturation* (New York and London: Routledge, 1992).

Primorac, Ranka, *The Place of Tears: The Novel and Politics in Modern Zimbabwe* (London: I. B. Tauris, 2006).

'The Poetics of State Terror in Twenty-First-Century Zimbabwe', *Interventions*, 9.3 (2007), pp. 435–51.

Puri, Shalini, *The Caribbean Postcolonial: Social Equality, Post/Nationalism, and Cultural Hybridity* (New York and London: Palgrave and St Martin's Press, 2003).

Quayson, Ato, *Postcolonialism: Theory, Practice or Process?* (Cambridge: Polity, 2000).

Raditlhalo, Sam, 'Rewriting Modernity', *Safundi: The Journal of South African and American Studies*, 9.2 (2008), pp. 225–31.

Ray, Sangeeta, 'Postscript: Popular Perceptions of Postcolonial Studies after 9/11' in Henry Schwarz and Sangeeta Ray (eds), *A Companion to Postcolonial Studies* (Oxford: Blackwell, 2005), pp. 574–83.

Read, Alan (ed.), *The Fact of Blackness: Frantz Fanon and Visual Representation* (London: Institute of Contemporary Arts; Seattle: Bay Press, 1996).

Richards, Thomas, *The Imperial Archive: Knowledge and the Fantasy of Empire* (New York and London: Verso, 1993).

Rigby, Peter, *Persistent Pastoralists: Nomadic Societies in Transition* (London: Zed Books, 1985).

Robinson, Cedric, 'The Appropriation of Frantz Fanon', *Race & Class*, 35.1 (1993), pp. 79–91.

Rosello, Mireille, 'The "Césaire Effect", or How to Cultivate One's Nation', *Research in African Literatures*, 32.4 (2001), pp. 77–91.

Roy, Arundhati, 'Fascism's Firm Footprint in India', *Nation*, 275.10 (2002), p. 18.

The Checkbook and the Cruise Missile: Conversations with Arundhati Roy, interviews by David Barsamian (Cambridge, MA: South End Press, 2004).

Rubin, David, 'Nirala and the Renaissance of Hindi Poetry', *Journal of Asian Studies*, 31.1 (1971), pp. 111–26.

Saad-Filho, Alfredo (ed.), *Anti-Capitalism: A Marxist Introduction* (London: Pluto, 2003).

Said, Edward W., *Orientalism* (New York: Vintage, 1979 [1978]).

The World, the Text, and the Critic (Cambridge, MA: Harvard University Press, 1983).

'Foreword' in Elias Khoury, *Little Mountain*, trans. Maia Tabet (Minneapolis: University of Minnesota Press, 1989), pp. ix–xxi.

'Figures, Configurations, Transfigurations', *Race & Class*, 32.1 (1990), pp. 1–16.

Interview with Jennifer Wicke and Michael Sprinker in Michael Sprinker (ed.), *Edward Said: A Critical Reader* (Oxford: Blackwell, 1992), pp. 221–64.

Culture and Imperialism (London: Chatto and Windus, 1993).

'Nationalism, Human Rights, and Interpretation', *Raritan*, 12.3 (1993), pp. 26–51.

The Politics of Dispossession: The Struggle for Palestinian Self-Determination, 1969–1994 (New York: Pantheon Books, 1994).

Representations of the Intellectual (London: Vintage, 1994).

Peace and its Discontents: Essays on Palestine in the Middle East Peace Process (New York: Vintage, 1995).

'East isn't East', *Times Literary Supplement*, 4792 (1995), pp. 3–5.

'An Interview with Edward W. Said' in Moustafa Bayoumi and Andrew Rubin (eds), *The Edward Said Reader* (London: Granta, 2000), pp. 419–44.

Reflection on Exile and other Literary and Cultural Essays (London: Granta, 2001).

The End of the Peace Process: Oslo and After, 2nd edn (London: Granta, 2002).

Culture and Resistance: Conversations with Edward W. Said, interviewer David Barsamian (Cambridge, MA: South End Press, 2003).

Humanism and Democratic Criticism (New York: Columbia University Press, 2004).

'Beginnings' (1976) in Gauri Viswanathan (ed.), *Power, Politics and Culture: Interviews with Edward W. Said* (London: Bloomsbury, 2004), pp. 3–38.

'In the Shadow of the West', interview with Jonathan Crary and Phil Mariani (1985), in Gauri Viswanathan (ed.), *Power, Politics and Culture: Interviews with Edward W. Said* (London: Bloomsbury, 2004), pp. 39–52.

'Culture and Imperialism', interview with Joseph A. Buttigieg and Paul A. Bové (1993), in Gauri Viswanathan (ed.), *Power, Politics and Culture: Interviews with Edward W. Said* (London: Bloomsbury, 2004), pp. 183–207.

'*Orientalism* and After', interview with Anne Beezer and Peter Osborne (1993), in Gauri Viswanathan (ed.), *Power, Politics and Culture: Interviews with Edward W. Said* (London: Bloomsbury, 2004), pp. 208–32.

'Language, History and the Production of Knowledge', interview with Gauri Viswanathan (1996), in Gauri Viswanathan (ed.), *Power, Politics and Culture: Interviews with Edward W. Said* (London: Bloomsbury, 2004), pp. 262–79.

'American Intellectuals and Middle East Politics', interview with Bruce Robbins (1998), in Gauri Viswanathan (ed.), *Power, Politics and Culture: Interviews with Edward W. Said* (London: Bloomsbury, 2004), pp. 323–42.

Salgado, Minoli, 'Tribal Stories, Scribal Worlds: Mahasweta Devi and the Unreliable Translator', *Journal of Commonwealth Literature*, 35.1 (2000), pp. 131–45.

San Juan, E., Jr, *Hegemony and Strategies of Transgression: Essays in Cultural Studies and Comparative Literature* (Albany: State University of New York Press, 1995).

Sanga, Jania C., *Salman Rushdie's Postcolonial Metaphors: Migration, Translation, Hybridity and Globalization* (Westport, CT: Greenwood Press, 2001).

Beyond Postcolonial Theory (New York: St Martin's Press, 1998).

'Fanon: An Intervention into Cultural Studies' in Anthony C. Alessandrini (ed.), *Frantz Fanon: Critical Perspectives* (London and New York: Routledge, 1999), pp. 126–45.

Sarkar, Sumit, 'Orientalism Revisited: Saidian Frameworks in the Writing of Modern Indian History' in Vinayak Chaturvedi (ed.), *Mapping Subaltern Studies and the Postcolonial* (London and New York: Verso, 2000), pp. 239–55; first published *Oxford Literary Review*, 16.1–2 (1994), pp. 205–24.

'The Decline of the Subaltern in *Subaltern Studies*' in Vinayak Chaturvedi (ed.), *Mapping Subaltern Studies and the Postcolonial* (London and New York: Verso, 2000), pp. 300–23; first published in Sumit Sarkar, *Writing Social History* (Delhi: Oxford University Press, 1996), pp. 82–108.

'The Return of Labour to South-Asian History', *Historical Materialism*, 12.3 (2004), pp. 285–313.

Saul, John S., 'The State in Post-Colonial Societies: Tanzania' in Ralph Miliband and John Saville (eds), *The Socialist Register* (New York: Monthly Review Press; London: Merlin Press, 1974), pp. 349–72; reprinted in John S. Saul, *The State and Revolution in Eastern Africa* (New York and London: Monthly Review Press, 1979), pp. 167–99.

Millennial Africa: Capitalism, Socialism, Democracy (Trenton and Asmara: Africa World Press, 2001).

Schell, Jonathan, 'Letter from Ground Zero', *Nation*, 5 May 2003, p. 8.

Schwarz, Roberto, *Misplaced Ideas: Essays on Brazilian Culture* (London and New York: Verso, 1992).

Scott, James C., *Weapons of the Weak: Everyday Forms of Peasant Resistance* (New Haven, CT: Yale University Press, 1985).

Sekyi-Otu, Ato, *Fanon's Dialectic of Experience* (Cambridge, MA: Harvard University Press, 1996).

Shankar, S., 'Midnight's Orphans, or, A Postcolonialism Worth its Name', *Cultural Critique*, 56 (2004), pp. 64–95.

Shohat, Ella and Robert Stam, *Unthinking Eurocentrism: Multiculturalism and the Media* (London: Routledge, 1994).

Siddiqi, Yumna, *Anxieties of Empire and the Fiction of Intrigue* (New York: Columbia University Press, 2008).

Sim, Wai Chew, 'Kazuo Ishiguro', *Review of Contemporary Fiction*, 25.1 (2005), pp. 80–115.

  Globalization and Dislocation in the Novels of Kazuo Ishiguro (Lewiston, Queenstown, Lampeter: Edwin Mellen Press, 2006).

  Kazuo Ishiguro (London and New York: Routledge, 2009).

Simatei, Tirop, 'Colonial Violence, Postcolonial Violations: Violence, Landscape, and Memory in Kenyan Fiction', *Research in African Literatures*, 36.2 (2005), pp. 85–94.

Sivanandan, Tamara, '"Lies of our own making": The Post-Colonial Nation-State in the Writings of Ngugi wa Thiong'o, V. S. Naipaul and Salman Rushdie', unpublished MA dissertation, University of Essex, 1993.

Smith, Neil, 'After the American *Lebensraum*: "Empire", Empire and Globalization', *Interventions*, 5.2 (2003), pp. 249–70.

Smith, Paul, *Millennial Dreams: Contemporary Culture and Capital in the North* (London and New York: Verso, 1997).

Sole, Kelwyn, 'South Africa Passes the Posts', *Alternation*, 4.1 (1997), pp. 116–51.

  'Political Fiction, Representation and the Canon: The Case of Mtutuzeli Matshoba', *English in Africa*, 28.2 (2001), pp. 101–22.

  'The Witness of Poetry: Economic Calculation, Civil Society and the Limits of the Everyday in Post-Liberation South Africa', *New Formations*, 45 (2002), pp. 24–53.

Sorensen, Eli Park, 'Postcolonial Melancholia', *Paragraph*, 30.2 (2007), pp. 65–81.

Soyinka, Wole, 'The Writer in a Modern African State' (1967) in *Art, Dialogue and Outrage: Essays on Literature and Culture* (London: Methuen, 1993), pp. 15–20.

  The Open Sore of a Continent: A Personal Narrative of the Nigerian Crisis (Oxford University Press, 1996).

Spencer, Robert, 'Fredric Jameson and the Ends of Art', unpublished Ph.D. thesis, University of Warwick, 2004.

Spivak, Gayatri Chakravorty, 'Can the Subaltern Speak?' in Cary Nelson and Lawrence Grossberg (eds), *Marxism and the Interpretation of Culture* (Urbana: University of Illinois Press, 1988), pp. 271–313.

  'Theory in the Margin: Coetzee's *Foe* Reading Defoe's *Crusoe/Roxana*' in Jonathan Arac and Barbara Johnson (eds), *Consequences of Theory* (Baltimore, MD: Johns Hopkins University Press, 1990), pp. 154–80.

  Outside in the Teaching Machine (London and New York: Routledge, 1993).

  A Critique of Postcolonial Reason: Toward a History of the Vanishing Present (Cambridge, MA: Harvard University Press, 1999).

'Mapping the Present: Interview with Gayatri Spivak' conducted by Meyda Yegenoglu and Mahmut Mutman, *New Formations*, 45 (2001), pp. 9–23.

Death of a Discipline (New York: Columbia University Press, 2003).

Sprinker, Michael, 'Introduction' in Michael Sprinker (ed.), *Edward Said: A Critical Reader* (Oxford: Blackwell, 1992), pp. 1–4.

'The National Question: Said, Ahmad, Jameson', *Public Culture*, 6.1 (1993), pp. 3–29.

Stafford, Andy, 'Frantz Fanon, Atlantic Theorist; or, Decolonization and Nation State in Postcolonial Theory' in Charles Forsdick and David Murphy (eds), *Francophone Postcolonial Studies: A Critical Introduction* (London: Edward Arnold, 2003), pp. 166–77.

Stora, Benjamin, *Algeria, 1820–2000: A Brief History*, trans. Jane Marie Todd (Ithaca, NY: Cornell University Press, 2001).

Suleri, Sara, *The Rhetoric of English India* (University of Chicago Press, 1992).

Szeman, Imre, 'Who's Afraid of National Allegory?', *South Atlantic Quarterly*, 100.3 (2001), pp. 803–27.

Zones of Instability: Literature, Postcolonialism, and the Nation (Baltimore, MD: Johns Hopkins University Press, 2003).

Szentes, Tamás, *The Transformation of the World Economy: New Directions and New Interests* (London and Atlantic Highlands, NJ: Zed Books, 1988).

Tabb, William K., 'Globalization is *an* Issue, the Power of Capital is *the* Issue', *Monthly Review*, 49.2 (1997), pp. 20–30.

The Amoral Elephant: Globalization and the Struggle for Justice in the Twenty-First Century (New York: Monthly Review Press, 2001).

Taylor, Patrick, *The Narrative of Liberation: Perspective on Afro-Caribbean Literature, Culture, and Politics* (Ithaca, NY: Cornell University Press, 1989).

Therborn, Göran, *European Modernity and Beyond: The Trajectory of European Societies 1945–2000* (London: Sage, 1996).

Thomas, Nicholas, *Colonialism and Culture* (Oxford: Polity, 1994).

Tomsky, Terri, 'Amitav Ghosh's Anxious Witnessing and the Ethics of Action in *The Hungry Tide*', *Journal of Commonwealth Literature*, 44.1 (2009), pp. 53–65.

Trotsky, Leon, *History of the Russian Revolution*, vol. 1, trans. Max Eastman (London: Sphere Books, 1967 [1932–3]).

Vallury, Raji, 'Walking the Tightrope between Memory and History: Metaphor in Tahar Djaout's *L'invention du désert*', *Novel*, 41.2–3 (2008), pp. 320–41.

Vambe, Maurice Taonezvi, 'Changing Nationalist Politics in African Fiction', *African Identities*, 6.3 (2008), pp. 227–39.

Vanaik, Achin, *The Furies of Indian Communalism: Religion, Modernity and Secularization* (London and New York: Verso, 1997).

Varadharajan, Asha, 'Afterword: The Phenomenology of Violence and the Politics of Becoming', *Comparative Studies of South Asia, Africa and the Middle East*, 28.1 (2008), pp. 124–41.

Vergès, Françoise, 'Chains of Madness, Chains of Colonialism: Fanon and Freedom' in Alan Read (ed.), *The Fact of Blackness: Frantz Fanon and*

Visual Representation (London: Institute of Contemporary Arts; Seattle: Bay Press, 1996), pp. 46–75.

Viswanathan, Gauri, *Masks of Conquest: Literary Study and British Rule in India* (New York: Columbia University Press, 1989).

Viswanathan, Gauri (ed.), *Power, Politics and Culture: Interviews with Edward W. Said* (London: Bloomsbury, 2004).

Wallerstein, Immanuel, *The Modern World-System: Capitalist Agriculture and the Origins of the European World-Economy in the Sixteenth Century* (New York and London: Academic Press, 1974).

Historical Capitalism with *Capitalist Civilization* (London and New York: Verso, 1996).

'Reading Fanon in the 21st Century', *New Left Review*, 57 (2009), pp. 117–25.

Warnes, Christopher, 'The Making and Unmaking of History in Ivan Vladislavic's *Propaganda by Monuments and Other Stories*', *Modern Fiction Studies*, 46.1 (2000), pp. 67–89.

Magical Realism and the Postcolonial Word: Between Faith and Irreverence (Basingstoke: Palgrave, 2009).

Waters, Hazel, *Racism on the Victorian Stage: Representation of Slavery and the Black Character* (Cambridge University Press, 2007).

Watson, Jini Kim, 'The Way Ahead: The Politics and Poetics of Singapore's Developmental Landscape', *Contemporary Literature*, 49.4 (2008), pp. 683–711.

Weate, Jeremy, 'Achille Mbembe and the Postcolony: Going beyond the Text', *Research in African Literatures*, 34.4 (2003), pp. 27–41.

'Postcolonial Theory on the Brink: A Critique of Achille Mbembe's *On the Postcolony*', *African Identities*, 1.1 (2003), pp. 1–18.

Weaver-Hightower, Rebecca, *Empire Islands: Castaways, Cannibals, and Fantasies of Conquest* (Minneapolis: University of Minnesota Press, 2007).

Wenzel, Jennifer, 'Epic Struggles over India's Forests in Mahasweta Devi's Short Fiction', *Alif: Journal of Comparative Poetics*, 18 (1998), pp. 127–58.

'Petro-Magic-Realism: Toward a Political Ecology of Nigerian Literature', *Postcolonial Studies*, 9.4 (2006), pp. 449–64.

Wilkin, Peter, 'New Myths for the South: Globalization and the Conflict Between Private Power and Freedom' in Caroline Thomas and Peter Wilkin (eds), *Globalization and the South* (London: Macmillan; New York: St Martin's Press, 1997), pp. 18–35.

Williams, Patrick, '"Faire peau neuve": Césaire, Fanon, Memmi, Sartre and Senghor' in Charles Forsdick and David Murphy (eds), *Francophone Postcolonial Studies: A Critical Introduction* (London: Edward Arnold, 2003), pp. 181–91.

Williams, Patrick and Laura Chrisman (eds), *Colonial Discourse and Post-Colonial Theory: A Reader* (Hemel Hempstead: Harvester Wheatsheaf, 1993).

Williams, Raymond, *The Country and the City* (Oxford University Press, 1973).

Marxism and Literature (Oxford University Press, 1977).

'Literature and Sociology' in *Problems in Materialism and Culture: Selected Essays* (London: Verso, 1980), pp. 11–30.

'The Welsh Industrial Novel' in *Problems in Materialism and Culture: Selected Essays* (London: Verso, 1980), pp. 213–29.

The Politics of Modernism: Against the New Conformists (London and New York: Verso, 1990).

The Long Revolution (London: Hogarth Press, 1992 [1961]).

Wing, Betsy, 'Introduction' in Édouard Glissant, *Black Salt*, trans. Betsy Wing (Ann Arbor: University of Michigan Press, 1998), pp. 1–13.

Winter, Joe, 'Introduction' in Jibanananda Das, *Naked Lonely Hand*, trans. Joe Winter (London: Anvil Press Poetry, 2003), pp. 9–18.

Wolf, Eric R., *Europe and the People without History* (Berkeley: University of California Press, 1982).

Wood, Marcus, *Blind Memory: Visual Representation of Slavery in England and America 1780–1865* (Manchester University Press, 2000).

Young, Elaine, '"Or is it just the angle?" Rivalling Realist Representation in Ivan Vladislavic's *Propaganda by Monuments and Other Stories*', *English Academy Review*, 18 (2001), pp. 38–45.

Young, Robert J. C., *White Mythologies: Writing History and the West* (London: Routledge, 1990).

Colonial Desire: Hybridity in Theory, Culture and Race (London: Routledge, 1995).

Postcolonialism: An Historical Introduction (Cambridge: Blackwell, 2001).

Zahar, Renate, *Frantz Fanon: Colonialism and Alienation* (New York: Monthly Review Press, 1974).

Zeleza, Paul Tiyambe, 'The Historic and Humanistic Agendas of African Nationalism: A Reassessment' in Toyin Falola and Salah Hassan (eds), *Power and Nationalism in Modern Africa: Essays in Honor of the Memory of the Late Professor Don Ohadike* (Durham, NC: Carolina Academic Press, 2008), pp. 37–53.

'What Happened to the African Renaissance? The Challenges of Development in the Twenty-First Century', *Comparative Studies of South Asia, Africa and the Middle East*, 29.2 (2009), pp. 155–70.

Zhang Longxi, *Unexpected Affinities: Reading Across Cultures* (University of Toronto Press, 2007).

Ziarek, Ewa Plonowska, 'Introduction: Fanon's Counterculture of Modernity', *parallax*, 8.2 (2002), pp. 1–9.

Index